BETWEEN THE RIVERS

HISTORY OF THE
LAND BETWEEN THE LAKES

BETTY JOE WALLACE

AUSTIN PEAY STATE UNIVERSITY

THE CENTER FOR FIELD BIOLOGY

DEPARTMENT OF HISTORY AND PHILOSOPHY

FRONT COVER: Photographs by Dr. Edward W. Chester, Professor of Biology, Austin Peay
State University.

BACK COVER: Illustration produced by Public Affairs office of Austin Peay State University.

CONTENTS

DEDICATION & ACKNOWLEDGEMENTS   ii

INTRODUCTION

     iii

Chapter I   EARLY HISTORY   1

Chapter II   THE FIRST SETTLERS   9

Chapter III   ORGANIZATION OF COUNTY GOVERNMENTS   21

Chapter IV   ECONOMIC DEVELOPMENT   33

Chapter V   CHANGES IN LIFESTYLE   53

Chapter VI   EVENTS LEADING TO CIVIL WAR   90

Chapter VII   THE WAR COMES TO THE LAND BETWEEN THE RIVERS   116

Chapter VIII   LIFE FROM 1890 TO WORLD WAR I   155

Chapter IX   WORLD WAR I AND THE DEPRESSION YEARS   175

Chapter X   WORLD WAR II AND CHANGES   193

Chapter XI   CREATION OF THE LAND BETWEEN THE LAKES   202

Chapter XII   TRIUMPH OF LBL   250

BIBLIOGRAPHY   282

INDEX   288

FIGURES
1   AN IRON FURNACE
2   IRON FURNACE STACK
3   SOW AND PIGS
4   GENERAL VIEW OF FORT DONELSON

DEDICATION

This study is dedicated to Dr. J. Milton Henry who was a superior teacher and a compassionate and distinguished man. It was in his history classes at Austin Peay State College that I first became intrigued with the study of history, and it was through his guidance and encouragement that I began my research into the history of Stewart County. Dr. Henry had the unique ability to inspire his students, and I thank him.

ACKNOWLEDGEMENTS

This work would not have been possible without the support of Dr. Benjamin Stone, Director of the Center for Field Biology and Chairman of the Biology Department at Austin Peay State University. His confidence in the value of my work and his encouragement during times of personal duress kept me working on this project.

I owe a debt of gratitude to Dr. Edward Irwin, Professor of Languages and Literature at Austin Peay. His careful reading and thoughtful criticism helped me to find most of my mistakes. My husband, John Chapman, deserves a medal for graciously listening to all my concerns for two years.

This book was improved with the contributions of all these people; its interpretations and weaknesses are mine.

INTRODUCTION

The purpose of this study is to describe the lives and views of those people who made the land between the rivers a distinctive region. The major emphasis is on the culture and lifestyle of these people. Because of geography they were isolated for many years from most of the settlements outside their area. The isolation resulted in a rather unique culture which retained many of the European traditions and speech patterns long after they had disappeared in other parts of the country. The people were faced with the unenviable difficulty of being forced from their homes and property because of the policies of the Tennessee Valley Authority. The trauma of displacement is mirrored in their actions from 1960 to 1970.

This study asks more questions than it answers about the actions of the agency and its use of the right of eminent domain. By asking questions we often seek answers to problems which affect people and their government. The policies of the Tennessee Valley Authority and the reaction of the people to those policies in the land between the rivers provide an excellent study of how easily a break-down in communication can cause negative responses.

Because of time and space, many events which affected the lives of the people in the land between the rivers have not been included in this study, and more research and writing are needed if we are to truly understand these people who lived and died. For generations their lives were a microcosm of the early frontier.

Dr. J. Milton Henry wrote The Land Between the Rivers, an excellent study of the area, and his book cannot be surpassed in its detail and scholarship. In this study every attempt has been made not to duplicate his work, but to bring new material to the reader. Unlike Dr. Henry's work, this study places emphasis on the events immediately preceding the removal of the people from the land between the rivers.

Some readers will notice that the material includes a very limited history of the Tennessee Valley Authority, an agency which has had an enormous impact on the lives of all the people surrounding the Tennessee and Cumberland Rivers. The activities of the agency have enabled many people to achieve more comfortable, healthy, and productive lives than they otherwise might have. Only a very small number of people criticize the general policies of the agency, and many people recognize an obligation to give the Tennessee Valley Authority credit for the many positive changes in the region.

CHAPTER I

EARLY HISTORY

Native Americans

At the dawn of time, as the geographical characteristics of the Western Hemisphere became stable, rivers formed and then pre-historic people moved into North America and named the lands, rivers, and streams. These same lands and waterways received new names when European explorers came into the interior regions of North America.

Flowing down toward a stream that was to be named the Ohio were two rivers that the explorers would name the Tennessee and the Cumberland. The Tennessee River was formed by the junction of the Holston River which rises in Virginia and the French Broad River which rises in North Carolina. As the Tennessee River continues in a placid flow southward it abruptly changes course several times and then turns northwest across Alabama. Fed by tributaries, it courses below Florence and then turns northward for nearly two hundred miles. After it crosses Tennessee a second time, it flows through Kentucky and empties into the Ohio. The Cumberland River begins in southeastern Kentucky and runs across northern Middle Tennessee. Then it parallels the Tennessee River on its way across Kentucky to the Ohio River. As the two near their junction with the Ohio River, an area of land approximately forty miles long and some six to sixteen miles wide lies between them. This land was inhabited thousands of years before the first European explorers visited the area. The terrain, made up of river-bottom land and covered by vast virgin forests, flooded annually. Hills and hollows were carved out by the creeks which flowed into both rivers.

There was no human life in North America before the last glacial period, which probably began twenty to thirty million years ago. Probably Ice Age hunters from Asia found North America and Asia connected by a plain at the present Bering Sea, and they traversed the land from Siberia to Alaska. They spread through Canada southward, and likely were in Tennessee and Kentucky before the Ice Age ended. Fluted points, cutting and scraping tools, and other remains have been found in the area to document the theory that they had migrated from North to South.[1]

The Archaic people, a name given to the descendants of the earlier hunters, probably inhabited the land from about eight thousand years ago to after the birth of Christ. Very little evidence is left to allow a comprehensive characterization of them and their way of life. But we know they settled in villages, built houses, cooked on open fires, and shaped and polished their stone spear points and other weapons and tools. They also domesticated the dog and hunted and fished. They used bone fishhooks, traps, and nets, and they fashioned ornaments from bone, shell, and copper. These people were probably hunters and gatherers moving often from area to area in search of food and water.

The Woodland Cultures inhabited the region from 1000 B.C. to approximately 500 B.C. They built ceremonial mounds and were called the Mound Builders. Evidences of these mounds

---

[1]Dan F. Morse, <u>Reports of 1962 Excavation In Stewart County, Tennessee Portion of the Lake Barkley Reservoir</u> (Knoxville, Tn.: University of Tennessee Press, 1963), 14-20.

can be found throughout the land between the rivers. The mounds were apparently built to serve as ceremonial sites and burial grounds, which indicates a belief in an afterlife. Because the bodies were buried in layers, the mounds reached heights of fifteen or more feet. Mounds were found near the communities of Tharpe and Indian Mound in Tennessee and Trigg County, Kentucky.[2]

These Woodland people gradually developed a life based upon agriculture. They were probably the first to cultivate corn in the region. They used bows and arrows as well as spears in hunting game and fighting their enemies. They made pottery, including large vessels for cooking. Their homes were circular huts or wigwams, made by pushing small poles into the ground and bending them to form a dome-shaped framework.[3]

The Mississippian Cultures, the name given to the primitive people who lived or hunted on the land between the rivers from 1200 A.D. to 1500, followed the Woodland culture. The Early Mississippian built large temple mounds for religious and community buildings. When the temples deteriorated, they were probably destroyed and another temple would be constructed on the site. The process was likely repeated several times if the people remained in the area. The top layers of these temples were probably added by Native Americans who either succeeded the Early Mississippian tribe or united with it.[4]

The tribesmen constructed rectangular dwellings by setting long poles upright in trenches. These poles were used to form walls, and the tops of the poles were tied together to hold a thatched roof. Their pottery was quite distinctive because of the design and decoration, and their crops included beans, potatoes, squash, and pumpkins as well as corn. Their diet was supplemented by wild berries and plants which were indigenous to the region. They hunted wild animals, large and small, and used their meat and skins for food, clothing, and shelter.[5]

The people of the late Mississippian culture divided themselves into tribal bands and adopted tribal names. Later, based upon their languages, the natives were classified into the Muskhogean, Caddoan, Iroquoian, Sioux, and Algonquin groups. Those who either lived or hunted in the land between the rivers were the Creeks, Chickasaw, and Choctaw because they belonged to the Muskhogean language group. Other tribes such as the Shawnee, Yuchi, and Cherokee were often classified in the Iroquoian tribe. As the language changed and tribes began to identify with a particular society, conflicts often developed among the groups.[6]

As the differences among the tribes grew, generated by language and cultural differences, the tribes adopted individual names, traditions and lifestyles. For example, unlike other tribes in the area, the Creek Indians operated two types of towns. The red town was devoted to preparing for war, and the white town was devoted to preserving peace. Ultimately, these

---

[2]Ibid.

[3]Ibid.

[4]Robert F. Berkhofer, Jr., The White Man's Indian: Images of the American Indian From Columbus to the Present (New York: Alfred A. Knopf, 1978), 22-107.

[5]Ibid.

[6]Ibid. The major conflicts in the land between the rivers centered on the violation of hunting agreements.

developing differences resulted in the inability to unite and form a strong confederation for defense.[7]

Life in the Creek towns was concentrated around the public square, with each dwelling open on the side facing the square. Council meetings were held daily, and the whole conference met periodically. Members of the tribe had to reach common agreement on such issues as war and the tribal site. The elders, both men and women, assigned chores, work, or duties by gender, and women were allowed some voice in the decision-making of the tribe.[8]

War and diseases kept the population of the Creek tribe relatively small in the Tennessee and Kentucky territories. Most died young and few reached the age of forty. The dead were buried in individual graves near the village.[9]

A few Yuchi (or Euchee) hunted or traded in the area even though they apparently lived in present day East Tennessee. These people were probably forced out of central Tennessee by the more powerful Cherokee.[10]

The Shawnee occupied part of the area and traded with the French, who referred to them as the Chaouanon. About 1715, the Cherokee and Chickasaw combined forces to attempt to drive them out of the Cumberland Valley, but they offered strong resistance and remained in the area for many years. The Shawnee had burial customs similar to those of the Creek tribe.[11]

Without doubt, the Cherokee were the most powerful tribe in Tennessee and Kentucky when the explorers and settlers entered the area. They called themselves the "Principal People" because they considered themselves superior to all other tribes. Cherokee village life was centered around the public square. Tradition dictated that the council house and temple had to be placed on the west. The dwellings, constructed with vertical logs, were grouped around the square. A fireplace, a shallow pit scooped out of the earth, was located in the center of the dwelling, flanked by a hearthstone used for baking corn bread. The beds, usually attached to the wall, were made from saplings and woven splints. When cold weather came the family moved into a cone-shaped winter home framed from saplings and then covered with dirt.[12]

The temple, used mainly for religious rites, was also the public hall for civil and military meetings. The structure had seven sides to correspond to the seven clans of the Cherokee

---

[7]The lack of Indian unity allowed the settlers to force them off their lands rather quickly. See Francis Jennings, The Invasion of America: Indians, Colonialism, and the Cant of Conquest (Chapel Hill: University of North Carolina Press, 1975), 56-76.

[8]Ibid.

[9]National Park Service, Survey of the Archeological Resources of Barkley Reservoir, Kentucky and Tennessee (Richmond, Va.: Department of the Interior, 1958), 22-23.

[10]Philip B. Hamer, Tennessee: A History 1673-1932, vol. I (New York: The American Historical Society, Inc., 1933), 13-28.

[11]Leitch J. Wright, Jr., The Only Land They Knew: The Tragic Story of the American Indians in the Old South (New York: The Free Press, 1981), 40-59.

[12]Ibid.

Nation. Seven large pillars lined the outer walls. People sat on tiers of benches built along the walls. An altar, usually made from stone, contained a ceremonial fire which was kept burning. Annually, the altar fire was extinguished and then quickly rekindled as a token of the continuity of the Cherokee.[13]

The Cherokee had one chief for the nation, but he was advised by seven counselors representing each division or clan. Other powerful officials in the tribe included the medicine men, priests, and the honored woman. The women, especially in time of war, played an important leadership function and had a vote through their honored woman on decisions about war. They exercised the power of life and death over captives taken in battle and it was not unusual for the women to decide the fate of captives even in time of peace. Stories abound of Cherokee women who saved the lives of white captives. The people had a concept of creation as well as life after death. The supreme being was called Yowa and periodically the people fasted, prayed, and offered sacrifices to the god. Since their religious life was closely associated with the civil government, the priests and medicine men were selected in early childhood and received special training for their role as adult leaders.[14]

The people were farmers and hunters. Although they depended on fishing and hunting for their meat supply and the skins of animals for clothing, they relied upon agriculture as well. The chief crops were corn, beans, gourds, squash, pumpkins, and sunflowers, and both men and women tilled the soil. Women usually did not hunt large game, but they often hunted and killed small animals for food and skins. They had developed skills in making pottery, stone pipes, and baskets. The artisans demonstrated their understanding of form and matter in their carvings in both wood and stone. They reproduced the shapes of birds, animals, and people. The people wove baskets and mats out of strips of cane, colored with dyes made from plants and berries. They wore clothing made from animal skins decorated with feathers, shells, and pieces of metal. Women wore skirts and shoulder mantles. The men wore breech cloths and sleeveless shirts.[15]

The Cherokee were somewhat taller and more robust than the other Native Americans of the region. They had coarse, black hair and an olive complexion. The men usually shaved their heads or had all of their hair plucked out by the roots. Some men left a patch of hair on the back of their head which they decorated with beads, feathers, wampum and other items. The women wore long hair with many types of ornaments woven into the strands.[16]

Marriage customs seem to have been influenced by the near-equality of the sexes. The matrilineal system predominated and elaborate negotiations were carried on by the kinfolk of the couple. Once marriage was agreed upon, the groom sent the bride a piece of venison as a pledge that he would provide an ample food supply. The bride sent the groom an ear of corn as a token of her commitment to help tend the crops and prepare the food.[17]

---

[13]Ibid.

[14]Ibid.

[15]Ibid.

[16]Ibid.

[17]Ibid.

The lives of most of these people appeared to be leisurely and pleasant. The forests teemed with game and the streams were stocked with fish. Without much cultivation, the fertile soil produced corn and other crops. The environment was wholesome, and the diet was nutritious. The culture and religion dictated that the people practice strict personal hygiene. Frequent bathing and the ritual cleansing of the body for religious ceremonies resulted in a more fit individual. The steam huts served as a way to purify the mind as well as the body.

Large-scale wars among the tribes in the land between the rivers were not prevalent before white men entered the area. Most of the ensuing conflicts resulted when they incited one tribe to war against another. Neighboring tribes engaged in commerce, transporting goods along trails and by canoe on the rivers. Usually the tribes shared hunting grounds in the land between the rivers because of dual claims and it was a choice hunting ground. It was exceptionally easy to trap the wild game between the rivers. The hunters would start a fire and drive the animals to the rivers and then kill as many as they wanted. The early conflicts usually arose between those tribes when someone violated the agreement over the hunting areas.[18]

European Explorers and Traders

American history, many people like to think, began with the arrival of the Europeans. They landed in a virgin land, and in making their way over the continent, they were impeded only by a shortage of labor and the savages who stood in the way. But this view overlooks the fact that Europeans invaded and eventually displaced somewhere between seven and ten million native inhabitants. The importance of these Indians, as they were called by the European explorers, is not due simply to the fact that they were here first. In a way their presence gave shape to the patterns of European settlement, impeding it for a full century and, thereafter, making some lands available and keeping others closed. They interacted with the explorers and hunters and instructed them on survival in the wilderness. They provided food supplies which were later introduced in Europe. They taught their language to the newcomers and many of those words were adopted into the language of the settlers. Trade relations were important to the Europeans, and many men made fortunes in the trade with Indians. Later, the threat of Indian attack forced men and women to become expert marksmen.[19]

Europeans succeeded in establishing permanent settlements in North America only after a century of experience with survival in the wilderness and trade with the natives. During the sixteenth century, brass and glass beads, mirrors, iron nails, awls, knives, axes, copper pots, cloth, and countless other European products were spread over eastern North America as natives came to appreciate their value.[20]

---

[18]Ibid.

[19]William Cronon, Changes in the Land: Indians, Colonists, and the Ecology of New England (New York: Hill and Wang, 1983), 19-54.

[20]"Indians in Colonial History," in The Impact of Indian History on the Teaching of United States History, D'Arcy McNickle Center for the History of the American Indian, Occasional Papers in the Curriculum Series 4 (Chicago: The Newberry Library, 1986), 1-26.

The effects of colonization spread far west of the narrow strip of colonial territory on the east coast of North America. Maps showing where Native Americans lived in North America are generally blank in the Ohio River Valley, not because it was unoccupied at the beginning of the colonial era, but because the Iroquois drove out the occupants before Europeans arrived to assign them names. Though the Iroquois exercised a loose sovereignty in the eighteenth century, refugee Indians from the north, south, and east converged on the Ohio, Tennessee, and Cumberland Rivers region to form a unique type of republic. The republic included a diverse people, most of whom rejected private property and accumulation of wealth.[21]

When the European explorers came, they were survivors of an age rampant with infectious disease, an era dating from the Black Death in the fourteenth century. Older diseases such as smallpox and consumption were overshadowed by the bubonic plague, syphilis, and typhus. Measles, mumps, and chicken pox were minor diseases compared to the epidemics of the plague which spread through the North American settlements. Plague came to mean any pestilence that killed large numbers of people. Native Americans were particularly vulnerable to these new diseases because they had developed no immunities.[22]

The diseases spread through the native population like wild fire, killing nine of every ten people during the period. Indians knew nothing of the principle of contagion; they could be seen picking body lice and killing them with their teeth. The people had ancient customs of visiting the sick, thus spreading the disease. Compounding the effects of the disease were the methods used to treat illnesses. The ill were placed in a sweatbox, followed by immersion in the nearest cold pond or river. When the plagues reached their apex, so many people were dying or incapacitated that there were no well survivors to bury the dead.[23]

How did the Native Americans react to the first foreigners? Certainly, few if any of them anticipated that these people would gradually take control of the land.[24] Thus, the Indians probably welcomed these people. This assumption can be documented only through the observations of the Europeans because none of the Indians had a written language at that time.[25] One would suspect that they looked upon these people as strangers who had bizarre customs and incomprehensible traditions. They likely feared those who carried guns, but generally they seemed willing to share their food and homes with the strangers.

Eventually, Indians attacked the explorers.[26] As early as 1675, natives in New England had responded to the Europeans with violence. They agreed that fighting was the worst way to handle the contest for land, but the plans for arbitration and mediation had been unsuccessful.

---

[21]Ibid.

[22]Ibid.

[23]William Cronon, Changes in the Land, 29-39.

[24]Ibid.

[25]Later Sequoia, a Cherokee, developed a syllabary and his people wrote a constitution. They had printing presses, newspapers, schools and churches in their settlements.

[26]Numerous accounts of Indian attacks can be found in the history of the settlement of Tennessee and Kentucky.

Metacom (King Philip) spoke to Rhode Island Quakers in 1675 about the impossibility of bargaining with the white men in any transaction. He expressed fear, bewilderment, and hostility toward the settlers.[27]

Some of the early explorers kept journals and wrote of Indian-white relations. They found many natives who willingly accepted Europeans, but who, unfortunately, did not receive the same hospitable treatment. Explorers usually wrote of the natives with condescension: they were savage, primitive, naive, and innocent creatures who would trade valuable furs for mere baubles. As might be expected, peaceful interaction between the races did not last long.[28]

Spanish explorers came as early as 1540 to find gold and trade. Soon the natives were telling them about the abundance of gold which could be found farther west.[29] In 1566 Juan Padro led a group into the Cumberland River region, and soon thereafter the Spanish began to make annual trips from their trading posts in the South to trade with the natives in the Cumberland and Tennessee areas.[30]

The French came into the region eager to barter for furs and spread the Catholic religion. As early as 1692, they had already established trading posts in the area. Martin Chartier, like many other French merchants, married an Indian woman and established a trading post on the Cumberland River.[31] The extensive French influence on the region can be seen in the many place names such as Paris, Louisville, and Frenchburg in Kentucky and Paris, French Lick, and DeMumbreun in Tennessee.[32]

All the traders seemed to get along with the Indians until around 1741, when incidents of attacks on trading parties increased. Antoine Bonnefey and a band of hunters were attacked by the Cherokee as they neared the Cumberland River. Only Bonnefey escaped the attack, and even though severely wounded he made his way to a French fort at the present site of Montgomery, Alabama.[33]

Of all the European countries, England ultimately was to exert the most influence over the region. After many failed attempts, English explorers were able to establish a settlement in the New World in 1607 after the London Company received a charter from James I. The sea to sea grant included all lands between the 34th and 41st parallels. A colony was established and the land became known as Virginia. Later in 1663, Charles II granted all the lands 30

---

[27]Charles M. Segal and David C. Stinebeck, eds., Puritans, Indians, and Manifest Destiny (New York: G. P. Putnam's Sons, 1977), 191-193.

[28]Ibid.

[29]A mythology of the existence of cities of gold existed throughout this period and survived even longer in the western regions.

[30]Goodspeed, Histories of Tennessee (Nashville, Tn.: The Goodspeed Publishing Company, 1886), 756-898.

[31]Ibid. Unlike other explorers, the French lived in the area. They married native women, learned the language, and conducted a thriving trading operation with the tribes in the region.

[32]Ibid.

[33]Ibid.

degrees and 36 minutes north to a group of his friends; this land became know as the Carolinas. At that time the land between the rivers became a part of the English claims in the New World.

For years, English merchants had wanted to enter the fur trade and they immediately sent traders and trappers into the land between the rivers. As soon as the colonists in Virginia heard of the lands to the west, they began to make their way into the wilderness and by 1740, Englishmen had settled in the area.[34]

Immediately following the first settlers were colonial government officials anxious to lay claim to western lands. An example of these visitors was Thomas Walker of Virginia who came to the area in 1748.[35] Walker and his party heard the Indians refer to the river as the Shawnee. Walker renamed it the Cumberland.[36]

Eventually, the Englishmen began to characterize the Indians as savages who had to be controlled. A few of the early traders viewed them as a primitive people who would become civilized from association with the white man. Many people tried to find an explanation of how these people came to the New World. James Adair, a Scottish fur trader, was convinced that the Native Americans were descended from the Ten Lost Tribes of Israel. To prove his theory, Adair described in great detail the customs of the Cherokee and other southeastern tribes among whom he lived. He described the burial customs of the Cherokee as more like those of the Hebrews than of Indians in South America. Like the Hebrews, they were very careful in the burial of their dead, but they did not include all of their individual riches in the grave with the dead. The general custom of Native Americans in North America was to bequeath the goods to someone in the family. Adair was adamant, even obsessive, about his theory of the ancestry of the natives.[37]

European explorers and traders opened the gateway for settlers to move into the wilderness. These were the people who created the environment for the development of hostility between the two races, but it was the settlers who would face the wars which later erupted in the region.

---

[34]The generally accepted theory is that as the hunters and trappers increased their activity, the Indians reacted with violence to protect their hunting grounds. In the land between the rivers it appears that settlers worried the Indians more than the hunters. When English settlers entered the area around 1740, the natives began to attack all outsiders. It is probable that the settlers cleared land and did more damage to the hunting grounds, thus the Indians reacted with violence.

[35]Thomas Walker served on the commission to draw an official boundary line in 1779.

[36]The River was named for the Duke of Cumberland.

[37]Samuel Cole Williams, ed., Adair's History of the American Indians (Johnson City, Tn: Watauga Press, 1930), 186-187.

CHAPTER II

THE FIRST SETTLERS

The Pristine Country

It is difficult to visualize the land between the rivers at a time when the first Europeans were arriving. Only a few accounts left by the first explorers survive, and those narratives provide few detailed descriptions of the terrain and vegetation. Some accounts made by travelers in the 1700s who had an interest in botany were preserved. The French botanist, Andre Michaux, traveled down the Mississippi in approximately 1794 and ventured up the Cumberland. The descriptions left by Michaux and others in his party describe the land between the rivers as a virgin state with varied woodlands and other areas covered with jungle cane and scrub. The terrain away from the rivers and creeks was blanketed with dense sward.[1]

Gerald McCrain and Aubrey Grubb in a 1987 study determined the types of vegetation indigenous to the Fort Donelson area by producing an inventory of the vegetation existing at the time of their study. They classified the vegetation into three general patterns: the upland oak forest, swamp lowlands, and prairie or barrens areas. The study provides us with some idea of what plants were seen by the first white men to enter the region.

The upland oak forest was made up of vast stands of mixed hardwoods, including the water oak, willow oak, white oak, sweet gum, and black gum. Ashes, poplars, and beeches were present, but these specie were not as numerous as some of the other hardwoods. Overcup white oak, chestnut oak, northern red oak, and others were located near the Cumberland River. Cedar was rare and pine was generally not found in the area. Scrubs and small trees such as alder, willows, buttonbush, and chokeberry were found in wet areas. May apple was observed in the deep woodlands. Vines, including grape, begonia, and trumpet flower were prolific.[2]

In the lowlands near the rivers and creeks, the settlers probably found cypress, plane trees, and tupelo gum. Frequently along creek bottoms were buttonbush, papaw, magnolia, box elder, and Carolina rose.[3]

In the prairie or barren area, which is often referred to as a part of the highland rim, there were treeless areas in the midst of black jack oak, Spanish oak, red oak, sourwood, and chestnuts. Shrubs such as the hydrangea, hazelnut, serviceberry, and huckleberry were present. It may be that some of the lands were barren because the Indians used fire to encircle their

---

[1] J. Milton Henry, <u>Land Between the Rivers</u>, 29.

[2] Ibid.

[3] Ibid.

game, drive off enemy war parties, to aid in their travel, and to improve conditions for good crops of nuts, seeds or berries. Also, early settlers burned large areas of timber land in order to convert it into croplands and pasture.[4]

A 1986 study of the Fort Donelson region by Dr. Edward Wayne Chester found that the area, which would be generally applicable to the land between the rivers, was made up of a plateau with narrow ridges, steep slopes, and stream valleys. Caves were not uncommon in the general area. Much of the area had a pattern of soil over Warsaw limestone of the Mississippian Age, and the limestone had weathered into a rocky soil in many areas. Of the many types of soil found in the general area, the most abundant was cherty, droughty, Bodine soils on steep slopes.[5]

The climate of the land between the rivers is a warm-temperate one generally with warm summers and mild winters. The average precipitation is 49.91 inches. The average annual temperature is approximately 58.1 degrees F. The average growing season is approximately 191 days.

The Europeans found that thousands of animals, especially the buffalo, roamed the land. Animal traces or trails connected the rivers and creeks. The buffalo traces were sixty to two hundred feet wide and crisscrossed the terrain.

The First Permanent Settlers

As John Donelson and the first group of permanent settlers made their way from present day East Tennessee into Middle Tennessee to establish a settlement at Nashborough (Nashboro) in 1779, they came up the Cumberland River on flatboats and passed by the land between the rivers. Navigation of the narrow Cumberland was exceedingly slow and the party had to make frequent stops along the way to replenish their food supply.[6]

Just as these people began their journey, a smallpox epidemic broke out. Those people who had the disease were separated from the others and placed on flatboats at the rear of the flotilla. Isolation of the smallpox victims was the only way they knew of to keep the disease from spreading. As the flatboats made their way slowly up the Cumberland River toward the land between the rivers, they were attacked by Indians, and the boats containing the smallpox victims were captured. The attackers killed the people, took all the provisions off the boats and divided them among the people of the tribe. They even stripped the dead and took their clothing. Since the Indians had no immunity from smallpox, their use of the captured blankets and clothing exposed them to the deadly disease, and later, a devastating smallpox epidemic

---

[4]Ibid.

[5]Edward W. Chester, The Vascular Flora of Fort Donelson National Military Park, Stewart County, Tennessee (Knoxville, Tennessee: University of Tennessee Resource Management Report 80, 1986), 1-85.

[6]Henry, 39.

broke out, killing hundreds of people.[7]

This wilderness area had the reputation of being a haven for criminals, but the Donelson party had not sighted anyone until they reached the Cumberland near the land between the rivers. At that point the expedition ran out of food, and they were forced to stop to replenish their food supply. When they went ashore they found evidence that white people had been there only hours before. Signs of abandoned camps and even the remnants of a cabin were found near the river. The next day the Donelson band sighted a woman and two men on the bank of the river and tried to determine who they were. But they would not respond to the greetings from the Donelson party. They were obviously hostile and it was apparent that they did not want a conversation with the travelers. The members of the Donelson party did not tarry in the area because they were afraid that a criminal band might attack them at any moment.[8]

Even though the country offered a wide variety of animals, the hunters in the Donelson party preferred bear meat over venison or buffalo. After days of eating dried meat and corn bread, they were particularly eager to find any plants which they knew were edible. A wild plant which they called Shawnee sallet was gathered along the banks of the river and boiled.[9] It is likely that the plant is known today as Poke sallet.

By 1779, the officials of the states of Virginia and North Carolina were impatient to establish a permanent boundary line between the two states and settle the older disputed colonial boundaries. The officials realized that settlers were moving into the disputed boundary areas and the state officials were concerned about which state should receive the revenue from the sale of land.[10]

Richard Henderson was commissioned by North Carolina; Thomas Walker[11] and Daniel Smith were commissioned by Virginia to conduct a survey to settle the boundary line. When the two commissions could not agree, Walker and Smith proceeded from the Clear Fork of the Cumberland River to a point at which the two states would reach the east bank of the Cumberland River. Walker and his team continued the survey westward to the Tennessee River. The irregular boundary line caused disputes between Virginia and North Carolina.[12]

Few records remain to document when the first settlers came to the land between the rivers. By 1750 a few people were already living in the area, and it appears that these people remained for a few years and then moved to other areas deeper in the wilderness. By 1779, settlers coming to the land between the rivers represented a cross section of the American people during and immediately after the Revolutionary War period. Some of the settlers came because they were poverty stricken, and they moved west with little more than what they could carry on

---

[7] Ibid.

[8] Ibid.

[9] Ibid.

[10] Hamer, 12-56.

[11] Thomas Walker had been in the area in 1740.

[12] Hamer, 42.

their backs. Many of the people had no formal education and were often unskilled. These people dreamed of owning land and becoming self-sufficient farmers. Adventurers came seeking gold and immediate wealth. They wanted to see the unexplored land and hunt the wild game. The adventurers often did not remain in the area. They tended to settle for a time and then move westward following the frontier.[13]

The peak period for settlement came when men received grants of land from the states of Virginia or North Carolina as payments for their services in the Revolutionary War. Both states followed similar plans in issuing land grants. A private could receive up to 640 acres; a fifer or sergeant 1,000 acres; a lieutenant 2,560 acres, and a captain could receive 3,840 acres. The veterans who did not want to settle in the west sold the land to people who did.[14]

Because it was difficult to survey the individual land grants, those people who were moving to the area often settled on farmland and later learned that they did not have a clear title to the property. They were then forced to leave their homesteads and move further west.

Boundary Disputes

Disputes between Tennessee and Kentucky which directly affected pioneers on the land between the rivers began when Tennessee became a state in 1796. Kentucky had joined the Union in 1792, and when Tennessee entered, the two states continued the boundary controversy that had started earlier between Virginia and North Carolina. Beginning in 1797, the officials of the new states agreed to discuss the Walker line and make an attempt to reach an acceptable compromise. The discussion went on for years and the people, not always sure if they were citizens of Tennessee or Kentucky, tended to identify themselves as citizens of the land between the rivers. State citizenship seemed to make very little difference in their lives.[15]

In 1819, the Kentucky legislature appointed a commission headed by Robert Alexander and Luke Munsell to study the Walker line and to make some determination of the legalities of the boundary. Andrew Jackson and Isaac Shelby had already negotiated a treaty with the Chickasaw Indians and the treaty had included a provision that set the existing line as the boundary between Kentucky and Tennessee.[16]

In the same year, the officials of the state of Tennessee were mostly concerned that there were to be no changes in the line east of the Tennessee River. The Tennessee officials requested a conference and when it was convened an agreement was made to accept the old Walker line from the Tennessee River eastward. Included in this agreement were the provisions that Kentucky would have the authority to dispose of all unappropriated land in the region between the rivers, but Tennessee would maintain political control of all land within her boundary set by

---

[13]Ibid.

[14]Ibid.

[15]Ibid.

[16]Ibid.

the old Walker line. Settlers in the land between the rivers continued to question the legalities of the line and forced further discussion in the legislatures of both states in 1827, 1831, 1844, and in 1858. The matter was finally concluded in 1860 when Kentucky ceded some 2,500 square miles of land mostly in the land between the rivers to Tennessee.[17]

The unique history of the disputed state boundaries resulted in an interesting attitude among those people who settled the land between the rivers. Because they identified with the local community and paid little attention to their state citizenship, they tended to look upon themselves as independent of state control. The area was bounded on three sides by water, and early roads were nonexistent; these conditions isolated the people in the land between the rivers. The geographic isolation led the people to be predisposed to preserve their old ways and develop traditions and customs which remained relatively unaffected by outside influences over the years.[18]

Early Settlements

As settlers moved into the land between the rivers, they tended to homestead first along both banks of the Tennessee and Cumberland because of the fertile soil, water supply, and ease of transportation. Later, as more and more people entered the region, they followed the animal traces and trails to find creeks and springs to establish their homesteads. The best farmland was near the rivers and creeks, and those people who were forced to settle inland often purchased several hundred acres of land in order to have access to fertile land and water.

People lived in a brush arbor called a "shebang" or in open camps until they could build their first cabins.[19] The first order of business after a camp was established was to clear land for planting. The trees were cut, and a small patch of land was tilled by hand. At this point settlers did not attempt to remove the tree stumps but planted around them. After the corn and any available vegetables were planted, the settlers began the construction of their crude cabins.[20]

The cabins were built from logs which were laid horizontally to form a square room. The spaces between the logs were chinked with a mixture of mud and animal hair. The first chimney was made from wooden slabs and sticks covered with the mud and animal hair compound. The roof of the cabin was made from wooden shingles usually called slabs, and

---

[17]Ibid.

[18]A survey of marriage records in Stewart, Trigg, and Lyon Counties indicates that most family names were constant from 1800 to 1865. The same records show several new family names appeared in the period immediately after the Civil War, but few new names appeared after 1879. During and after WWII approximately twenty new names were listed, but the most obvious flood of new citizens began around 1965 probably resulting from the activities of TVA.

[19]The word "shebang" is still used in the region. "He destroyed the whole shebang." is a commonplace expression.

[20]A survey of the county records in Frankfort, Kentucky and Nashville, Tennessee provides some information about the first land claims in the land between the rivers. A map plotting these settlements indicates that the river settlements were the first, followed by creekside settlements.

animal skins and wooden shutters covered the windows.

The use of animal skin, especially from a young deer, to cover the windows evolved into an interesting craft. Settlers soaked the skin, called a hide, in mild lye water or a solution made from the bark of a hardwood tree to make it malleable. The skin was scraped to remove the hair and then cured by rubbing it with animal brains or even human urine. The skin was then stretched until it became so thin that it was almost transparent and used to cover the windows to substitute for glass. Many types of window coverings were used because it was often several years after they were settled before families were able to add stone chimneys, extra rooms, and glass windows to their cabins. When the log home was covered with a plank siding, it was an indication that the family was prosperous.[21]

The staple foods for the first years on the land were meat from wild animals, bread from the corn crop, and any wild plants, nuts, and berries which the settlers learned were safe to eat. In 1780 a hunting party from Nashborough killed 105 bears, 75 buffaloes, and 80 deer for a part of the winter meat supply. Because these people had salt licks nearby, they were able to preserve the fresh meat with a combination of salt and smoke. Pioneers learned to follow animals and observe where they licked the earth. Most likely the animals had found salt. Even small quantities of salt in the soil could be extracted and used. If no salt was available, people were forced to dry the meat. Preservation of meat for the winter months was important because the larger animals moved south when the snow and ice covered their food supply. Hunting small animals for the winter rations did not always guarantee enough food for the family.[22]

Corn was the most valuable crop because it provided bread and whiskey for the family. Without grist mills, it was almost impossible to grind the corn into meal for bread. The common practice was to make the corn into hominy and then crush the hominy for bread.[23] The hominy block, commonly made from the stump of a nearby tree, was indispensable for making bread. The preparation of the hominy block included selecting the stump of a tree near the cabin, then shaping a hollow indentation about the size of a large bowl in the center of the stump by chipping and burning. Once the bowl was shaped, a pestle made from a block of wood was fashioned to fit into the depression. The pestle was either lifted by hand or if it were extremely heavy, the handle was fastened to a sapling and it was pulled up or down by a leather rope or grapevine.

To make hominy, the corn was soaked in lye water to soften the husk surrounding the kernel. The corn was boiled to soften the husk so that it would split away from the heart of the corn. Also, the boiling removed the lye residue. Once the husk was removed, the corn was called hominy. The hominy was placed in the bowl fashioned in the stump and crushed with the pestle. The pulverized, lumpy, viscous, and bland hominy was mixed with water to make

---

[21]Maude Ward Lafferty, The Lure of Kentucky (Detroit: Singing Tree Press, 1971), 5-49.

[22]Goodspeed, Histories, 432.

[23]Lafferty, Kentucky, 50.

14

a concoction which they called bread.[24]

Settlers devised many ways of using the hominy meal. Desserts were made with honey, fruit, and the corn mixture. The corn was also made into flat cakes which were cooked in ashes of the campfire. When it was necessary to cook the bread in a hurry in the field, a mixture of meal and water was placed on the blade of a hoe and held over a fire.[25] The bread was called fritters when it was made from the meal and water and fried in animal fat.[26]

Lye was an important commodity in the home. As was mentioned, it was used to make hominy and it was used as well in the preparation of other foods. The most important use was for making soap. The lye soap was used to clean the body, clothes, walls, and floors. A practice of using strong lye water to kill insects, especially ticks, lice, and fleas was found throughout the frontier. A lye or ash hopper was built very soon after the construction of the cabin. A container made from two slanted logs or planks fastened together to form a trough was fitted with legs so that it would be a few feet off the ground. The legs on the trough were shortened in the front to allow the trough to slant toward one end. The ashes from hardwood trees were placed in the trough and a small amount of water was poured over them each day. The water would leech the lye out of the ashes and the liquid lye dripped into a container.[27]

To the settlers fermented beverages were indispensable. When they moved into the land between the rivers, they brought with them the knowledge and accoutrements to make beer, wine, and whiskey. The settlers who were primarily from Scotland, Ireland, Wales, and northern England came with strong traditions in the production and consumption of alcohol. These people knew how to produce a supreme brew, and great pride was taken in producing the best whiskey in the community.

The earliest settlers produced many different types of fermented drinks. When they first settled on the land, they used whatever was available, including vegetables, fruits, and grain to make wine, beer, and other brews. Among other things, they used wild grapes, blackberries, persimmons, sassafras bark, birch bark, hickory nuts, pumpkins, turnips, potatoes, apples, peaches, plums, and cherries for their fermented drinks.

The stillhouse or tavern was one of the first public establishments built in a community. It often served as the local community center, and the entire family patronized the business. The local government regulated the price of the drinks and food sold at the establishment.[28]

---

[24]Ibid.

[25]The word "hoecake" likely came from this custom.

[26]Lafferty, Kentucky, 52.

[27]In interviews with residents in the land between the rivers in 1956, lye was mentioned as one of the most important items found on the farms until after the 1930s. The interviews are in the hands of the author.

[28]Stillhouses were regulated as soon as county governments were established. Owners were directed by the magistrates of the county courts to charge a standard fee for their alcohol. It appears that the stillhouses were able to draw customers because they were served good whiskey but other types of alcohol were brought in as well. Rum was a standard drink served in Stewart County, but there is no evidence that it was made there. It is likely that it was brought in via the Cumberland.

Whiskey was the drink of choice for the people. Initially, the settler built a still to produce whiskey for family consumption, but it was not long before the settlers were competing over who produced the best whiskey. The contents and techniques of brewing were family secrets. The real art of whiskey making, according to the makers, was in the control of the fermenting stages of the process. The grain, malt, and water had to be added at just the right time to produce a superior drink. Stirring the mash was considered by some as the most critical step in the process. The mash had to stirred with just the right momentum and at the right time; otherwise the whiskey would not be perfect.[29]

The quintessence of whiskey could only be achieved if the producer sprouted the corn and ground it into malt which would be used to generate the fermentation. The use of sugar or yeast to initiate the fermentation was intolerable. Most of the drinkers could tell by the taste that it was not even good corn liquor.

Preparing the malt was a complicated task within itself. The corn for the malt had to be placed in burlap bags called tow sacks and soaked with hot water. The bags of corn had to be kept warm and at a constant temperature. The bags of corn were placed in sawdust or straw until the corn sprouted. Disagreements abounded over what constituted the correct size of the sprouts to use for the malt. The general consensus was that the sprouts should reach about three inches in length before they were ground into malt. Sprouts with any imperfection had to discarded.

In the land between the rivers, the pure corn whiskey was referred to as corn squeezing, white mule, white lightning, or corn liquor. The purists agreed that the stills must have copper pots and worms and the right type of water, with as few minerals as possible, in order to make a superior whiskey.[30]

If a still owner made an excellent whiskey, he could sell to his neighbors. If that were the case, the operator used at least a fifty gallon copper pot and placed his still near a stream with clean, clear, soft water. In the land between the rivers, creeks rising from underground springs and supplemented by rain water often flowed over chert and limestone rocks which produced a clear, cool source of water for the whiskey.[31]

The furnace and the still were as individual as the person making the whiskey. The furnace, constructed from the rocks near the stream, was by necessity located near a wood supply. The configuration of the worm or copper condensing coil, made from copper pipe, was determined by individual preference. Regardless of the curves in the coil it had to be shaped by hand from one length of copper pipe. The usual practice was to fill the pipe with sand, then bend the filled pipe around a tree, until the desired pattern and length had been achieved. The coils were placed in the creek, just below the surface of the water, so that the running water

---

[29]For a good study of whiskey production see Joseph Early Dabney, Spirits: A Chronicle of Corn Whiskey (New York: Charles Scribner's Sons, 1974), 31-199. Information about the production of whiskey in the land between the rivers was gathered from interviews with people who lived in the area. Mr. Joe Dill, Mr. Frazier Riggins, and others talked with the author in 1955 and 1956. Other interviews were conducted in 1990.

[30]Ibid.

[31]Ibid.

flowed over them as the whiskey was produced.[32]

Eight bushels of corn meal were needed to make a run in a fifty gallon pot. Eight empty barrels had to be readied for the run. A half bushel of meal was put in each barrel and another four bushels were put in the copper pot, already filled with water, to cook. The meal and water mixture was warmed until it reached the mush stage. The mush was then transferred from the pot to the barrels. The pot was cleaned several times to remove any trace of the mush which could contaminate the next run. The mush in the barrels was left to ferment. The time necessary for fermentation depended on the opinion of the operator, but when it was ready, the mash, as it was now called, was thinned with water and stirred. Again depending on the producer, about two gallons of malt were poured into each barrel. The mash had to be kept warm and allowed to ferment. The operators determined the proper amount of time by watching the bubbles at the top of each barrel and the amount of clear liquid which had come to the top of the barrel.[33]

In the last stage of production, the content of each barrel was run through the still. The first run from each barrel yielded about six gallons of siglings or beer. At the beginning of the second run, the whiskey was about one hundred and sixty proof and dropped to about one hundred proof near the end of the run. The run had to be stopped at exactly the right point or the dregs would give the whiskey a sour taste and smell. An expert could tell the proper time to stop by watching the liquid as it came from the end of the worm. Good drinking whiskey was at least one hundred and twenty proof.[34]

Most of the drinkers could determine the proof of the whiskey by the size of the bubble or bead. To determine the bead, a jar of whiskey was sealed and turned upside down and the bubbles or beads, as they were called, slowly rose to the top. As the bubbles formed and moved toward the surface, the size of the bead and the time it took to reach the surface determined the proof. Good drinking whiskey, one hundred and twenty proof, had a bead the size of a bb shot.[35]

A swallow of the best whiskey could leave the inexperienced drinker breathless, so a few drinkers had to cut the whiskey with water in order to swallow it. A small number of people added sugar and water to the whiskey to make toddies. Toddies were most often given to very small children and the very ill. Because children began to consume the whiskey at an early age, a healthy adult was expected to take the whiskey straight, and most of the people, men and women, drank whiskey every day.[36]

When more and more settlers entered the region, the whiskey producers sold their goods to neighbors and shipped the whiskey to consumers outside the area. Corn, which was easily produced on the farm, made the cost of the production quite low and farmers often made

---

[32]Ibid.

[33]Ibid.

[34]Ibid.

[35]Ibid.

[36]Ibid.

whiskey as a way of increasing their income. The reputation of the region's whiskey grew until it was understood in several states that some of the best corn whiskey in the United States was found in the land between the rivers. The word spread that whiskey was available in large quantities. Later, the reputation resulted in farmers turning to corn and whiskey production to remain financially secure.

Pioneers made cloth from animal hair and wild nettles as a substitute for woolen cloth. The cloth was coarse, prickly, and extremely irritating to the skin. It is no wonder that the people preferred animal skin clothes, which they fashioned much like those worn by the Native Americans.

When the settlers used the homespun cloth, they often changed the somber color of the material by using homemade dyes made from plants and berries. A dye was made from the inner bark of the white walnut tree to produce an interesting yellow shade. The bark from the black walnut tree produced a brown or tan dye. Berries from sumac and cedar were used to make brighter colors such as red, purple, and green.[37]

Pioneers, out of necessity, were obliged to use all available materials and supplies found in their surroundings. For years sugar was unobtainable and honey became the replacement. Colonies of bees were found in hollow trees throughout the area. Even though the wild honey appeared to be readily available, farmers did not like the total dependency of relying on the capriciousness of mother nature to provide enough for their needs.

Farmers established bee hives to guarantee an adequate supply of honey by catching wild bees when they swarmed or hovered together. The bees swarmed when the colony was disturbed or they were in the process of establishing a new colony. As the bees flew away from the old hive, they were easily sighted, and people prepared to capture them. A loud persistent noise would attract the bees and they would hover atop the sound. A common practice was to beat on a tin pot or pan to attract them. The bees were coaxed to hover on a tree limb near the ground. Special care had to be taken in order to keep the bees from swarming on the person making the noise.

As soon as the bees had settled, they could, with great care, be moved to a previously prepared hive on the farm. A novice in handling bees was often in for a nasty surprise. The bees were unpredictable, and extremely dangerous. Children were warned not to try to attract bees while they were swarming because the multiple stings would kill them. This method of establishing hives continued until insecticides destroyed most of the wild bees in the area.[38]

Bee-keeping was a relatively easy activity because of the climate and the availability of food. The mild spring weather produced early food sources and the first warm winds in February brought out an abundance of flowers from the red maple, plum, peach, spicewood, dogwood, sassafras, pear, cherry, gooseberry, and apple trees. Plants including red and white clover, blackberry, dewberry, catnip, peas, golden rod, and many others furnished the nectar for the bees. Because of the mild and relatively short winter, the hives held an accumulation of honey. Normally, the summer months were not extremely hot and the food supply for the

---

[37]Ibid.

[38]According to the people in the area, the sightings of swarming bees ceased in the decade of the 1950s. Interviews by the author with former citizens in the land between the lakes in 1990.

bees was constant.

Whether the bees were making their honey in the hollow tree or in a prepared hive, they protected it from the people. Robbing the hive was dangerous and certain settlers built a reputation around their proficiency in handling wild bees.[39] Some individuals simply walked to the colony and placed a hand among the bees and removed the honey comb without a sting or even agitating the bees. These people were said to have special powers to charm the bees. Because these charmers often hummed while they were gathering the bees, it was believed that they had the ability to communicate with the queen bee.[40]

For those who were not bee charmers, the routine was to build a small fire at the base of the tree which contained the beehive and force the smoke into the hive. The smoke would drive the bees away from the hive. These people did not dare hum or make any kind of noise which would agitate the bees. Gloves and cloth masks were worn for added protection and while the bees were trying to escape the smoke, the honey was removed from the hive. A number of bees were killed or injured in the process of removing the honey, and because the people enjoyed chewing the honeycomb as soon as it was removed from the hive, attention had to be paid to removing the injured bees else the person was stung in the mouth or lips.[41]

The honeycomb was a useful commodity in the household. The honeycomb was heated, strained through a thin cloth, and a sealing wax, which served many purposes in the home, was rendered. Wax could be reheated and used to seal jams, jellies, and other bottled goods. Pots or crocks were filled and the wax provided a protective covering. Wax, placed in a shallow dish with a wick made from cotton or linen fibers, served as a crude source of light. Because the wax was absorbed very slowly into the wick, the odor and thick smoke were unpleasant. Many people preferred a tallow or fish oil light to the wax light.[42]

By 1780 as the number of settlers increased and cleared more land to plant their crops, the Native Americans launched a campaign to force them out of the land between the rivers. Raids became a constant threat to the settlers, forcing men, women, and children to go armed. Skill in using guns became an important part of adaptation to the frontier.[43] Their crude cabins did not provide enough safety from the raids, and the settlers built blockhouses in a central location in the community. The blockhouse, made from large logs, was built with small openings in the walls from which the defenders could shoot at the Indians. Food supplies and water were kept at the blockhouse in case the raiders laid siege. If a settler was not able to use

---

[39]Information about handling bees can be found in letters from the members of the Joe Heflin family from 1820 to 1850. The information is in the hands of the author.

[40]Ibid.

[41]Ibid.

[42]Ibid.

[43]It was mentioned earlier that hostility between the races escalated in direct relationship to the number of settlers who entered the area. The raids in the region increased rapidly after 1780, and seems to support the thesis that Indians resented settlers who cleared the land and interfered with the hunting grounds.

a blockhouse, he often constructed his cabin with very narrow windows so that he could defend himself from attacks. The Boyd house built in 1809 in the Blue Spring Community near Fort Henry had windows in the attic shaped much like port holes. Rifles could be mounted in these windows to ward off an attack.[44]

Throughout the early settlement period, battles between the Native Americans and the settlers resulted in heavy death tolls and many injuries. People were scalped; incredibly, some of them survived. Persons who survived a scalping endured horrifying pain and for the rest of their lives, they suffered from the effects of the hideous scars about the face and head.

---

[44]Pictures of the house are owned by the descendants of James Boyd.

CHAPTER III

ORGANIZATION OF THE COUNTY
GOVERNMENTS

Portions of Stewart County, Tennessee, along with Trigg and Lyon Counties in Kentucky eventually made up the local political units in the land between the rivers. All three counties had many things in common, including the fact that they were settled at about the same time by people moving to the frontier from Virginia and North Carolina. These people were Celtic in origin and very anxious, for whatever reason, to start a new life in the wilderness.[1]

The soil and mineral deposits were similar in all the counties. The region was covered with virgin forests and the soil was especially fertile in the creek and river bottom lands. The topography was uneven with many hills and ravines. Limestone cliffs jutted out of hills, and clear, sparkling spring water bubbled from underneath limestone, forming numerous creeks and small pools of water. The mild climate, along with the annual rainfall, made life pleasant for the colonists.

Stewart County

Stewart County was a part of Davidson County, North Carolina from 1783 to 1788. During the period from 1789 to 1796, it was a portion of the Tennessee County of the Southwest Territory.[2] From 1796 to November 1, 1803, the sector was a part of Montgomery County, Tennessee. On November 1, 1803, the state legislature, sitting at Knoxville, passed a statute which partitioned Montgomery County with a line which commenced with the Kentucky line thirteen miles west of the meridian of Clarksville and ran south to the state boundary. At that time, Stewart County extended south to the Alabama boundary and west to the Tennessee River.[3]

Duncan Stewart, a Scottish immigrant who had first settled in North Carolina, was one of the earliest settlers in the area. He acquired vast tracts of land and was instrumental in bringing several families to the locality. It was Stewart who negotiated with officials and eventually arranged for the founding of the county.[4] It was only fitting that the area should be named for him.

From 1795 to 1803, at the time that Duncan Stewart was acquiring land, several other

---

[1] By tracing family names through the census records from 1790, the author was able to determine that a large majority of the early settlers came from Ireland, Scotland, Wales and Northern England.

[2] Tennessee County, along with the other counties of the area became Tennessee in 1796.

[3] Goodspeed, Histories, 756-898.

[4] Ibid.

men were issued grants from the government of North Carolina. Thomas Armstrong, Caleb Fisher, Abner Lamb, Henry Turner, Robert Hays, Benjamin Shepherd, Brittian Sexton, Sam Boyt, Elisha Dawson, James Andrews, and James Martin came to establish farms on their land.[5] Smaller grants, approximately 274 to 640 acres, were awarded to Martin Armstrong, Lewis Pipkin, John Baker, John McNeese, Joseph Brach, Nathan Alexander, Arthur Tynor, Thomas Campbell, Charles Griggs, John McNairy, James Mills, Anthony Hart, John Rice, Henry Johnston, Thomas Sharp, Jesse Massie, Hayen Wells, James Coglin, Joshua Doris, James Lack, Abner Lamb, John Collins, Bryan Whitfield, and Jesse Burton.[6]   Around 1800 a wave of immigrants, numbering around one hundred, entered the area, stayed a short time and then moved farther into the wilderness.   Of this group, homesteaders such as John Kingings, Christopher Brandon, and Etheldred Wallace remained in the area.[7]

Etheldred Wallace, a tall, stern man, left Edinborough, Scotland with parents, William and Susanna, and seven brothers to settle in Virginia around 1770. For some reason Etheldred went back to Scotland but later returned to settle in North Carolina around 1774. While there he married Amy Taylor who owned land in Martin County, North Carolina. Around 1800, Etheldred with his family, which included his father, moved to Saline Creek near Bumpus Mills. Three of Etheldred's brothers joined him there, but for some reason, they moved in 1805 to Ashland, Kentucky.[8]

George Brandon came to Stewart County from North Carolina around 1800. He settled at Tobacco Port and quickly became a thriving businessman and farmer. His was the first general store in the area. His son, Christopher Brandon, inherited his father's ability to expand his real estate. Nathan Brandon, the grandson of George Brandon, became one of the first attorneys in the county, and was influential in the history of the area during the Civil War. At his death in 1891, his property in Dover went to the city for a cemetery.[9]

John Kingins and his mother came from North Carolina to Stewart County and settled at Tobacco Port around 1800. He married Martha Manning, and they had ten children.[10] The size of the Kingings family was characteristic of the large families of these early settlers. It was not uncommon for a family to have ten to fifteen children.[11]

---

[5]Land grants of 1000 to 1500 acres were given these men and others who entered the region from 1796 to 1803. Many of the descendants of these men live in Stewart County in 1992.

[6]A listing of names from the Stewart County Court Records of 1803, Book 00, compared to the telephone directory in 1990 shows all of these family names. Goodspeed, Histories of Tennessee includes some of these names on page 896.

[7]These men are typical of many of the early settlers in that they came from Europe to Virginia or North Carolina and then moved to settle in Stewart County.

[8]Stewart County Historical Society, The Stewart County Heritage: Dover, Tennessee (Dover, Tennessee: Stewart County Historical Society, 1980), 441.

[9]Ibid., 93.

[10]All of the early family members are buried in the family cemetery near Tobacco Port.

[11]Stewart County Historical Society, Heritage, 232.

Originally, Stewart County encompassed Houston, Humphreys, Perry, Wayne, and a part of Hardin and Lewis counties, and when the Western District was added to Tennessee in 1819, its jurisdiction was extended to the Mississippi River and encompassed approximately 425 square miles or 270,000 acres of the richest agricultural land in the state. Subsequent reorganization of the counties in 1821 resulted in the creation of thirteen new counties.

The legislative act creating Stewart County stipulated that a boundary line dividing Stewart and Montgomery had to be drawn, and in 1803 James Elder was appointed by the state as the surveyor to run the boundary between the two counties. James Huling, James Elder, Amos Bird, Harry Small, and John Blair were appointed to serve as commissioners to choose the site of the permanent county seat. While the men were trying to decide on the location, the first session of the county court was held at the home of William Martin who lived near Bald Island. As directed by the state legislature, the taxes for the fiscal year 1803 were presented to the commission by the sheriff of Montgomery County, and a state appointed commission which included George Petty, Caleb Williams, and James Tagert began to acquire the property for the county seat.[12] The commission was empowered to purchase thirty acres of land and to design the town. It was not an easy task to determine the location of the town. Ideally it would be in the geographical center of the county but more importantly at the time, the site must be near the settlers, and they were living along the Cumberland. Also that waterway gave the people easier passage to the towns of Clarksville and Nashville.[13]

The land on the Cumberland was chosen and eventually purchased from Robert Nelson in 1805.[14] A plot of one and one half acres was reserved for a court house, a jail, and stocks. The land around the public square was to be divided into lots which were to be sold to individuals who wished to establish businesses or homes within the confines of the town. All of the revenue from the sale of the lots had to be used to begin the immediate construction of the public buildings. After considerable argument, the commissioners agreed that the lots could be sold on credit because capital was required to pay for drawing the construction plans for Dover and the construction of the buildings.[15]

For more than two years, the members of the county court planned for the development of the region. The members of the court and other elected officials regulated many of the projects. Citizens were encouraged to build gristmills, sawmills, and ferries. In 1805 permission was granted to Jesse Denson to erect a public sawmill and gristmill on Long Creek,

---

[12]Ibid.

[13]Stewart County Court Records, no number given, 12. Located at the Court House in Dover, Tennessee.

[14]The records of the second session of the county court referred to the county seat as Dover even though the land had not yet been acquired. The name was mentioned several times in the Stewart County Court Records, Book 00, 19. Citizens who trace their ancestry to the earliest settlers have two explanations for the change. One story is that the settlers thought that their settlement, perched on the limestone cliffs of the Cumberland, looked much like Dover, England. These people most certainly had a vivid imagination. Another legend is that one of the settlers was named Monroe and he wanted his name given to the town. A meticulous study of the existing records does not show any settler by that name.

[15]Stewart County Court Records, Book 00, 13. Stewart County Court Records, Book 001, 19.

four miles east of Dover on the Cumberland River. John Elliott was granted permission to keep a ferry on the Cumberland River and the rates were set by the court.[16]

The only hint of impropriety among these early county officials came in 1805 when Samuel A. Smith, the county clerk, was indicted by the grand jury and tried on charges of misdemeanor in office. He was acquitted of the charges, but he resigned his office after the trial. William Nelson, who had qualified for the position before the trial ended, took the job. At the next election, Thomas Clinton was elected to fill the position. He served until the March term of the court in 1806 and resigned. Robert Cooper was elected to fill the vacancy and served his full term.[17] It was no surprise that all of these men were large property owners and businessmen, indicating that merchants and farmers shouldered the responsibility of managing the county in these early days. The puzzle was why so many of them resigned their particular office before the expiration of their term. The answer that emerged was that they were exasperated and discomfited because they were censured for the lack of progress in the area. The leaders claimed that they were disparaged for the limited growth while the real problem was the lack of revenue and the apathy of the citizenry. Their rejoinder was a call for more taxes, but the citizens were resolutely opposed to any increase in taxes. Many elected officials became so perturbed with this dilemma that they resigned.[18]

Little progress was made in the construction of public buildings in Dover for more than two years. Money was not available to pay for building materials or pay the workers. The courthouse, a one story, double-log building, cost $600, and was completed in June, 1806. Later that year, the jail, also a log building, was completed for a cost of $300.[19]

The permits for gristmills and taverns increased during each session of court from 1803 to 1806. Beginning in 1806, the county court appointed inspectors for cotton gins and set rates for taverns. All tavern keepers were directed to impose the following rates: a meal for twelve and one-half cents; one-half pint of whiskey--twelve and one-half cents; horse feed--twelve and one-half cents; lodging for one person--six and one-half cents; one-half pint of rum--three and one-half cents, and one-half pint of brandy--twelve and one-half cents.[20]

Trigg County

Trigg County, the second oldest county in the land between the rivers, had settlers around 1778 when people from the Carolinas came on flatboats down the Cumberland and Tennessee Rivers and raised primitive cabins. It seems that most of these pioneers remained in the area for a few years and then migrated farther west. In 1779, several men obtained grants of land

---

[16]Ibid. 1805, Stewart County Court, Book 002, 12-14.

[17]Ibid.

[18]Ibid., 1805, Stewart County Court records, Book 002, 22; 1806, Book 003, 21.

[19]Ibid, 22.

[20]Stewart County Court records, Book 003, 21, 22.

and relocated their families in the area.[21] They constructed cabins and planted crops, but again for some unknown reason, these people did not remain in the area for more than a few years. Apparently they had such great apprehension about possible Indian raids that they left. Another conjecture is that these people often relocated because they assumed that they could locate better farmland in the wilderness.[22] Some of these people seemed to have had a wanderlust and continually moved to the edge of the frontier.

As early as 1782 and 1783, the first permanent settlers were moving into the area. Robert Goodwin and his sons Samuel and Jesse came from North Carolina to settle near Cerulean Springs. These men, like the other settlers who followed, were good hunters who dreamed of owning farms. The Goodwin family liked the territory and decided to locate there. They cleared fields, burning most of the trees they had cut, planted, and cultivated crops. Within a year, a small herd of cattle was imported, and the Goodwin brothers soon developed the largest herd of beef cattle in the region.[23] In 1783, Allan Grace, Moses McWaters, Robert Fergeson, Abraham Lash, Robert Feutrell, James Benham, and Eli Kilgore settled and cultivated crops.[24]

Settlements on Dyer's Creek, Donaldson's Creek, Casey's Creek, and Sinking Creek were made by 1798. John Mayberry settled near Dyer's Creek. R. Thedford built a gristmill near the head of the creek in 1798. John Grasty came from South Carolina and started the first school in 1799.[25]

Even though most of these early settlers used the rivers to enter the area, others came in wagons and walked in with pack-horses. Transportation by land was extremely difficult and dangerous. There were few trails, and during periods of heavy rain, the travelers were not able to move their wagons because of the mud. They were often forced to interrupt their journey for several days or even weeks to wait for the ground to dry. These people brought in nothing but their most treasured family heirlooms because heavily loaded wagons could not complete the journey.

The Kentucky state legislature established Trigg County from appropriated land from Christian and Caldwell Counties in 1819-1820. The legislature, sitting in its winter session, conducted its business from December through January. The area was named for Stephen Trigg of Virginia who had come to the district of Kentucky in 1779 as a member of the Court of Land Commissioners.[26] He had decided to remain in Kentucky at that time, and built a home which later became known as Trigg Station on Cane Run Creek, the present site of Cadiz, Kentucky.

---

[21]These people came after the Court of Land Commissioners headed by Walker surveyed the region.

[22]Lewis Collins, History of Kentucky (Cincinnati: Lewis Collins and J. A. and U. P. James, 1847), 222-229.

[23]Ibid.

[24]All of these family names were included in the Trigg County Court Records, Book I for 1820-1830, located at Cadiz, Kentucky.

[25]Ibid.

[26]Ibid. Collins, Kentucky, 230.

The station was used by most of the people who traveled through the area and served as a meeting place for farmers. Stephen Trigg prospered as a businessman and land speculator, but at the height of his career, he was killed in a fight with the Native Americans on August 19, 1782 at the battle of Blue Lick. The settlers, especially on Cane Run Creek, considered Trigg a hero. Not only had he been a prominent leader of the community at Cane Run Creek, but he had died in the defense of his friends. His benefactors wanted to honor Stephen Trigg and make sure that his name was not overlooked in the history of the region. This group petitioned the state legislature to name the county in his honor.[27]

Dickson Givins, William Thomson, Lander Sharp, and Benjamin Vance were appointed as commissioners to choose the site of the county seat. Property on the Main Little River which belonged to Robert Baker was chosen as the best location. Baker agreed to sell fifty acres to the commissioners, but the construction of the public building would have to be delayed until he removed his stables from the site. After some protracted discussions, the name Cadiz was adopted for the county seat.[28]

Records show that one of the fastest growing settlements in Trigg County was at Golden Pond, and most of the settlers were ordinary folk who accommodated to the conventions of their community, although some did not. By 1804, the settlement was used as a hideout for a group of horse thieves who stole horses throughout the area and brought them to Golden Pond. They remained there until it was safe to transport the horses out of the region. Eventually, the more honest settlers banded together to force the thieves out of the settlement, and by 1820 it was a peaceful place to live.[29]

Folklore has it that Josuah Newberry, a courtly, educated, moral gentleman, came with his wife and son to Golden Pond in 1805. Financially independent, he built a large, beautiful home, surrounding it with immense, formal gardens. His rose garden soon became an attraction in the community. Soon after he moved into the community, he was invited to attend worship services at the local church but he declined, and informed the people that he and his wife did not believe that there was a god. Immediately, the man was referred to as "The Infidel," and thereafter his home was known as "The Infidel's House." Newberry's major shortcoming was his lack of circumspection. He did not hesitate to discuss his philosophy with anyone who would listen. The wife, who agreed with her husband's convictions, sensed the circumstances

---

[27]Ibid.

[28]Trigg County Court records, Book I, 19. These records show that the citizens argued for Cadiz because they had some knowledge of the Spanish city. It is not clear if they had ever visited the city. There is no indication that they had ever lived in Spain. One story is that they wanted to establish the fact that the Spanish had preceded them into the region. Another account is that a small group of Spanish settlers were living in the land between the rivers when the English settlers arrived, but no evidence can be found to support this belief.

[29]Caldwell County Court records, 1804 to 1819, Books III through XX. 1804, Book III, 17; 1805, Book IV, 12; 1806, Book V, 7; 1806, Book VI, II; 1807, Book VII, 5; 1808, Book VIII, 2; 1809, Book IX, 7; 1810, Book X, 3; 1811, Book XI, 14; 1812, Book XII, 1; 1813, Book XIII, 5.; 1814, Book XIV, II.; 1815, Book XV, 5.; 1816, Book XVI, 2; 1817, Book XVII, 8; 1818, Book XVIII, 10; 1819, Book XIX, 6; 1820, Book XX, 9.

more clearly and refused to discuss the topic outside the family.[30]

The couple completed the construction of their home and settled into the community, and even though they were considered unusual, there seemed to be no malevolence toward them. When Mr. Newberry completed his house, he placed a marble slab at the front gate. Several admonitions were carved into the marble: Limit Your Family; In the Brief Daytime of Life-Love; In the Long Dark of Night of Death-Oblivion. People strolled and rode by the grounds just to read the messages chiseled in the stone.

All of these things about the Newberry family fascinated the members of the community and generated gossip and whispered predictions that God would punish the man, but the citizenry continued to include the couple in all the community affairs. Then one day the couple's only child, a son, fell ill with consumption (or tuberculosis). After a time, it became apparent that the boy was not going to improve. One morning, the father demolished all the rose bushes in the rose garden. He then announced to all who passed by the house that the devil had been peeping from behind the rose bushes at him. The wife upbraided her husband for the loss of his convictions and accused him of surrendering to superstition.

When the son soon died from the disease, the couple could not cope with their anguish. They argued with anyone who would listen that mankind was overly superstitious about the devil and people should not believe in a god. The members of the community did not openly censure the couple, even though they expressed the belief that their God would eventually show himself to the couple. The citizenry seemed to feel remorse over the death of the child, but they could not comprehend the reactions of the parents.

Finally, the couple turned the marble slab face down, sold their home, and moved out of the region. They refused to tell anyone where they were going, and nobody was able to determine where they went. But from that time until the twentieth century, the house, regardless of who owned it, was always referred to as the Infidel House in Golden Pond.[31]

The first session of the Trigg County Court met at Cadiz in October 1820 to conduct business, including the tax structure. While the meeting was in progress, the assembly heard a gunshot. They were not alarmed at the noise because gunshots were a common occurrence and continued their discussion, but they were sufficiently astonished when a wounded bear lumbered into the room. All the men except the county court clerk scrambled over one another trying to get out of the one door and window in the building. Everyone realized that the wounded bear was enraged, and extremely dangerous. William Cannon Jr., the county court clerk, remained in his seat and exhibited an inordinate lack of concern about the bear. The animal lunged out of the room and the people returned to find Cannon still seated in his chair waiting for them. He was the only one who came out of the encounter without a scratch. The others had injured themselves running from the bear. Cannon became a celebrity because he

[30]The story was told to many people in the land between the rivers. It was told to the author first in 1956 and in other interviews in 1990.

[31]According to Mr. John Newberry, a descendant of Josuah Newberry, the family moved to Stewart County. The story was repeated in the Newberry family which lived in Stewart County. In a small history of Golden Pond compiled by high school students, the story is recorded. The material can be found in the Visitor's Center Library at Golden Pond.

was portrayed as an individual who took his responsibility so seriously that he would not abandon his records even if it meant he had to face a wounded bear.[32]

Most of the business of the court was about establishing offices and monitoring businesses. Licenses were granted to officials to solemnize matrimony, as well as establish taverns. Rates at these establishments were fixed and in order to become the first tavern operator, Robert Baker had to prove that he was of good moral character by presenting witnesses to the proper authorities. The court fixed the first tavern rates as follows: for French or Cognac brandy, thirty-seven and one-half cents per half pint; for rum or domestic gin, twenty-five cents per half pint; for Holland gin, thirty-seven and one-half cents per half pint; Madeira Wine, fifty cents per half pint; for port or sherry, thirty-seven and one-half cents per half pint; for peach or apple brandy, eighteen and three-fourth cents per pint; for whiskey, twelve and one-half cents per half pint; for a quart or bottle of port, twenty-five cents, and for a quart of cider, twelve and one-half cents. A person could find lodging for a night for twelve and one-half cents. Either breakfast, dinner, or supper could be purchased for twenty-five cents. The stallage cost for a horse which included the feeding of corn, oats, hay or fodder for twenty-four hours was fifty cents. Putting a horse to pasture for twelve hours cost thirty-seven and one-half cents. A gallon of oats or corn for an animal cost twelve and one-half cents. A person could find lodgings and food for himself cheaper than he could care for his horse.[33]

The court ordered that a mill was to be erected on Sinking Fort Creek, and twelve men were appointed to supervise the procedure for building the mill. The plans for the first public road were discussed, and it was concluded that the road should be laid out from Cadiz to intersect with the existing road to Dover. Later in the same session, plans were discussed about the possibility of building a road to Princeton and Hopkinsville.[34] The early Circuit Court records involved a number of interesting cases. Men were sentenced to jail for non-payment of debts, beatings, assault, and using profane language. It was better not to curse on Sunday because those men who did received a significant fine, and after the second offense, a jail term of four weeks.[35]

For many reasons the people of Trigg County did not regard Cadiz as a suitable location for the county seat. Cadiz was inaccessible to travelers using the rivers. The Little River was no more than a large creek and other sites would be more central to the people who lived in the county.[36] The argument over the location of the county seat became so heated that in December, 1821, an act was passed by the Kentucky General Assembly to allow the citizens of Trigg County to decide by ballot where they wanted to place the county seat. At the March

---

[32]Trigg County Court records, 1820, Book I, 3. All County Court records from 1820 to the present can be found in the courthouse in Cadiz, Kentucky.

[33]Ibid.

[34]Ibid.

[35]Trigg County Circuit Court records 1819 and 1920, 1819, Book O, 2,4, 8, 19, and 20; 1820, Book OI, 1, 12, 15-19. These Circuit Court records for Trigg County are in the courthouse in Cadiz, Kentucky.

[36]Trigg County Court records 1820, Book OI, 1-8.

term of the court in 1822, an election was ordered, and George Street, Richard P. Dawson, and Beman Fowler were appointed election judges. Cadiz, Boyd's Landing, Warrington, and Center were all considered as places for the government. When the election was held in Cadiz on March 6, 1822, the voters came out in full force. Cadiz received 295 votes, Boyd's Landing received 204 votes, Warrington received 69 votes, and Center had only 59 votes. The controversy did not cease; for many years attempts were made to move the county government to Canton. But each endeavor was obstructed by the people of Cadiz. They were successful because the village continued to grow and most of the voters were determined to keep the county seat. None of the other sites could band together and generate enough votes to change the location.[37]

The rivalry among the small towns in Trigg, Stewart, and Lyon Counties is a part of the history of the area. Each village wanted to be designated as the county seat because large numbers of people came to the meetings of the county and circuit courts. Listening to the trials was a great source of entertainment; while the proceedings were not in session the people could visit, trade, and traffic. These people spent a considerable amount of money while they were in the town, and merchants could make larger profits.[38]

Lyon County

Lyon County, Kentucky was a part of Caldwell County until 1854. But the residents of the county who lived within the boundaries of the land between the rivers had settled there as early as 1791.[39] Burchwell Fuetrell, Elsa Downs, and Joseph Jones were able to establish farms in the area around 1792.[40]

In 1798, the man who would become very instrumental in the development of the land between the rivers had just decided to move to the area. Matthew Lyon, a congressman from Vermont, was embroiled in a public confrontation with the leaders of the Federalist Party. Lyon, who supported the political views of Thomas Jefferson and the Democrat-Republican Party, had delivered speeches in which he denounced John Adams and the leading Federalists. When the Sedition Act was passed, it in effect disallowed any criticism of the Federalist Party or the officials of the government, including John Adams, the President of the United States. Lyon was seeking reelection and openly accused the administration of mishandling foreign affairs. This was not the first time that this Irish immigrant had angered his opponents. On the floor of the House of Representatives, Lyon once spit in the eye of a Federalist congressman from Connecticut. Lyon was immediately labeled the "Spitting Lyon," and became the brunt

[37]Trigg County Court records, 1820, Books OI, 11; 1821, Book OII, 9; 1821, Book OIII, 5; 1822, Book IV, 6.

[38]Ibid.

[39]Caldwell County Court records. 1800, Book 2, 7.

[40]Ibid.

of numerous spitting witticisms.[41]

Lyon continued his verbal and written condemnation of John Adams, the members of his administration and anyone who had supported the Sedition Act, and tempers erupted in a fistfight between Lyon and Roger Griswold on the floor of the House of Representatives on February 15, 1798. Lyon had referred to John Adams as an individual who continually grasped for power, and who also had an unbounded thirst for ridiculous pomp. These denunciations pleased the Federalists who now arrested Lyon and charged him with violation of the Sedition Act. He pleaded not guilty and posted a thousand dollar bond.[42]

While he was awaiting trial, Lyon continued to publish his attacks, but he also decided that he was going to leave Vermont and move to the frontier. He corresponded with his friend Andrew Jackson and considered acquiring property near Nashville, Tennessee, but after he made contacts with landowners in the land between the rivers, he purchased 5800 acres of land between the Tennessee and Cumberland Rivers.[43]

Lyon stood trial and a jury found him guilty as charged. The court sentenced Lyon to imprisonment for four months, and the payment of a one thousand dollar fine and court costs. Lyon went to jail, spending his time denouncing the Federalists and making plans to move his family to the land between the rivers. John Messenger and George Catlett, who were married to his daughters, Ann and Pamela, were persuaded to move to the property in the land between the rivers. A small community called Eddy, later renamed Eddyville, had grown up on the banks of the Cumberland and Lyon sent his daughters and their husbands to the same location. The advance party was to construct cabins and plant corn and the others would follow as soon as Lyon was released.[44]

In the meantime, Lyon was publicizing his scheme of leading a group of settlers to the frontier. He heard from his daughters and their husbands, and talked in glowing terms about life in the wilderness. Lyon recruited a number of skilled artisans and managers and persuaded them to move with him to his property in Kentucky. He wanted boat builders, ironworkers, cabinet makers, farmers and others to go with him and build their homes on his property. He guaranteed the people a house and lot and all the work they wanted if they would accompany him. While he was in jail, his constituents in Vermont, trying to persuade him that he was needed there, voted him into office for another term. Lyon resigned his seat because nothing could dissuaded him from trying to establish his ideal community on the frontier.[45]

Lyon and ten other families constructed a flotilla of flatboats for the expedition from Vermont to Kentucky. They built ten flatboats, each approximately sixty feet long, covering a portion of each flatboat with canvas to serve as shelter. A temporary home was constructed on

---

[41]Aleine Austin, Matthew Lyon: "New Man" of the Democratic Revolution 1749-1882 (University Park: The Pennsylvania State Press, 1981), 1-51.

[42]Ibid., 59.

[43]Ibid.

[44]Ibid., 59-62.

[45]Ibid.

each flatboat, and all the flatboats were loaded with household goods, tools, animals, food supplies and weapons. The sides of the boats had been built to six feet heights, and several of the boats were lashed together so that the people could move freely from one flatboat to another. The formation of connected flatboats resembled a floating community. Over one hundred people began their journey to Kentucky after the inauguration of President Thomas Jefferson in 1801.[46] Lyon seemed satisfied that Jefferson's inauguration meant the end of Federalist domination. Pragmatically, Lyon wanted to tighten his affiliations with the leading Republicans.

Matthew Lyon has never been considered as a leader, or even a member, of the communitarian element which flourished in North America from the colonial era until after the Civil War. Historical accounts of the European immigrants, such as the Rappites of western Pennsylvania, and the Shaker Communities organized by Ann Lee abound because these communities were unique in their quest for economic simplicity and gender equality. Yet many communities, such as the one established at Eddy, Kentucky have not been studied as experiments in community development. Lyon's plans to diversify the economy of Eddy by combining agriculture and industry do not tell the full story. He recognized the importance of transportation even in 1798. His experiment was an indication that frontier leaders had already realized that the marriage of raw materials, skilled labor, and transportation were indispensable to economic prosperity.[47]

Lyon established several farms as soon as he arrived in Eddy. His plans were to ship pork, bacon, lard, corn, venison, hams, and cotton to New Orleans, New York, Boston and Philadelphia. Within a matter of months, merchant boats had been built and goods dispatched from river ports on the Tennessee and Cumberland Rivers to New Orleans and Philadelphia.

Lyon used his political connections with Thomas Jefferson and the members of Jefferson's administration to receive an appointment as Commissary General of the Western Army. As soon as he received the appointment, he and his workmen were able to sell an ever increasing amount to the Western Army. Within a few months, Lyon began to recruit more people in the Northeast to settle in the land between the rivers.

Lyon went into partnership with Matthew Carey, a prominent book dealer, publicist, and economist, and they instituted an operation which the people referred to as a moving book store. Books were shipped up and down the Cumberland and Tennessee, and people came to the river landings to meet the boats and purchase books. Many people were obviously avid readers because the floating book stores became so profitable that more boats were put into operation to expand the business. Large profits ensued and the money was used by the men to purchase

---

[46]Ibid.

[47]For more information on communitarian movements see: Arthur E. Bestor, Backwoods Utopians: The Sectarian and Owenite Phases of Communitarian Socialism in America, 1663-1829 (Philadelphia: University of Pennsylvania Press, 1950); Whitney Cross, The Burned-Over District: The Social and Intellectual History of Enthusiastic Religion in Western New York, 1800-1850 (Ithaca, N. Y.: Cornell University Press, 1950); Rosabeth Moss Kanter, Commitment and Community: Communes and Utopias in Sociological Perspective (Cambridge, Mass.: Harvard University Press, 1972); Alice Felt Tyler, Freedom's Ferment: Phases of American Social History to 1860 (Minneapolis: University of Minnesota Press, 1944).

more land. Lyon's farming operations were enlarged, and a sawmill was built.[48]

Although he said he was disenchanted with government, Lyon kept the lines of communication open with his friends and acquaintances in the national government. Through these connections he was able to obtain contracts to build barges, sloops, and gunboats for the federal government. He established a shipbuilding company and recruited more workers from Vermont to run the business. In a short time, the business had expanded and was able to meet the demands of the government contracts and sell vessels to merchants in Philadelphia and New Orleans.

In 1803, when Matthew Lyon was elected to the U.S. Congress from Kentucky, he turned the supervision of his businesses over to his son, Chittenden Lyon. The young man had as much business acumen as his father and soon expanded the family business by building a gristmill, a cotton gin, and a paper mill. He founded a newspaper and purchased a printing press that had been used by Benjamin Franklin. Linden trees, which were plentiful near the rivers, were processed at the paper mill and used by the newspaper.[49]

Clearly, by the turn of the century , the area had taken on the aspects of a permanently settled region with its local governments, its variety of businesses, its agriculture, and its steadily expanding population.

---

[48]Aleine Austin, Matthew Lyon, 140-80.

[49]Ibid.

CHAPTER IV

ECONOMIC DEVELOPMENT

Waterways

The rivers were both a blessing and a detriment in the settlement era. People were often restricted by the lack of roads, so much so that it was often impossible to travel into and out of the region. Without bridges, the Tennessee and Cumberland Rivers so isolated the area that people usually limited their junkets to the locale. As means of water transportation became obtainable, people used the rivers as their highways, ignoring the need for roads. During many months of the year, especially during periods of heavy rains in the spring and fall, the paths and wagon roads turned into quagmires. Mud and water made travel impossible and many settlers were forced to abandon wagons and buggies and walk. Businesses which had to ship goods overland had to halt operations until the weather changed. Within a few years, transportation, especially railroads, was crucial to economic advancement, but the area had fallen too far behind to compete with adjacent regions.

Taxes and Government

One consistent attitude of the people was their aversion to any taxation. All duties were considered insufferable, and even though leaders often argued that progress demanded that the local governments use tax revenue to initiate community projects, the county courts repeatedly refused to levy new taxes. This attitude demonstrated the indigenous value system of the people. They loathed any restriction over their lives, and local government was the potential villain by legislating what they could or could not do. The ultimate control, they concluded, was the requirement to pay taxes.[1]

Added to the abhorrence to powerful government was the view that individuals must assume responsibility for themselves, but it was not the responsibility of taxpayers to care for the indigent. True, people should be charitable and take care of the poor and disabled, but their philanthropic gestures should be private and a matter of individual choice. It was generally agreed that most needs of the community, including schools, should be supported by private donations, not taxes. Altercations arose periodically over the role of government in the maintenance of roads, asylums, and paupers.[2]

---

[1]After a survey of records in Lyon, Trigg, and Stewart Counties the author became convinced that a majority of the people did not want any strong government to have jurisdiction over them.

[2]Ibid.

Agriculture and the People

These self-sufficient farmers expected to produce all that was needed on the land, and any ingredient not obtainable there was often regarded as a luxury. In the attempt to have a self-contained environment, the early settlers used wild plants as substitutes for the more familiar types of vegetables used in Europe. As a result new food products came into use from experimentation with seeds and plants. This is not to say that they did not try to import the familiar plants. Letters to friends and relatives in Europe and in other parts of the country usually included a solicitation for the exchange of seeds. The frequency of the requests shows that the people were anxious to acquire as many seeds and plants as possible.[3]

By 1805, the larger landowners were planting corn, hemp, and cotton for sale, as well as for use in the home. Cotton was the major money crop until the late 1830s, when tobacco became the largest export item. From the beginning, the most prosperous farmers did not rely on one money crop. They were inclined to diversify their crops and raise cattle, hogs, mules and horses for sale. Fruit harvests were usually limited to home consumption, although some fruits were bought and sold within the communities. Chickens, geese, ducks, and other fowl were used at home and in some cases bartered to merchants for other goods.[4] Small farmers encountered many problems when they tried to make enough money to purchase land. They realized that several hundred acres of land were needed if they expected to enlarge their annual production. Cotton proved to be an arduous crop to produce because it required a large, constant labor supply and depleted the soil. Fertile soil along the rivers and creeks was soon worn out and new crop lands were needed. Virgin forests were cut and the land was used as new ground for cotton. Soon, these lands returned low yields per acre. Small farmers did not have forest lands available, and they stood to lose their land if they suffered two second-rate growing seasons in succession. These farmers soon became disheartened and sold their land or left it and moved to another area of the country. A population decline in the land between the rivers in 1830 can be traced to the adverse weather conditions and depleted cotton fields in 1828 and 1829.[5]

Soil conservation was not a priority among the early settlers anywhere on the frontier. The farmers seemed to assume that fertile lands could always be found, and if their fields lost their productivity, it was a simple matter to clear a new field or move away and find farmland in another part of the country. Many farmers considered it a waste of time to rotate crops or try to use manure or other fertilizers. The more prosperous farmers often bought the exhausted land from the farmers who wanted to leave the area and practiced some forms of crop rotation. Farming practices often made the difference between success and failure among the small farmers. County records indicate that many of the original settlers stayed on the farms at least

---

[3]Letters from the Nathan Brandon family dated 1836 mention the desire to exchange the seeds for both fruits and vegetables.

[4]J. B. Killebrew, An Introduction to the Resources of Tennessee (Nashville: Travel, Eastman and Howell, 1874), 1-49.

[5]Census Records indicate the decline in 1830.

until the Civil War era and after. Overworked cotton fields were turned into pasture lands, and they cleared new grounds for use until the cotton fields were more productive. One of the reasons for increasing the size of their farms was so the overused land could lay fallow for a period of years. Thus, farmers tended to own more and more unproductive land. During periods when the harvests were poor, they often had to go further into debt.[6]

Hemp was produced for both rope and cloth. Because chains were often difficult to obtain, farmers and craftsmen used specially constructed ropes instead. Farmers could sell ropes as a way of making extra money. No evidence is left to indicate that any ropes were exported. The hemp fiber could be processed and used for making linen. Women usually had two spinning wheels in the home, one for hemp and one for cotton. The larger wheel was used to spin the cotton fibers; the smaller wheel was used for hemp. Cotton cloth was usually preferred for clothing, but linen was used for canvas which was useful on the farm and in other businesses. The linen cloth was durable and could withstand harsh weather conditions.[7]

There is no indication that the people realized the narcotic effect of the hemp leaves. Stories abound about how the citizens smoked everything from grapevines to corn silks when tobacco was unavailable. If the people smoked the leaves from the hemp plant, no notice was taken by the community.

Grape arbors could be found on most farms, although farmers did not seem interested in developing vineyards. The grapes were grown primarily for wine or jelly for home use. In 1844, P. F. Travel, a native of Switzerland, bought land in Stewart County and attempted the first vineyard in the state. During the fall of 1845, he planted two acres of grape vines on his farm, two miles from Dover. The assortment of vines, imported from Europe, failed to produce as well as he had anticipated. Finally, he realized that if he did not prune the vines too closely, the yield was more bounteous. He experimented with the vines and found that if they were allowed to run on trellises, the harvest was more abundant. For a time, Mr. Travel ran a successful winery, making and selling enough wine for him to consider his grape and wine production as a money crop. But none of the other farmers in the area considered his experiment important enough to emulate.[8]

As was mentioned earlier, the farmers in the land between the rivers had the advantage of two rivers for transportation. It was not too laborious during dry periods to haul produce from the farm to the rivers for transportation to larger markets. Communities along the Cumberland and Tennessee Rivers developed as shipping terminals. Such landing sites grew into villages as the years went by. Warehouses, gristmills, and retail businesses were often built

---

[6]Survey of all County Court Records, Estate Sales, and a comparison to Census Reports 1800 to 1860 indicate a correlation between poor harvests and the number of farmers who lost land because of mortgage foreclosure. Many of the bankrupt farmers moved out of the land between the rivers, and their land was purchased by the farmers already living in the area.

[7]Stewart County Court records 1803 to 1850; Trigg County Court records 1819 to 1850; Caldwell Court records 1830 to 1850.
A survey of estate sales and probates of wills establishes the types of crops and household items found in the land between the rivers.

[8]Stewart County Court records 1845, Book XXX, 16.

nearby in order to take advantage of the trade. It was convenient to take goods to the port for shipment and purchase supplies in one trip. Tobacco Port, in Stewart County, is a good example of this type of community.

The Iron Industry

The most important industry not connected directly to agriculture was the iron industry. The land between the rivers had a rolling terrain incised by valleys and dissected by numerous streams. Topography elevations averaged between five hundred and one thousand feet above sea level. The area was within the great Western Iron Belt which varied from fifteen to forty miles wide and stretched from north to south through the land between the rivers. Although its western boundary was, for the most part, the Tennessee River, it crossed over and occupied portions of two counties on the west side of the river.

In Tennessee, this iron region includes portions of Stewart, Montgomery, Houston, Humphreys, Dickson, Perry, Hickman, Lewis, Wayne, Lawrence, and the edges of Cheatham, Maury, and Williamson Counties. Lesser ore deposits were found in Benton and Decatur Counties. In Kentucky the belt extended into parts of Trigg, Lyon, Livingston Counties, and south into Alabama to include the counties of Lauderdale, Colbert, and Franklin. In total, the iron ore region encompassed an area of approximately 5,000 square miles. The ore deposits varied in size and depth. One of the best deposit areas was in Stewart County, Tennessee.[9]

The rocks underlying the iron belt were limestone containing chert masses, with siliceous and clay impurities. The deposits or banks of iron ores were hematite (red), limonite (brown), and magnetite (magnetic ore). The brown iron ores appeared to be a mixture of hydrous ferric oxides in which the iron was present in the form of sesqui-oxide. We now know that the limonite was made up of a variable composition of several minerals including goethite, lepidocrocite, and even hematite. Researchers have referred to the ores as brown hematite which they divided into grades according to the amount of water they contain. Tables have been devised to list the minerals hematite, turgite, goethite, limonite, and xanthosiderite according to the amount of water and iron content.[10]

The demand for iron on the frontier provided the impetus for establishing the earliest ironworks. Since the demand was so great, state governments felt compelled to aid in the development of the earliest ironworks. As early as 1788, the North Carolina legislature passed an act to provide that the proprietor of an ironworks could receive a grant of 3,000 acres of state land by filing an entry form proving that he had produced a certain quantity of iron in a three year period immediately prior to filing the form. This law was used as a model for a Tennessee law which went into effect in 1809. The grants of land were exempt from taxation for ninety-

---

[9]Killebrew, An Introduction to the Resources of Tennessee, 932. William Hogan, An Economic History of the Iron and Steel Industry in the United States, vol. I (Washington, D. C.: Heath and Company, 1971), 3.

[10]Ibid.

nine years.[11]

Grants of land were not the only incentives for investing in iron production. Profits were good, and local governments granted a tax exempt status to most of the iron furnaces. Later, local governments granted exempt status from local restrictions for iron workers. Workers in the iron industry were not forced to serve on the county work force which maintained roads.[12] Another example was the petition in 1827 presented by Richard C. Napier, E.W. Napier, Thomas Yeatman, Simon Bradford, Anthony Vanleer, Wallace Dixon, E. D. Hichs(Hicks), Samuel Stacker, John Stacker, Robert Baxter, Nicholas Perkins, and Montgomery Bell to the Tennessee legislature requesting that in times of peace, iron workers be exempted from all militia duty. Compliance with the request was needed, according to the petitioners, because the workers returned to work after their militia duty still intoxicated and incapable of attending to their duties. Iron, they said, was so essential that the workers had to be fit for work every day. The legislature acquiesced, and the men were exempted.[13] Apparently, the Tennessee legislators appreciated the growing significance of the iron industry.

As early as 1796 settlers found the brown iron ore in the region, but it was not until 1820 that developers became interested in the mass production of iron in the land between the rivers. By that time developers and investors were eager to buy the land which contained both the iron ore and the contiguous forests because iron products were in great demand in the world as well as domestic markets. In the United States, iron products were costly, and on the frontier the prices were often prohibitive. Sad irons cost six cents each, and iron tea kettles sold for ten dollars a dozen. Entrepreneurs with accessible capital could anticipate significant profits from the production of crude iron.[14]

Other factors which made the iron ore in the land between the rivers an attractive investment were the relative accessibility of the ore and the forests. The iron ore was near the surface of the earth and the virgin forests would provide the enormous amount of wood needed to generate the heat for the iron furnaces. Limestone, needed in processing ore, was readily available. The determinant which first drew the entrepreneurs to the area, and would later hurt the industry, was the availability of water transportation. The Tennessee and Cumberland would allow the shipment of crude iron to diverse markets. In the 1840s, railroad transportation assumed preeminence because interior domestic markets were procurable and the foreign markets had dwindled because of new processing techniques. However, the investors and producers could not generate enough interest among railroad companies to bring lines into the land between the rivers. The iron industry could not finance the railway systems because it lacked the capital;

---

[11]Harriet Simpson Arnow, Flowering of the Cumberland (New York: MacMillan and Company, 1963), 295-297.

[12]This practice was adopted in Stewart County in 1922. County Court records, 1922, Book 32, 17.

[13]Buena Coleman Daniel, "The Iron Industry in Dickson County, Tennessee" (unpublished Master's Thesis, Austin Peay State University, 1970), 38-42.

[14]Merchant records from Walters and Company Dover, Tennessee 1822. Can be located in the Court House in Dover, Tennessee.

consequently, the iron industry languished after its initial prosperity.[15]

Montgomery Bell, Anthony Vanleer, William Stacker, William Kelly, Thomas Yeatman, and Samuel Vanleer were among the initial investors who began to purchase land in the land between the rivers even before the iron furnaces were constructed. These men had experience in developing the industry in other parts of the country, and they envisioned a network of furnaces in Tennessee and Kentucky. A part of their strategy was to encourage local farmers, businessmen, and professional leaders to invest in the industry. They wrote to members of the county courts encouraging them to advise the populace about the merits of the industry.[16]

In 1815, Matthew and Chittenden Lyon began the construction of the first furnace in the land between the rivers near Eddyville. Businessmen in Stewart County began the operation of a furnace in 1820, and a Trigg County operation followed in 1832. The industry reached its peak operational phase during the decade of the 1850s and at least one furnace operated intermittently until 1927, but for all practical purposes, the iron industry ceased to function as an important economic factor after 1860.[17]

One of the largest iron companies in Stewart County was the Cumberland Iron Works. The company began production in the late 1820s under the leadership of Joseph and Robert Woods, Thomas Yeatman, and Samuel and John Stacker and was known as the Woods, Yeatman, and Company. The company owned over 60,000 acres of land, on both sides of the Cumberland River. During its history, the Cumberland Iron Works was composed of different combinations of partners who were involved with several different iron production sites. The company owned a rolling mill and nailer. During the more profitable period, works included the Bear Spring Furnace, the Dover Furnace, the Randolph Furnace and Forge, the Bellwood Furnace, and the Saline Furnace.[18]

In 1828 The Cumberland Iron Works included two puddling furnaces, seven heating furnaces, and four steam driven trains. In 1834, after the death of Thomas Yeatman, the company was sold at auction. The "Nashville Republican," a daily newspaper published in Nashville, Tennessee, on June 25, 1834 advertised for sale at auction five nail-making machines, a Rolling Mill and Furnaces, dwelling houses, Negro houses, work shops, stables, two hundred slaves, and an unlisted number of horses, mules, and oxen. Supplies including wagons, paraphernalia for work animals, carts, and implements including tools for digging ore were sold. Also, all the household and kitchen furniture, milk cows, and milking accoutrements were sold.

---

[15]Stewart County Court records from 1840 to 1845 contain comments regarding the need to finance the construction of railroads in the area. 1840, Book 40, 1-4; 1841, Book 41, 5; 1842, Book 42, 11; 1843, Book (no number) 7; 1844, Book 44, 10; 1845 Book 45, 3-7.

[16]Stewart County Court records; 1822, Book 22, 7, 9; 1823, Book 23, 12; 1824, Book 24, 1, 4, 6-9.

[17]Caldwell County Court records; 1815, Book 02, 5; Stewart County Court records; Book 20, 7; 1927 Book 90, 25.

[18]Information about the company can be found in a collection of miscellaneous records with no title or binding in the Court House in Dover. The records cover the period from approximately 1819 to 1850 and include information about certain business operations in the area. These records do not appear to be the files of the county courts, real property, or tax assessments.

38

One keelboat and two boats, not described, were also sold at the auction.[19] Immediately after the auction, the company reorganized and Jane Erwin Yeatman, the widow of Thomas Yeatman, became actively involved in the operation of the Cumberland Iron Works.[20]

Jane Yeatman was obviously not a typical woman of the 1830s. When her husband died she quietly became involved in the operations of the businesses she had inherited. She later married John Bell, a farmer and congressman from the Nashville district. Before the marriage, John Bell agreed to a premarital contract that enabled Jane Erwin Yeatman to own and operate her business affairs without any interference from him. According to the state law at the time, John Bell, as the head of the family, could have assumed control of his wife's business. The premarital contract stated that John Bell would receive an allowance from his wife, but he in no way would intrude upon or question her business decisions. It was agreed that after ten years, Jane Bell could allow John Bell to become personally involved in the management of the business. For eleven years Jane Bell ran her family business, and the profits were substantial. Eleven years after he signed the agreement, John Bell was brought into the business. He purchased ten slaves and constructed a residence near one of their furnaces on the Cumberland River. The community became known as Bellwood.[21]

In 1852 an inventory of the Cumberland Iron Works showed the company owned 51,000 acres of land, a Rolling Mill, furnaces at Bear Spring and Bellwood, and the Randolph forge. The company owned 365 slaves and employed 300 workers.[22]

It was not unusual for a parent company to extend its operation into another county or state and develop furnaces. An example of this operation was the LaGrange Iron Works which was based in Benton County. That company owned and operated the Clark, Eclipse, and LaGrange furnaces in Stewart County.[23]

The Rough and Ready Furnace was constructed about 1846 and ceased operation in the 1880s. The Cobb, Bradley Company operated the furnace until the mid-1850s. The Barksdale, Cook Company purchased the operation some time after 1856, introduced a steam-powered furnace operated by at least eighty-one workers, and had an annual production of 1,400 tons of pig iron. The Company owned about 16,000 acres of land and a furnace, with a brick and stone stack, which was approximately twenty-eight feet high and nine feet across. The stack had a horizontal engine, a seventeen inch steam cylinder, and a six foot stoke with two blast cylinders. Adjacent to the furnace stack was a field used to produce charcoal. The company owned several

---

[19]Ibid. A copy of the newspaper item was included in the file.

[20]Ibid. A brochure listing the auction was found in the file.

[21]Ibid.

[22]Tax Assessment records for Stewart County. 1852, Book A-52, 7.

[23]Stewart County Court records, 1839, Book XXXIX, 9.

horses, wagons, and other supplies.[24] After the battle of Fort Donelson, the furnace ceased production and did not reopen until 1868. The old furnace stack had been damaged and when the furnace reopened the new stack was forty-five feet high and nine feet across the bosh. By 1878, the furnace had been purchased by I. Westheimer of Pittsburgh and continued operations until 1880.[25]

The Great Western Furnace stack was built in 1854 by Brian, Newell and Company.[26] In 1855, the Great Western was generating about 1,350 tons of iron from brown hematite located near the site. The furnace ceased operation in 1856 because of a rumored slave uprising. It was owned at that time by the Newell and Pritchett Company of Clarksville, Tennessee.[27] There is no evidence to indicate that the furnace was in jeopardy, but it was typical of that time period to counteract the most insignificant rumor.[28]

The Cross Creek Furnace located on a branch of North Cross Creek was also known as the Blue Spring Furnace. It was built in 1853 and owned by Jordan, Brother, and Company. The original owner of the site was probably the Newell, Irwin Company. The Stewart County Tax Books show that in 1853 the company owned by Newell and Irwin had assets of 3,400 acres of land valued at $5,800 in Civil District No. 1. By 1855, they owned less than 3,000 acres of land, but the assessed value of the property was $15,400, indicating vast improvements of the property at the furnace site. The company had also acquired sixty-three slaves, and they employed approximately forty white workers.[29]

In 1857, a partnership was arranged between Newell, Irwin, and Quarles, owners of the Cross Creek Furnace, and W. and G. H. Jordan, owners of the Valley Forge Furnace in Montgomery County. This agreement joined the two operations and specialized in the production of pig iron and blooms under the name Jordan, Irwin, and Company. The agreement stipulated that the company was to continue operation for four years before any changes could be made, but the operations were to remain under the control of their respective owners. The finances and business contacts were to be handled by Dr. D.S. Newell.[30] Due to undisclosed problems explained as mismanagement, the partnership faced financial trouble within six months. By September of 1857, the Bank of Tennessee and the Commerce Bank of Kentucky had both obtained judgments against all the partners in the Company. A court action resulted in the cessation of production at the furnace and the business venture went bankrupt. All the property

---

[24]Jerilee S. Davis, "The Charcoal Iron Industry of Montgomery and Stewart Counties, Tennessee" (unpublished Master's Thesis, Austin Peay State University, 1976), 48-52.

[25]Ibid.

[26]This information is inscribed on a limestone block above the arch on the west face of the stack.

[27]Davis, Charcoal, 47.

[28]Ibid.

[29]Stewart County Tax Assessment records, 1853, A-53,11; 1955, B-55, 12-13.

[30]Stewart County Court records, 1857, addendum to Book, LVII, 9.

belonging to the company was sold at public auction in 1857.[31]

The Saline Furnace was built in 1853 and operated until the Civil War. It was owned by Lewis, Erwin, and Company and first appeared in the Stewart County Tax Books in 1853.[32] At that time, the company owned 2,485 acres of land, but Stewart County Deed records indicate that the company rapidly acquired many individual land tracts on the Beech Fork of Saline Creek during 1852 and 1853.[33] The Company acquired a right of way across farm land to the Cumberland River, and approximately 7,000 acres of land were purchased by the Company in Civil District No. 4. The company obviously expected to expand production but for some reason this expansion did not take place.[34] When the furnace closed in 1860, it was not producing a sufficient quantity of iron to warrant continued operations, and in 1865, when G. T. and E. H. Lewis began buying tracts of land in the vicinity of Saline and Cross Creeks, they listed their interest in mining various minerals, including coal, water, oil, salt, lead, and zinc, but iron was not included in the list. Evidently, the company tried to expand its mining operation to other minerals. One could assume that several small furnaces were becoming unprofitable at that time.[35]

The Peytona Furnace began operation in 1846 and was active until the time of the Civil War. The first furnace was replaced by a forty-two foot high structure in 1856. Thomas Kirkman and his son were listed as the owners and operators of the furnace. The steam-powered operation employed some ninety persons and was producing 1,700 tons of pig iron in 1850. At that time, the Kirkman operation owned eighty-three slaves who appeared to be the majority of the labor force at the furnace.[36]

In 1850, a household described as the Thomas Kirkman Boarders was adjacent to the home of H. Milton Atkins who was the manager of the Peytona Furnace. The list of boarders indicated that several men and their families lived next to the manager of the furnace. The description of the house did furnish information about the number of rooms which housed some twenty people. It appeared that the manager and most of the supervisors or skilled workers lived at the furnace site. The occupations were listed as manager, founders, colliers, clerks, and laborers. The furnace was at full production when it was destroyed by Federal troops immediately after the fall of Fort Donelson.[37]

From 1815 to 1860, Stewart County had eighteen furnaces operating at one time or another, while Trigg County and Lyon County each had two furnaces. In 1852 the iron industry

---

[31]Ibid. Stewart County Circuit Court records, 1857, Book, 61, 19.

[32]Stewart County Tax Assessment records, 1853, Book A-53, 27.

[33]Stewart County records, 1852, Deed Book 99, ll; 1853, Deed Book, 102, 17.

[34]Stewart County Court records, 1853, Book LVIII, 19.

[35]Stewart County Court records 1852, Book LVII, 30 1859, LIX, 37.

[36]Stewart County Tax Assessment records, 1846, B-42, 19; 1852, A-52, 34; 1853, A-53, 42.

[37]National Census records, Population Schedule 1850 for Stewart County.

owned 145,000 acres of land in Stewart County.[38] The Stewart County industry was more extensive because the Tennessee legislature had already provided inducements to bring investors into the state. Also, the investors were attracted to the area because of the extensive deposits of both limonite and brown hematite scattered over the entire county. The ore was relatively free of impurities and was usually concentrated in banks or beds. Even though most of the deposits were small, they lay just below the surface of the earth or were exposed on the sides of bluffs. The fact that the ore was easily mined was a big incentive to the businessmen, and even if a furnace were limited to a few years of production, the profits were extensive, and the investors could afford to terminate the work at one furnace site and move to another.

The entire iron industry in the land between the rivers was interrelated or connected because the same individuals held stock in most of the furnaces. At one time or another, the businessmen bought and sold stock in each of the companies. When capital was needed at any particular furnace, the businessmen sold interests in the furnaces to friends who owned other furnaces or to citizens in the region. The iron masters, a term applied to businessmen who had experience in the industry, were eager to sell shares in the industry to farmers, doctors, lawyers, and merchants who wanted to invest their money for quick returns in the enterprise. It was not unusual for stockholders to sell their shares to an acquaintance who, for whatever reason, had money to invest.

Often the absentee owners of the furnaces were involved in many businesses and did not become personally involved in the day to day operations of the furnaces. This type of management was used with the larger furnaces in the land between the rivers which included the Empire Furnace, the Fulton Furnace, the Mammoth Furnace, the Peytona Furnace, the Great Western Furnace, the Iron Mountain Furnace, the Laura Furnace, Saline Creek, Clark, Brunsoni, Byron Forge and Furnace, Ashland, Union, and the Center Furnace.

The Center Furnace, in Kentucky, was kept in operation during the Civil War, and was typical of the operations of a larger furnace. The labor force was made up of slaves, Chinese and Irish immigrants, and citizens of the region. The village of Hematite grew up at the furnace site, and as the village grew it included a post office, commissary, a public meeting hall, housing for the workmen, and a public kitchen. A farm, owned by the company, supplied the food for the workers who lived on the site. The trail from Hematite to the Cumberland River was known as the Silver Trail because the paymaster traveled the road each week to bring the wages, usually in silver, to the workers.[39]

In the early years, the iron industry used the cold-blast charcoal furnace to produce the crude iron for pig iron and other cast iron products. The older furnaces were often referred to as the hillside furnaces. They were built into the side of a small hill in order that ore, limestone flux, and charcoal could be more easily placed into the stack from the top, using a wooden ramp built from the hill to the stack opening. The furnace was usually in the shape of a truncated pyramid and constructed by applying the rule that the base of the furnace was equal to its height. The body of the furnace was fashioned into three layers: the interior wall section was made up

---

[38]Stewart County Tax Assessment records, 1852, Book B-47, 29.

[39]William H. Perrin, ed., Counties of Christian and Trigg, Kentucky (Chicago: F. A. Battery Publishing Co., 1884), 5-117.

of five brick walls, known as the core; a space between the core and outer masonry wall was filled with sand, stone chips, clay, coarse mortar, or furnace cinders to provide insulation for the outer wall; usually hand-hewn limestone blocks were used to construct the outer wall surrounding the structure. The furnace stack was simply a type of container for the reduction of iron ore, which occurred when a continuous blast of hot air caused the charcoal to burn with sufficient temperature to melt the iron present in the ore.[40]

The furnace owners usually made the brick from either red or grey clay located near the furnace. The bricks measured about eight inches in length, four inches in width, and about two inches thick. The core of the furnace made from the five layers of brick formed a circle which was approximately thirty-two inches thick with the addition of mortar for the bricks. The core bulged in the middle and was narrow at the bottom and top. At the base of the core was the hearth which was often fitted with an iron base and was about six feet across. The widest section of the core, located near the middle, was called the bosh. The widest part of the bosh was about six to ten feet from the hearth, depending on the height of the stack. The bosh measured about nine or ten feet across, and it began to narrow gradually from the middle of the stack to the top.[41] [See Fig. 1 and 2]

The space outside the core was filled with sand or other insulation material to contain the heat and protect the outer walls from the intense temperatures generated by the furnace. A few of the later furnaces had a metal jacket around the core to further insulate the outer walls. The outer limestone walls were built to form a pyramid and the average furnace had side walls of about twenty-seven feet. The walls tapered to about twenty-two feet at the opening for the furnace. The height of the stack was usually twenty-eight feet.[42] Because the furnace required intensive heat to melt the ore and separate the iron ore from the other elements, charcoal was needed in large amounts, and it had to be immediately available to keep the blast at a constant temperature. The ideal site for the furnace was adjacent to a large forest area.[43] [Fig. 1 and 2]

The furnace had an open hearth at the base, and bellows, much like an oversized fireplace bellows, forced the outside air into the stack. To load the furnace, a charcoal fire was started on the hearth, then more charcoal was added from the top. The limestone, followed by the iron ore, was dumped into the core. As air was forced into the furnace, the oxygen was combined with the hot charcoal to form carbon monoxide. The gas and the heated air rose to the top of the stack where the heat turned the iron ore into liquid. During the blasting process both molten metal and slag accumulated near the hearth at the base of the furnace. Slag, formed from the impurities in the ore combined with the limestone flux, floated on top of the molten

[40]For details on iron making see Buena Coleman Daniel, "The Iron Industry in Dickson County, Tennessee," M. A. Thesis located at Austin Peay State University; Jerilee S. Davis, "The Charcoal Industry of Montgomery and Stewart Counties," M.A. Thesis located at Austin Peay State University, and Betty Joe Wallace, "The Economic Effects of the Civil War in Stewart County," M.A. Thesis located at Austin Peay State University.

[41]Ibid.

[42]Ibid.

[43]Ibid.

iron. The slag was tapped off first through the slag notch, and as it cooled it was broken or crushed into irregular lumps and usually discarded near the furnace. The glass-like slag varied in color and texture from a clear sky-blue color, indicating the presence of manganese, to a gray color, indicating a high grade iron, rich in graphite carbon. Dark slag indicated that the iron was low in graphitic carbon. The material formed large mounds near the furnace, and after a time it was used as a foundation for roads.[44]

The molten metal was drained off through the iron notch and allowed to run onto a casting floor adjacent to the run-out arch. The floor was covered with sand and was usually roofed or enclosed in a casting shed. Impressions were made in wet sand with wooden patterns to form sand molds. Great care was given to allow the exact amount of the molten iron to run into the molds. If the molds overflowed, the iron hardened into a mass that was difficult to break. The main trench was usually called a feeder trench or sow. The sand molds along each side of the sow were called pigs and as the molten iron drained into the sow it was directed by a skilled worker into pig molds. Because the iron workers often referred to the sand mold as the pig bed, the term pig iron became a common term used in the industry.[45] [Fig. 3]

At the same time that the molten iron was directed into the pig beds, functional cast iron objects were made at the site. These articles included hollow wares such as pots, pans, skillets and kettles. Solid items such as firebricks, stove parts, cannon balls, grave markers, water pits, and mill parts were produced. Nails, knives, fenders, stoves, farm implements, railroad ties, and decorative items were made from the iron.[46]

If the blasting process were not efficient, there was a considerable loss of iron in the slag. Some ironworks utilized stamping mills for crushing furnace slag, sometimes referred to as forge cinders, in order to run it through the furnace again to obtain the iron which it contained.[47]

If the furnace used steam power it had to be located near a dependable stream. As soon as the site was chosen, a dam was constructed and a water wheel was used to power the air blast machinery. Steam engines were used in the early 1840s but within a decade they were no longer in use in the land between the rivers.[48]

The labor force was perhaps the single most important factor in guaranteeing the success of a furnace operation. Iron masters had to have an available, constant labor force of both skilled and unskilled workers. The iron masters preferred to create a community around the furnace site and keep as many of the workers as possible on the site. If the furnace owner did not live at the furnace, he hired a supervisor who had the responsibility to act in his behalf. The furnace community was clearly based on the ideology that division of labor and special incentives to workers resulted in a more stable, efficient labor force and a superior product, thus

---

[44]Ibid.

[45]Ibid.

[46]Ibid.

[47]Ibid.

[48]Ibid.

more profits for the company.[49]

The labor force could be described as an occupational pyramid with the iron master at the top and the unskilled slave workers at the base. Unskilled and semi-skilled laborers were used to dig ore and limestone, clean the furnace area, work on the farms, prepare the food for the workers, cut timber, care for the animals, repair the broken equipment, and drive the wagons and carts. Between the iron master and the workers a chain of command was essential, especially if the owner did not live on the site. Clerks, who were responsible for all the records, were directly responsible to the owners of the furnace. The founder, who was responsible for keeping the furnace running at peak efficiency, was perhaps the most important individual in the daily operation of the furnace. He had assistants called keepers who worked in shifts to keep the operation running night and day. If the production rate fell below expectations, the founder was held responsible. The fillers were responsible for collecting and maintaining all the raw materials for loading the furnace. Guttermen prepared the sand beds on the casting house floor. Molders and their helpers were responsible for casting the iron into usable forms, either on the casting house floor or in special molds made for casting utensils.[50] Colliers prepared the charcoal and supervised the men who delivered the wood to the coaling field. Miners who dug the iron ore and limestone, teamsters who drove wagons loaded with the iron ore or charcoal, and woodcutters who prepared the logs for charcoal were usually included in the unskilled category along with those workers who did odd jobs around the furnace. The number of individuals in each of the categories varied with the size of the operation. In many instances the occupations below the level of founder were often held by slaves and immigrant workers.

During the periods of peak operations, owners were forced to bring in workers from outside the states of Tennessee and Kentucky to meet the labor demands. By 1820, immigrant workers from Ireland were already a part of the work force. Large numbers of immigrant workers were employed until the Civil War. Stewart County reached a population of 6,550 white, 1,352 slaves, and 48 free African Americans in 1820.[51] The companies made contracts with many of the immigrant workers to pay their expenses to the land between the rivers area if they would agree to work for a designated length of time.[52]

It is difficult to determine the exact number of immigrants who worked at a furnace in any given year, but at the peak of the iron production period in the 1850s, several hundred Irishmen were living and working in the land between the rivers. The wages for the Irish immigrant workers appeared to be the same as those for other white employees at the furnace. The single men were usually housed in dormitories owned by the company. Small cabins were

---

[49]Ibid.

[50]Utensils including pots, pans, skillets, and tubs were molded. Two types of kettles became very well known. The wash pot kettle was soon found in most homes. The sugar kettle was shipped to Louisiana for use in the sugar industry. Implements from hammers to sad irons were molded at the furnace.

[51]U. S. Population Census records 1820.

[52]Partial contracts were found for 1840 among the documents described in footnote 18.

available for the workers who had families. Some of the Irishmen married into families who already resided in the area, and these individuals often purchased land and became permanent residents of the counties in the land between the rivers.[53]

Chinese immigrants were brought into the Center Furnace area around 1820. Very little is known about the wage agreements which were made with these individuals, but it appears that they were segregated in the furnace community and often received lower wages than other workers. Most of the Chinese came to work for a short time and return home, but some of the men arranged for their families to come later. These workers did eventually leave the employment of the iron masters and entered other occupations, including farming and gardening.[54]

A considerable number of the iron workers were African American; the majority were slaves, either owned by the iron master or by farmers in the area. Usually, the iron masters hired slaves from farmers when they needed more laborers on short notice or when they had expectations of increasing the production at a particular furnace. The work contract was negotiated with the slaveholder, but the primary components were standard arrangements for the region. The owners received from $150.00 to $200.00 a year for the services of each male slave, the higher figure being for skilled slaves. The employment term normally ran from the beginning of January until early December. The iron master had to specify that he would provide adequate food, shelter, clothing, and medical care for the slave. The contracts were usually vague when it came to determining the term adequate, but the slaveholder was usually concerned that his slave be well fed and kept healthy. Medical attention varied from year to year and from furnace to furnace, but because the iron master needed healthy workers, most furnace operators hired at least a part-time physician for the workers. Taking into consideration the amount of medical care available to all the people in the area, the workers in the iron industry received above average care.[55] The slave was provided with two suits of clothes, one hat, three pairs of shoes, one blanket and in some cases, one overcoat each year. The amount of food was traditionally set at seven pounds of pork, a jar of molasses, and a peck and a half of cornmeal per week. This amount was the most generous of the food allotments. The amounts were usually smaller but the type of food remained rather constant. In some cases, the slaves were allowed to eat in a segregated, dining hall provided by the furnace owner.[56]

The information about the role of the female workers in the iron industry is practically non-existent, even though women made up a large segment of a furnace community. Furnace owners provided houses and garden plots so that the workman's family could live near the furnace. Iron masters owned married slaves and it was not uncommon to provide a separate

---

[53]Study of U. S. Population Census records 1820-1850.

[54]U. S. Population Census records were compared to Stewart County and Trigg County Tax Assessment records and it was found that if the Chinese workers left the iron industry, they sometimes bought land and farmed. The names gradually disappeared from all the records after 1860. It is possible that some of the names were changed.

[55]In some areas the only doctor available in the community was employed at the furnace.

[56]The contracts were validated by magistrate signatures from 1840 to 1860. For an example see Stewart County Court records, 1841, Book IVI, 30.

residence for the couple and their children. These slave women were employed in the furnace operation as cooks and farm workers. On occasion, the wives of the white employees were paid a wage to work for the company, but it seems that these women worked intermittently as the need for extra laborers expanded. Sewing, cooking, washing, and cleaning were the customary jobs which women performed. Women and children worked alongside men on the company farms. There is no evidence that women were ever used as a part of the skilled labor force.

Charcoal Production

Since iron furnaces could not operate without charcoal, a number of furnace workers and farmers in the region cut timber for the furnaces. As time went by, the furnace owners were forced to purchase more and more forest lands for charcoal production. If the timber was not nearby, the furnace owners made arrangements with farmers to haul logs from their land to the charcoal pits. [Fig. 3]

The production of charcoal was a tedious, time-consuming, and complex task that demanded both skilled and unskilled labor. Colliers were the specialists who supervised the production of charcoal. As already indicated the early furnaces required large amounts of hardwood for charcoal. At least 400 tons of charcoal were needed to produce a ton of iron. A furnace in full operation might consume from one to two acres of timber per day. Frequent accidents in the coaling areas consumed hundreds of tons of charcoal periodically.[57]

The preparation of the wood for the coaling fields employed scores of unskilled workers.[58] Once the trees were cut, the limbs were removed and the logs were cut into four foot lengths and stacked in cords--four feet wide, four feet high, and eight feet in length. The wood was hauled by sleds or wagons pulled by oxen, horses or mules to a coaling field. Careful attention was given to the location of the coaling field because a charcoal pit could malfunction, explode, and kill workers in the area. Another danger was that the explosion could start a forest fire and burn many tracts of timber.[59]

Once the wood was available for the coaling field, the workers were ready to begin the tedious task of making the charcoal. The first task was to determine how many coaling pits could be produced from the available wood. Then the location of each pit was determined, and the entire area was swept clean with brooms. Even the smallest twigs were gathered and removed from the site. Skilled workers constructed the conical or circular pits, each about thirty feet in diameter. Approximately sixty cords of wood were needed for each pit. The act of placing the wood in the pit was exacting and only skilled workmen were allowed to attempt the task because the quality of the charcoal was determined by how well the fires burned, and a poorly constructed pit could explode. The workmen fashioned a tepee out of poles and built

---

[57]Daniel, "The Iron Industry," Davis, "The Charcoal Iron Industry," 39, and Wallace, "The Economic Effects of the Civil War," 92.

[58]In the industry the site where charcoal was made was called the coaling fields.

[59]Daniel, 41.

a three-cornered pen in the center to form a hearth. The prepared wood was then set on end around the pen in a circle two lengths high. Then another length was placed on top of the pen. This technique was followed very carefully until the pit was about twelve feet tall.[60] [See Fig. 3]

Workers, using wagons with extra large frames and tall beds, hauled wet or dampened leaves to the newly constructed pits. Slowly and meticulously, workmen covered each pit with the wet leaves. One blunder could cause the collapse of a whole pit, and if an accident happened, the whole area had to be cleaned, and the construction of the pit was started again. By this time workmen had wagon loads of wet clay, which had been dug from the hills in the area, ready to cover each pit.[61] The sides of the pit had to have at least six inches of clay, and the top area had to have at least eighteen inches, packed very carefully. If the top was not prepared precisely, the pit could literally blow its top during the burning process. Since there were usually several pits burning at a given time, the explosion of one pit could result in a chain reaction in all the pits. Workers feared such accidents because the burning charcoal could rain over the entire coaling field, and any workers nearby would be unable to escape the fire.[62]

Workers totally encased the pits in leaves and clay and then allowed them to dry. The weather conditions determined how long the pits were left before they were ready to cook. During this period, workers feared rain storms because the pit could become water logged and crumble. If that happened, the work had be done all over again.[63]

The firing process, considered the most critical step in the production of charcoal, was controlled by a skilled workman. He used a special ladder, about twelve feet long, to climb to the top of the pit, and with great care so that he did not disturb the pit in any way, he used a specific type of shovel to open a hole in the top of the pit. When the hole was opened, kindling, comprised of small pieces of wood and wood shavings, was then gently dropped into the pit to settle in the hearth. A fire, kindled into flames on a long-handled shovel, was lowered into the pen or center of the hearth at the base of the pit.[64]

When it was apparent that the fire had caught and a satisfactory draft or current of air would cause the fire to continue burning, the hole in the top of the pit was covered. Two holes about six inches across were made on each side of the pit at the base to permit the gas and smoke to escape, and to allow just enough air to char the wood.[65] After the pit burned for four days, other holes were made around the base and at the top of the first length of wood; then the pit was allowed to burn for four more nights. Each pit was expected to produce a thousand

---

[60]Ibid, 44.

[61]The workmen called the clay green dust.

[62]Wallace, Economic Effects, 102.

[63]Ibid.

[64]Ibid.

[65]Ibid.

bushels of charcoal if the burning process had worked well.[66]

When the coal was ready to draw, or to be removed from the pit, an opening was made at the base and an experienced workman, called a drawer, removed the charcoal from the pit with a shovel made for that purpose. When the charcoal came from the pit, it had to be quickly and completely covered with water to ensure that no sparks ignited any material which could cause a flame. After all the charcoal had been removed from the pit and soaked with water, the pit was drenched with water and raked over by the workmen to extinguish even the smallest coal of fire.[67]

After the charcoal had been cooked and cooled, it was ready to be hauled to the furnace. Workmen filled large flat baskets with the charcoal and loaded them on wagons. Each bushel of charcoal weighed about twenty pounds, and each wagon was designed to haul one hundred bushels per load. Transporting the charcoal was dangerous because the smallest spark could ignite the basket and wagon. As a safety measure, large buckets and barrels of water were placed along the road to the furnace, but even these precautions did not always protect the charcoal and wagons.[68]

Different estimates are recorded relative to the amount of charcoal needed to keep a furnace in operation over a period of time. On the average the furnaces in the land between the rivers needed at least 10,000 cords of wood, representing at least 500 acres of good timber to keep a furnace running during a typical blast period of eight to ten months. Records of the numbers of accidents in the production of charcoal and the amount of timber that furnace owners purchased indicate that much more than 500 acres of timber were used by each furnace during an annual operation.[69]

The people of the region wanted to purchase items made from the pig iron. Responding to that market demand, Chittenden Lyon and other financiers formed a company and brought in a rolling mill. The rolling mill and a slitting mill were combined under one roof, producing iron strips cut by water-powered crocodile shears. When the strips were heated to a red heat, they were passed through rollers until they were pressed into the calculated thickness needed for the rod or sheet that was required for a particular product.[70] After the rods or sheets were reheated, they were sent to the slitters, which consisted of small grooved rolls, set so that the rims of one roll entered the grooves of the other. In the slitters the strips were divided into several rods. Blacksmiths and other iron workers could heat, bend, and hammer the rods into useful items for the home and farm.

The increased use of steam engines severely affected the iron industry in the land between

---

[66]Ibid.

[67]Ibid. The coaling fields destroyed the productivity of the soil. The combined heat and acid from the burned wood destroyed all vegetation and nothing would grow in the soil for many years.

[68]Wallace, 103.

[69]Iron furnace owners purchased large tracts of timber each year in Stewart and Trigg Counties. Once the timber was cut, the land was often sold to farmers in the area.

[70]Caldwell County records 1832 (no book number was shown).

the rivers. British innovations during the last quarter of the eighteenth century changed the whole industry. The innovations included using coaked coal to smelt the iron ore into pig iron and the development of puddling and rolling techniques to refine the pig iron into usable wrought iron.[71] Even though the local iron industry tried to use the latest technology, they lagged behind the British and other regions in the United States. By the late 1800s the rolling mills had converted and included the puddling furnaces as part of their operation. Instead of heating the pig iron in a charcoal fire, workers melted it in a reverberator furnace using coal. As the pig iron melted, a worker stood at the door of the furnace and stirred the molten iron with an iron bar. The carbon in the iron was burned out through contact with the air as the stirring took place. The iron then stiffened into a lump which could be taken from the furnace with the aid of tongs and passed through a pair of rolls, emerging as a bar suitable for sale to merchants, blacksmiths, and the slitting operations. The iron masters were not able to convert to steam before the Civil War. That delay and the war itself helped to destroy the industry.

Lumber Industry

The vast forest lands, which the settlers found in the land between the rivers, led to the development of profitable lumber industries. Sawmills were located throughout the countryside and provided employment for workers as well as profits for lumbermen. Lumber was used in construction, and white-oak staves were produced for barrels. The lumber and staves, not purchased in the local area, were shipped out by way of the Tennessee and Cumberland. The staves, barrels, or hogsheads were needed in the iron industry and by farmers who shipped their produce to various markets. But tobacco and whiskey producers became the best customers for barrel makers. A hogshead would hold as much as two thousand pounds of tobacco. The demand became so great that the hoop shops were soon located near the stave mill.[72]

Many of the communities had spoke factories which manufactured hardwood spokes for wagons and buggies. One of the oldest of these factories, which operated until 1904, was at Carlisle in Stewart County.[73]

Huge forest lands were needed for the iron industry and the lumber industry. As expected, these forest lands were cut to provide for those needs; land was often cleared indiscriminately in a process called clean cutting. Fire was often used to facilitate the process. Farmers simply burned scrub timber in order to clear the land for planting, and little attention was given to protecting the forests.[74]

---

[71]Puddling is the process of making wrought iron from pig iron by heating and stirring it in the presence of oxidizing agents.

[72]Hoop shops produced the iron rings called hoops for the barrels. Merchant records indicate that the barrels were a popular commodity in all three counties.

[73]Stewart County Tax Assessment records, 1904, Book 109, 44.

[74]According to interviews with former residents of the area, the burning practices were quite common in the area until well after World War I.

Tanning Industry

The tanning of animal skins, an industry that was at one time of considerable importance to the region, began around 1800 at Eddyville, and a little later in Dover. Because the tanning process required an abundant quantity of water, it was necessary to locate the business near a river or large creek. Farmers and hunters were proficient in supplying the animal skins, and there was an ample supply of trees to provide the bark for the tanning process.[75] The mountain oak bark was considered the best. The bark was collected in the fall when the sap in the trees was falling, and again in the spring while the sap was rising. The bark was pulverized, using a machine designed for that purpose, and placed in vats to steep.[76] The earliest vats were nothing more than shallow wells dug into the ground and paved with stone or brick. Later, more elaborate metal vats were used. When the tanner was ready to treat the skins, he filled several vats with a solution of water and lime in proper proportions. The skins of the animals were placed in the solution and soaked until the hair could be removed. The skins, now called hides, were scraped clean and placed in another vat that had a stronger solution of lime and water, soaking for several days.

When the hides were properly soaked, they were placed in vats and covered with tannin which had been extracted from the bark.[77] The hides were left in the tannin solution for several days and then immersed in clear water for an even longer period. After this processing, they were stretched on frames designed for that purpose and worked, scraped and pounded, to make them strong and pliable. The final steps consisted of rubbing the hides with a ball of glass or wood to give them a polished appearance, and then to massaging a small quantity of oil into the skin to produce a glossy finish.

Craftsmen in the area bought the hides and made articles of clothing and aprons which were sold locally. Cobblers made the shoes to fit on either foot, and the wearer was encouraged to rotate his shoes to insure that they lasted longer. Most of the hides were shipped out of the area to other states and even to foreign markets.[78]

Gristmills

As early as 1797, gristmills were constructed for the purpose of converting grain, such as corn and wheat, into meal and flour. The people were anxious to have local mills established

---

[75]Information about tanning was supplied by Mr. Tom Martin and others in Stewart County who had first hand information about the process.

[76]The people in the area called these vats ground tubs.

[77]Some tanners simply placed five to six pounds of tree bark in the vat with the hides.

[78]Tanning operations continued in Dover and Bumpus Mills in Stewart County and Eddyville in Lyon County and Cadiz in Trigg County until around 1927. The author was able to interview several men who had worked in the tanning business. These tapes and written reports are in the hands of the author.

because of the arduous job of grinding the grain at home. The mills were located on streams or creeks, and the early dams were not more than fifteen feet in height. The water-powered mills were geared so that the runner stone would revolve at a greater speed than the water wheel. The grain was poured into a hopper, the wheel was started, and the grain was forced under the grinding stone. As the grinding stone pulverized and forced the corn or wheat into a trough, the miller stood ready to catch the flour or meal in bags. Farmers raised both corn and wheat, and they often bartered with the miller, giving him a percentage of the grain to mill their crops. The miller usually sold his shares to people who did not farm for a living and to small landholders who could not produce enough wheat or corn on their farms. The milling enterprise allowed the owner of the mill to pursue his trade and also to operate a store. Frequently, a small business community developed around the mill. General stores, blacksmith shops, and inns were built in the locale in order to take advantage of the traffic to the mill.

The mill owners were licensed by the county courts, and until 1850 the mill owner's prices were regulated by the courts. Like the stillhouse, the gristmills were necessary if the community was going to survive, and the public attitude was that no individual could charge exorbitant prices for grinding the corn or wheat which made their daily bread.[79]

---

[79]Two gristmills operated in Bumpus Mills in Stewart County until the 1950s. The mills at Eddyville and Cadiz, Kentucky operated until around 1945. Stewart County controlled the prices at the mills until 1850. The county courts in Trigg and Caldwell appear to have stopped the practice in 1848 or 1849.

CHAPTER V

CHANGES IN THE LIFESTYLE

Development of a Distinctive Culture

During the first quarter of the century, people in the land between the rivers were founding farms, industries, and communities. They relied upon farming and hunting to provide them with the necessities of life. Extensive time and energy were devoted to acquiring the essential food, shelter, and clothing. News of world affairs was learned by word of mouth, and the few newspapers brought into the area arrived days and even months after the events had transpired. The clannish traditions plus the geographical isolation because of the rivers resulted in a continued concern with local affairs and a passionate pride in the family, community, and local traditions.

Although they found transportation extremely difficult, many people travelled by boat on the Tennessee and Cumberland Rivers to places outside the region. The first steamboat to reach Dover was the "General Jackson" in 1818.[1] Ferries, regulated by the county courts, moved people across the Tennessee and Cumberland Rivers to visit towns and cities in the region.[2] By 1830, it was not unusual for the more affluent to travel to Philadelphia, New Orleans, and even to Europe.

The people exhibited a passionate sense of self-esteem and family pride.[3] A common comment was that a person's word was his bond and there was no need for written contracts. The protection of family honor often led to militant behavior, including duels and physical attacks. If an individual's honor was questioned, he was forced by community pressure to make the record clear. The predisposition toward violence remained a cultural undercurrent in the society for generations.[4]

Because the rivers separated the people from the seats of local governments, they tended to develop a general resentment toward their leaders. The county officials usually lived in or near the county seat and the people in the outlying areas seemed to feel that they were not adequately represented in the county seats at Dover, Cadiz, or Eddyville. They accused the

---

[1]Stewart County Heritage, 15.

[2]County Court records indicate that the magistrates set the ferry rates at each session of the County Court. The rates varied from year to year.

[3]New immigrants from Germany, Switzerland, and Holland made an effort to maintain their farm buildings and fences. They landscaped their yards and developed herds of milk and beef cows. Another wave of people from Ireland, Scotland, Wales, Cornwall, and the English uplands came at about the same time, but even with the new immigrants, the Celtic culture continued to dominate the area.

[4]These conclusions were reached after a study of the charges and resulting trials for misdemeanors and felonies in the County Courts and Circuit Courts. For a study of the Celtic people see Grady McWhiney, Cracker Culture and Celtic Ways in the Old South (University of Alabama: University of Alabama Press, 1988), 1-320.

townspeople of feeling superior to the rural people. The oddity in this situation was that the county seats were so small they certainly could not be called cities nor should the citizens have boasted about the amenities of the towns, but they did. No matter how small the county seat might be, it was still the most important town in the county.

The people were independent and pugnacious, with little regard for rules which they did not make for themselves. For example, they did not believe that governments, state or local, had the right to force them to build fences to contain their livestock. When the state of Tennessee tried to force the farmers to comply with a fencing law, they refused.[5]

Growth in Villages and Communities in the 1830s

After 1830, many thriving villages and communities were settled and grew in the area. Dover, Cadiz, and Eddyville were joined by communities which took their names from settlers, businesses, or from incidents which happened at the site.

Bear Springs got its name when settlers moved to the locale and found a large cave with a spring. The settlement might have been known as Cave Spring, but one night the settlement was aroused by barking dogs. When the settlers investigated, they found a huge bear treed in the spring. From then on, the community was known as Bear Springs.[6]

A big limestone rock, measuring at least one hundred feet tall and about the same width, with a cave and ever-flowing spring, drew settlers to Big Rock.[7] A tree was growing out of a crevice in the rock and cave explorers found strange fish in a lake deep inside the cave. Big Rock became a thriving community with a gristmill, stores, blacksmith shops, a carding mill, and a tobacco prizing warehouse.[8]

Bumpus Mills was named for Andrew Jackson Bumpus, an early settler in the area. The community was known for the sawmills, gristmills, and planing and machinery shop. The mills produced excellent flour and the community became quite famous for a time after 1900 because of its Bobwhite Flour. The brand name was developed by Gilbert Williams who was a partner in the Saline Milling Company in Bumpus Mills.[9]

A commissary furnished food and supplies for the furnace workers at Bellwood Furnace and it was an important location for many years.[10] People referred to the area as Commissary

---

[5]County Court records in Lyon, Trigg, and Stewart Counties. Stewart County Court records, 1847, Book 48, 1-9; Stewart County Circuit Court records, 1848, A-52, 11-17.

[6]Stewart County Heritage, 30.

[7]Citizens refer to the village as "The Rock."

[8]Stewart County Heritage, 30-31.

[9]Ibid.

[10]The Bellwood community grew up around the Bell Furnace owned by John Bell.

54

Ridge. In more recent times, people have called the area Can't Find It Ridge.[11]

One of the oldest communities in Stewart County is Cub Creek. The first settler saw a bear cub wading in the creek and the place had a name. Nathan Parker gave land to build a church and a thriving community began to grow by 1830.[12]

Indian Mound got its name from the Indian burial mounds scattered over the site. The early settlers were Caleb and John Williams, Mark McGregory, James Wilson, Hezekiah Rorie, and Richard Bagwell. The community grew to include gristmills, sawmills, stores, churches, a tobacco prizing house, and a drug store.[13]

Pot Neck was one of the more colorful names for a community. The name has caused considerable discussion since the early 1800s. Residents disagree on how the community got its name. Two of the most often repeated stories are indeed interesting. It is said that around 1819 a picnic was held at the Gatlin Sand Bar on the Cumberland for residents on the north and south side of the bar. People came from miles around, and after several hours of drinking the good domestic corn liquor, the people from the north side of the river started an argument with the people from the south side. A fight erupted and a man from the south side hit his opponent with a pot, and the man from the north side hit his opponent with a skillet. From that time on, the southern side of river was called Lick Skillet and the northern side was known as Pot Neck.[14]

Some of the residents of the Pot Neck community declare that the fight story is wrong. They maintain that the community got its name when a family who lived near a rock quarry disturbed the whole community with their fighting. On one occasion, the husband was nearly killed when his wife threw an iron pot at him, hitting him on the head and nearly breaking his neck. Other residents say the bails of the pot were caught around the man's neck and killed him. Regardless of the origin of the name, the community was remembered became of it.[15]

Some of the earliest mills were in the communities at Hickman Creek, Well's Creek, Lick Creek, Gatlin Point, and Tharpe on Barrett's Creek. Prosperous communities developed in the areas surrounding these communities and the residents took great pride in their settlements.

---

[11]Local residents insist that the community is Commissary Ridge. Can't Find It is located near Needmore Community. The reader can imagine the local jokes about the names of the communities. "Indian Mound Needsmore and Can't Find It." has been heard too many times by the author.

[12]Evidence indicates that the names of the first families in Cub Creek were Brown, Harris, Crockarell, Norfleet, Lewis, and Parker.

[13]Stewart County Heritage, 32-33.

[14]The community ceased to exist when the Cumberland River was flooded to form Barkley Lake. Interviews with residents of Pot Neck in 1956.

[15]Ibid.

Crimes and Punishments

Around 1830, the instances of crimes such as robbery and horse stealing seemed to increase in the area. Horse stealing could send a man to prison for three to five years and carried a fine of twenty-five to fifty dollars. The Circuit Court session in Dover in 1835 recorded that men were charged with kidnapping of slaves, rape, stealing horses, assault, grand larceny, and murder. The punishments for crimes were interesting because they were so varied. A man could be sent to prison for three years for larceny, eight years for stealing a horse, twelve years for rape, and two years for first-degree murder. On December 7, 1846, the first case of hanging by law in Stewart County occurred when Bob Wood, a slave belonging to Stacker, Wood, and Company, was convicted of murder, and then hanged before a large crowd.[16]

Lifestyles and Politics

The residents remained frugal and self-supporting even though their lives had been changed by the growing industries in the region. The region was more prosperous, but the people seemed to resist conspicuous consumption. They did not build extravagant homes or wear elegant apparel.[17] One tradition tenaciously persevered even though the environment was changing. A bountiful supply of food was the badge of success. Food seemed to symbolize the accomplishments of the family. A family had to have a full smoke house, root cellar, and pantry. A widespread custom was that food was made available to visitors at any time of the day or night. The custom of offering food to even a casual visitor was an indication of acceptance or friendship. A guest who was not offered food was not welcome. The visitor who refused to eat risked offending his host.[18]

The practice of eating only with equals was an integral part of the tradition. Individuals were very selective about sitting down at the dinner table with another person. The attitude was that food was offered to just about anyone who came to your door, but you did not necessarily eat at the same table with that person. Even in the family women did not eat at the table with the men. The women served the food and waited until after the men had left the table before they ate. In many households the children did not eat with adults.[19]

An ordinary farmer had seven sheep, ten cows or calves, two mules, four or five horses,

---

[16]Stewart County Circuit Court records, 1835, Book A-35, 11-16; 1847, Book B-41, 16-27.

[17]In interviews with the residents in 1959 and former residents in 1989, comments were made about how the wealthiest people in the community dressed and behaved as if they were ordinary people. Anyone who tried to appear wealthy by the way he dressed or the home he built was often ostracized by the community.

[18]1960 interviews with residents of the land between the rivers in the hands of the author. Supplementary interviews with former residents of the area in 1989 are in the hands of the author.

[19]These attitudes also existed in those areas which immediately surrounded the land between the rivers. Interviews with citizens in Lyon, Stewart, and Trigg Counties in 1989 indicate that these views about food are still held.

and at least one yoke of oxen. He owned chickens, ducks, geese, and hogs. The farm equipment included wagons, carriages or buggies, plows, saws, axes, hoes, planers, shovels, trowels, and chisels, knives, scythes, grindstones, a vice, augers, hammers, wedges, drawing knives, hooks, chains, turning tools, spikes, braces, and bits. Even small farmers owned gear for their horses, mules or oxen. Steel traps to capture wild animals were common. Lanterns and many types of molds to make such things as shot, spoons, and hammers were found in almost every household.[20]

The typical house was very modest. The building was usually of log construction with additional rooms added as the family grew larger. The additional rooms were often constructed from lumber and were added to either side of the original log structure. The kitchen was not attached to the main house.[21] Around 1830, people began to build their homes with a wide hall, usually referred to as the dog trot, through the center of the structure. The hall was open at each end and the living quarters or front room was on one side of the hall and bedrooms on the other. The open hall served as a porch and allowed for ventilation during the summer months. The front room or parlor contained the best household furnishings the family could afford because it was for visitors. These furnishings included tables and chairs made by family members or artisans in the area. Spinning wheels and a loom were standard in most homes.

Standard supplies included several containers of honey; bushels of Irish and sweet potatoes; barrels of peas, beans, fruit, flour, meal, sugar, rice, hominy, oats, corn and pickles; and coffee, salt, pepper, allspice, tallow, and soap were kept in various amounts. A nearby smokehouse contained lard and pork. The housewife kept supplies of fabrics, thread, cotton, hemp, and the skins of cows, deer, sheep, and horses in her work room.[22]

Of course each household was different, but the basic annual provisions for an individual of moderate means might seem limited today. Jane Mizell, the wife of Stephen Mizell, became the responsibility of the Stewart County Court when her husband died without a will in 1840. She was awarded a widow's yearly allowance for food which included: five hundred pounds of pork, ten bushels of corn, fifty pounds of sugar, two hundred pounds of flour, fifty pounds of soap, two pounds of black pepper, a half pound of allspice, two bushels of salt, and five bushels of sweet potatoes. Jane Mizell was expected to raise vegetables and perhaps to acquire wild game to supplement her diet, but it is apparent that her household was not able to provide a wide variety of food.[23]

Politics was a serious concern and a form of entertainment. The preoccupation with candidates did not mean that all the eligible voters went to the polls. Often people refused to vote because they did not like any of the candidates. These same people waited and watched the elected officials and chided them about every action they took.

---

[20]The information was collected from a survey of wills and auctions from the County Court records from Caldwell (Lyon), Trigg, and Stewart Counties from 1830 to 1860.

[21]Most of the household fires started in the kitchen. To protect the house, the kitchen was a separate building.

[22]The list of supplies was compiled from data from allotments made by the county courts in Caldwell, Stewart, and Trigg Counties to widows in 1840-1850.

[23]Stewart County Court records July, 1840, Book 41,29.

The genesis of a two party system in Kentucky and Tennessee occurred around 1824. Previously the two states had been Jeffersonian Republicans, or Democratic as the party later became known. People in the land between the rivers took a special interest in the election in 1824. The election marked the first contest in which Henry Clay, Kentucky's long time favorite son, and Tennessee's Andrew Jackson entered the list for the presidency. Clay and Jackson were worthy opponents in the contest for support in Tennessee and Kentucky.

During the period from 1824 to 1860, voter participation in Kentucky and Tennessee was not large. On the average, no more than one in four potential voters actually went to the polls. Even though the turnout was low, the voter participation in the two states was not much below the average for the nation, which was about 28%.[24]

In the Presidential election of 1824, Clay's major opposition came from the supporters of Andrew Jackson. Kentucky counties in the western portion of the state, especially those such as Calloway County which had been a part of the Jackson purchase, supported Andrew Jackson. Caldwell, Trigg, and Stewart Counties also voted for him.[25] Jackson seemed to exemplify the background of most of the settlers in the area because of his ancestry and his flamboyant disregard for England which endeared him to these people.[26] His reputation for dueling and his staunch defense of the reputation of Rachel was appreciated by the people.

In 1828, Caldwell and Trigg Counties followed the rest of the state and voted against John Quincy Adams, the National Republican.[27] During the campaign, Clay, although not a formal candidate, was an issue in the contention because he had allegedly made a bargain with Adams to defeat Jackson in 1824.[28] Clay threw his whole support to Adams because his prestige was at stake, and he wanted the presidency in 1832. Over 70% of the voters in Caldwell County voted for Jackson. Trigg County supported Jackson with about 60% of the votes and Stewart County gave Jackson 80% of the votes. In this election, the rate of voter participation ran higher than usual in both Kentucky and Tennessee.[29]

Henry Clay ran again for the presidency in 1832, and once more he had to challenge the popularity of Andrew Jackson. By this time, the two parties were better organized and more issues were discussed during the campaign. Deliberately, Clay made the United States Bank one of his principal issues against Jackson. Clay carried Kentucky in the election, but Jackson took 56% of the Caldwell County voters and 54% of the Trigg County voters. Stewart County

---

[24]Jasper B. Shannon and Ruth McQuown, Presidential Politics in Kentucky (Lexington: University of Kentucky Press, 1950), 1-24.

[25]Ibid.

[26]Andrew Jackson was Scotch-Irish. He was described as a self-made man who was quick to fight, but loyal to his friends.

[27]At this time Caldwell County still owned the land that would become Lyon County.

[28]In the election in the House of Representatives, Clay had been accused of supporting Adams in return for an appointment as Secretary of State.

[29]Shannon and McQuown, Presidential Politics, 18.

continued to vote heavily for Jackson, giving him 80% of the votes.[30]

Voter participation declined in both Kentucky and Tennessee in the election of 1836. In Kentucky the voters were faced with making a choice for Van Buren with Richard Johnson of Kentucky as the running mate or voting for General William Henry Harrison who was supported by Henry Clay. Again the three counties in the land between the rivers voted for the Democratic candidate even though Van Buren was never as celebrated as Jackson.[31]

Clay, still Kentucky's favorite son, was thrust aside by the Whig party in 1840 when they nominated William Henry Harrison. Tennessee and Kentucky had suffered from the Panic of 1837 and the Whigs spent a great deal of energy trying to convince the voters in the two states that Martin Van Buren, a rich man, did not recognize their problems. Voter participation ran higher than usual in the two states; approximately seven out of ten voters went to the polls. Caldwell was the only county in the land between the rivers which gave William Henry Harrison more votes.[32]

"Prince Hal," "The Sage of Ashland," or "The Compromiser," as Henry Clay was familiarly and widely known, made his last formal bid for the presidency in 1844. When the Whig party split after Tyler succeeded to the presidency following Harrison's death in 1841, Clay had assumed the position as the leader of the Whig party and retired from the Senate. The annexation of Texas became a central issue in the campaign in 1844, and to his chagrin, Clay was confronted by a neighboring Tennessean, this time in the person of James K. Polk. The campaign was hotly contested and resulted in the highest voter participation in Tennessee and Kentucky until long after the Civil War. Caldwell, Trigg and Stewart Counties voted for Polk, and Polk won.[33]

When Zachary Taylor won the nomination from the Whig party in 1848, Henry Clay did not seem to support him. Southern Democrats did not seem especially happy with Lewis Cass of Michigan as their candidate. Free-Soil Party advocates were not enchanted with Martin Van Buren on the ticket. The election brought Taylor into office. Caldwell, Trigg, and Stewart Counties voted for the Democratic candidate by a small margin.[34]

The Whig party made its last bid for the presidency in 1852. Death had taken a severe toll on its leadership when Taylor and Calhoun died in 1850 followed by Henry Clay and Daniel Webster in 1852. Even though he was near death, Clay had indicated that he supported General Winfield Scott for the presidency. The Whigs relied on the old political technique of offering a military hero as their candidate. Franklin Pierce, the Democratic candidate, also claimed that

---

[30]Ibid, 20.

[31]Ibid, 21; Stewart County Court records, 1836, Book 37, 22.

[32]Note in the Caldwell County Court records, January 1841, Book 51, p 17; 1841, Trigg County Court records, Book 41, 27; 1841, Stewart County Court records, Book 42, 23.

[33]County Court records in Caldwell, Trigg, and Stewart Counties, January 1845. Caldwell, Book 45-II, 27; Trigg, Book 45, 32; Stewart, Book 47, 19.

[34]County Court records in Caldwell, Trigg, and Stewart Counties, January 1849; Caldwell, Book 49-A, 23; Trigg, Book 49, 19; Stewart, Book 50, 21.

he was a military hero in the Mexican War. The Whigs turned to personal assaults against Pierce, claiming that he was too fond of alcohol. Caldwell, Trigg, and Stewart Counties gave more than 50% of their votes to Pierce.[35] Perhaps they did view the charge of excessive drinking as a problem.

From 1832 to 1856, the counties in the land between the rivers had remained loyal to the Democratic candidate even though most of the rest of the parent state voted for the opposition. In 1856 both Tennessee and Kentucky went to the Democratic party. In Lyon county, which had been formed in 1854, over 60% of the votes was for James Buchanan. Trigg and Stewart Counties were closer to 70% for Buchanan.[36]

The division within the political parties in 1860 resulted in bewilderment among the voters. The Democratic party was in disarray and as a result, nominated two candidates. John C. Breckinridge from Fayette County, Kentucky was nominated to lead the southern wing of the party, and the northern wing nominated Stephen A. Douglas from Illinois. The Republican party, still trying to organize its following, nominated Abraham Lincoln from Illinois.[37] The Constitutional Unionists nominated John Bell from Tennessee. With this confusing array of choices the voters in Kentucky and Tennessee were baffled and apparently unhappy.

Kentucky and Tennessee voters wanted to preserve the Union and protect slavery in 1860. They did not want the "either or" doctrines of some politicians; they wanted to preserve the status quo. Kentucky gave a substantial plurality vote of 45.2% to John Bell. John Bell, a native son of Tennessee, received 47.5% of the vote in his state. In the two states Bell seemed to do well in the old Whig counties as well as the former Democratic strongholds. Bell received all of the electoral votes in Tennessee and Kentucky.[38]

In the land between the rivers, the people were almost evenly divided between Breckinridge and Bell. In all three counties approximately 70% to 80% of the registered voters actually voted in the election. Lyon County voters preferred Breckinridge, while both Trigg and Stewart County preferred Bell.[39] The election returns indicate that those counties in Kentucky and Tennessee which had the largest number of slaveholders tended to vote for Bell instead of Breckinridge. The old Jacksonian Democratic regions went with Breckinridge.[40]

---

[35]County Court records in Caldwell, Trigg, and Stewart Counties, January, 1853; Caldwell, Book 53-C, 32; Trigg, Book 53, 22; Stewart, Book 54, 29.

[36]For the Kentucky counties see Shannon and McQuown, Presidential Politics, 34-35. For Stewart County returns see County Court records, Book 55, 29.

[37]Lincoln was born in Kentucky less than a hundred miles from the land between the rivers.

[38]Ibid., Shannon and McQuown, Presidential Politics, 32-34.

[39]Original election returns are in the Archives of Kentucky and Tennessee. Kentucky Archives Frankfort, Kentucky; Tennessee Archives Nashville, Tennessee.

[40]Ibid.

Development of Education

Education has always been a concern to many citizens, but finances and the view that education was the private responsibility of the family hampered the development of public schools in Tennessee and Kentucky. In the early days, tax payers refused to support public education, and for those people who wanted training for their children, private, formal education was the only possibility. As early as 1806, John Ferrell established a common or subscription school for the elementary grades in Dover. His school was typical of all the schools operating in the area. Ferrell had moved from North Carolina to the Saline Creek area to organize the first Baptist Church in the region. He lived near Bumpus Mills for the rest of his life and was buried at the Morgan Cemetery near there in 1849. The school was designed to teach the basics to children of parents who were willing to pay a fee for their children's education.[41]

The common schools had a limited term, usually three or four months of the year. The schools were not well attended because the subscription fee had to be paid at the beginning of the term, and money was not always available. Arrangements were made with some teachers to pay the fees in kind which meant the teachers took produce in exchange for the instruction. Church schools were organized as soon as the ministers had established a congregation and built a church in the community. The general practice was for the minister or his wife to hold school sessions for children during the evening or on Sunday to teach them how to read the scriptures.

In 1806 Congress agreed on the Compact for Academies in Tennessee.[42] Professor R. McDougal, educated at Yale, established an academy in Dover because he had understood that some funding would come from the state. It is not clear if any of the state funds ever made it to Stewart County. The curriculum in his academy was similar to the offerings of a junior college, and the school term was four to seven months each year. By 1826, Alexander Coppedge had started the second school in Dover.[43]

In 1815 the General Assembly in Tennessee passed a law which provided schooling for orphan children whose fathers had been killed in the War of 1812. Stewart County Court tried to find the resources to educate all of these children because no money was coming from the state. The citizens refused to levy taxes to support these children. For a time, money from a budget for repairs was shifted to pay fees for these children.[44]

By 1830 the county courts in each of the counties had made attempts to establish public education for the elementary grades. Kentucky and Tennessee legislators had made several attempts to establish a common school law. By 1854 legislation in Tennessee provided for a twenty-five cents poll tax and a two and one-half cent tax on each one hundred dollars of taxable

---

[41]Stewart County Heritage, 16-17, 22, 24; Henry, Land Between the Rivers, 34.

[42]At the time of the agreement among the states in 1806, Tennessee promised to reserve areas of land for the use of public education. A tract of 100,000 acres was to be reserved to support academies in each county.

[43] Stewart County Heritage, 35. Tax Assessor records show that a school was located near Hematite in 1846.

[44]Stewart County Court records: 1815, Book 19, 30.

property.[45] In 1854 Stewart County allocated $279.62 and Trigg County set aside $292.00 for all the educational expenses in the schools, but at the end of the year both counties owed the entire amount. The debt was for the salaries of the teachers because the schools were using available buildings, usually churches, for schools. Only four schools were operating in the land between the rivers from 1850-1854. The top salary was $70.00 for the four month school term and it was owed to Mr. MeCalls in Civil District No. 3, in Stewart County and the lowest salary of $9.00 was owed to Littleberry Biushle in Civil District No. 8 in the same county. The average salary was around $30.00 for a term of four months in all the counties in the land between the rivers.[46]

The typical curriculum for the private and public school of that period of history placed emphasis on reading, spelling, mathematics, and penmanship in the elementary grades. Higher mathematics, science, literature, and philosophy were added to the curriculum in the academies, but in each grade the children were taught politeness, rhetoric, and morality, especially honesty.

Growth of Churches

The Baptist, Methodist and Presbyterian circuit riders followed the first settlers, and by 1830 they had established churches in most of the communities. The Dry Creek Baptist Church established by H. L. Craig was the parent church for all the Baptist churches in the area. The Reverend John Ross from the Dry Creek congregation helped to establish the first church in the area. The church was first known as the Barren Creek Church, but by 1808 it was known as the Crockett Creek Baptist Church.[47]

The Methodist congregation, second in number to the Baptist, built several churches in the region. Smaller numbers of Presbyterians and Christian church members organized congregations as the population grew. These groups and the Christian church eagerly competed for the reputation of having the largest membership.

In the period around 1830, church revival services called camp meetings were held annually to increase the church membership. Some of these meetings such as the services led by Peter Cartwright were protracted and inspiring. When the camp meetings were announced, it was not unusual for people from all the denominations to travel many miles to attend the services. Cartwright was known as a superb speaker, and the camp meetings he sponsored were acclaimed as the best. Hundreds of people came from the most remote areas to hear him preach.

The camp meetings served not only to energize the churches and increase membership but also to provide the opportunities for meeting people, renewing old friendships, and establishing new relationships. For some people, the most important feature of the meeting was the social gatherings before and after the church services. The camp meetings often lasted for

---

[45]The education bill came about because of the insistence of Governor Andrew Johnson.

[46]Henry, Land Between the Rivers, 59; Stewart County Court Records, Book 54, 19-21.

[47]Henry, Land Between the Rivers, 27.

several days, and preachers, working in succession, delivered sermons from early morning until late in the evening.

The organizers of the camp meetings encountered some problems with young ruffians who took great delight in disrupting the services. Local stories relate that on one occasion, several young men burst into a service and tried to stop the preacher by shouting and threatening the congregation. They waved their guns and cracked their whips, challenging any man present to fight. Members of the congregation did not intervene because they felt that the young men were dangerous. When the preacher realized that no one was ready to assist him, he seized the leader of the group and wrestled him to the ground. Then, some of the other men in the congregation rushed to support the minister. They successfully restrained the boisterous young men, and the minister ordered that the miscreants be caged in a pen until a local magistrate could be summoned. Eventually, the young men were arrested, charged with disorderly conduct, and removed from the site.[48] The land between the rivers moved out of the settlement period in the 1830s, and for the period from 1800 to 1860, with the exception of the decade of the 1830s the region had maintained relative prosperity. The rural, agricultural setting was the rule. The farms were generally efficient and the homes and buildings were in good condition. The most obvious blight on the landscape was in the general locations of the iron furnaces. In those areas, the forests had been destroyed and the land showed signs of serious soil erosion. Charcoal production had resulted in acres of worthless land.

Prosperity and Change

In the decade preceding the Civil War, the region entered a boom period. Farm commodity prices were good. The iron and lumber industries were prosperous. Small secondary industries were moving into the area and the population was growing. Immigrants from Prussia, Spain, Germany, and Bavaria joined those who were coming from England, Scotland, and Ireland.[49]

Even the smallest community had a stillhouse. General merchants established stores in the larger communities and sent peddlers to all the homes in the region. Blacksmith shops were located throughout the region. Cabinet and furniture makers sold their wares to farmers and merchants. Dress makers and tailors established shops to meet the growing demand for clothing made outside the home. Apothecaries were opened in the larger communities from which druggists dispensed medicine and often received the title of doctor.

The people enjoyed travel, and travel they did even though the journey could prove to be very difficult, even dangerous. The county courts continued to set the rates for the ferries, but the rates on the Cumberland were lower than those on the Tennessee. In the summer of

---

[48]Stewart County Court records, 1846: Book 15, 19, noted that eight young men were arrested for disorderly conduct at a revival in the Tharpe community in August 1846.

[49]U. S. Population Census records for the land between the rivers for 1840 and 1850. County Court records for Stewart, Trigg and Caldwell Counties, 1840-50.

1840 the ferry rates for the Cumberland were posted as follows: one man and horse- twenty five cents; one horse and carriage- thirty five cents; two horses and a carriage- fifty cents; four horses and a carriage- seventy five cents; six horses and a wagon- one dollar; a cart and ox-forty cents; and footmen- ten cents each. After nine p.m. the ferryman could double the rates.[50]

The recreational activities often were both fun and work. Neighbors came together to build houses, barns, and other buildings, turning the job into a community party. The men worked on the building and the women prepared the food. When the workday ended the adults relaxed and had fun playing games, drinking, and talking. Horse racing, even from the earliest days, was a recreational event that brought people from far and wide. People took great pride in their horse. Peer status was linked to having a beautiful, trained horse which could beat all the other horses in a race. Betting on the favorite horse was common and races were held almost every week.

Marksmanship and physical prowess were highly regarded in the community. The ability to shoot well was a sign of accomplishment. Barking a squirrel was a test of the best marksmen.[51] Wrestling and fighting were usually regarded as forms of entertainment. Wrestling matches did not have many rules, and contenders were often hurt. People liked to drink their whiskey at the matches, and as a result, fights broke out among the spectators. These altercations resulted sometimes in bloodshed and death. Disagreements were settled with firearms or fists. The free-for-all included punching, jabbing, biting, and gouging. Combatants often lost fingers, ears, a nose or other parts of the face in these brawls.[52]

Men took immense pride in displaying their ability to lift heavy objects. A stone, weighing up to fifteen pounds, was thrown from one shoulder to the other to demonstrate dexterity of movement. Lifting heavy objects, especially if the individual could walk with the object, was hailed as an accomplishment.[53]

Some forms of recreation were quite brutal. The gander pull was considered great fun. The neck of the gander was greased with lard, suet, or wax and the players grab the neck and pull it from the body. Cock fighting was another form of entertainment.[54] People raised and trained fighting cocks and attended fights. A common practice was to fashion a steel spur and strap it to the rooster's leg to insure that each thrust would injure and draw blood from its opponent. Dog fighting was used as entertainment but was not as widely acceptable as the cock

---

[50]Stewart County Court records, 1840: Book 40, 29. Information from County Court records in Trigg and Caldwell Counties show much the same rates were charged there.

[51]Expert marksmen were able to bark a squirrel. The marksman aimed at the tree limb instead of the squirrel. The blast would stun or paralyze the animal and it would fall to the ground. The animal was killed and not filled with shot.

[52]Letters from the Brandon family written in 1856 indicate the forms of amusements. Copies of the letters in the hands of the author. Interviews with residents of the area. Tapes in the hands of the author.

[53]Ibid.

[54]Cock fighting became illegal in the area in 1850. Many people openly disregarded the law.

64

fighting.[55]

The people had a mixture of insensitivity and compassion for animals. The hunter who wounded an animal and left it to die was not considered responsible or acceptable. In the slaughter of farm animals, a shooter must kill the animal with the first shot or blow. It was intolerable to hear a pig squeal after it had been shot. The attitude was that the animal should be killed so quickly that it could not make a sound.[56]

The largest slaveholders in the land between the rivers were the iron masters. Therefore, the largest concentration of the slave population was on or near the furnace sites. Although most of the farmers did not own slaves, those who did had on the average of six to seven slaves each.[57] About three-fourths of one per cent of the farmers in the land between the lakes had enough farm land to support owning more than five slaves.[58]

Rumors of slave uprisings had occurred periodically, but they seemed to circulate more frequently after 1830. As these recurrent rumors circulated, slave owners tried to determine their accuracy. If it were determined that the rumors were unfounded, then people settled down into an uneasy sense of safety. One of the strongest undercurrents in public attitudes seemed to be that eventually the slaves would rebel.[59]

The relationship between whites and blacks in the region was strained because of the constant fear of rebellion. Black codes, laws which restricted blacks, were strengthened as the numbers of slaves increased in the area between 1830 and 1850. Slaves or freedmen were not allowed to own weapons, horses, or other animals. By 1850, slaves were not allowed to hold their own religious services and could not travel from one farm to another without written permission from their owners.[60]

By 1850 an apprehension, bordering on paranoia, about possible rebellions blanketed the area. Slaves who worked at the iron industries were suspect because of the large numbers who lived in a small area.[61] Even though all the counties had restrictions against selling alcohol to all blacks, the records show that the illegal sales continued and local restrictions were hard to enforce. Gambling with slaves was forbidden, and several men were arrested for violating the

---

[55]Hunting dogs were too valuable to use in these dog fights. The men had a special attachment to these animals.

[56]Ibid.

[57]U. S. Population Census records from 1820-1850.

[58]Ibid.

[59]These rumors are mentioned in the county records from 1830 to 1861. See Stewart County Court records, 1850: Book 51, 29.

[60]Survey of Circuit Court and County Court records in Stewart, Trigg, and Caldwell Counties from 1830 to 1850. See Stewart County Circuit Court records, 1835: Book 35-A, 22; Caldwell County Court records, 1842: Book 47, 29.

[61]Stewart County Court records, 1850: Book 51, 11.

law.[62]

County courts made provisions to more strictly regulate those individuals who were given licenses to tipple. The laws restricted more than three slaves meeting in a group. Whipping was the usual punishment for slaves who disobeyed these rules. The county courts ordered the arrest of any individuals who allowed blacks to meet on their land. Irvin Brandon and John Cherry of Stewart County were arrested and charged with allowing an unlawful assembly of slaves on their land. Each man had to pay a fine of ten dollars.[63] William Davis was arrested when he was found drinking with a slave in Stewart County, and when he did not pay his fine, he went to jail. Several merchants who were arrested and convicted of selling whiskey to slaves lost their licenses to tipple.[64]

The threat of rebellion resulted in stronger action in the January session of the Stewart County Court in 1850. It was ordered that all free persons of color in the county had to register with the county court and make bond to keep the peace. An individual had to have property sufficient to cover the bond, or someone, usually white, had to co-sign the bond. The co-signer took responsibility for the actions of the freedman. In the February session, the county court expressed concern that only five free persons of color had complied with the court order and reacted by ordering that the justices of the peace, or magistrates, in each district compile a true and accurate list of all the free persons of color living in the county. There is no record of the list, but in April, 1851, the county court ordered the clerk of the court to notify all free persons of color to appear at the July session of the court and give bond as the law required. In July and August of 1851, thirty-two men and women appeared before the court, and bond was made for them and their families.[65]

Approximately one hundred freedmen were living in the county at that time, mostly outside the land between the rivers, and about a third of the freedmen complied with the court order. It does not appear that freedmen left the county when the bond rule was put into effect, since the freedman population increased to one hundred and fifty-five in 1860.[66]

In 1852, the increasing fear about the activities of blacks resulted in a change in policy in Stewart County. It was required that a responsible white man must co-sign the bond with a freedman. Up until this time, a freedman with property could sign his own bond. Because white men were not willing to sign the bonds, tensions grew. By 1856 some of the freedmen in the Stewart County portion of the land between the rivers moved out of the land between the rivers into Trigg and Lyon Counties. A small number of freedmen moved from Stewart County

---

[62]County Court records in Caldwell, Trigg, and Stewart Counties. See Stewart County Court records, 1840: Book 41, 24. James Alsop was arrested for playing cards with slaves.

[63]Stewart County Court records 1850. See Book 49, 37.

[64]Circuit Court and County Court records 1820-1860 in Stewart, Trigg, and Caldwell (Lyon) Counties. See Stewart County records, 1851, Book 52, 24.

[65]1850, Stewart County records, Book 51, 23-27; 1851: Book 51, 32-39; U.S. Population Census, 1850.

[66]U. S. Population Census, 1860.

just across the county line in Montgomery County.[67]

The tensions in Stewart County reached a climax in November, 1856. For months, rumors that freedmen and slaves were organizing a rebellion had been raging throughout the region. Slaves were said to be holding secret meetings and making plans to execute all the white people and escape to a free state. It was said that the slaves wanted to escape to the north by way of Hopkinsville. Slaveholders tried to keep their slaves from meeting without white supervision, but some of the slaveholders who did not seem to take the stories about rebellion seriously, allowed their slaves to assemble for certain religious meetings. These slaveholders were arrested and fined for not controlling their slaves, and public sentiment against lenient slaveholders and their slaves became widespread.

The fear of black violence triggered intense reactions among some of the white men in the area. An extra-legal group, calling itself the Committee of Safety, was organized in Stewart County and recruited members in Trigg and Lyon Counties. The Committee of Safety adopted as its major responsibility the need to locate and seize all blacks who were conspiring in a planned rebellion.[68]

During November and December, the Committee apprehended several suspected revolutionaries and interrogated them. One slave was beaten and questioned and eventually confessed that he and several others were in fact leaders of a planned rebellion. The reaction to the confession was swift and brutal. At least nine slaves were executed by the Committee of Safety on December 5, 1856. The other blacks who were accused of being involved in the conspiracy were marched to jail.[69]

By the evening of December 5, the Committee of Safety had contacted all slave owners in the area and ordered them to force march all slaves to Dover. Legend has it that at dusk, the Committee of Safety presented the heads of some of the rebel leaders impaled on spiked poles to the assembled blacks. The area was then illuminated with pine torches and the lifeless heads of the black leaders were placed in front of the crowd. Committee members forced the blacks to stay all night without moving and watch the heads. The next morning the blacks were marched back to their homes.[70]

All blacks who were thought to have had a role in the rebellion were jailed in Dover. The exact number of prisoners is not known, but an item in the January 1857 session of the county court of Stewart County gives an indication of the possible numbers involved. The court

---

[67]When these people moved to Montgomery County they most likely farmed. The U. S. Population Census for 1850 and 1860 for Stewart and Montgomery Counties in 1850 and 1860 show that black families with identical surnames disappeared in Stewart County and five of those names appeared in Montgomery Court.

[68]1856: Stewart County records, Book 57, 11,14,22, 16-27; Book 58, 1-8.

[69]Ibid.

[70]There is evidence in the County Court records in Stewart County for November and December of 1856 and January, February, and March of 1857 to place some credibility in the story. The fear of black rebellion was noticed in Montgomery County at the same time. Newspapers contain news items about the possibility of a race war. There is no evidence to determine the exact number of people who were executed in the incident. See Book 59, 21; Book 60, 32.

ordered that O. P. Thomason be allowed one hundred and forty dollars for boarding Negro prisoners during the excitement in the county during November and December, 1856. At that time, the average cost for boarding a prisoner was approximately fifty cents a day. When the court stipulated that amount for the black prisoners, it indicates that approximately forty-six slaves were held in jail during the crisis. At the same session the county court ordered that E. P. Lancaster be allowed the sum of seven dollars and fifty cents for the making of three coffins for the Negroes executed by the county.[71] Law enforcement officials took no action against any member of the Committee of Safety for taking the extra-legal initiative in putting an end to the possible rebellion. Yet, some members of the county court did express concern about the possibility of further violence from their slaves. The court ordered that two white men from each of the civil districts be chosen to serve on a patrol to keep the peace among the slaves and the free people of color. The patrol was to check the blacks to make sure that they were not traveling without their master's permission.[72]

The consequence of possible revolution and violence affected the iron industry immediately. The Great Western Furnace was closed in 1856 because of the rumored rebellion, and other furnace owners organized special patrols to watch the slaves working in the industry. Even though the rebellion had not transpired, or for that matter had not even been planned, the fear that the close proximity of the slaves at the iron furnaces would breed rebellion caused negative reactions from the white workers. The iron masters who faced these additional problems in their work force often closed the furnaces. When the furnaces closed the unemployed white workers blamed the blacks for their unemployment. Apprehension, wrath, and resentment fed on the erratic employment practices and the rumors of rebellion. In the minds of many people the blacks were the cause of all the problems.[73]

Without doubt, the incidents of racial tensions increased during the period, yet the county officials protected some of the slaves. In 1856 John McBride was indicted by a Grand Jury in Trigg County for whipping a slave. The case was continued for several sessions of the court but was never brought to trial.[74]

Samuel Elam of Stewart County was an example of the slaveholder who was confident that he could control the fate of his slaves during his lifetime but worried about them after his death. At his death in 1855, his will stipulated that his slaves would be turned over to the protection of the Stewart County Court. The court was charged with the responsibility of finding jobs for the slaves for two years. At the end of that time, the slaves were to be sent to Liberia. The passage fee to Africa was provided by the Elam estate and the money the slaves had earned would be given to them when they reached Liberia. The Stewart County court accepted the responsibility, and recorded its attempts to find employment for the slaves, but no

---

[71]Stewart County Court, January, 1857. (Book is not numbered but if the sequence was followed it should be numbered 59) 12,13.

[72]Ibid., 17-19.

[73]These concerns were mentioned in the Stewart County Court records, February 1857, Book 59, 13-19.

[74]Trigg County Circuit Court records, July 1856, Book LIV, 17.

record was found that indicated that the court did send the slaves to Africa.[75]

Evidences of Class Structure

The people in Tennessee and Kentucky, as elsewhere in the United States, did not live in a classless society. By 1840 modest displays of wealth could be seen among the people. Those who owned land and industries, especially the iron industry, made up the elite class, and their homes reflected their economic status in the community. The wealthier citizens built brick houses, which were usually copies of the Federalist architecture. By 1852 approximately twenty homes of this type were standing in the land between the rivers.[76] The majority of the people continued building log homes even though frame-construction homes were becoming popular by 1850. Many people added rooms to existing log cabins instead of building new homes. No particular plan was used when the rooms were added to the cabin. Some people simply built frame structures around the original log cabin and then added a second floor.[77] Other builders chose to copy the dog trot plan.

A study of the sales of personal property shows that the more affluent citizens were interested in acquiring certain trappings of wealth. Estate sales in the period from 1830 to 1860 mention the type of carriage a family had acquired. The finest carriage was an ornate covered vehicle pulled by matched carriage horses. Men and women were quite particular about the horses that they owned and used. Young men wanted a fine saddle horse to demonstrate to the community that they had reached adulthood. Young women wanted matched horses for their buggies.[78]

Even though most of the household furnishings were not usually imported, the estates of wealthier individuals contained several objects that would be considered luxury import items. Ornate chests from China, spice racks from India, and furniture from France were mentioned in the records.[79] The people seemed to assume that a family with a certain economic standing would acqure more extravagant household furnishings, but the very wealthy people continued to take pride in the fact that they lived as most of their neighbors, and an outsider would not

---

[75]A survey was made of the court records for four years after the item appeared in August, 1855, Book 56, 19, to determine if the court sent the freedmen to Liberia. No record of the transaction was found.

[76]Property tax rolls in Stewart, Caldwell (Lyon), and Trigg Counties in 1852 provided a brief description of the homes.

[77]A good example of construction around a log house can be seen in a home in Dover, Tennessee. The house belonged to the Stone family and is now owned by the Wallace family.

[78]Estate of E. H. Brandon and Robert Futrell are examples of estates sold from 1850 to 1860. 1850, Stewart County records of Real Property, Book 109-C, 28-32; 1860, Trigg County records of Real Property, Book 199, 45-46.

[79]Estate of N. H. Brandon, and Robert Futrell, and others. Located in Trigg and Stewart County records, 1850-1860.

recognize that they were wealthy.[80]

Many of the tools used for operating the farm were still made mostly from wood or crude iron. Mallets and shaving horses were common implements on the farms.[81] Even though a variety of new agricultural implements were on the market, the farmers imported only a few of them. Cast iron and steel plows were found on most farms. Seed drills, threshers, mowers, reapers and other devices of this kind were not yet widely used. Perhaps the sufficient labor supply and the cost-prohibitive price of these machines kept many farmers from using them.[82]

Since people continued to make many tools and their furniture from wood, they needed specific tools. Most households had a broadaxe, a foot adze, a pole axe, and a chalk box. The timber was cut and the logs were hewn with these tools. The craftsmen had to develop skill in hewing in order to make the rounded sides of a log flat. Hewing logs by hand for the construction of buildings or crossties for the railroads was a simple but arduous task. The log was placed on blocks and wedges were placed under the ends to keep the log from rolling. Then the workmen made guideline marks along the side of the log so they could hew it in a straight line. The guideline boxes contained either ground charcoal or a mixture of pokeberry juice and lime. The line, coiled in the box, was pulled out the length of the log, laid on the log where the hewing was to be done, stretched tight, and then twanged or snapped. A straight marked line became clearly visible along the length of the log. Using an axe, the worker would score the log at two to three-inch intervals. Then, he used a broadaxe to slice the chips off the log. The broadaxe had a curved handle to keep the workman from skinning his hand against the side of the log. An inexperienced workman could easily miss the log and cut his leg or foot. Such accidents often proved fatal because the man could bleed to death before help arrived.[83]

Regardless of wealth, most farmers used the same implements and tools in planting and harvesting crops. Usually, mules or oxen pulled the iron plows and planting and harvesting were done by hand. The farmers who owned river bottom or creek bottom land had an easier time tilling the soil than those farmers who tried to plow the hillsides. The top soil on the hills was thin and rocky. Chert and clay combinations made the land unusable without fertilizer.

---

[80]Ibid. The author found that out of fifty people interviewed in 1956 (average age was 77) about their recollections of their ancestors, 90% of them mentioned that their family did not welcome an ostentatious display of wealth.

[81]Mallets were made by hand from a two-foot section cut from the limb of a hardwood tree. While the wood was still green, two-thirds of the limb was hewn into a handle and then smoothed by sanding and rubbing. The head of the mallet was formed, and it was allowed to cure. Wooden mauls were made the same way. The shaving horse was constructed out of lumber and designed to hold logs or any item that was to be sawed or shaped. A simple shaving horse had one main brace with two short legs at the front and two longer legs at the back. One arm, one block, and a foot pedal were attached to the main brace.

[82]A survey was made of estate sales from 1830 to 1861.

[83]By 1840 farmers and lumbermen had contracts to furnish the crossties to railroad companies outside the counties. The ties were shipped by the rivers to the buyer. From about this time until after World War I, area lumber companies and farmers sold ties to the railroads.

Money Crops

By 1850 the economic practice for many families was to own enough land to produce one money crop plus the animals, fruits, and vegetables which the family would consume each year. Extra income was made in secondary industries around the iron furnace or the lumber industry. In the years after the Civil War and the cessation of the iron industry, these farmers looked to the whiskey and lumber industries for supplementary income.

Both tobacco and cotton were crops which demanded a large, stable labor supply because of the importance of the planting and harvesting seasons. By 1850 tobacco had replaced cotton and hemp as the money crop in the land between the rivers. Tobacco farmers were forced to spend many days preparing the land for planting and working against time to harvest the crop in the autumn. Early in the spring, tobacco beds were prepared, and seeds were planted to produce seedlings which were then transplanted to the tobacco fields after the last frost. The tobacco had to be planted in rows called hills to allow for cultivation with plows and hoes. The tobacco setters used a wooden peg to made a hole in the center of a hill, placed a young tobacco plant in the hole, then packed soil around the roots and stalk of the plant. Behind the setter came the workman with buckets of water to pour ever so gently around the young tobacco plant. Throughout the growing season the tobacco was plowed and hoed to clear out the weeds and grass.[84] The adult tobacco plant had sprouts which grew where the leaf stem and stalk joined. Workmen had to "sucker" the tobacco which meant they had to remove all the sprouts along the stem so that the tobacco leaf could receive all the nourishment from the roots.[85]

Throughout the growing season, the tobacco plants had to be plowed, hoed and wormed. A one-horse plow was used to plow down the center of the tobacco rows. The farmer was constantly working to rid the area of weeds and turned the soil to keep it loose around the tobacco stalk. Weather was an all-important factor in the success of the crop, especially during the early growing season. Since worms could destroy the crop, the entire farm family worked to pull worms off the plants.[86]

When the tobacco leaf was ripe, it had to be harvested on sunny days before a frost. Farmers needed a large labor supply for the harvest because cold weather would damage the leaf. Cutting and hanging tobacco was a dirty, back-breaking job. Tobacco sticks made from a hardwood tree or cane were cut to fit the length of the tier-poles in the tobacco barn.[87]

Tobacco cutters first sliced the plant from the top to within two feet of the roots. The plant was cut evenly across at ground level and hung across the tobacco stick. Depending on the size of the tobacco plants, each stick would hold from five to six plants. The cutter had to

---

[84]With the exception of the use of a mechanical tobacco setter, tobacco crops are planted in much the same way today.

[85]Chemicals are used today to control the suckers.

[86]Today farmers use tractors to plow the crop, and chemicals are used to eliminate the weeds and worms.

[87]The tobacco sticks were about six feet long and about two inches in diameter.

handle the plant carefully because the leaves and stalk were tender and easily broken.[88]

Once the tobacco stalks were cut and placed on the sticks, the plants were hauled on wagons or carts to the tobacco barn. Three to four men were needed to properly hang the tobacco in the barn. The hanging started at the top of the barn and was tiered down to ten or fifteen feet from ground level. The tobacco plants were hung to cure in such a way as to keep the leaves from touching each other or the ground.

If the farmer had a small tobacco crop, he might elect to remove the leaves from the stalk and string them on wire or thread. The strings were allowed to hang in the barn or shed to cure. Either method required careful handling of the tobacco. If the weather were dry the tobacco leaf could shatter with too much handling or if it were too wet the tobacco would mold.

Once the barn was filled, the farmer allowed the tobacco to dry slowly until it was time to complete the curing process. Short logs or sticks of wood were placed on the ground under the tobacco and set on fire. The wood had to be placed with care so as to achieve just the right balance of wood to the size of the fire. Too much fire could scorch the tobacco plants or even catch the barn on fire. Once the wood had been placed and the fire was started, the flames were quickly extinguished with just the right amounts of water. Billows of smoke were kept going constantly until the tobacco was cured. A watchman had to stay with the fires so that flames would not erupt from the smoldering wood. From time to time, new wood was added in an attempt to keep continual smoke.[89]

Each farmer timed the curing process according to his own method, but after the curing, the farmer had to wait for a wet season in the late fall or early winter to get his tobacco ready for market.[90] Stripping tobacco was one of the more skilled phases of crop production. Tobacco strippers had to cull or sort the leaves and place different grades of leaf in a separate bundle called a hand. The culls or scrap tobacco brought the least money when it went on the market. The best leaves had a certain color and texture which meant they could be sold as first grade. The tobacco stripper had to be able to pick out the best leaf at a glance and wrap it together in a hand. If a hand of tobacco was mixed with good and poor grades, it brought the lower price on the market.[91]

The stripping could not be done while the tobacco was dry and brittle. If the weather turned too cool the tobacco would go out of order and the stripping had to stop. The farmer might have to wait for days for the right season of warm, wet, humid weather to continue the stripping. The capricious weather in the land between the rivers could mean that the farmer had

---

[88]Depending on the size of the tobacco plant, a stick of tobacco could weigh up to a hundred pounds.

[89]Farmers who had barns near the roadway were often besieged by strangers who were not familiar with tobacco barns. They stopped to warn the farmers that their barns were on fire. Workmen complained of nausea when they tended the tobacco barns.

[90]When the tobacco was in order, it was damp and pliable. It would not shatter when removed from the stalk and tied into small bundles called hands or culled and placed in baskets.

[91]The term "hand of tobacco" meant just that. It was the number of stems of the tobacco leaf which could be held in the hand. Once the hand had been selected, a leaf of tobacco was folded and wrapped around the stems to bind them together. Strippers took great pride in the amount of time it took them to tie a tightly wrapped hand.

72

to rush to get all his tobacco stripped within a week. Often workers worked by lantern light in order to complete the task.

When the tobacco was ready for market, the farmer took the tobacco to a prizing factory to be sorted, pressed, and packed in barrels called hogsheads for shipment to market. Each hogshead could hold two thousand pounds of tobacco. Tobacco merchants came to the prizing factories or to the farm to make bids on the tobacco. Farmers tried to determine the best price for the tobacco, and it was often more economical to sell to the merchant than to ship the tobacco to an outside market.[92]

Women's Work

Many homes were larger by 1840, but they had not become more convenient or comfortable. Kitchens were still separate from the main house, and the bedrooms did not have fireplaces or stoves. Women cared for homes, minded children, prepared food, and produced most of the necessary items for the family. They needed warm bedding in the winter, and feather beds or straw ticks, placed on boards or springs, were the usual beds. Women made the ticks or covering to hold the feathers or straw. Quilting was a very necessary task, but it was to be recognized later as an art form. By 1850, women traded quilt patterns from community to community. Journals, newspapers, and even quilt pattern companies spread the quilt patterns throughout the country.[93]

Women formed quilting bees to produce coverings for the beds, but it was also a social activity. Most women could not afford to attend meetings just for entertainment, and quilting bees allowed them the opportunity to do productive work and interact with other women. Many customs and beliefs grew up around the quilts. For example, grandmothers were expected to make a special quilt for each of their grandchildren, to be passed on to the next generation. Young women were presented with several quilts to put in their hope chests, and some of these were kept to give to their sons or daughters when they married.[94] Many of the quilts were works of art and special significance was attributed to some of them. A belief grew up that if a young girl slept under a new quilt, she would dream of the boy she was going to marry.[95]

No matter how beautiful the bedding might be, it was a breeding ground for bed bugs

---

[92]A prizing factory was located in most of the communities along the rivers. For a fee the company assumed the responsibility of handling and shipping. By 1850, specific landings along the Cumberland and Tennessee became the central ports because of the good docks. Tobacco Port in Stewart County was one of these sites.

[93]Patterns were swapped by the women. In every community one woman seemed to develop the skill of making patterns. Quilt making allowed women to express their artistic abilities. It might have been unacceptable for women to spend time painting pictures, but designing and sewing quilts was a necessary task.

[94]According to several interviews with people who lived in the land between the rivers, the practice of making these family quilts was carried on well into the twentieth century. 1959, Interview with Mrs. Emma D. Riggins, in the hands of the author.

[95]Interview with Mrs. Lois Lee Heflin in 1956. Interview in the hands of the author.

and other insects. Commercial insecticides were not in existence, and the homemaker constantly worked to kill the pests. Tobacco, sulphur, and lime were used to kill the bugs or to chase them out of the house. It became a ritual in the spring to empty and wash the bedding in lye water to kill the insects. During the winter, the beds were aired in the sun in an attempt kill some of the bugs and to make the bedding smell better.[96]

Women made lye soap at home, and the skills in making good soap resulted in community recognition. Usually only one woman in the community had the reputation of making the best soap and her techniques were copied by others. Essential ingredients for the soap included grease, lye, and water. The technique was to develop the correct mixing of these ingredients. Some women insisted that the lye that they extracted from ashes was better than the lye purchased at the stores. The lye and water were stirred together until it was well mixed and then the grease was added. The mixture was brought to a boil and stirred until it thickened. The soap was cooled, cut into bars and used for cleaning the body as well as washing the clothes.[97]

Forms of Entertainment

Forms of entertainment had changed very little from the settlement period to the Civil War. Men still found recreation in hunting, riding, and fishing. They wrestled and ran races to demonstrate their physical prowess. Because both men had women had little leisure time, the usual activities of barn raisings, husking bees, and quilting parties were held periodically. During the winter they met to sing and dance. The Celtic background lent itself to self-taught musicians performing on guitars, harps, and fiddles, and almost every family had several musicians.

Women and Medicine

The scarcity of doctors resulted in women and other family members treating illnesses and accidents at home. Home remedies were developed because medicine was unavailable.[98] Women made the medicines in their kitchens. They used turpentine and sugar or kerosene oil and sugar to treat many problems. A number of these worked, but some of the treatments were deadly. A large body of lore developed in the region about the types of home treatment to use for each illness.[99]

---

[96]1959 interviews with women residents of the land between the rivers. Interviews in the hands of the author.

[97]Lye soap was considered an excellent shampoo.

[98]In 1850 there were only three doctors in the land between the rivers. People had to rely upon doctors in Dover, Bumpus Mills, and Indian Mound in Tennessee and Cadiz and Eddyville in Kentucky for help.

[99]Hundreds of treatments were mentioned to the author in the interviews with people in Lyon, Trigg, and Stewart Counties. Interviews are in the hands of the author.

Some of the remedies such as the one for rheumatism included several treatments. The person drank a mixture of honey, vinegar, and whiskey to ease the pain and bring down the swelling in the joints. The amount of whiskey used in the drink often determined how soon the person's pain eased. Another remedy was to pass a magnet over the body to remove the pain. No doubt the liquid concoction was preferred to the magnet treatment.

A person afflicted with asthma used a medicine which included a pint of gin and several pieces of the heartwood of a pine tree. The wood had to soak in the gin for several days, then the patient took a healthy swallow of the gin three times a day.

Bleeding was stopped by placing a spider web across the wound. If that cure did not work, then a poultice of turpentine and brown sugar was applied to the wound. Some people applied lamp black or soot directly to the cut. Kerosene or pine resin was used to stop the bleeding. In some cases the wound was infected by the treatments used to stop the bleeding.

When individuals did not feel well or looked porely (which meant they looked downright awful), they took a mixture of sulphur and molasses. Another treatment for feeling porely was to drink the liquid from the parboiled leaves of a young pokeberry plant. The people believed that sassafras tea, made from the roots of a sassafras tree, cleaned the blood and made people feel better.

For treatment of a burn, people used a mixture of lard and flour or the scrapings from a raw white potato. Another treatment was to mix castor oil and egg whites and bind them on the wound. The most painful treatment was to put hot coals on the burned places and pour water over them. The steam was supposed to draw the fire out of the burn.[100]

The usual treatment for chest congestion, which could be anything from a cold to tuberculosis, was the application of a poultice of kerosene, turpentine, and lard. To make the poultice, a wool cloth, soaked in the mixture, was placed on the chest.[101] Goose grease was recommended as a way to clear the chest as well as prevent a person from catching a cold. Some of the people made a vest, then applied a thick layer of goose grease to the upper torso and sewed up the vest. The vest was not removed during the winter months. Whether the therapy cleared the congestion was questionable, but there is little doubt that the odor would keep most people so far away that they were not likely to catch a cold. The most widely acclaimed cough medicine was made from the bark of a wild cherry tree.[102]

It was believed that a cold could be cured if the person ate an onion roasted in ashes. Honey and vinegar or whiskey was said to cure colds. Red pepper tea was used to heal anyone suffering from a cold. Asafetida bags, placed on a string and worn around the neck, were said to cure coughs, colds, colic and many other afflictions. Again, the odor of asafetida was so unpleasant that people who wore the bags were shunned. People chewed ginseng root to cure many of their ills including infertility.

---

[100]The author was surprised at the use of hot coals. But the people who mentioned this cure were insistent that hot coals had to be used.

[101]The people called this particular poultice a "flannel cloth."

[102]It makes one wonder if that is the reason that manufacturers of cough medicine still insist that their product should be cherry flavored.

Conceivably, some of the medication which the people used had some medicinal value, but many of the treatments were mere superstitions. For example, it was thought that an eye ailment could be cured by running the tip of a black cat's tail over the eyes. A headache would stop if the person tied a white flour sack around the head. Heart trouble could be cured if the person ate onions. It was believed that whiskey would cure snake and spider bites. A mixture of buttermilk and stump water was used to remove freckles. A wool string wrapped around the toe would cure foot itch, probably athlete's foot. A tea made from cow dung was used to cure the measles. To prevent a nosebleed, people wore a necklace made from small pieces of lead, threaded on a string. A buckeye was used as a preventive measure to ward off most illnesses.[103] Flint rocks soaked in water produced a liquid which cured stomach pains. A person could rid himself of warts by placing his hand in a bag and binding it and then the person who removed the bag would get the warts. If an individual had a tapeworm, he could capture the worm if he starved himself for several days and then held some warm milk up to the nose and breathed deeply. The tapeworm would crawl out through the nose to get the milk.[104]

Motherhood

The nineteenth century has often been called the century of the child. Americans focused not only on the importance of children within individual families but also on their critical role in the nation's future. It was believed that the country could not progress without healthy, vigorous, and moral citizens. A new interest in reform during the antebellum period heightened the concern surrounding children.[105] By the 1850s, many people believed that improving the child's character, mind, behavior, and physical fitness would create a better society. If this dream were to succeed, mothers stood at the center of the perceptions. The significance of motherhood had grown, and women were told that they could guide and influence the future of the country from within the domestic sphere by focusing their time and energy on bearing and rearing children. From the pulpit, from the published materials, and from polite conversation came an endless stream of comments magnifying the role that mothers were to assume.[106]

Women in the land between the rivers, like many of their sisters throughout the country,

---

[103]The use of the buckeye had a mixed history. Some people carried one for good luck, but other people declared that a buckeye brought bad luck.

[104]People who lost weight even though they had a healthy appetite were thought to have tapeworms.

[105]For a discussion of the significance of the child in recent history, see Phillipe Aries, Centuries of Childhood: A Social History of Family Life (New York: Knopf, 1962), 1-245; Carl Degler, At Odds: Women and the Family in America from the Revolution to the Present (New York: Knopf, 1980), 72-74; Linda K. Kerber, "Daughters of Columbia: Educating Women for the Republic, 1787-1805," in Linda K. Kerber and Jane DeHart Mathews, eds., Women's America: Refocusing the Past (New York: Oxford University Press, 1982), 82-94.

[106]Kerber and Mathews, eds., Women's America, 80-120.

undoubtedly adopted much of this ideology.[107] An intrinsic element within this theory was that all women were to become wives and mothers regardless of the dangers of childbirth, and any woman who gave birth during the nineteenth century was in grave danger.[108]

For thousands of years, women had regarded childbirth as a natural, though painful event, and relied on midwives and female friends and relatives to assist them in giving birth. Infant health care had traditionally fallen within the province of domestic medicine and homemade cures. The traditional attitudes began to change around 1850. Doctors wishing involvement came to consider childbirth a pathological condition. By viewing the situation of expectant women as diseased, they could argue that science rather than nature should assume a primary role during labor. Doctors rather than midwives gradually assumed the leading role in maternal and infant medicine.[109]

Until well after the Civil War, doctors in the South practiced allopathic medicine. Even when many doctors around the world disagreed with the practices, many southern doctors contended that vascular tension caused disease. The most effective way to ease that tension and rid the body of undesirable substances was to include the drastic measures of venesection, leeching, cupping, blistering, purging, and extensive medication. If one dose of medication was insufficient, doctors intensified their treatment and experimented with a variety of techniques until they achieved success or the patient died.[110] These techniques and the strong medications were prescribed for pregnant women because it was believed that the fetus would not be affected by the medications. Only luck or a strong constitution allowed a patient and her baby to survive such extreme remedies.

In rural southern households such as those in the land between the rivers, home remedies and herbal cures had stood the test of time and continued in use throughout the nineteenth century. Published volumes offered cures to the public, including pregnant women, and they were found in many households. One of the most popular guides was Gunn's Domestic Medicine; or, Poor Man's Friend, published in Tennessee in 1830. The book included a

---

[107]In the interviews with people in the area, they were asked to discuss what they knew of their female ancestors. In many of the interviews the importance of motherhood was mentioned as having high priority in their families.

[108]This sentiment about motherhood and the duty of women was mentioned in the interviews.

[109]The modification of opinions about childbirth and the change from female midwives to male doctors has been widely studied. See Irving S. Cutter and Henry R. Viets, A Short History of Midwifery (Philadelphia: Saunders, 1964); Jane B. Donegan, Women and Men Midwives: Medicine, Morality, and Misogyny in Early America (Westport, Conn.: Greenwoood Press, 1978); Richard W. Wertz and Dorothy Wertz, Lying-In: A History of Childbirth in America (New York: Free Press, 1977); and Judith Walzer Leavitt, Brought to Bed: Childbearing in America, 1750-1950 (New York: Oxford University Press, 1986).

[110]For a discussion of medical treatments, see Judith Walzer Leavitt and Ronald L. Numbers, eds., Sickness and Health in America: Readings in the History of Medicine and Public Health (Madison, Wisc.: University of Wisconsin Press, 1978), 77-186; William G. Rothstein, American Physicians in the Nineteenth Century: From Sects to Science (Baltimore: John Hopkins University Press, 1972).

compilation of Southern herbal recipes and it received high praise from its readers.[111]

During the period from 1840 to 1850, southern doctors attempted to convince female patients that masculine skills were essential in the delivery room. These doctors blamed midwives for women's sufferings during childbirth. It was a common practice for doctors to accuse midwives of ignorance which could result in the death of a newborn child.[112]

Doctors tended to overestimate their capabilities and interfere prematurely during childbirth.[113] Infecting the patient was always a possibility, because hands and instruments frequently went unwashed and street clothes were worn by the doctor during delivery. Bloodletting continued as a common practice because the doctor maintained that it was a technique which lessened pain during childbirth.[114]

In 1850, Tennessee had a total of 1,523 physicians which meant that there was one doctor for approximately 660 people. That number placed Tennessee close to the national average for medical service.[115] Census information indicates that approximately one out of twenty-five white women in the South who died in 1850 died in childbirth, twice the maternal mortality rate in the rest of the country.[116] Cemetery and census records indicate that deaths for women in the land between the rivers fell slightly below the state and national average.[117]

Mortality rates for women between the ages of twenty and forty were significant. The number of white women who died in Tennessee in 1850 was approximately 3,877; it is estimated that 2% of that number died in childbirth.[118] The rate was slightly higher than the national average.[119] There are a number of possible explanations why these women died in childbirth. The lack of proper medical attention was only one of the factors. Tennessee and Kentucky, like

---

[111]John C. Gunn, Gunn's Domestic Medicine; or Poor Man's Friend, Shewing(sic) the Diseases of Men, Women and Children, (Madisonville, Tennessee:_____, 1834). Five estate sales in 1850 in the land between the rivers listed this book. Stewart County, Book 108-B, 41, 49, 55, 67, and 74.

[112]Donegan, Women and Men Midwives, 67.

[113]Doctors were not required to have medical training. They had to "read medicine" with some older doctor and possibly attend some lectures in Lexington, Kentucky. Joseph H. Parks and Stanley J. Folmsbee, in the Story of Tennessee (Norman, Oklahoma: Harlow Publishing Corporation, 1973), 180, described the doctor of this period: "any farm boy who was too lazy to plow corn might procure a horse, a pair of saddle bags, a lancet, a few dollars worth of drugs, and hang up a shingle naming himself a doctor, and begin the practice of medicine." Not until 1889 were doctors required by Tennessee law to have a medical license.

[114]Donegan, Women and Men Midwives, 67.

[115]_____, "The Medical Profession," Nashville Journal of Medicine and Surgery, VII(1854), 410-414.

[116]Federal Population Census 1850.

[117]Records from Lyon County Historical Society, Trigg County Historical, and Stewart County Historical Society include a listing of grave sites and dates of death.

[118]U. S. Federal Census, Mortality Statistics of the Seventh Census of the United States 1850, ed. J. D. B. De Bow (Washington, D. C.: U. S. Government Printing Office, 1855).

[119]Wertiz, Lying-In, 108.

the rest of the South, could not boast that their climate was healthy. Malaria, dysentery, and a host of fevers were endemic in the South. Settlement patterns along the rivers and streams made these diseases more likely.

The women in the land between the rivers were probably more likely to contract malaria and typhoid fevers because of geography, and these fevers could cause them to abort the fetus. Also, during the nineteenth century, southern women bore more children than women living in the Northeast, thus putting their lives at risk more often. Women had to worry about the safety of their unborn child as well as the many diseases which they would have to fight. Women in the land between the rivers could have had an advantage over other southern women because they worked long hours and were often in good physical condition when they became pregnant. This fact would have made them more able to withstand the rigors of pregnancy and childbirth.

Even if a woman experienced a healthy pregnancy, labor brought suffering. In letters and journals written by women during this period, numerous references were made to their confinement as painful or dreadful.[120] Frightening medical problems such as convulsions or hemorrhages occurred during or shortly after delivery. Part of this problem was the number of southern women who gave birth to large babies, thus augmenting the risk of sepsis and maternal and fetal death.[121]

Internal damage to reproductive organs could produce long-term negative effects. Fallen wombs were common, and women suffered from fevers, chills, headaches, and severe pain for months after delivery. The physical suffering contributed to postpartum depression for these women. The custom was for women to remain in bed for two weeks to a month after the delivery. The higher the socio-economic class, the more likely the woman was to lengthen her recovery period.[122]

Infant mortality was alarmingly high in the 1850s and American physicians were concerned. The 1850 federal census, directed by Dr. Edward Jarvis, of Massachusetts, was the first nationwide effort to determine systematically the death rate and the causes of death among Americans. In the introduction to the census report is the observation that mortality figures were unusually high in urban areas because of the severe cholera epidemic which had affected the country in 1849. In the report the editor commented that at least one-fourth of the whole number of deaths were not reported at all.[123]

By 1860 the statistics showed an increase of 3% in the number of children who died under the age of one: 17% died in 1850 and 20% died in 1860. In 1850, 38% of those under five years of age died, while the number had increased to 43% in 1860.[124] Families did not

---

[120]Kenneth Kiple and Virginia Himmelstreib King, <u>Another Dimension in the Black Diaspora: Diet, Disease, and Racism</u> (New York: Cambridge University Press, 1981), 1-56.

[121]Usually the birth weight of babies born in the South was higher than those born in the rest of the country. See Sally G. McMillen, <u>Motherhood</u>, 190-195.

[122]Ibid.

[123]<u>U. S. Federal Census, Mortality Statistics of the Seventh Census of the United States,1850</u>, 8.

[124]<u>U.S. Federal Census, Mortality Statistics</u>,9.

need statistics to prove that children's deaths were common, and often recurrent within a family. The leading causes of death among children from birth to five years of age, ranked in order of occurrences, were cholera, dysentery, unknown reasons, scarlet fever, croup, fever, pneumonia, whooping cough, worms, external causes, teething, convulsions, typhoid fever, measles, small pox, bronchitis, and enteritis.[125]

Women in the South could expect to lose at least one child at birth or before it reached the age of five. The cemetery records show that many children were stillborn or died within a few months after birth. The tombstones often had only a last name for the stillborn child, making it impossible to determine the gender of the child. Markers for older children bore the full name and span of life. One of the problems in the records is to determine who was buried without markers. Cemetery records show a grave site but there is no marker to indicate the age or gender of the deceased. Oral history is the only method that one can use to determine who the individuals were.[126]

In compiling the cemetery records, every effort was made to determine the names of the people who were buried in the cemeteries. An interesting tradition emerged from a study of these records. A practice of naming two children in the family the same name was not uncommon. If a child was born, named, and died before one year of age, later another child would be given the same name.[127]

The high mortality rate must have had an effect on the lives and traditions of the people. Mothers and fathers had to learn to accept the deaths of their children and live with the feeling of loss. No records are left by these people to reveal to us how they felt when a child was born and they knew that there was a good chance that it would not live past the age of five. Women often expressed their worry and grief to other women. This practice allowed some release of their emotions, but men did not seem to express their grief in the same manner. Men had few outlets which would give them some way of handling their sorrow.

Leadership in the Counties

By 1840 the leaders were men who were professionals and land owners. The ministers exerted a great deal of influence because the church was a strong social institution. Most people valued education, and the educated man was looked upon with favor unless he flaunted his knowledge. Intellectual arrogance was unacceptable because people had dignity and pride, and any implication that a person was inferior resulted in swift retribution.[128]

---

[125]Ibid.

[126]Cemetery records for Lyon, Trigg, and Stewart Counties.

[127]Ibid.

[128]In over one hundred interviews with the people, an interesting concept about the necessity of education emerged. Beginning at some point in the history of the region, people began to form resentments toward higher education. The author got the impression that there was a particular reservation about intellectuals. Ministers, for example, should be "called," not trained.

The influence of men who owned slaves was apparent. Even though the majority of the people did not own any slaves, their actions indicated that they found no difficulty with the concept of slavery. Also, there is no evidence to indicate that abolitionists spoke out against slavery in the two decades preceding the Civil War. One can assume that most of the people desired the status of slave owner for themselves. These men ran the world around them. They decided who would serve in most of the elected offices. They had money to send their children to school. They supported the churches and philanthropic organizations. In other words, these men either personally ran the governments or decided who would be elected. Because none of the local offices provided a salary large enough to support the family of an officeholder, the elected officials usually had to have another income large enough to enable them to serve the community.

A study of the records from the settlement period until the Civil War provided information which suggests that during that entire period the men in the land between the rivers did not seek many of the county offices. They often served as magistrates, county surveyors, and school board members, but they did not demonstrate any interest in the other offices. The evidence does not determine how much influence these men had in the nomination of the individuals who sought the other county offices; however, it could be expected that they consulted with the farmers and slave holders in other parts of the region and reached an agreement on the men who should hold the office.

Effects of Prosperity

The people in the land between the rivers thrived except for short economic recessions during the 1830s. The national economic scene was not always an indicator of how the people lived because so many of them lived on farms and maintained a self-sufficient economy. Holding on to old economic values, they still tried to produce all they needed at home. Of course, their annual income was affected by the price of agricultural goods during any given year, but they often produced one or more money crops. The sale of estates during any given period reflected local problems more than national depressions. A few individuals without sufficient assets tried to enlarge their farm acreage and lost everything. Most of the farms were sold because owners died without a will and their children sold the farm. A few businesses failed because of expansion within a limited sales area.

The period of general prosperity from 1850 to 1860 was reflected in the price of farm goods. The only decline was in 1857 when three iron furnaces were closed, and the national economy was dropping. Land on the average sold for a dollar an acre. The average price of a prime slave, a male twenty years old in excellent physical condition, was five hundred dollars. Male slaves who were younger, ranging in age from fifteen to twenty, sold for as much as eight hundred to one thousand dollars. The sale price for a slave in the land between the rivers was somewhat lower than the going price in the deep South.[129] Not only were slaves cheaper in the land between the rivers, but the number of slaves decreased from 1840 to 1860. One

---

[129]Records of Estate Sales in all the counties. On the average, these slaves in the deep South were selling for one thousand to fifteen hundred dollars.

explanation for this decrease could be the fear of slave rebellion and the decline in the iron industry.

The economic conditions of the era led to an increase in the demand for more and varied goods, especially products and merchandise which were not made at home. Merchants purchased the supplies and goods which the people wanted to buy, and ordered them from wholesalers in northern cities and from New Orleans. The Woods and Bacon Company of Philadelphia, Pennsylvania was representative of a wholesaler which served the merchants. A survey of the purchase orders made by the merchants from 1850 to 1859 indicates the demand for various types of goods and the prices the people paid for the goods. Purchase orders from William M. Cook, one of approximately twelve large retailers in the area, give some indication of the variety of goods imported into the region.[130]

The merchants generally made their purchases quarterly and sent orders to different wholesalers at different times of the year. In general, merchants in all the communities ordered the same types of products. The following is a partial list of the goods ordered by the Cook Company in 1852:

72 yds. Blue and Orange Prints @ 9 cents per yard.
72 yds. Black and White Prints @ 8 and one-half cents per yd.
69 yds. Fancy Black and White Print @ 9 and one-half cents per yd.
85 yds. Fancy Print @ 7 and one-half cents per yd.
207 yds. Fancy Purple Print @ 7 cents per yd.
35 yds. Purple Print @ 5 cents per yd.
30 yds. Solid Colored Print @ 10 cents per yd.
68 yds. Neat Plaid Print @ 10 cents per yd
104 yds. Fancy Plaid @ 17 and one-half cents per yd.
27 yds. Red Plaid @ 17 and one-half cents per yd.
29 yds. Turkey Red Prints @ 16 and one-half cents per yd.
33 yds. Purple Print @ 10 cents per yd.
42 yds. Erlston Gingham @ 14 cents per yd.
40 yds. Turkey Red Gingham @ 25 cents per yd.
24 yds. Printed Lawn @ 14 cents per yd.
32 yds. Printed Lawn @ 2 cents per yd.
30 yds. Figured Alpaca @ 42 cents per yd.
28 yds. Figured Alpaca @ 42 cents per yd.
48 yds. Silk Striped Alpaca @ 42 cents per yd.
48 yds. Linen Lustre @ 35 cents per yd.
47 yds. Brown Linen Drill @ 35 cents per yd.
72 yds. Color Cambric @ 8 cents per yd.

---

[130]Merchant records for 1852 are more complete than any other year. The author found a bundle of these records in the Stewart County Court clerk's office. They were not bound or titled.

37 yds. Union Linen Check @ 17 and one-half
cents per yd.
60 yds. Linen Check @ 20 cents per yd.
34 yds. Cotton Chambray @ 9 and one-half cents per yd.
42 yds. Plaid Cottonade @ 9 and one-half
cents per yd.
40 yds. Blue Cottonade @ 13 cents per yd.
29 yds. Blue Chambray @13 cents per yd.
11 yd. Verona Twills @ 17 cents per yd.
30 yds. Orleans Cottonade @ 17 cents per yd.
42 yds. French Cottonade @ 37 cents per yd.
47 yds. Drab Satinet @ 75 cents per yd.
25 yds. Doeskin Satinet @ 75 cents per yd.
74 yds. Tweed Satinet @ 52 cents per yd.
29 yds. All Wool Tweed @ 37 cents per yd.
 6 yds. Plaid Cassimere @ 75 cents per yd.
 6 yds. Pale Cassimere @ 60 cents per yd.
12 yds. Black Cassimere @ $1.20 cents per yd.
26 yds. Scarlet Flannel @ 35 cents per yd.
24 yds. White Flannel @ 35 cents per yd.
54 yds. Shirting Check @ 12 and one-half
cents per yd.
46 yds. Power Loom Stripe @ 9 cents per yd.
43 yds. Ticking @ 17 cents per yd.
37 yds. Bleached Muslin @ 8 cents per yd.
51 yds. Bleached Muslin @ 7 and one-half
cents per yd.
47 yds. Bleached Muslin @ 10 cents per yd.
51 yds. Bleached Muslin @ 13 cents per yd.
25 yds. Striped Irish Linen @ 40 cents per yd.[131]

1 doz. Bordered Linen Handkerchiefs	$ 4.00
2 pr. Saddle Blankets	$ 3.00
2 Marseilles Vests	$ 1.75
3 Fancy Silk Vests	$ 5.75
6 Figured Mohair Vests	$ 6.75
3 pr. Mixed Cottonade Pants	$ 2.85
2 pr. Fancy Cottonade Pants	$ 3.00
1 pr. Summer Cloth Pants	$ 2.00
2 pr. Fancy Cassimere Pants	$ 6.00

---

[131]Lawn is a fine, sheer cloth of linen or cotton, used for handkerchiefs, blouses, curtains, etc. Cottonade is a tightly woven cotton fabric. Satinet is a strong cloth of cotton and wool, made to resemble satin. Cassimere is a thin, twilled woolen cloth, usually used for men's suits. Muslin is a fabric of fine cotton of plain weave, often dyed or printed. Mohair is made from the hair of the Angora goat.

2 pr. Black Cassimer Pants	$ 6.75
8 Brown Linen Coats	$ 6.40
5 Brown Linen Coats	$ 5.00
1 Straw Linen Coat	$ 1.75
5 Gingham Coats	$ 4.38
1 Black Alpaca Coat	$ 2.25
2 Black Cloth Coats	$15.00

This order contained more than two thousand yards of fabric. If the merchant supplemented this amount in his next order, an enormous amount of fabric was purchased each year in the region. One could conclude that many households were no longer spinning thread and weaving cloth.

On March 31, 1855 the William M. Cook Company received an order of goods from the Babbit Good and Company of Philadelphia, Pennsylvania which included the following goods:

25 bbl. S. and F. Flour @ 3.65	$18.00
2 boxes Hunt and D. Axes @.14	$28.00
1 box S.C. Soda @ .8	$ 2.00
1 bag No. 500 yarn @ .9	$13.05
1 bag No. 600 yarn @ .8	$13.33
1 reel Hemp Cordade	$ 4.08
1 Doz. Fancy Buckets	$ 2.20
1 Doz. Zinc Washboards	$ 1.38
1 Doz. Shaker Brooms	$ 1.50
1 Doz. Wire Gilt Brooms	$ 2.00
2 Boxes Lord Byron Cigars	$ 4.00
2 Boxes El Neptuno Cigars	$ 5.00
3 Boxes Prime Cheese @ .10 lb	$ 7.10
1 Copy "Weekly Times"	$ 1.00
Fray .38 [132]	

On March 31, 1855 the Wright Brothers & Company of Philadelphia, Pennsylvania, shipped an order to the William M. Cook Company which included the following:

6 Cotton Umbrellas	$ 2.70
4 Cotton Whalebone Umbrellas	$ 2.60
2 Sup. Gingham Whalebone Umbrellas	$ 1.90
3 S. Scotch Gingham Umbrellas	$ 2.40

Another dozen umbrellas selling for one dollar each were included in the order.[133]

In April of 1855, William Cook ordered goods from the McFerrin and Hunter Company of Nashville, Tennessee. The order included:

Aunt Philas' Cabin	$ .45
Robinson Crusoe	$ .20
Poetry and Love	$ .25
24 Lithographs	$ 1.24

---

[132]Fray seems to be a contraction for shipping cost. Merchant records in Dover.

[133]Ibid.

One-half Ream letter paper	$ 1.90
1 Box envelopes	$ .90
1 Doz. Spelling Books	$ 1.65 [134]

An order from Whelan and Company of Philadelphia, Pennsylvania was delivered to a store belonging to William Cook and Company at Indian Mound in March of 1855 which included the following items:

12 pr. Men's Calf Boots @ 3.25	$39.00
12 pr. Men's Calf Boots @ 2.75	$33.00
12 pr. Boy's Hip Boots @ 1.50	$18.00
12 pr. Men's Hip Boots @ 2.00	$24.00
30 pr. Men's Brogans @ 1.07	$32.25
24 pr. Men's Hip Brogans @ 1.00	$24.00
24 pr. Men's S. & B Brogans @ 85	$25.50
12 pr. Men's Calf Brogans @ 1.35	$16.20
6 pr. Men's Goat Slips @ .55	$ 3.30 [135]
12 pr. Men's Enam Brogans @ 1.30	$15.60
12 pr. Men's Goat Brogans @ 1.25	$15.00
18 pr. Child's Hip Boots @ .55	$ 9.90

The order included another request for one hundred dozen boots and shoes at the same prices, and added to the order was a gross of shoe strings for thirty-one cents.

In April of 1856 William Cook and Company received a mixed order of goods from A. H. Hicks & Company of Nashville, Tennessee and the items received included:

one-half dozen Chambers	$ 2.00
one-half dozen Chamber Covers	$ 2.50 [136]
one-half dozen Dippers and Pitchers	$ 3.25
20 sets Common teas	$11.00 [137]
24 Dishes	$ 7.20
1 dozen Bowls	$ .60
one-half dozen Molasses Cans	$ 1.00
50 Marbles	$ 1.00 [138]
2 dozen Tumblers	$ 2.70 [139]

Several other types of dishes and glassware were included in the order and delivered in good

---

[134]Ibid.

[135]The Goat Slips were most likely house slippers.

[136]The chamber covers cost more than the chambers, and it appears that the error was not noticed by the merchant.

[137]Common teas were usually six cups and saucers. In some instances a tea pot was included.

[138]These were probably taws or large fancy marbles used to shoot with in a game of marbles.

[139]Tumblers were drinking glasses.

condition to the store in Model, Tennessee.[140]

The accounts of the William M. Cook Company, along with the five or more merchants in the area, indicated that the people had a wide selection of goods from which to choose. It seems safe to conclude that since the merchants repeated orders for the merchandise, it was selling quickly, and even the more expensive imported goods were in demand.

Apparently, men purchased more of their clothing from the merchants than from tailors. The clothes appeared to be relatively inexpensive compared to the price of fabrics sold at the same stores. The surviving merchant records, of which the William Cook stores are the most complete, indicate that women and girls were unable to find a variety of clothing. From the description of the amount and types of fabric shipped to the stores monthly, it appears that females bought the fabrics for their clothes, and the items were either made at home or by dressmakers.

The one mystery was the absence of any record of purchases of women's shoes. It is true that cobblers had establishments in the larger villages and women could have their shoes made there and it is possible that their footwear was still made at home. However, it would appear that if men's shoes were competitive in price with the shoes made at home, it would have been true for shoes for women and girls.

The merchants carried a variety of goods such as vases, jewelry, hair pins, face powder, furniture, handkerchiefs, kitchen utensils, books, pins, scissors, thread, and a thousand other items which people could buy. Food supplies were available, and merchants often bought produce from the farmers to sell in the stores. Flour and salt were sold by the barrel and whiskey was sold by the keg. These general merchants often competed with items sold in the drug stores, harness and blacksmith shops, and dressmaker's shops.

The people did not change their diet a great deal from one generation to another. In the decade before the Civil War, grains for corn meal and flour were grown on the farm. Pork was the principal meat eaten by the people, and wild game was the second source and beef was last. There were no slaughter houses in the area so farmers killed and processed the animals. A celebration around hog killing day was a common practice. Farmers chose the day in the late fall as soon as it was cold enough to preserve the meat. Neighbors and relatives were invited to come and help in the slaughter and the preservation of the meat. Women brought covered dishes and prepared the noon meal while the men slaughtered and dressed the animals.[141]

Cattle and wild animals were skinned, but the hogs had to be scalded in hot water and the hair scraped off. Since a large quantity of boiling water was needed, fires were built before daylight on hog killing day. Water was heated in large pots and poured into large barrels or vats. In the meantime, a hog was killed, its throat cut, and hung head down from a pole or tree limb.[142] When the blood had drained into a container, the hog was dipped in the hot water. The temperature of the water and the time the hog was immersed in the water were watched

---

[140]Ibid.

[141]All the information gathered about the slaughter of animals was collected from former residents of the land between the rivers. Copies of these interviews are in the hands of the author.

[142]The hog was either shot in the brain or hit in the head with a large hammer called a sledge.

closely. The purpose of scalding was to loosen the top layer of skin so that the hair could be scraped off the carcass, but it was important that the second layer of skin remain intact. Almost every part of the hog was saved and used.

Souse, scrapple, and hog's head stew were made from the head after the brains and eyeballs were removed. The eyeballs were usually discarded but the brains were later cooked with eggs. Scrapple was a particular type of dish or bread that many people liked. Once the cook had removed the eyeballs, brain, and ears from the head, it was placed in a large pot to boil. When the meat fell away from the bones, the larger bones were removed from the pot, and the liquid was strained to remove small bones. Then the liquid was poured back into the pot and the meat from the head was picked through and returned to the liquid. Sage, pepper and other seasonings were added to the pot, and brought to a boil. Corn meal was added to the mixture, and allowed to thicken. When it was just the right texture, the mixture was poured into a mold to cool. It was cut into slices and eaten with vegetables.[143]

Hog jowls, tongue, brain, snout, and ears were prepared by the cook. Internal organs, such as liver, heart, lights (lungs), and stomach were cooked and eaten. The intestines, called "chitlins" (chitterlings), were cleaned, soaked in salt water for three to four days and then cut into small pieces and fried or boiled. The feet, backbone, ribs, tail, and skin were prepared in various ways and eaten. The fat was trimmed from the lean meat and used to make lard. Even the bladder was used.[144]

The hams, shoulders, and tenderloins, which were considered the choice parts of the hog, were salted and smoked. Farmers developed different techniques to cure the hams. The most common practice was to use salt, sugar, and hickory smoke as preservatives and to give the ham a certain flavor. Farmers experimented on the ways to cure a ham to make it less salty while maintaining a good flavor. Those who preferred a sweeter taste added more sugar. Most of the people preferred the salty taste in the meat.

An integral part of an established farm was a large vegetable garden. Vegetables, including potatoes, onions, tomatoes, carrots, turnips, okra, and a variety of peas and beans were planted in all the gardens. Orchards, usually contained a variety of fruit trees. Salt and pepper were the standard seasonings, but many herbs and spices were cultivated in kitchen gardens.

Wild animals such as the raccoon, rabbits, groundhog, squirrels, bears, and deer were still commonly used to supplement the pork. Turkey and quail were plentiful and cooks prepared delicious dishes by combining several meats and vegetables. Turtles, frogs, and fish were in or near all the creeks and rivers.

Most farmers adhered to two familiar Bible quotes, Genesis 1:14 and Ecclesiastes 3:1-2, when they chose a time to plant or harvest their crops.[145] Farmers followed the twelve signs

---

[143]The recipe was used on most farms until World War II. The women mentioned that it took too much time to make souse and it wasn't that good anyway.

[144]A common practice was to inflate the bladder into a balloon for the children.

[145]The quotes were from Genesis 1:14: Let there be lights in the firmament of the heavens to divide the day from the night; and let them be for signs and for seasons, and for days, and years. The other from Ecclesiastes 3:1-2 said, To everything there is a season, and a time to every purpose under heaven: a time to be born, a time to die; a time to

of the zodiac and the movement of the sun and moon to decide when to plant and harvest their crops. Early wise men, believing that there was an intimate relationship between the celestial bodies and mankind, identified the twelve signs of the zodiac with various parts of the human body. Charts which illustrate this relationship have been noted as far back in history as 1300 B.C. In the nineteenth century, farmers in the land between the rivers purchased almanacs which gave them the signs to follow in cultivating their crops. These signs were studied and followed because the farmers believed in their value.[146]

The almanacs show that each day of the month is dominated by one of the twelve signs of the zodiac. All good planting almanacs labeled each day with the sign that ruled over it. The sign depended upon which constellation was foremost in the sky at the time. Each of the signs was known as being either masculine, feminine, airy, dry, barren, fiery, earthy, moist, watery, fruitful, or very fruitful. In general, any activity which required a dry atmosphere, such as planting, would be done in the dry signs. The best time of all to conduct an activity was when a day fell on both an ideal sign and a good phase of the moon.

One of the more obvious signs of prosperity was the growth of the villages and communities. In the settlement period the farms were isolated and people had difficulty traveling from one homestead to another. By 1850 the area boasted about their communities at Hematite, Eddyville, Tharpe, and Model. Communities grew as roads were built. A road to Dover was passable during most of the year. Ferries along the Cumberland and Tennessee Rivers made it easier to travel to Cadiz, Bumpus Mills, Paris, and Clarksville. People used the Cumberland to reach Nashville and other towns. Travel to Philadelphia and New Orleans was increasing.

The history of the town of Model is a good example of the determination of the people to make progress. Model developed later than some of the early villages but the citizens were determined to make it the best. Model, located near the Great Western furnace, was in the settlement period called Pryor's Creek, named for the first settler who came to the area in 1803. Around 1845, it was called Great Western for the Great Western Furnace which was established by Brian, Newell and Company. The community was large enough to have a postoffice by 1846 and it was called Bass because Jethro Bass was the first postmaster. The city fathers encouraged merchants to establish their businesses in the community. The people dreamed of creating a little utopia or a model town to serve as an example of how people could design a positive environment for themselves. Model was not used for the name of the community until after the Civil War. A real estate operation by the Cincinnati Cooperage Company which made staves came to the area. The businessmen agreed that the community could be a model for others to follow, and they joined the movement to develop the area. A committee planned the construction of sidewalks and a public square. From 1850 to 1860, the community continued to work

---

plant and a time to pluck up that which is planted.

[146]The Bible was the most common book in the home and the almanac was second.

toward the goal of becoming the most important town in Stewart County, but the goals were interrupted by the Civil War. The people tried to regain their zeal after the battles but they never recovered the momentum.

CHAPTER VI

EVENTS LEADING TO THE
CIVIL WAR

The Tennessee State Legislature ordered each county court in the state to appoint and raise a home guard, on the following day entered into a military alliance with the Confederacy, and on June 8, 1861, ratified the Ordinance of Secession. The enlistment period in Stewart County was for three months. As it turned out, the period was much too short and recruiting was a problem. Stewart County had a population of some 1,613 adult white males who might qualify for service in the home guard, yet only about 300 of these men joined. The others either joined the Confederate army, the Union army, left the area, or somehow managed to evade enlistment.[1]

The home guard had the responsibility of obtaining warrants and arresting all persons suspected of being disloyal to the county and the state. Officially, the guard was not an army, yet the people seemed to expect the men to stop any outside enemy that might appear. Individuals were arrested by the guard and brought before civil authorities for trial. The guardsmen also disarmed all slaves and made sure that they did not congregate in large numbers. The guard had the responsibility of maintaining peace and order and acted as an extra, more powerful police force.[2]

Stewart County began preparing for war, but Trigg and Lyon Counties were still in the Union. People in all three counties realized that they were likely to suffer if any invasion came from the Cumberland or Tennessee Rivers.[3]   When Union forces moved into Illinois and Kentucky the environment changed very quickly because people were no longer concerned with the philosophical arguments about secession. Invasion was the new reality. People remained undecided about their governmental allegiances and changed their minds from time to time as the months went by. It appears that a vocal minority remained loyal to the Union throughout 1861, but the majority expressed strong support for the Confederate cause.[4]

Officially, only Stewart County had to rush to meet the directives for reorganization as a part of the Confederacy, but all the people became entangled in the drama and excitement about the possibility of an impending invasion from the North. As has been noted earlier, the people had little real concern with whether they lived in Lyon, Trigg, or Stewart Counties because they identified with the community, thus when Stewart County began to mobilize under the orders from the state authorities, all the people felt the effects of the action.   Reactions

---

[1]Names on the U.S. Population Census records of 1860 show the numbers who might have been eligible to serve in the guard. The guard rosters are listed in the County Court records.

[2]County Court records from June 1861 through January 1862 mention numerous enforcement activities of the home guard: Book 60: 23, 24, 29, 32, 46; Book 62: 9, 10, 13, 27, 29, 22, 23, 30.

[3]Both of the Kentucky counties expected to go with the Confederacy. Lyon County Court records, Book 62: 10-14.; Trigg County Court records, Book 70: 1-14.

[4]Ibid.

seemed to depend upon what the people did for a living, upon religious beliefs, and on attitudes toward the role of the government. The most critical concern was the perceived effect that the fighting would have on the people. Few people cared about what had transpired in Washington D. C., or what President Abraham Lincoln believed. They were much more aware of the possibility of a war and they had to decide whether they were going to involve themselves in the fighting or not. The period of uncertainty lasted for almost a year. After that time, the war came and people had to respond.[5]

The threat of invasion changed the concerns of the people. They did not spend their time contemplating opinions about states' rights, slavery or nationalism. Self-preservation was their major concern, and the immediate goal was to control the panic which spread throughout the region. The people were afraid and anxious. People were unequivocal in their belief that they had the right to protect their property, but they were tentative over the merits of secession. Citizens cooperated in most of the preparedness plans, but it took weeks to appoint men to supervise the tasks of arming the county.[6]

The Home Guard

The county court appointed Henry H. Erwin as the General Commander of the home guard. A total of one hundred and twenty men were chosen from the twelve districts of the county. A special tax of seven dollars and one-half cents was levied on each one hundred dollars of taxable property to support the families of the men who had volunteered for the Confederate Army and to support the home guard. To meet the immediate financial needs of the county, primarily the upkeep of the families of the guard, the court authorized the issuance of county bonds, or script, not to exceed one thousand dollars. The court guaranteed the script at par rate.[7]

Organizing the guard took an inordinate amount of work. At the same time, the county court was inundated with requests for aid from the families of the volunteers who left to join the Confederate Army. Money became a serious problem and the court established a committee made up of three men in each of the twelve civil districts to attend to the needs of the families of men who had volunteered for the home guard and the Confederate army.[8] From the spring of 1861 to January of 1862, the constant complaint from the committee was that there were

---

[5]These attitudes can be seen in the comments in the records in the counties. See Book 27: 12, 13.

[6]A thorough search of all county records resulted in a clearer picture of the confusion in the minds of the people. Those citizens who lived outside the land between the rivers in Stewart County seem strongly supportive of the Confederacy. In 1861 it appears that the majority of the people in Lyon and Trigg counties were in favor of the Confederate cause.

[7]1861, Stewart County Court records, Book 60: 1-11.

[8]Ibid.

insufficient funds to meet the needs of the families of the volunteers.[9]

The need for an organized home guard was soon apparent even to those citizens who argued that war would never come. No one expected the guard or the sheriff and two deputies to stand against an army. Rumors began to circulate in June of 1861 that an invasion was imminent, and many people felt the quickest solution was to arm themselves to protect their homes. Some of the people thought that it might be wise to move their families out of the area.[10]

The county court ordered that the Clerk of the Court, M. C. McGee, purchase one hundred and twenty guns for the guard. Authorization was made for extra script to cover the purchase price, and ten dollars was appropriated for the purchase of twenty pounds of powder and twenty pounds of lead to use in training the home guard. Twenty five dollars was allocated for the purchase of ten copies of Hardie's Rifles and Infantry Tactics. Since ten copies of the book were all the court could afford, only the officers had manuals. The county court ordered the captain of each of the guard units to teach the material contained in the manual to the individuals under his command. Without books for each guardsman, the officer had to resort to reading the material to his men.[11] None of the men knew much about military discipline or procedure. They could shoot but they did not want to take orders.

The county court and the General Commander of the home guard had some difficulty in maintaining a guard in 1861 and 1862. Many of the men had expressed the desire to volunteer for the Confederate army because they did not want to remain in the home guard for a period of three months. Yet, when they were exempted from the home guard, not all of them volunteered for the Confederate army. The court admitted that it had no legal way to force the men into the home guard or the Confederate army. For the duration of its tenure, the court argued over the amount of power it had to force the men into local service.[12]

Problems of organization and discipline threatened the effectiveness of the guard. The men were displeased with the appointed officers because they wanted to elect their own. They rejected the order that they were to supply their own provisions while they were in training. One of the biggest complaints was that they had to pay the expenses of getting to and from the training sessions. They refused to pay the fee to use a ferry to get to the training grounds. Finally, the county court ordered that the guardsmen were to be ferried to and from the training fields free of cost.[13] Since the court did not specify who would pay the ferry fees, it must be assumed that the ferry owners were forced to absorb the expense.

---

[9] 1862, Stewart County record Book 61: 18.

[10] Stewart County Court records, Book 61: 25. It is not known if action followed this discussion.

[11] Stewart County Court records June, July, and August 1861. Book 61: 5, 7, 12, 17. The court members discussed the general conflicts in the guard. The guardsmen were present to complain to the court, and they commented that the officers were responsible for the problems.

[12] 1862, Book 63: 14-22.

[13] 1861, Stewart County Court record Book 60: 30, 31; Book 61: 19-20; Book 63: 9-11.

In October 1861, approximately fifty members of the home guard were in training under the command of J.C. Cook. Officially, the guard had a total of 120 men, but it was almost impossible to get all the men together at one time. Captain Cook complained to county officials that it was impossible to organize the men because all of them wanted to make the decisions. In letters written to a friend of his, Major Nathan Brandon, who was at that time stationed at Big Springs, Virginia, Cook enumerated the obstacles he had confronted in training the guard. He said that when he had been involved in trying to train volunteers for the Confederate army, he had run into similar problems. The problem was, he said:

> We have great trouble here lately in organizing companys the greatest number of men wish to be captains or lieutenants. I wish the present legislature would make it legal for them all to have an office then we would have plenty fiting men. There have been some three or four companies broke and deposed in our county on account of dissatisfaction about office.[14]

He also indicated that there were problems with keeping the men in the guard. He had lost several men who had simply walked away because they did not like the officer in charge.[15]

For months following the order to arm the home guard, the people in the land between the rivers were involved in enthusiastic preparations for war. The total activity was protracted, ineffectual, and chaotic. For example, the Fourteenth Tennessee Infantry Regiment, made up of volunteers from Trigg and Lyon Counties in Kentucky, and Stewart County in Tennessee, was eager to join the Confederate army. The men did not want to wait around playing at being a soldier. Their first priority was to halt any invasion of their homes, but if that invasion was not coming immediately they wanted to search out the enemy. Three companies led by Captain Nathan Brandon, Captain Hiram Buckner, and Captain Wash Lowe were sent to Camp Quarles located near Clarksville, Tennessee on June 6, 1861. The Fourteenth Tennessee Infantry Regiment did not remain in the area to defend Tennessee. The Regiment was sent to Virginia and later fought in the battles of Seven Pines, Chancellorsville, and Cold Harbor, among others.[16]

Loyalty and Finances

In July of 1861, the county court discussed a problem which they had not anticipated. It was learned that some of the men who had told their families that they were leaving to join the Confederate army had joined the Union forces. The family members had applied to the court for assistance and the court had responded. Now, the court had the added difficulty of trying to determine which families actually merited assistance. The men were determined that

---

[14]Letters by J. C. Cook, Confederate Collection, Manuscript Account No. 801, Tennessee State Library and Archives, Nashville, Tennessee.

[15]Ibid.

[16]Ibid.

no family of a Union soldier would get aid from the county.[17]

From the tone of the sessions of the county court throughout 1861, the families of those men who had joined the Union Army must have faced severe condemnation from their neighbors. Even though individual family names were omitted from the records it appears that at least fifty men joined the Union army.[18] Of the two thousand potential soldiers in the region, a group of fifty men did not constitute an alarming number of Union sympathizers, yet the outraged reaction from within the county is apparent.[19] It had not taken the people long to require that everyone had to follow the will of the majority. The problem of divided loyalties added to the tension in the area.

In January 1862, the county court declared that the expenses for the care of the families of the volunteers were more than the county script would cover. The court ordered that a special property tax of thirteen cents on one hundred dollars of taxable property be paid by the property owners of Stewart County. The property owners argued that they could not pay the additional tax and meet their own debts. They argued that they were being forced to assume the total cost of the preparedness efforts, and they could not shoulder the financial responsibility.[20]

When the men in the Fourteenth Tennessee Infantry Regiment complained about the orders to leave for Virginia, they were told by their commanders that they were needed in the East more than in Middle Tennessee. The general attitude was that the orders were ill founded because of the rumored invasion by way of the Tennessee and Cumberland. The civilians were convinced that the men should remain and protect their homes. When some of the soldiers realized that they were leaving the area, they simply walked away from the army.[21]

The first people to feel the effects of the war were the families of the volunteers. Many families were soon without food and clothing, and the government could do very little to help. It would be logical to assume that church groups and neighbors tried to help these people, but there was another problem. It would be one thing for these people to get money that the government owed them, and quite another to take charity from neighbors. Charity carried a stigma in the area, and some people had rather suffer severe hardship than ask for assistance.

Statistics are not available to indicate how many men left the land between the rivers to join the Union army. It has been theorized that Union and Confederate loyalties in the area were almost equal.[22] Yet the local records do not indicate that people supported the Union cause. The general attitude seemed to be that they could not support a government which forced

[17]Discussed in the July, 1861 session of the Stewart County Court. Found in Book 59, 134-140.

[18]1861, Stewart County Court record Book 60: 24-31.

[19]Ibid.

[20]1862, Book 63: 19-21.

[21] Cook, Confederate Collection, Brandon Letter sent to Cook dated 1861. Throughout the war, desertion was a problem for both armies. How these men survived for the remainder of the war is clouded in confusion of the time.

[22]In 1862 General Ulysses S. Grant made such a statement in a message to General Halleck. See Leslie Perry, Joseph W. Kirkley, The War of the Rebellion: A Compilation of the Official Records of the Union and Confederate Armies, vol. I (Washington D. C.: Government Printing Office, 1898), 145.

them to denounce their local power. The southern states had decreed their right to withdraw from the federation, and the federal government could not revoke that decree. Loyalty was given, not demanded.

By October 1861, rumors of an immediate attack by way of the Tennessee or Cumberland Rivers were rampant throughout the countryside. Fewer citizens argued that the Federal government would not attack civilians, and loyalty shifted even more toward the Confederate cause when the news of Union mobilization at Cairo, Illinois and Paducah, Kentucky reached the people in the land between the rivers.[23]

In November 1861, the members of the Stewart County Court and other leading citizens of Dover requested all available men and resources to defend the town. Stockpiling a quantity of guns and ammunition for the defense of Dover was the first priority. The county court ordered that all guns be requisitioned from private citizens. When agents of the county court went throughout the county to seize the guns, the citizens often threatened the agents and ordered them to stay off their land. The citizens argued that they needed the weapons for their own defense, and they had no obligations to sacrifice their safety to protect Dover.[24]

An agent of the court complained to the court at the November session in 1861 that Ruben Wallace would not surrender his guns to the agent and he even denied that he owned any guns. The agent assured the court that Wallace was not telling the truth. Later in the December session of the court, the same agent reported that Wallace had been hiding his guns. The agent reported that he had been skeptical when Wallace said that he did not own a gun; everyone owned guns. The agent watched the man's home and caught him concealing his guns by placing them in a bucket which he then lowered into a well each time anyone visited the farm. The agent decided to watch Wallace and surprise him in the act of hiding the guns, and he confiscated four guns from Wallace which he subsequently turned over to the home guard. There is no record that the court prosecuted any of the citizens who did not follow the order to relinquish their guns.[25]

Men from Montgomery, Cheatham, and Stewart counties in Tennessee along with Trigg and Lyon counties in Kentucky organized the Forty-Second Confederate Regiment in October 1861. These men were later ordered to serve at Fort Donelson. Men from the land between the rivers joined the Fiftieth Tennessee Infantry Regiment on December 25, 1861. Later, they assisted the civilian work crews at Fort Donelson.[26]

---

[23]Ibid.

[24]Stewart County Court records November, 1861.

[25]1861, Stewart County Court records, Book 62: 27, 49.

[26]Approximately 275 civilian workers were at Fort Donelson by October 13, 1961. These men were supported by Colonel R. W. McGavock with three companies of Tennessee troops on October 16, 1861; General Service Schools, Fort Henry and Fort Donelson Campaigns February 1862: Source Book (Kansas: General Services School Press, 1912), 202-250. Bromfield L. Riley, Battles and Sketches of the Army of the Tennessee (Mexico, Missouri: Missouri Press, 1906), 6.

Plans to Repel an Invasion

The strategic geographic location of Stewart County did not escape the attention of Isham G. Harris, governor of Tennessee. The governor was also knowledgeable about the importance of the iron industry to the military strength of the Confederacy. Therefore, the assumption that the land between the rivers could be the strategic point of attack by Union forces drew the attention of state officials. For months, the people in the land between the rivers had written letters and sent messages to state and Confederate authorities warning that a growing Union force in Kentucky posed an immediate danger to the Tennessee and Cumberland Rivers. These rivers led directly into the heartland of the South, and their homes lay in the path of any invading force. They advised the civilian and military leaders that the construction of fortifications on the rivers should begin immediately.[27]

Governor Harris had also learned from Confederate authorities, and civilians who had traveled in Kentucky and Illinois came to Nashville to report that a large Union force was in Cairo and Paducah. The people expressed amazement at the activity and size of the force in the two towns.[28] The people commented on the vulnerability of the northwestern border of Tennessee. It was hardly news that the easiest way to invade the heart of the Confederacy was to open the rivers leading into the interior of the country. Geographically, the land between the rivers appeared to be the perfect passageway into the South. Since the Ohio River was already in the hands of the Union forces, it seemed a simple matter to send gunboats up the Tennessee and Cumberland Rivers.

Local leaders and the governor sent numerous messages to Confederate authorities defining the need to construct fortifications on the two waterways. The argument was that the area was important to the Confederacy because of the iron industry. The area produced approximately 42,500 tons of iron per year. Here was an almost incalculable resource for the Confederate war effort, but it must be protected, properly developed, and utilized for the war effort. Thriving communities lay within the area, and the new Memphis, Clarksville, and Louisville Railroad provided an important transfer link between Louisville and Memphis. The land between the rivers had important ports at Dover, Lineport, and Tobacco Port. These places and others shipped grain, pork, beef, tobacco, and whiskey out of the area. The messages stressed the conviction that the whole western Confederacy depended on keeping the Tennessee and Cumberland Rivers free from federal control.[29]

Confederate leaders including Jefferson Davis and Albert Sidney Johnston expressed interest in the need to fortify the rivers, but they appeared to believe that other concerns should take priority. In the meantime, no one in authority made any effort to determine the need for

---

[27]Notes in the Stewart County Court records, Book 64: 11, 19, 21, 19.

[28]Ibid.

[29]Governor Harris sent several messages to General Albert Sidney Johnston about the fortifications. See O. R. Series I, vol. I, 87, and Benjamin Franklin Cooling, Forts Henry and Donelson: The Key to the Confederate Heartland (Knoxville: The University of Tennessee Press, 1987), 69-80.

the strongholds on the Tennessee and Cumberland Rivers.[30]

When Governor Harris could not get a positive response from the Confederate government in Montgomery, Alabama or Johnston, he took action in May 1861. Adna Anderson, a civil engineer, and Wilbur Foster were sent to locate a site for a fortification on the Cumberland River. Governor Harris instructed the men about the neutrality of Kentucky. He was adamant about any violation of the neutrality. The only possible sites for the fortification were in Tennessee.[31]

Anderson selected a site about one mile from Dover for the fortification on the Cumberland. The site was adequate; it lay eleven miles south of neutral Kentucky and approximately sixty miles from the mouth of the Cumberland. The installation could protect Clarksville which was thirty miles upstream and Nashville which lay upstream some seventy miles. A hill rising seventy to one hundred feet overlooking the Cumberland was chosen as the center of the fortification. The hill was surrounded by deep gullies offering barriers to land assault. Several country roads linked the fort site with Dover and led to other Middle Tennessee communities and railroad lines on both the Cumberland and Tennessee.[32]

While Anderson was choosing the site on the Cumberland, Governor Harris decided that a fortification was needed to protect the Tennessee River. The selection of the best possible sites for placement of the fortifications was a difficult task, and Adna Anderson requested assistance. The lowlands along the Tennessee River were considerably flatter than on the Cumberland and posed a real problem of flooding. Eventually Anderson chose a location below Standing Rock Creek which was almost opposite the mouth of Sandy Creek. Work teams were not available and Anderson returned to Nashville to brief Governor Harris on his decisions.[33]

Governor Harris wanted detailed information about the sites, and he selected one of his military authorities, a West Pointer and former militia veteran, Brigadier General Daniel S. Donelson to study the sites. General Donelson, a nephew of Rachel Jackson, found work underway at Dover and he approved the site, which subsequently was named for him. When he reached the Tennessee, Donelson decided that no suitable site was available. He disliked the site at Standing Rock Creek and moved to an alternate position at Kirkman's Old Landing which was almost twelve miles due west of Fort Donelson. Donelson was considering a third site across the river at Pine Bluff which offered better protection from a land assault, but the bluffs were deemed too high to permit proper cannon installation to cover the river. On June 9, Major Bushrod Rust Johnson arrived to advise General Donelson, and he voted for the site at Kirkman's Old Landing.[34]

Harris knew that time was running out and his priority was the construction of fortifications anywhere near the entrances to the rivers. Arrangements for construction crews

---

[30]Ibid.

[31]Ibid.

[32]Ibid.

[33]General Service Schools, Fort Henry and Fort Donelson, 19.

[34]Ibid.

had to made so that work could begin immediately, but very little work was done that summer because local workers were not available. Eleven companies of Stewart County men departed for Virginia in July with the Fourteenth Tennessee. The construction of the forts was left to slaves and mill hands.[35]

General Donelson and Major Johnson bore the stigma of selecting very poor sites for the forts. Bushrod Johnson, an 1840 graduate of West Point, had fought the Seminoles and Mexicans before being forced out of the army on a charge of smuggling. He was associated with the Western Military Institute in Nashville, and he became chief engineer of the Tennessee state forces in 1861. Johnson has remained an enigma in American history. He does not appear in many of the historical accounts of the events at Fort Henry and Fort Donelson. It is not unusual to see his name omitted in accounts of the selection of the sites for the forts. It must be noted that both Donelson and Johnson advised Governor Harris that they did not like the site on the Tennessee River. They reported that they did not have enough information at their disposal, and because time was of the essence, they had made their decision without checking other locations. Governor Harris consulted with Gustavus A. Henry and decided to accept the sites that Donelson and Johnson had chosen.[36]

A young man, Captain B. D. Bidwell of the Thirtieth Tennessee Infantry Regiment, was a member of the first construction crew at Fort Donelson, and he made notations in his journal about the work. Later, Captain Bidwell was in command of one 4-gun section of the river batteries which defended the fort. Just before the battle, he described the fort as an entrenchment encircling the crest of a hill on the south bank of the Cumberland. The fort was about one mile below the little town of Dover. He observed that running back from the river for at least a mile was a ravine or gorge filled with backwater. Away from the backwater was another deep hollow, which ran behind the fort. Above the main part of the fort, a hollow extended from the river and ran diagonally across the fort. The inner entrenchments made the fortifications into a hollow and on the side of a hill.[37]

The first work force began construction on Fort Donelson on October 2, 1861. William Stacker, one of the owners of the Cumberland Iron Works, brought workers, including approximately five hundred slaves, to Fort Donelson. The records show that most of the slave masters sent their male slaves to work at the fort. The numbers of workers, black and white, varied from day to day because owners took their slaves when they needed them to work for them. The person in charge of the work crews at the fort never knew exactly how many workers would be available for work on any given day.[38]

Even though it seemed that agreement had been reached that construction on the forts was

---

[35]Cooling, Forts, 90.

[36]General Service Schools, Fort Henry and Fort Donelson, 215. Fort Henry was named for Gustavus A. Henry who was a friend of Governor Harris and a Confederate Senator from Tennessee. His letters to the governor were instrumental in forcing the Confederate leaders to recognize the importance of the defense of the Tennessee and Cumberland.

[37]Portions of the journal are in the Tennessee State Library and Archives, Civil War Collection.

[38]Stewart County Court records, Book 62: 29-30.

critical because of a possible invasion, very little construction was completed and only a small military force was sent. The military authorities relied upon Confederate units training out of Clarksville to handle any emergency that might arise, and the first military garrison at the Fort spent more time regulating river traffic than digging trenches.

On the Tennessee River, Colonel Adolphus Heiman's 10th Tennessee began work on Fort Henry. Seven hundred and twenty men armed with flintlock rifles had the responsibility of constructing the fort and repulsing any attack. Heiman was of German descent and had come to the forefront of Nashville society as a well-known architect, and he had shown valor in the Mexican War. He was joined in October 1861 by Colonel Randal W. McGavock, with three companies of Tennessee troops. At this time, some two hundred and seventy-five white workmen were assembled to begin construction of the fortification. Supplies came in by boats from Nashville and Clarksville. The work force was disorganized and construction proceeded at a very slow pace. Because of the lack of plans and general disarray, precious time was lost.[39]

Even as Colonel Heiman and his men assumed the task of constructing the fortifications at Fort Henry, rumors spread like wild fire that Union gunboats were advancing toward Fort Henry. On Monday, October 14, 1861, Union gunboats did appear within full view of the workers, but the gunboats turned back without offering a challenge. The citizens of the land between the rivers fired on the gunboats as they withdrew below the fort. The citizens reported that they had hit at least one man on a gunboat. They were sure that they had killed him because he had been looking out a window (porthole) at the time. The gunboats remained within a few miles of Fort Henry for several days. During that time, they reported daily on the progress being made on the construction at Fort Henry.[40]

More attention than ever before centered on the situation on the rivers. Numerous messages were transmitted about the lack of construction on the forts. Johnston ordered that a force under Kentuckian Lloyd Tilghman assist at Fort Donelson. Major Jeremy Gilmer and Senator Henry set out to inspect the forts. Gilmer and Henry agreed that Fort Henry was progressing but Fort Donelson was another matter. While at Fort Donelson, Gilmer decided that the armaments should be doubled, and he also wanted a single battery of bronze field pieces, plus two small iron guns made in Clarksville installed.[41]

In October 1861, Union troops came ashore in the land between the rivers and took provisions, including food, cattle, and horses from farmers in the area. The soldiers treated the people in Lyon and Trigg County the same way they treated people in Stewart County. The Union soldiers did not have a physical, geographical line to help them determine if they were in Kentucky or Tennessee. Once again, the people made adjustments in their attitude toward the war. Until October 1861, war did not seem to be a reality to many of the people. There could be no doubt, however, when Union gunboats and Union troops entered the region that war had begun. The people called upon the Confederate forces for protection, but not enough men

---

[39]Ibid. O. R. Series I, vol. I, 132; O. R. Series I, vol. LXII, 122; O. R. Series I, vol. I, 134.

[40]Ibid., 146.

[41]O. R. Series, I, vol. IV, 496-97.

were available to provide that protection. McGavock, Heiman and others in the region expressed concerns over the treatment of the civilians in the land between the rivers. These people were being robbed and brutalized and no help was offered. They speculated that these people would turn against the Confederate cause if actions were not taken immediately.[42]

More importantly at this time, the people considered the action an encroachment on their individual rights. These people, because of their culture and traditions, were extraordinarily sensitive to property rights. Now, the federal government had proved what the antagonists had been saying earlier that the government no longer respected the rights of the state or the private citizen, and it was ready to use an army to destroy property and kill innocent citizens in order to exert its control over the states. For the first time, some of the people began to fear the power of the federal forces, and became impassioned advocates of the Confederate cause.[43]

Tennessee state officials warned citizens of Stewart County that they could expect an advance of an organized, well-equipped Union army into their region at any time. The officials of Kentucky did not warn the people in Trigg and Lyon Counties that they should identify themselves as Unionist. The farmers in Stewart County received instructions from the county officials to move their tobacco, cotton, and grain away from the Tennessee and Cumberland and hide it in the hills to prevent the Union soldiers from seizing their produce. Iron masters received information from the Confederate authorities that they could expect to lose their goods if they tried to ship them down the Tennessee and Cumberland. Authorities told the people that they could expect physical abuse and bloodshed when Union soldiers entered the area. The citizens of Lyon and Trigg Counties in the land between the rivers received no instruction about what to expect from the Union force. These people in Kentucky did not hide their food and valuables until they were raided by the Union soldiers.[44]

Stewart County officials issued statements about the need for workers at the forts. Few men volunteered, and the court issued a statement that all available men would be impressed into the work gangs. Men grumbled about this order, and the officers in the home guard expressed concern that some of the people were not being loyal to the Confederate cause. They wanted more personnel to watch these people. Because it was very difficult to gauge the emotions of the people, some Confederate leaders reacted too quickly. Their attitude was that it was necessary to control the people even before solid evidence about acts of disloyalty had been gathered. The strident Confederate supporters felt that the Unionists, if they had the opportunity, would transmit important military information to the Union forces. The home guard, with authorization from the county court, began a house-to-house probe and interrogation of the people. They wanted to determine if anyone living in the area was a Union sympathizer. If any individual was deemed a suspect by the home guard, he was disarmed and his guns and ammunition were confiscated. Neighbor watching neighbors was detrimental to the spirit of the

[42]O. R. Series I, vol. IV, 481,491-92,495,511, 513-14, 519, 522, 524-25, 539, 543.

[43]Ibid. A sense of this change in attitude can be obtained from the records in Caldwell, Lyon, Trigg, and Stewart Counties in 1861.

[44]Lyon and Trigg County records had no discussion about what to expect from the Union Forces. Stewart County Court records, Book 62: 12, 34, 39, 42.

community. Suspicion bred suspicion. Also, the people developed deep resentment against the home guard. The guard, which represented the Confederate government, invaded the people's privacy, and they often arrested people with little or no evidence of wrongdoing. People were often undecided about which government was the most dangerous to their freedom.[45]

During this period, the construction at the forts was moving too slowly, even though several additional units of soldiers had arrived to supplement the work force. In November 1861, the people of Stewart County received an order from the county court to present themselves, along with their slaves and work animals, to the directors of work crews at either Fort Henry or Fort Donelson. The rains in October and November delayed the work at both fortifications and turned the roads into quagmires. It was difficult to reach the construction sites even if the individuals had been willing to work in the cold rain. The cold weather made work even more difficult in November and December. Sickness spread through the forts. Men died from measles, pneumonia, dysentery, jaundice, typhus, and meningitis.[46] Sickness and disease were to become major problems for the military for the duration of the war.

Supplies for the soldiers and workers were a problem. Even though many men had relatives or friends living nearby who would provide them with some help, they needed food and clothing. Some of the men such as John Nolin, David Sills, and Christopher Columbus Stewart knew the area because their family homes were only a mile or so away. They hunted and fished during their off duty hours. At Fort Henry, Smith Crutcher and others visited friends and relatives on Rushing Creek. Even if the men could leave the confines of the forts for visits with friends and relatives, the weather and short supplies made life miserable for most.[47]

The Confederate leaders began sending weapons to the fortifications in November. The men unloaded the heavy guns from the boats with little difficulty, but as soon as the guns reached the shore, they sank into the mud. The men spent days, during what was to be a most critical period, trying to maneuver the guns into position. After several days, they decided that they were unable to move the guns into the fortifications until the weather changed. They waited for weeks until the temperature dropped and the ground froze, allowing the guns to be pulled to the fortifications.[48] The delay resulted in unfinished sections in the defense line even as the Union forces moved into the area.

After the rains in October and November, the ensuing flood waters should have alerted the Confederate planners to the fact that Fort Henry was likely to be submerged under the back water. Fort Henry was below the flood line and Fort Donelson was partially surrounded by creeks which could flood the ravines in the area. Because the planners were under such a strain of trying to build the forts so quickly, they seemed to lose sight of the potential hazards of flooding.

The constant demands by the Stewart County Court to contribute more and more men

---

[45]Stewart County records from October, 1861 through January 1862. Book 62: 39, 45, 56; Book 63: 21, 22, 29, 32.

[46]1861, Stewart County Court records, Book 62: 42; Henry, Land Between the Rivers, 42-44.

[47]Ibid.

[48]O. R. Series I, vol. I, 152.

and money to the war effort angered many citizens of the region. They often grumbled that they did not know which was worse, their compatriots or their adversaries. Both groups, they felt, seemed to disregard the essential prerogatives of the individual to protect his own financial interests and meet the needs of his family. Some of the people began to argue that the whole story of an impending invasion by a federal force was a hoax. Those people who denied that a threat was forthcoming refused to contribute to the work at Fort Henry or Fort Donelson.[49] When civilian workers or slaves were removed from the work gangs it was difficult for the local officials or the Confederate military to force the men back to work. The local records provide evidence of a number of threats that official action would be taken, but there is no indication that any worker or slave owner was charged with a crime.

When Albert Sidney Johnston assumed command of Department No. II in September 1861, it was a vast area including Tennessee and Arkansas. He had quickly agreed with Governor Harris, Senator Henry, and others that the construction of Fort Henry and Fort Donelson should take top priority because the forts were strategic to the control and safety of the Western Confederacy. General Johnston became quite distraught whenever he received messages from September through December that work at the forts had progressed so slowly. He reacted by choosing a subordinate to study the situation and initiate changes. These men always responded that they needed more of everything including workers, equipment, weapons, and supplies to complete the work. Yet, identifying the needs did not result in a resolution of the problem.[50] Communiqués between General Johnston and the President of the Confederacy, Jefferson Davis, indicated that President Davis did not understand the importance of the fortifications on the Tennessee and Cumberland Rivers. The messages sent by General Johnston did not convince the Confederate leader that it was of critical importance to complete the construction of Fort Henry and Fort Donelson.[51] During the most crucial time, the construction workers did not receive the resources, material, or extra manpower they needed to complete their work.

The preparations for war affected the citizens of the area in several ways. The tranquility of the area was completely disrupted when hundreds of soldiers arrived at the fortifications. Rumor ran rampant that the impending invasion had begun, and the extreme brutality of the Union soldiers had to be met with fervor and sacrifice. People were soon in a frenzy because they did not know how to prepare for the crisis. Workers were coming and going constantly. Housing and food supplies were not available to meet the demands from the soldiers and the workers. Even the animals at the fortifications had been displaced because people needed the stables for shelter. Work crews built approximately fifty crude log huts to house some of the workers. Fifty small cabins did not meet the need, and men and animals continued to work with short rations and inadequate housing. The working conditions, hunger, and fear combined to

---

[49]1861, Stewart County Court records, Book 62: 48.

[50]O. R. Series I, vol. 7, 159.

[51]O. R. Series I, vol. I, 159-162.

spawn disorder and impaired the progress of the construction.[52]

The lack of leadership was one of the problems at the construction sites. No individual had the authority to supervise the construction of shelters for the civilian workers. The top priority was given to the construction of trenches and barricades around the gun batteries. No one seemed to anticipate the problem of feeding the civilian workers and soldiers. Leaders seemed to assume that needed supplies would arrive by water. The men needed large stores of food and other supplies, but supply vessels did not arrive on schedule. At first, the farmers in the land between the rivers were elated to sell their commodities to the Confederate soldiers. They became concerned, however, when the army tried to pay for the goods with Confederate currency; they wanted gold or silver. Soon, the farmers had sold all their surplus supplies and feared that goods which they needed at home would be confiscated by the Confederate army or the county officials.

Boats, appearing in convoy fashion, loaded with supplies and men moved into the Tennessee and Cumberland Rivers. Soon, both streams became congested with the traffic. The boats, bringing supplies, also brought friends and relatives of the soldiers and workers to the forts. The people who came to visit found that they could not find shelter or food in the area. Supply boats could not off-load the goods because they could not reach the docks.[53] No one was placed in charge of assigning priority to which boats could use the docks. Confusion and frustration caused delays in getting supplies and equipment to the workers. The visitors simply exacerbated the problems.

Roads, that a few months before had been empty, were now crowded and difficult or impossible to travel. The citizens of the area sensed the frantic atmosphere, and they expected the enemy to appear at any minute. The tumult of preparation and the pandemonium resulting from all the people rushing to and fro certainly changed the lives of the people in the land between the rivers. The area took on the appearance of a medieval circus.

The military encouraged the farmers in the area to sell their produce to the Confederate soldiers at Fort Henry and Fort Donelson. They were told that Union soldiers would appropriate the produce as soon as they entered the region. Afraid of losing their goods, the farmers moved everthing including farm goods, animals, and valuables deep into the wooded areas. Within a matter of a few weeks, farm produce became scarce and the prices increased. Inflation remained a serious problem until the end of the war.[54]

Merchants in the towns and villages in the area were doing a booming business, and the demand for goods was always more than the merchants could supply. Suppliers and shippers

---

[52]The Stewart County Court records provide a sense of the troubles, but for a more detailed understanding see: Bruce Catton, Grant Moves South (Boston: Little, Brown and Company, 1960); Thomas L. Connelly, Army of the Heartland; The Army of Tennessee, 1861-1862 (Baton Rouge: Louisiana State University Press, 1967);_____. Autumn of Glory; The Army of Tennessee, 1862-1865 (Baton Rouge: Louisiana State University Press, 1971); James Hamilton. The Battle of Fort Donelson (New York, New York: Yoseloff, 1968); Stanley F. Horn. Army of Tennessee (Norman, Oklahoma: University of Oklahoma Press, 1941); _____, compiled and edited. Tennessee's War 1861-1865 (Nashville: Vanderbilt University Press, 1965)

[53]Ibid.

[54]Ibid. See Stewart County Court records, Book 63: 19.

had serious problems when they tried to ship their goods to the merchants. River traffic on the Ohio River was interrupted by the Union navy. Military supplies did not arrive on schedule and the shippers complained that they did not have merchant ships available to meet the demand. The river traffic was hectic. Accidents often caused delays and the time schedules were capricious. During this period, every message sent by Confederate officers at Fort Henry and Fort Donelson to their commanders included a request for more supplies.[55]

Slave owners became more and more concerned when county officials and the Confederate army ordered them to send their slaves to the work force at Fort Henry and Fort Donelson. The iron masters, who had more slaves than most other individuals in the area, complained that they could not keep their iron industries in operation if their workers were forced to work for the government.

General Johnston realized that more workers were needed, and he requested that a slave force of some five hundred men from farmers in West Tennessee and Northern Alabama be sent to supplement the work force at Fort Henry and Fort Donelson. Slaves came in from both regions and approximately nine hundred reached the construction sites at Fort Henry and Fort Donelson on November 28, 1861.[56]

Still more workers, both slave and free, were recruited from the surrounding counties in Tennessee and Kentucky. They were needed to supplement the existing work force and fill the work quotas when workers left the site to attend to matters at home. The exact number of black and white workers who came to the fortifications is difficult to determine, but a conservative estimation is that at least one thousand workers came by November 1861.[57] There is no way to determine how long they stayed. Certainly, some of the workers stayed for a few days or weeks and then left to care for things at home. Slaves were brought to work for a few weeks and were moved back to their original jobs.

The Confederate officers, in official communications to their superiors, reported that they were having a difficult time trying to buy provisions from the local farmers and merchants. The people did not want to accept the Confederate currency because they could sell their goods to buyers and merchants in Kentucky and receive better prices in gold and silver. They had learned that Union forces in Cairo and Paducah were actually sending buyers to the land between the rivers to purchase goods. Regardless of an individual's loyalties, farmers sold to the people who offered the highest price.[58]

The sudden increase in the population resulted in concerns about law and order. The soldiers and workers, both white and slave, were impossible to control with the number of available guardsmen. The Stewart County Court ordered that the number in the home guard be increased to two hundred men. The county officials ordered the guard to make more frequent

---

[55]O. R. Series I, vol. I. 182.

[56]O. R. Series I, vol. 7, 169-172.

[57]Estimate made after a study of all the numbers suggested by researchers and the activities of the officials of Stewart County.

[58]O. R. Series I, vol. I, 192.

patrols, especially at night. They were instructed to stop and search any suspicious person.[59]

It seemed as if the whole countryside had changed radically in a few weeks, and the accompanying economic inflation stunned the citizens. The escalating prices for goods caused the officials in Trigg, Lyon and Stewart Counties such consternation that the courts held special sessions to discuss the additional economic strain. In Stewart County, the problem of providing goods and services to people who had come to the county was impossible to solve. The greatest financial difficulty was providing support for the growing numbers of families who qualified for assistance because the head of the household had volunteered for service in the Confederate army. The taxes collected by the county had not met the cost before inflation, and now, the court was forced to consider the feasibility of levying new taxes. Most of the members of the county court opposed any proposal for additional taxes, and even though the court continued to discuss the problem, it had not reached a decision by the spring of 1862. At that time, the county government was disbanded by the invading Union army.[60]

By January 1862, the Confederate army stationed at Fort Donelson and Fort Henry was essentially without food. The irony was that food was available, but it was on the merchant ships headed for the forts. The lack of adequate management of railroad and river traffic resulted in supplies being shifted to sidings and ports and soldiers were in desperate need.[61] Reports made by civilians and the military indicated that the Confederate soldiers were stealing produce from farmers and merchants in the area. General Albert Sidney Johnston received requests from Confederate officers asking him for permission to appropriate the supplies they needed, but General Johnston opposed the plan. He wrote on one occasion, "whether among friends or foes it has always resulted prejudicially (sic) to the public interest" to impress supplies.[62]

This message was a direct order to stop the pillage by Confederate soldiers in the land between the rivers. There is little doubt that the officers at Fort Henry and Fort Donelson ordered their men not to take merchandise from the citizens, but the men usually disregarded the order and took whatever they wanted.

In January it was brought to General Johnston's attention that very little work was being done on placing galvanic mines, chains, trees, and sunken boats in the rivers. Johnston dispatched messages to General Tilghman to get the work done.[63] General Tilghman was mildly reprimanded for not adequately supervising the construction of an installation now called Fort Heiman which lay directly across the Tennessee River from Fort Henry. Little work had been completed by January and when the number of sightings of Union gunboats increased in

---

[59]1861 Stewart County Court records, Book 62, 42. The author got the impression that the officials were concerned with workers who were staying around the town of Dover.

[60] December 1861, Lyon County Court records, Book 63: 22; December 1861. Trigg County Court records, Book 70: 29; Stewart County Court records, Book 62: 29-30; Book 63: 23.

[61]O. R. Series I, vol. VII, 544,563, 828-29, 852-55.

[62]O. R. Series I, vol. VII, 197.

[63]O. R. Series I, vol. VII, 74, 75, 144-45, 834-35.

December and January, the impact was felt in Johnston's headquarters.[64]

In January Bushrod Johnson and Lieutenant Colonel Milton A. Haynes were sent to the forts. Colonel Haynes was to assume control of gunnery instruction at the two forts. The only positive account in the reports sent back to General Johnston was that telegraph lines had been strung and communications were very good.[65]

Once again, General Johnston had requested that officials in Richmond send more supplies and men to Fort Henry and Fort Donelson. The officials acknowledged the requests, but they took no action to meet the General's supplication.[66] In January 1862, General John B. Floyd with four regiments from Virginia and one from Mississippi, and General Simon B. Buckner were finally ordered to Fort Donelson. General Gideon Pillow was placed in command of the Confederate force at Clarksville, Tennessee. He was ordered by General Johnston to stand ready to support any needs at Fort Donelson.[67]

Just as these military forces were arriving at Fort Henry and Fort Donelson, the spring rains began. The numerous creeks which fed the Tennessee and Cumberland accelerated the flow of water from the hills to the rivers. The water from the creeks soon covered the lowlands and the river waters began to rise.

With growing apprehension, the Confederate leaders watched the water rise around Fort Henry. The Fort was still under construction as the water slowly edged its way into the breastworks. On January 22, Lt. Colonel Haynes in a report to General Tilghman observed:

Fort Henry is untenable and ought to be forth-with abandoned, first because it is surrounded by water, then it is cut off from support by the infantry and it is on the point of being submerged: second, because our whole force amounting to a little over two thousand men is wholly inadequate to cope with that of the enemy, even if there is no extraordinary rise in the River.[68]

Every day new rumors reached the area that the Union soldiers in Kentucky were standing poised to invade the region. For weeks, civilians and Confederate soldiers sighted Union gunboats just downstream from Fort Henry. The gunboats were careful to remain outside the range of the guns at the fort, but they were in position to begin an attack at any time.[69]

On January 22, 1862, the backwaters of the Tennessee River overflowed the breastworks at Fort Henry. In another report to Tilghman, Haynes observed that Fort Henry ought to be abandoned immediately. His observation was that since the Fort was surrounded by water which in a short time was expected to cover the outer edge of the fortification, the men could not fall

---

[64]Ibid.

[65]Ibid.

[66]O. R. Series I, vol. I, 195.

[67]Ibid.

[68]O. R. Series I, vol. VII, 145.

[69]Ibid.

back to Fort Donelson because the water would cut them off above the Fort.[70]

At that time, Fort Henry was a bastion fort of solid constructed earthworks enclosing an area of a little more than three acres. The ditch surrounding the fort was twenty feet wide and on the average ten feet deep. The height of the parapet from the bottom of the ditch was about eighteen feet. The line of the parapet was some two thousand, two hundred and seventy feet long. The armaments consisted of six thirty-two pound field pieces, two twelve pound field guns, and one six pound field piece. Four of the thirty-two pound pieces ranged down the Tennessee River, and the fifth could be trained on boats that passed along the channel between Fort Henry and an island that lay in the river. The island was about one and one-half miles from the shore battery at Fort Henry. Five guns protected the fortification on the land side. Infantry entrenchments, thrown up on a rise or hillside protecting the land side of Fort Henry, controlled the road to Fort Donelson. Since the entrenchments were still under construction, they would be easily overwhelmed if Union forces should attack.[71]

Fort Donelson had river batteries and an outer land defense system that was nearer completion. The river batteries had been constructed first, and the military considered these batteries as the best preventive measure aimed at keeping the Union movement out of the Cumberland River. The Confederate officers seemed to agree that the attack on Fort Donelson would be by gunboats on the Cumberland. The lower water battery was approximately one hundred and fifty yards long. It had been constructed of logs and sod found on the site. The base of the parapets was approximately sixteen feet thick and ten feet across the top. The upper battery was designed in a semicircle and located about one hundred and fifteen yards southeast of the right edge of the lower emplacement.[72]

The trenches and earthworks, which encircled the land side of the Fort, were designed as a secondary line of defense against the Union attack. The people expected that the initial invasion would be by Federal gunboats which would come up the Cumberland River from the Ohio River, and it was conceivable, but not likely, that Union soldiers would come ashore just below the fortification and attack by land. The earthworks were approximately sixteen feet wide at the base, four feet thick at the top and sixteen feet high. The earthworks were built to enclose approximately fifteen acres of land which was made up of large sloping hollows.[73]

The main line of defense on the land side of Fort Donelson consisted of a line of rifle-pits which extended from the Fort in a two and one-half mile semicircle. The pits ran from west to east and ended just south of the town of Dover. The soldiers described these pits as ditches dug some five feet wide and two feet deep. Small trees called saplings were cut and placed around the pits and clay dirt was thrown over the saplings to form a five foot barricade. Trying desperately to provide as much defense as possible for the forts, some twenty thousand soldiers, two thousand slaves, and five thousand white workers had cut trees and thrown a barricade of

---

[70]Ibid., 200.

[71]General Services School, Fort Henry and Fort Donelson, 202.

[72]O. R. Series II, vol. III, 290-294.

[73]Ibid.

107

fallen timber and brush outside the perimeter of the forts. The cleared area would provide the Confederates some warning if the Union force attacked. Also, Union snipers could not use the trees as easily to pick off Confederate soldiers within the fort. In his memoirs, General Ulysses S. Grant described the outer defenses as an area where trees had been cut outside the rifle-pits for some distance. The trees were felled so that their pointed tops pointed outward toward his army. The limbs had been trimmed and the ends were pointed in order to hinder the attack against the fortification.[74]

The Confederate leaders had anticipated that the Union navy would play an important role in the rivers in the western theater. Several technological changes in naval construction had heralded a revolution in methods of naval warfare. Among the changes were an increasing reliance on steam rather than sail power and the employment of rifled ordnance and other guns firing explosive shells. The exploding shell could easily destroy wooden ships. The competition between the Confederate and Union navies led to the construction of the ironclad warship.[75]

During the winter of 1861, the Union leaders completed their plans to secure control of the Mississippi line by moving either on the river itself or parallel to it. They planned an offensive with a combined land and naval operation. Union land forces in the West were under the direction of two departmental commanders. One army, with its base at Louisville, was led by General Don Carlos Buell. He was in control of all of Kentucky except the western tip. The western tip of Kentucky and the area west of the Mississippi was under the command of General Henry W. Halleck, with headquarters in St. Louis. General Halleck stationed an army under Grant near Paducah. All the Confederate troops in the West were under the command of General Albert Sidney Johnston. General Johnston's headquarters were at Bowling Green.[76]

The number of Union troops in Kentucky increased to about 100,000. Threats of invasion loomed as an impending disaster to the leaders of the Confederacy. Rumors about atrocities committed by Union soldiers against the people in Kentucky horrified and angered the Confederate soldiers and civilians. Daily, travelers gave verbal accounts of affronts against people and damages to property which those in close proximity to Union troops had to tolerate. Many of the stories had some foundation in fact.[77]

A soldier attached to General C. F. Smith's command wrote to the headquarters at Paducah, Kentucky concerning his march across Calloway County, Kentucky, some twenty-five miles from Fort Donelson, and described what he had encountered:

> The country through which we have passed, and that in which we are, is intensely session. There is scarcely a Union man to be found, at least in the immediate vicinity. Deserted houses are common and have been since we left Graves County. The rebels are flying in utter confusion at the first intimation of our approach. Fortunate, indeed,

---

[74]Ulysses S. Grant, Personal Memoirs, vol. 2 (New York: Webster, 1894), 192.

[75]For a complete discussion of the navy see Charles B. Boyton, The History of the Navy During the Rebellion. 2 vols. New York: 1870; George Rogers Taylor, The Transportation Revolution 1815-1860. New York: 1951.

[76]Cooling, Forts, 212.

[77]A search of the O. R. Series indicates that many protests from civilians were sent to Union commanders about the conduct of the soldiers.

were those who remained at home, for a house without a tenant was quickly despoiled of its contents of any value. In some instances, the white males alone have fled, leaving their wives and children, with their niggers, to the mercy of those who were such a terror to them-selves. In such cases the households were sacred. In other cases, the niggers alone were left, and these were called upon to furnish a meal for the tired and hungry soldiers. The panic is universal among all who are in the least involved with secession politics.[78]

According to the rest of the letter, the roads were muddy and the people seemed intensely loyal to the Confederate cause. He guessed that people were leaving Calloway County and moving to Tennessee. He assumed that they were seeking the protection of the Confederate forces.[79]

The same soldier reported that the countryside was in poor condition because very little food was available. He noted that tobacco seemed to be the only crop produced on the farms and none of the families had coffee to drink. He did not like the ground rye that was substituted for coffee. The usual meal for people, both black and white, consisted of salt meat, hominy, hoe cake, molasses, and rye coffee. Butter, sugar, and wheat bread were rarely found. Vegetables were very scarce. Farmers had large crops of tobacco and money was scarce.

It is unknown just how much of the soldier's report mirrored the actual circumstances. It is quite likely that some of the people had concealed their provisions if they were aware that troops were in the vicinity. Also, the men were apt to hide until the soldiers left the area because rumors had already circulated that men were being impressed into service if they were found by the Union forces.

General Smith was concerned with the actions of Union troops in Kentucky, especially those around Paducah, and in the area of the land between the rivers. In January 1862, General Smith expressed his concern over the "outrages committed by the men in the numbers of hogs and poultry killed." He suggested that more discipline be imposed upon the men. Brigade and regimental commanders ordered their men to stop stealing from civilians, but soldiers seemed to ignore the orders and continued to pillage and steal. When the complaints from the citizens continued, the Union army took action and arrested several men. It does not appear that the action taken by the Union officials diminished the looting in the area.[80]

Some people, mostly women and children, were leaving the area by January of 1862. They were afraid that they were too close to both forts. They realized that they would undoubtedly be caught between two armies when the fighting started because any confrontation erupting between Union and Confederate forces meant a move across the land between the rivers. These people wanted to move out of the area and find a refuge with relatives or friends in other parts of the country. Loyalties to the North or South did not seem to matter at this point. They were trying to protect themselves. Quite often, it was a matter of finding anyone who would allow them to visit for an undesignated period of time. The very poor did not have

---

[78]General Services School, Fort Henry and Fort Donelson, 108, 109, 110.

[79]Ibid.

[80]Ibid., 212-230.

the resources to leave the area, and some people did not have relatives or friends who would take then in. Some people simply chose not to leave.[81]

On January 7, 1862, Lieutenant S. L. Phelps, Commander of the U. S. gunboat "Conestoga" sent a reconnaissance report to his superiors in Paducah. In the report, he described his activities on January 6, 1862 as follows:

Sir:

Yesterday I ascended the Tennessee River to the state line, returning in the night. The rebels are industriously perfecting their means of defense both at Dover and Fort Henry. At Fort Donelson they have placed obstructions in the river 1 and one-half miles below their battery, on the left bank in the bend where the battery comes in sight. These obstructions consist of trees chained together and sunk across the river with the butts upstream, the heads floating near the surface, and are pointed. They have four 32 S mounted on the hill, and a large force of negroes at work.[82]

In the same report, he mentioned that several hundred blacks were counted working at the fortifications at Fort Henry.

While Lieutenant Phelps was watching the construction of the fortifications at Fort Henry and Fort Donelson, the Confederates were planning to block access to the Tennessee and Cumberland Rivers by sinking old boats in each channel. Lieutenant Phelps had underestimated the number of black workers involved in construction of the fortifications. About five hundred to six hundred additional slave workers had reached the area in January of 1862. These men had been put to work building log huts and the breastworks around Fort Donelson. The workers were not visible from the Cumberland River. General Johnston had to insist vigorously that the extra labor force was needed, because those slaves involved in the iron industry were sorely needed there; furthermore, the iron production had to be increased as quickly as possible.[83] The owners of the iron industries were quite willing to continue their production. Later after the Union forces overran the area, some of these men swore that they had tried to stop the production of iron in order to handicap the Confederate military. All the military and county records indicate that none of the men had any moral trepidations about assisting the Confederacy.[84]

John W. Murphy was at Fort Donelson on January 27, and wrote to a friend about the his life at the fort:

After we eat our breakfast, myself and John Benton went to look at our fortifications and you may be sure it was something new to me and I would be glad you could hear and see how they are construct. They are formed by a deep ditch about 8 feet deep, and an embankment about 10 feet wide and about every 50 yards or 100 yards a big cannon was

---

[81]Stewart County Court records mention that some citizens would like to leave the area. In this same book, some loose leaf notes dated 1862 are included but not signed. There are notations about people wanting to leave for Kentucky. See Book 63: 44.

[82]O. R. Series I, vol. V, 121.

[83]Ibid., 121-149.

[84]Cooling, Forts, 121.

110

planted in the embankment and whar our company is stationed ther is a 32 pounder planted about 20 feet and one 128 pounder. We fired 4 cannon this evening and anyone had have told me that I could have seen the ball I would have told them it was not so. But I could see the ball so plane as you see a bird flying.[85]

One of the soldiers who was assiduously digging trenches at Fort Donelson was determined not to appear fatigued. The motive was neither an attempt to impress the officer in charge of the detail nor an endeavor to demonstrate physical prowess. The soldier was afraid to admit that the work was extremely difficult, because to complain would mean that the other soldiers would pay more attention to the amount of strain the soldier was under.

This particular individual did not want to be observed too closely because someone might guess that the soldier was a woman disguised as a man. The soldier, Loreta Velasquez, had come to Fort Donelson as a part of Brigadier General Pillow's force, and she hated digging trenches. The story of how she came to Fort Donelson is not an easy one to tell because historians have been unable to piece together all the details, but by putting bits and pieces of evidence together, some of the story can be told.[86]

Loreta Velasquez was born in Cuba where her father held a diplomatic post. She lived in Mexico and the British West Indies before she moved to New Orleans to attend a school conducted by the Sisters of Charity. She learned to speak English as fluently as Spanish and French. Before she turned fourteen, Loreta Velasquez married a young American Army officer whom she referred to as William. There is no record of the man's last name.[87]

By 1860 when she was eighteen, she had three children, all of whom had died. When the Civil War broke out, Loreta Velasquez was determined to be a soldier, and she had no intentions of becoming a mere private in rank. The best way in those days to obtain a commission was to raise a troop of soldiers, which was not too difficult to do if you had money. Loreta Velasquez had plenty of money and she raised the troop and emerged from the recruiting office in New Orleans as Lieutenant Henry T. Buford of the Independent Scouts.[88]

At that time in the Confederate Armies of the South regular troops and volunteers had not become assimilated. The regular soldiers tended to scoff at the undisciplined volunteers, but they were probably a little jealous of the freedom given them. Loreta Velasquez as a volunteer officer classified herself as a guerrilla.[89]

She had her chance at front line action in the first Battle of Bull Run, July 20, 1861. She was attached to the command of Brigadier General Bernard Bee who appeared to want to enter

---

[85]Stewart-Houston Times, February 10, 1965. The letter was printed in an article about Fort Donelson.

[86]John Laffin, Women In Battle (New York: Abelard-Shuman) 123-132. See also Sheila Rowbotham, Hidden From History: Rediscovering Women in History From the 17th Century to the Present (New York: Pantheon Books), 212. Jeanne Holm, Women in the Military: An Unfinished Revolution (Novato, California: Presidio Press), 5-7.

[87]Ibid.

[88]Ibid.

[89]Ibid.

battle as much as she. Immediately after the battle, Loreta Velasquez asked for a promotion which was refused. Offended, she summoned her servant and rode off to Richmond. She was sure that opportunities for advancement could be found there.[90]

She was anxious to get to Richmond because she had developed a plan which she wanted to present to the Confederate leaders. When she encountered some difficulty in presenting her plan, she found a billet for her servant in Leesburg, Virginia and told him to keep a low profile until she returned. She disguised herself in a calico dress, woolen shawl, sunbonnet, and rough shoes and bribed a boatman to ferry her across the Potomac River to the Maryland side. She was now in enemy territory without any contacts. She rode to Washington D. C. and took a room at Browne's Hotel.[91]

She was pretty and also charming enough to attract the attention of Union officers. Talking and flirting with the soldiers, she was able to gather information. Within a few days, she had reached the conclusion that the Union intended to capture the Upper Mississippi River and to blockade the mouth of the river at New Orleans.

Thirteen days after leaving Virginia she was back. She had no trouble at all in crossing the Union and Confederate lines, either going or coming. By begging, bluffing, and buying her way, she was able to get into the Army Headquarters at Leesburg and present her information. The officers thanked her politely and warned her of the dangers of espionage. Loreta Velasquez was furious at her treatment, but she reminded herself that she was dealing with dull men.[92]

She decided to transfer her allegiance to the Army of Tennessee and with a forged letter of introduction presented herself as Lieutenant Buford to Lieutenant General Leonidas Polk. She was just settling into her duties when word was received from General Simon Bolivar Buckner, the commander at Fort Donelson, that reinforcements were needed. Loreta Velasquez was sent as a part of Brigadier General Pillow's force to reinforce Fort Donelson.[93]

On the stormy night of February 13, 1862, Loreta Velasquez volunteered to take another officer's tour of duty in the outpost line at Fort Donelson. That night the Union forces attacked the fort. For forty-eight hours the fighting went on almost continuously in sleet, snow, and violent wind.[94]

The Union drive was spent when General Pillow led about 11,000 men--including at least one woman--in a massive seven-hour counter-attack to break through the Union line. The Confederate force pushed the Union forces back, but General Pillow gave the order to retreat to the original position.[95]

Surrender was discussed but some of the officers did not want to remain at the fort.

---

[90]Ibid.

[91]Ibid.

[92]Ibid.

[93]Ibid.

[94]Ibid.

[95]Ibid.

With some two thousand soldiers, Loreta Velasquez left Fort Donelson and marched toward Clarksville. During the retreat, Loreta Velasquez was accidentally shot in the foot. Even though the wound was not dangerous, she was ordered to see a doctor. Knowing that a doctor would discover her disguise, she decided to ride off to New Orleans.[96]

Staying in New Orleans to convalesce turned out to be a very bad idea. In a very short time, people became suspicious of the young army officer who lived privately. The young man should be in the military. An officer arrived at her door one day to ask her to accompany him to the provost-marshal's headquarters. She was suspected of being a Union spy. Loreta Velasquez talked her way out of the charge, but as she was leaving the headquarters, she was arrested again. This time the charge was that she was a woman masquerading as an officer. She was taken to a Dr. Root at the Charity Hospital in New Orleans for an examination. Knowing that she would be found out, she confessed and explained her activities in the army. To her disgust, she was sentenced to ten days in jail and a fine of ten dollars.[97]

Loreta Velasquez was not yet ready to sit home and wait for interesting things to find her. Within days after her release from jail, she dressed in male civilian clothes and enlisted in the Twenty-first Louisiana Regiment, but she soon decided that she did not like the infantry. Since she still had her original documents of commission, she wrote to the army of East Tennessee requesting an appointment as a cavalry officer. She received her appointment.[98]

Loreta Velasquez had finally found the assignment she had desired. Leading patrols was dangerous, exciting, and challenging--all the ingredients which made life interesting for Loreta Velasquez. One day while leading a small scouting patrol, she came under routine unaimed enemy artillery fire. A shell burst overhead, killing one man and badly wounding Loreta in the shoulder and right arm. She led her patrol out of the area and back to camp. Her wounds were too serious for her to retain her command and she was put on a hospital train. The train was delayed at Corinth, Mississippi where doctors came aboard to treat the serious cases.[99]

The doctor who stopped at Loreta's berth soon discovered that she was female. Not be deterred, Loreta Velasquez convinced the doctor that he must keep her secret. Not only did he not report her, he found quarters for her in Corinth. He later arranged for movement orders for her to Louisiana. Thus, Loreta Velasquez ended her military career.[100]

Were there other women fighting at Fort Donelson and in other battles of the Civil War? The answer is unknown, but a good guess is that Loreta Velasquez was not the only female who refused to wait at home for the husband, father, brother, or son who had gone off to fight. Throughout American history, women have become actively involved in the military defense of the country. Those females who disguised themselves as men in order to fight have been the most difficult to trace.

---

[96]Ibid.

[97]Ibid.

[98]Ibid.

[99]Ibid.

[100]Ibid.

Most of the soldiers at Fort Henry and Fort Donelson were inexperienced male recruits. They had never been in combat, and they were not inclined to take orders. Awestruck by the new and exciting life in the army, they were boisterous and undisciplined. Control was very difficult, if not impossible at times, to maintain. Soldiers wandered in and out of the forts at will. The new life with the exciting possibilities of battle caused many of the soldiers to disregard any concern for the citizens of the area. A general sense of fear and anticipation resulted in a peculiar disregard for common values.[101]

As the cannons boomed and the rifle shots resounded through the hills, the people became even more terrified. As mentioned before, some people had left to live with relatives and friends in other parts of the country, but many families either did not desire to leave or had no family members who were willing to take them in; thus, many civilians were forced by circumstances to remain in the area. They could do little, if anything, to protect themselves from the confrontation that would surely come. The only course of action was to try and arm themselves to fight or to hide in the woods if any strangers appeared in the vicinity.

Around the fires and dining tables, people told stories of the horrors that could be expected from those fiends wearing Union uniforms. The general fears intensified when the people realized that the very large slave population, now housed in the area, might be encouraged and even assisted by Union soldiers to attack the white people. They were sure the slaves would attack if the opportunity presented itself. There is every reason to believe that the slaves were as afraid of the Union soldiers as the white citizens were. The slaves believed, because they had been told by the white people, that the Union troops would not hesitate to kill them. At this time, very few slaves were willing to jeopardize themselves and their family members by seeking sanctuary behind Union lines.[102]

Severe flooding presented another problem by January. The flood waters destroyed the use of the vaunted mines which had been laid in defense of the river. The mines were constructed of sheet-iron cylinders about five and one-half feet long and one foot in diameter. Each mine held seventy pounds of black powder and was anchored to the river bottom. A tipped rod from the top of the mine activated a musket lock that fired the weapon when a vessel brushed the rod. At least twenty of these mines had been placed in the river channel where Panther Island divided the river below Fort Henry and Fort Heiman. When the river rose to flood stage, the mines became useless. The men began a frantic attempt to lay more mines but they did not succeed.[103]

Even though the two men did not realize it, both General Halleck, Union Commander in the West, and General Grant had the idea that they should invade the Confederacy through the Tennessee and Cumberland.[104] Apparently the two men could not communicate even in

[101]Letters found in the Tennessee Civil War Collection in the Tennessee State Library and Archives in Nashville, Tennessee. The letter did not have an address and was signed John B.

[102]Joseph C. Carter, Magnolia Journey: A Union Veteran Revisited the Former Confederate States (University: University of Alabama Press, 1974), 170-90.

[103]Cooling, Forts, 213.

[104]O. R. Series I, vol. VII, 121-123, 149, 153-55, 843, 855.

person.

On January 30, Halleck ordered Grant who was at his Cairo headquarters to attack Fort Henry. Grant was surprised at the command because he had been led to believe that General Halleck did not support the plan.[105] Halleck ordered that the attack was to be a combined naval and ground assault under the commands of Foote and Grant. General Grant, anxious to move immediately, was ordered by Halleck to maintain absolute secrecy concerning the location of the target at Fort Henry. Grant instructed General John McClernand to ready the military personnel to travel light with rations for three days. Steamboats to transport 10,000 infantry, four artillery companies, equipment, and rations were to be made ready. Only thirteen steamers were drawn into service, including the "Aleck Scott," "Minnehan," "City of Memphis," "Chancellor," "Fanny Bullett," "Keystone," "Lake Erie," "Iatan," "Illinois," "D. A. January," "Wilson," "W. A. B.," and "Uncle Sam." The "Uncle Sam" was fitted as a headquarters boat. It was a difficult task finding these steamboats because the merchants were reluctant to turn them over to the military.[106]

Meanwhile, Flag Officer Andrew H. Foote was having great difficulty obtaining personnel for his naval vessels. With a good amount of grumbling and complaining about the quality of his recruits, he finally was ready with the "Cincinnati," "Essex," "Carondelete." "St. Louis," " Conestoga," "Tyler," and the "Lexington." When the expedition turned into the Tennessee River on February 6, 1862, the men realized that Fort Henry was the target. Until that time, absolute secrecy had been maintained.[107]

---

[105]Ibid.

[106]Cooling, Forts, 91.

[107]O. R. Series I, vol. XXII, 522-34.

CHAPTER VII

THE WAR COMES TO THE LAND
BETWEEN THE RIVERS

At daybreak on the morning of February 4, 1862, the people of the land between the rivers were truly alarmed when they sighted a number of Union gunboats and steamboats on the Tennessee River just below Fort Henry. They had no way of knowing that seven gunboats under the command of Flag Officer Andrew H. Foote and about 12,000 Federal troops under the command of General Ulysses S. Grant were approaching Fort Henry ready for an assault. Union gunboats had been observing the activities at Fort Henry for months and at first the people probably thought that the Union was once again spying on the fort.

The Union soldiers began going ashore on the east bank of the Tennessee River below Bailey's Ferry. General Grant did not know exactly where he wanted the men to land, but he attempted to move as close to the fort as possible. Both the gunboats and the transport vessels slowly moved up the Tennessee River.[1]

The Union men knew that the Confederate forces had attempted to mine the river, and they scrutinized the surface of the river looking for traps. Mines had been placed in the river, but the floodwater had forced them to the surface of the water making them harmless. As soon as the mines were noticed, the men on the gunboats and transport vessels fished them out of the water. The Confederate plan, which the Union forces knew about, was to sink old boats, barges, trees, and stretch heavy chains across the Tennessee and Cumberland to protect the forts, but the Confederates had only partially completed the task. The obstructions which had been laid were useless because the flood waters allowed the Union boats to pass over them.[2]

At 4:30 a.m. on February 6, Grant was still trying to decide where to off-load his men. He was wary of the gunners at Fort Henry, and he wanted to insure that his men were outside the range of fire. He halted the transport vessels just above Bailey's Ferry and boarded the "Essex" commanded by W. D. Porter to reconnoiter the river closer to Fort Henry. The "Essex" did not draw fire and proceeded slowly up the river. The gunboat drew even closer until it was about two and one-half miles below the fort. Suddenly, a twenty-four pounder shell passed over the heads of the officers and flattened trees on the opposite side of the river. In a matter of seconds another shell crashed through the stern deck and smashed into Porter's quarters. Grant and Porter could have easily been killed, and Grant decided to move all his men back to Bailey's Ferry.[3]

Brigadier General Tilghman, commander at Fort Henry, was not at the fort when the Federal Army came ashore. On the night of February 3, he and Colonel Gilmer had left Fort Henry to inspect the construction work at Fort Donelson. Colonel Heiman was in command at the fort, and he and his men sighted the Union activity below the fort and made a token effort

---

[1] O. R. Series I, vol. VII, 312.

[2] Ibid.

[3] O. R. Series I, vol. VII, 126.

to warn the enemy to keep their distance.[4]

When Heiman realized that the army was grouping at Bailey's Ferry, he sent a message to inform Tilghman of the danger. The message did not reach Tilghman until late in the evening, and by that time the men at Fort Donelson were aware that something was amiss because of the activity of the gun batteries. Tilghman did not reach Fort Henry until 11:30 P. M., and any opportunity to keep Grant's men from going ashore just two miles below the fort was lost.[5]

In the meantime, Heiman tried to manage the situation. He sent a steamboat to collect four hundred men at Paris Landing and Danville. He positioned some of the men at Fort Heiman and sent others to block the ford at Panther Creek and to guard the road leading inland for Bailey's Ferry to Boyd's house. The balance of the force was put to work to strengthen the rifle pits.[6]

When Tilghman reached Fort Henry, he called a meeting with his staff. After a short conference, he sent a message to General Johnston reaffirming his conviction that Fort Henry was capable of withstanding an attack. He ordered the evacuation of Fort Heiman leaving a battalion of Alabama cavalry and a spy company to halt the Union forces on the Fort Heiman side of the Tennessee River. Later that day, the officers and staff held another conference. They re-evaluated their position and agreed that Fort Henry would not be able to repel the Union gunboats. The problem was the backwater from the Tennessee River which had flowed into the fortifications. Tilghman waited to see what Grant planned to do.[7]

Grant was not having a very good time. Delays in putting his men ashore aggravated him, and he observed some of his men staggering down the ramps, drinking liquor which they had acquired during one of the stops for firewood.[8] He had more than adequate time to plan his attack, and ordered McClernand to take a position on Bailey's Ferry road and move to the Telegraph road which linked Fort Henry and Fort Donelson. McClernand was ordered to cut the telegraph lines and determine if Confederate forces were in the area. General Smith was ordered to take Fort Heiman and then move to reinforce McClernand.[9] Union and Confederate soldiers were anxious about the inactivity. The atmosphere in both camps was one of dread and anticipation. It was obvious that a fight was coming, and the men hated the delay. Snow and heavy rains had turned the lowlands along the river into a quagmire, and it was impossible to find dry land for a camp. Union soldiers had consumed their rations and were hungry. The day took on a dreamlike quality when the Union regimental bands began playing "Yankee Doodle,"

---

[4]Ibid., 153.

[5]O. R. Series I, vol. VII, 124-125.

[6]Ibid.

[7]Cooling, Forts, 121.

[8]Ibid.

[9]O. R. Series I, vol. VIII, 125-26.

"Hail Columbia," "Star Spangled Banner," and "St Patrick's Day in the Morning."[10]

Fort Henry

At 10:20 A. M. on February 6, Foote was ready to begin the attack. He notified Grant and then waited thirty minutes, but he did not hear from Grant. Foote decided to begin the attack whether Grant's men were ready or not. The boats moved through the Panther Island chute and formed into divisional lines without mishap. Foote formed his vessels into two lines, the ironclad "Cincinnati," the "Carondelet," the "Essex," and the "St. Louis" forming a front rank. Slowly and cautiously the boats approached the fort, firing as they went, the guns on the parapet answering those of the fleet. Shots were exchanged for over an hour.[11]

At 12:30 the gunboats moved forward and the guns at the fort commenced firing. For over an hour the battle raged. Cannon balls decapitated sailors and exploded boilers. The scalding steam killed and seriously wounded any sailors near the boiler explosions. The "Essex" was disabled and drifted out of the battle line. At the zenith of the battle, the twenty-four pounder rifle in Fort Henry burst. Within a few minutes, the Columbiad was spiked when a priming rod bent, and at least two of the thirty-two pounders were disabled.[12]

The moment of truth had arrived. The Confederates had to decide whether or not they could defend the fort against the Union guns. Both Heiman and Gilmer expressed the opinion that Tilghman should surrender the fort, but Haynes opposed the surrender. Tilghman hesitated until 2:00 P.M. because he did not want the reputation of giving up the fight.[13]

Heiman and Gilmer had already announced that they intended to retreat to Fort Donelson. Tilghman agreed that Heiman should lead the main Confederate force of approximately 3,000 men to Fort Donelson. Fifty-four men of Company B of the First Tennessee Artillery remained at Fort Henry to provide time for the men to evacuate the fort.[14]

Tilghman carried a white flag onto the parapet to signal the Union boats, but Foote could not see the flag because the smoke from the battle was so heavy. Tilghman then ordered his men to lower the Confederate flag which was flying over the fort. As the flag was lowered,

---

[10]Ibid.,138-39, 153-54, 858-59. On February 6, Grant had approximately 12,000 soldiers below Fort Henry. The following complement was present: thirty-seven regiments and one company of infantry; eight artillery batteries; two cavalry regiments, and four independent companies. Tilghman had between 2,700 and 3,300 men organized into six infantry regiments plus a battalion, three batteries of light and heavy artillery, two battalions and one company, and miscellaneous cavalry.

[11]Ibid., Cooling, Forts, 102-132.

[12]Ibid., O. R. Series I, vol. VII, 129, 134, 140, 144, 151.

[13]Cooling, Forts, 116; O. R. Series I, vol. XII, 122-23.

[14]Ibid.

Foote realized that the Confederate forces were ready to surrender.[15] The navy took Tilghman and his men captive.

To Grant's consternation and to Foote's delight, Fort Henry was a naval victory. Grant and his men arrived at the fort after the Confederate force had surrendered. Gleefully, Andrew Foote sent a message to the Union commanders announcing that he had turned the captured installation over to Grant after his naval victory, and he was returning to Cairo with his gunboats.[16]

Later, Grant explained that he had been late in arriving at Fort Henry because his men had been bogged down in the slush, mud, and backwater and could not travel fast enough to coordinate with Foote. Indeed the delay had kept the army from participating in the battle of Fort Henry, but it had also allowed some 3,000 Confederate soldiers to retreat and strengthen the force at Fort Donelson.[17]

The outcome of the battle at Fort Henry affected Grant's reputation. General Halleck, Grant's immediate superior, was not pleased with the fact that the navy received recognition for the defeat at the Confederate fort. In his opinion, Grant had delayed his orders and had allowed the navy to trounce the army. Halleck had never been pleased that Grant was the commander of the army, and he was involved in a series of manipulations to replace Grant. Rumors about Grant's drinking problem emerged once again, and the word spread that Grant was drunk and did not properly lead his men. Absolutely no evidence has been found to authenticate these charges.[18]

During the battle at Fort Henry, the civilians were extremely anxious. Some people took their personal belongings and fled the area. They were not really sure of their destination, but they wanted to run. These people tried to find a boat that was going upstream. If they did not have the money to pay their passage by water, they traveled on horses, by wagon, and on foot. Those people who remained in the area went into hiding in the wooded areas. From the requests sent to the Union officers from the civilians, it appears that the civilian population expected massive retribution.[19]

Almost immediately after the Union soldiers arrived below Fort Henry, they began to pilfer and loot the countryside. The actions of the soldiers were so obviously destructive that

---

[15]Ibid. The white flag used at Fort Henry was a bed sheet. When Tilghman called for the flag, none could be found. Soldiers found a white sheet for him to use.

[16]O. R. Series II, vol.III, 542.

[17]Grant, Memoirs, 182; General Services School, Fort Henry and Fort Donelson, 235-245; O. R. Series I, vol. 7, 274, 275.; Edwin C. Bearss, "Unconditional Surrender," (Washington D.C.: U. S. Department of the Interior, 1960), 88. A copy of this article can be obtained at Fort Donelson Military Park, Dover, Tennessee.

[18]Ibid.

[19]Conclusion based on letter written to Nathan Brandon from his parents, and the notations in the O. R. about the battle. The Brandon letters and notes are in the hands of the Brandon family in Stewart County.

General Grant issued a command to protect the lives and property of the citizens.[20]

General Field Order No. 5, issued by Jonathan A. Rawlins, Assistant Adjutant General, on February 9, 1862 from Fort Henry for the District of Cairo, ordered that brigade commanders would be held accountable for the conduct of their brigades, regimental commanders would be responsible for their regiments and company commanders would be responsible for their companies. The order admonished the officers to make examples of those men who disobeyed the orders and cautioned the men about their deportment. They were reminded that they were now in enemy country and they should be careful not to convince the enemy that the causes of the Union forces were not just. The order expressed great surprise that "men can be found so wanton as to destroy, pillage, and burn indiscriminately, without inquiry."[21] The official orders were read to the troops. For a time, the orders seemed to diminish the more conspicuous acts of destruction. In a matter of a few days, however, soldiers had begun to ignore the directives.[22]

The land between the rivers appeared uninhabited, and when the Union army went through the countryside looking for black workers, slaves or freedmen, for assignment at Fort Henry, none could be found. Grant wrote to his headquarters: "There are no Negroes in this part of the country to work on the fortification."[23] Grant soon realized that the blacks had been moved behind the Confederate lines above Fort Donelson.

In their hasty retreat from Fort Henry to Fort Donelson, the Confederate soldiers had neglected to carry away a quantity of supplies that had just reached the fort. When Federal soldiers occupied the area, they found tents and camp equipment along with 2,500 bushels of wheat, large quantities of corn and about 200 hogsheads of tobacco that farmers in the area had brought to Fort Henry for shipment to markets or for use by the Confederate military.[24]

With the news of the attack and fall of Fort Henry, the people working at Fort Donelson began a feverish attempt to get every available person to help in the completion of the defenses around Fort Donelson. Workmen cut more trees around the perimeter of the fortification making it more difficult for the enemy to approach the outer breastworks undetected. The branches of the trees were left in a tangled mass in order to further impede the advancing enemy.

---

[20]One of the most unruly groups with Grant's forces were the Jesse Scouts. They caused so much trouble that Grant ordered McClernand to ship them back to Cairo.

[21]O. R. Series II, vol. 3, 401.

[22]From February 10th until the Union army left the area, complaints were filed with the Union army and reproduced in the O. R. files. For example see Series II, vol. 3, 507.

[23]O. R. Series II, vol. 3, 602; General Services School, Fort Henry and Fort Donelson, 355, 521.

[24]General Services School, Fort Henry and Fort Donelson, 358-360.

Fort Donelson

Fort Donelson had two batteries of thirteen guns facing the Cumberland River. At the crest of the bluff above the river, a big rifled gun and two cannonades were trained on the water. Halfway down the hillside toward the river the batteries included a ten-inch columbine and eight smoothbore thirty-two pound guns. Each of the guns was protected by hastily constructed earthworks. At the top of the hill the main portion of Fort Donelson had been constructed of irregular earthworks enclosing about fifteen acres of land. Rows of twenty-five to thirty crude log huts, built by slaves and the men of Tilghman's garrison, were strung along the edge of the hill.[25]

Military reinforcements, arriving at Fort Donelson daily, came ashore at Dover, which then consisted of a court house, a two-story tavern, a jail, and some twenty houses scattered about the river landing. As the reinforcements arrived with their officers, the command at Fort Donelson was transferred to the ranking officer. At the time that Fort Henry surrendered, there were some 18,000 men under the command of General John B. Floyd, late Secretary of War in the cabinet of James Buchanan. In ranking order under his command were Generals Pillow, Buckner, Bushrod Johnson, and Colonel Nathan B. Forrest.[26] [See Fig. 4]

Pillow and Colonel Gilmer worked night and day trying to complete the defenses at Fort Donelson. They were attempting to complete the construction before Union troops could make their way to the fort. The outer defenses of Fort Donelson were constructed primarily as field support for the water batteries because a Union attack by land had not been expected. At this point they realized that the fall of Fort Henry would allow the Federal troops to march the twelve miles overland to Fort Donelson.

The leaders at Fort Donelson were counting on the rugged terrain between Fort Henry and Fort Donelson to hinder the Union march. The area was principally a chain of deeply wooded hills and ridges with deep gullies and hollows. At that time of the year, many of the gullies and the low lands were filled with backwater, and as expected, the Union soldiers had a difficult time marching over the terrain.

Colonel Gilmer had positioned rifle pits along the ridges west and back of the fortifications to enable his soldiers to observe and respond to any attack from that direction. The pits followed the crest of the hill to the southward edge of the fortification and then they curved back across the Charlotte Road to the Cumberland River above Dover. Just north of Dover, Hickman Creek flowed into the Cumberland, and to the south of Dover, Indian and Lick Creeks emptied into the Cumberland River.

The Confederates knew that all the creeks had overflowed their banks and water was backing into the low fields. One problem was the possibility that the rising waters would cut off the right wing of the Confederate fortification from the main battlements. General Floyd also believed that the flood waters could surround the fort and close any escape route out of the

---

[25]Cooling, <u>Forts</u>, 122.

[26]Ibid.

121

area.[27]

When Floyd had arrived from Clarksville to take his command, his officers were informed that a meeting must be held to plan and prepare for the Union attack. Even as Floyd discussed his arrangements for a meeting, an advance Union force was arriving at Fort Donelson.[28]

The Union army under Grant was divided under the respective commands of Generals Smith, McClernand, and Lew Wallace. Smith and McClernand marched across country and arrived at the fort during the night of February 12 and the morning of the 13th. Smith stationed his men on the left while McClernand moved his men to the extreme right, near the town of Dover. Wallace was expected to move his men into the open space in the center. The firing began on February 13th while Floyd was involved in the meeting with his commanders.[29] [Fig. 4]

Floyd demonstrated that he had little inherent aptitude in ascertaining and calculating a strategy for repulsing an offensive force. He did not send men to determine the approximate number of Union soldiers under Grant's command. Even though there were rumors that Grant was waiting for at least 20,000 soldiers to arrive from Paducah, Floyd made no attempt to determine the truth of the rumors. From his actions, it appears that he believed the rumors. Floyd was more than a little concerned about the outcome of the attack because he was under indictment by a federal grand jury, accused of stockpiling weapons in southern fortifications while he was serving as Secretary of War with James Buchanan. Floyd was convinced that he would be hanged if he were captured by the Union forces. His actions during the battle at Fort Donelson indicate that above all else he did not want to be captured.[30]

Years later, when Grant reflected on the events of February 1862, he commented that General Johnston had made a fatal mistake when he gave the command of Fort Donelson to Floyd, "who he must have known was no soldier even if he possessed the elements of one."[31] General Grant's hindsight should be taken for what it is worth. At the time he wrote his memoirs, Grant was no longer considered a powerful public figure. His attitude toward the battle at Fort Donelson was affected by the criticism he had suffered immediately after the battle. It is true that Floyd lacked experience, and he was at a tremendous disadvantage when he took command at Fort Donelson. He did not seem to comprehend the verity that the fort was in an excellent defensive position. He was never able to judge the fighting capabilities of the men under his command. He seemed to believe that it was only a matter of time before Fort Donelson would have to surrender. To say the least, Floyd was indecisive and lacked the

---

[27]Ibid.,126.

[28]O. R. Series I, vol. VII, 168. Floyd had approximately 15,000 to 21,000 men at Donelson. The complement included twenty-seven infantry regiments plus one battalion and two companies, nine artillery batteries, and two cavalry regiments plus one battalion.

[29]Grant had approximately 25,000 men under his command on February 16, and more recruits were arriving daily.

[30]Cooling, Forts, 137.

[31]Grant, Personal Memoirs, 189.

conviction that the fortification could or even should be held against the Union assault.

Later, military historians concluded that the loss of Fort Henry and Fort Donelson fatally crippled the Confederacy.[32] Under great duress, Floyd was trying to comprehend the scope and magnitude of his command. In the meantime, Grant ordered his men to gain control of the road which linked Fort Henry to Fort Donelson. For the most part, the road led along the ridges through densely wooded hills. It was no more than a cart path which twisted and turned through the steep hills and deep valleys. The area was densely wooded and thinly populated. The water-logged hillsides turned into mud pits as soon as Union soldiers began their march. As the army marched, the ruts and mud became almost impassable.[33]

On February 6 and 7, Grant and Foote designed their combined assault on Fort Donelson. Foote's gunboats were to move from the Tennessee to the Ohio and then advance up the Cumberland to assist Grant's attack. Grant was to move his men overland from Fort Henry to Fort Donelson and be in position to attack when Foote's gunboats arrived. The gunboats reached Fort Donelson on February 14, but Grant's army had already made initial contact with the Confederate forces.[34]

A reporter for the Chicago Tribune was aboard one of the gunboats as it travelled from Eddyville to Fort Donelson. The reporter described the actions of the people of the land between the rivers as they assembled on the banks of the river to watch the gunboats go by. Some of the people were waving U. S. flags and cheering the Union gunboats onward, while the others stood in sullen silence. Once again, the people were making choices about which side they would support[35]

As the Union troops marched over the hills and gullies the weather grew quite warm. The temperature climbed to about seventy degrees. Most of the Union soldiers, thinking they were truly in the South, threw away their extra coats and blankets. As the day grew warmer, men threw away any extra clothing, and any heavy articles in their packs.[36]

The skirmish on February 13 between the advancing Union force and the men positioned on the outer edge of the defense works had lasted only a few hours. The chief action involved the attempt to capture a battery on a hill, near the center of the Confederate line, known as Maney's Battery, commanded by Captain Maney of Tennessee. This battery had annoyed General McClernand greatly, and he delegated his third brigade to capture it. The charge was led by Colonel Morrison and his men from Illinois. As they ran up the hill, firing as they went, their numbers were rapidly thinned by the paralyzing cross fire from this battery and two others

---

[32]For further discussions of the Civil War see Allan Nevin's The War for the Union, 4 vols. (New York: Scriber,1959) or the works of Bruce Catton including Mr. Lincoln's Army (Garden City, New York: Doubleday , 1951). David Donald, ed., Why the North Won the Civil War (Baton Rouge: Louisiana State University Press, 1960) is a fine collection of essays analyzing the differences in resources, tactics, and morale.

[33]O. R. Series I, vol. VII, 159.

[34]Ibid., 135-38.

[35]O. R. Series II, vol. IV, 192.

[36]Cooling, Forts, 139.

on adjoining hills. They came within forty yards of the goal and suddenly near the battery, a barrage of bullets from Confederate muskets stopped the assault. The dry leaves caught fire, and Union soldiers, impeded by the smoke, retreated.[37]

As the Union forces ended their march and assumed the attack position, the weather became a vicious enemy. The weather turned colder: it began to rain and the cold, misty rain turned into sleet, then into a heavy rain. The temperature dropped and the rain turned into ice and snow. In the below freezing weather, soldiers who had discarded their coats and blankets during the march were in danger of frostbite. They could not build fires because their encampment was too close to the Confederate rifle pits. Confederate snipers could pick off any soldier who built even the smallest fire. Some of the men burned ropes, which would smolder and produce heat with little light to keep their fingers and toes from freezing. When the morning came, the soldiers were extremely cold, hungry, uncomfortable, and ill.[38]   On the morning of February 14, Foote's gunboats were within range of the guns at Fort Donelson. The "St. Louis" serving as the flag ship led the way followed by the "Louisville," the "Carondelet," and the "Pittsburg." Following his concept of a precise naval strategy, Foote ordered the gunboats to commence firing when they were about a mile below the fortifications. As the gunboats pushed forward, they were to continue firing until they were within a hundred and fifty yards of the Confederate batteries. When the Confederate soldiers returned the fire, the Columbian and the rifled guns proved to be formidable weapons against the gunboats.[39]

Within a short time, the "St. Louis" had been hit fifty-nine times, the pilot house taking a direct hit. The wheel of Foote's flagship was blown away by the direct hit and the pilot was killed. Foote was severely wounded in the leg, but continued the order that the gunboats move forward and maintain a constant barrage of fire. After firing for more than an hour, all the gunboats had sustained extensive damage. When Foote gave the order to withdraw, he was injured and fifty-four of his men were either dead or severely wounded.[40]

There were no casualties among the men at Fort Donelson nor had the gun batteries been seriously damaged. Foote, who had hoped to win another naval victory, was thwarted by the expert use and position of the gun batteries. The guns, positioned on the bluff overlooking the narrow river, were able to disable the boats and destroy Foote's strategy.

The Confederate gunners, even though they had never been in a battle, were able to manage the guns quite effectively. They often exhibited a courage and reason which many untrained soldiers would not have been able to summon under fire. During the battle, the guns often jammed, and the gunners had to ram a rod into the cannon to clear the barrel. The Confederate gunners did not let a jammed barrel stop them. On several occasions, they were

---

[37]Ibid.

[38]Ibid.

[39]Ibid.

[40]Ibid., O. R. Series I, vol. VII, 432. Foote was standing next to a sailor who was decapitated by a shell. The decks of the gunboats were slick with blood.

exposed to enemy fire when they repaired their guns.[41]

Grant's army did not commence a major offensive when Foote's gunboats began firing. No explanation was ever given as to why he did not follow the coordinated plan of attack. Many years later, Grant wrote that Foote began the attack before he notified the army of his plans. Grant accused Foote of trying to claim another naval victory. From Foote's messages immediately after the battle, it is clear that he was outraged that Grant had not cooperated and his strategy had not resulted in a Union victory.[42]

On the night of February 14, the Confederate staff planned the deployment of men for the battle which they anticipated the next morning. The official consensus was that the Confederate army would attack the Union line. Pillow was to advance toward and break the line that was under the command of General McClernand. Buckner assumed command of the area from Hickman Creek to Indian Creek, and the area from Indian Creek to the Charlotte road was under the command of Pillow and Bushrod Johnson.[43]

Pillow began his advance at 5:00 a.m. on February 15. The Union troops, anticipating an attack sometime the next day, had made hasty preparations by throwing up earthworks to provide as much protection as possible. The Confederate soldiers, carrying shotguns and squirrel rifles, moved silently toward the enemy line. They had to be within very close range in order to achieve accuracy with their weapons. The wild terrain provided excellent cover for the Confederate forces who were able to come near enough to the Union line to rain deadly fire on the sleeping enemy. The Union forces were not ready for any attack at 5:00 a.m., and much less prepared to resist the ferocious unseen enemy. The troops scattered and the officers were unable to maintain control.[44]

Nathan B. Forrest and his men worked their way around the Union right flank and moved to the rear. When a break opened in the Union line occupied by Oglesby's Illinois Brigade, Colonel Forrest led a spectacular charge straight into the wavering line. Terror and pandemonium broke out among the Union soldiers near the Confederate charge.[45]

At the same time, Pillow's forces broke through the Union line. The Union forces were in a general chaos as the day came to an end. Grant had arrived on the scene at about three o'clock in the afternoon, but he had not been able to halt the retreat of his soldiers. Where had Grant been when the Confederate force broke through his line? His absence is a mystery.[46]

McClernand had sent a courier to Wallace asking for aid when the Confederate force broke through his lines, but Wallace was unable to send reinforcements because he could not find Grant. Earlier, Grant had issued an order that no commander was to make a move without

---

[41]Ibid.

[42]Grant, Personal Memoirs, 200; O. R. Series I, vol. 1, 206.

[43]O. R. Series I, vol. VIII, 432.

[44]Ibid., 346-47.

[45]Ibid., 349.

[46]Ibid.

further orders from him, and then he had left the field. Later, when Grant was questioned about his absence, he declared that he was in a meeting with Foote. There is no reason to doubt Grant's veracity, but since that day he has stood in the shadow of the rumor that he was drinking when he should have been on the battlefield with his troops.[47]

As darkness descended, Pillow ordered the Confederate forces to fall back to their original positions within the earthworks at Fort Donelson. The advantages the Confederate forces had gained that day were lost. No explanation was ever given to explain why General Pillow was ordered to retreat, thereby losing the advantages he had won. The supposition is that Floyd had believed the rumors that Grant had been reinforced by several thousand troops on February 15. He was convinced that the Confederates would not be able to withstand a counterattack on February 16.

The effects of the battles at Fort Henry and Fort Donelson were to remain with the people for generations. The death and devastation was evident any way one looked. Men and animals were strewn over the ground, and the realities of war had come to the region. Eyewitnesses made comments about the odor coming from the dead animals. Little was being done to clean the area.[48]

One rather extraordinary woman helped to alleviate some of the misery for the sick and wounded men at Fort Donelson. When the war began, Mary Ann Bickerdyke had come on her own initiative to work at the smallpox hospital in Cairo. She was determined to improve the sanitary conditions in the Union hospital.[49]

Mary Ann Bickerdyke was a widow in Galesburg, Illinois when she heard of the deplorable conditions in the Union army hospitals in Cairo. With five hundred dollars from her church congregation, she came to Cairo to help the sick and wounded soldiers. She started by washing and scrubbing everything in sight, thereby antagonizing the entire hospital staff. The military personnel complained to General Grant, but he was hesitant to interfere with Bickerdyke because she was such an impressive woman who got the job done.[50]

When the expedition to Fort Donelson was announced, Bickerdyke decided to follow the army to the battlefield. Without asking for authorization, she came to Fort Donelson on February 16 with the hospital ship, the "City of Memphis." She waited all night for the military to bring the wounded to the ship, but none came.[51]

Field hospitals, spotted here and there over the hillsides, were nothing more than abandoned farmhouses or crude shelters. She was told that army surgeons and doctors could

---

[47]Cooling, Forts, 236. John Allen Wyeth, That Devil Forrest: Life of General Nathan Bedford Forrest, 231.

[48]Ibid.

[49]For more information on the details of the services of Mary Ann Bickerdyke see: Nina Brown Baker, Cyclone in Calico (Boston: Little Brown and Company, 1952). Julia A. Chase, Mary A. Bickerdyke, "Mother" (Lawrence Kansas: Journal Publishing House, 1896). Florence S. Kellogg, Mother Bickerdyke as I Knew Her (Chicago: Unity Publishing Company, 1907).

[50]Baker, Cyclone in Calico, 12-34.

[51]Ibid., 34.

not treat all the men who needed their help. Surgeons were amputating frozen arms and legs, but men were bleeding to death before the doctors could get to them, and wounded soldiers were still on the battlefield.[52]

The next morning, some of the wounded were brought to the hospital ship in farm carts and Bickerdyke went to work. She washed and clothed the men and fed them soup. To the wounded and dying, she was like the mothers they had once had. It was during this time, that the men began to refer to her as "Mother." From that day forward, she was known as Mother Bickerdyke.[53]

Learning first hand from the men that many wounded soldiers were still on the battlefield impelled her into action. She was told that some of the men had frozen to the ground and were too weak to cry out for help when the medics came by. The officers assured her that all the wounded had been found, but she was not sure the report was correct. Without authorization, she decided to go herself and check the area. With only a lantern, she walked from one field hospital to another checking the bodies on the battlefield to see if any wounded men were there among the dead. She found several.[54]

Mother Bickerdyke had problems with the doctors in every army hospital where she worked. She often had to disobey a direct order in her effort to help the sick and wounded, but she did not let any of these problems deter her from her mission. She followed the Union army to the battlefields at Shiloh and Chickamauga, and overcoming angry protests from the military, she accompanied General Sherman on his march to the sea.[55]

Many other women came to the battlefields to help the soldiers through the bloody years of the war. The names of these women were never recorded in the chronicles of the Civil War. They saved lives and mourned the dead, and waited for the madness to end.

On the evening of February 15, General Floyd called his staff together and initiated a discussion on the next course of action. He began the deliberation even before all of his officers were present. The officers who were present agreed that Grant would launch a massive attack as soon as he had regrouped his men. Floyd introduced the suggestion that the fort should surrender. The suggestion seemed to take everyone by surprise. Floyd had obviously considered surrender for some time. Before the meeting, he had sent a wire to Johnston saying, "The fort can not hold out twenty minutes."[56] Forrest, who had arrived late to the staff meeting, found the officers discussing the possibility of surrender. He angrily denounced the plan, stating emphatically that he would not allow his men to surrender. Initially several of the officers spoke against surrender. After a time the officers, except Forrest, seemed to agree with Floyd that Fort Donelson could not withstand an assault by the superior Union forces, and it was

---

[52]Ibid.

[53]Ibid., 35-40.

[54]Ibid.

[55]June Sochen, Herstory: A Woman's View of American History, vol. I (New York: Alfred Publishing Company, Inc., 1974), 162-64.

[56]Ibid. O. R. Series II, vol. IV, 198.

best to surrender before the full impact of the assault   nched. None of the men
questioned the inaccurate data about the number of Federal troops under Grant's command.
Pillow suggested that if the fortification could not repulse the assault then the officers should
evacuate their men as quickly as possible. In his opinion, evacuation was clearly better than
total surrender.[57]

The discussion on the feasibility of evacuation continued for some time. The men
disagreed over whether the roads east of Fort Donelson were covered with water. Someone
suggested that the information could be gotten from men who lived in the area. Surely, they
knew whether or not the army was isolated within the Fort. The biggest worry was the flood
waters which could prevent a march up the Cumberland River toward Clarksville. Floyd asked
his aide to contact J. W. Smith, a medical doctor who had a farm a mile from Dover on Lick
Creek, and to invite him to the meeting. Dr. Smith, in a sworn statement in January 1897, gave
his recollection of the event:

I am seventy-eight years of age, and have resided in Dover, Tennessee since 1853. My
occupation has been practicing medicine up to a few years ago, when I retired. I was
born and reared on a farm one mile from Dover, near the ford of Lick Creek, on the
Dover and Clarksville road. My father and I have owned this farm and this ford, now
known as Smith's ford, for over seventy-five years. From my earliest boyhood I have
been familiar with this road and creek. On the night of the 15th of February 1862 about
eleven o'clock, I was required by my fellow-townsman, J. E. Rice, to go with him to the
room of General J. B. Floyd. I was accompanied by him to Floyd, finding him in his
private quarters with his aides. As soon as I reached General Floyd he placed before me
a map of the battle-ground of Fort Donelson, which had been drawn by General Buckner.
Finding that I understood the map and was familiar with the ground, roads, and creeks,
General Floyd requested me to go out on the Clarksville road and investigate and
examine the ford of Lick Creek. He requested me specially to ascertain the depth of the
water and to report as soon as practicable to him at the residence of Mr. Rice in Dover,
where he went to hold a council of war. I went to said ford, examined carefully, and
found water just high enough to reach the saddle-skirts on a horse of medium size. It was
easily fordable. There were no Federals in that locality, and I returned by the way of
the big road to the city, and found General Floyd, Pillow, Buckner, and Colonel Forrest
holding a conference at the house of Mr. Rice, and made my report, assuring him that
the road was open and that the creek could be crossed.[58]

Even after Floyd received this report from Dr. Smith, he insisted that the fortification
could not be evacuated, and the only course of action was to surrender. Forrest refused to
accept this conclusion and announced that he intended to take his men out by way of the
Clarksville road. More than 1,500 soldiers left Fort Donelson and followed Forrest's men out

---

[57]This picture of the events at Fort Donelson can be found in Wythe's, That Devil Forrest. See also the O. R. Series I, vol. VII, 175-80.

[58]Wythe, Forrest, 581-82; O. R. Series I, vol.7, 239,253.

of the area.[59]

While the officers were meeting, the Confederate soldiers heard rumors that they were going to surrender. Their first response was disbelief, surely they would stand and fight. When Colonel Forrest and his men began to leave, many soldiers began to believe the rumors. They met in small groups to deliberate on whether or not they wanted to remain at Fort Donelson. During the night and early morning, small groups of men quietly left and made their way toward the Clarksville road or disappeared into the forest.[60]

In the meantime, Floyd ordered that about 1,100 sick and wounded soldiers should be sent by boat to Nashville. Generals Floyd and Pillow made the decision that they must leave the fortification immediately. Once Floyd made his decision to leave, he dashed around in a frenzy commandeering boats to evacuate his men and their equipment. When he reached the docks at Dover, he found two steamboats that had just anchored with about 400 reinforcements. He forced the captains of the boats to transport him and his men up the river. Floyd and Pillow with about 1,500 men scrambled aboard the boats and headed toward Nashville.[61]

When the rumor circulated the fortification was ready to surrender to the enemy, the civilians were confused. They, like the soldiers, could not believe that the fort would be abandoned without a fight. Civilians and soldiers gathered around Fort Donelson and Dover trying to determine what was going to happen. No official announcement was made to the people.[62]

Spot F. Terrell of Company H. Forth-Ninth Tennessee Infantry wrote in a journal about what he described as the great confusion and fear that seemed to grip the people, including the soldiers, when it was rumored that the Confederate officers were leaving and Fort Donelson would surrender without a fight. According to the journal, many soldiers were determined not to surrender and they took it upon themselves to find a space on boats leaving the fortification. Some of the soldiers took their possessions and walked away. Civilians tried to load their property on carts and wagons in preparation for evacuation.[63] Months later, Bushrod Johnson reflected on the scenes he witnessed at Fort Donelson and wrote that many of the men and officers commenced to leave as soon as they heard that there was a possibility of surrender. Hundreds of them, no doubt, made their way home and to other areas where they had relatives. As the men left the Fort, none of them came into contact with the enemy.[64]

During the night and early morning, 1,134 wounded Confederate soldiers were sent up the Cumberland River toward Nashville. Many of them were placed in private homes in Clarksville. Women tended the wounded and helped to bury them when they died. At the time

---

[59]O. R. Series I, vol. VII, 275; Cooling, Forts, 132.

[60]Ibid.

[61]O. R. Series I, vol. VII, 276-280.

[62]Ibid.

[63]Journal owned by Mrs. Goldie Barrow of Dover, Tennessee.

[64]O. R. Series I, vol. VII, 364.

that the wounded were leaving, reinforcements were continuing to arrive at Fort Donelson.[65]

On the morning of February 16, Buckner, who was now in command of the Fort, sent a Confederate bugler to the parapets to sound the call for a truce. An affirmative answer sounded from the Union lines. Buckner sent a written message under a flag of truce to Grant. Buckner offered capitulation and asked for terms of surrender. Grant responded with a demand for unconditional and immediate surrender. For the first time in a major battle, the conquering army did not give terms of surrender. Buckner had no recourse but to meet the demand. The Union army could now move into Fort Donelson and take an estimated 14,000 prisoners.[66] Grant got his surrender and the Confederacy lost not only a position of major strategic significance but also what was quite as important in the long run, a whole army. Manpower shortage was to be one of the major causes of the downfall of the Confederacy.

Occupation Forces

On the whole the contemporary press did a very creditable job of reporting the fall of Fort Donelson. Harper's Weekly picked up eyewitness accounts from correspondents at headquarters, with the Second Iowa, and with the batteries of artillery. The paper had an artist aboard the gunboat "Louisville." All the reporters sent reports and sketches to the newspapers and people in the northern states knew more detailed information about the battles than people in the land between the rivers. Because it was early in the war, the newspapers tended to miss the strategic importance of the victory, but they fully appreciated the capture of the army.[67]

The exact numbers of men killed, wounded, or taken prisoner at Fort Donelson vary with each report on the battle. The official records list Union losses at 500 killed and 2,000 wounded. The Confederate losses are listed as 400 killed and 1,500 wounded. Only 365 of the Confederate wounded were captured at Fort Donelson. Most accounts list the total number of Confederates killed at 2,000 and the Union loss at 3,000.

The Confederate prisoners were kept standing all day in the bitter cold without food or fires waiting for orders. For some unknown reason, it was late in the day, when Grant finally issued orders concerning the captured soldiers, but nothing was mentioned about the civilians. The soldiers were to be searched and disarmed. Officers were to remain with their units. Prisoners were allowed to retain their personal baggage, and the officers were allowed to keep their side arms. Later that same evening, the men were told that they would be transferred to Cairo and Chicago and each Rebel would be issued two days' rations. The prisoners would be allowed to retain their clothing, blankets, and any of their private possessions which they might have with them. Several days passed before the men were actually moved.[68]

---

[65]O. R. Series I, vol. VII, 279.

[66]Ibid.

[67]For a collection of the sketches and pictures see: Fletcher Platt's Civil War in Pictures, (Garden City New York: Garden City Books, 1957).

[68]O. R. Series II, vol. III, 266.

The records indicate General Grant and his officers were unable to determine the exact number of prisoners taken at Fort Donelson because the numbers changed each time the count was made. For several days after the surrender, men vanished without a trace. They slipped through the Union lines and disappeared. A whole company, Company H. of the Fifty-third Tennessee Infantry, left the camp and dispersed before the Union forces realized that the prisoners were leaving the fortifications.[69] When Grant realized that the prisoners were leaving the area, he made an attempt to stop their exodus. He positioned his men around the perimeter of Fort Donelson in an attempt to contain the prisoners. On February 19, Grant sent a message to General Halleck saying:

Generally the prisoners have been treated with great kindness, and I believe they appreciate it. Great numbers of Union people have come in to see us, and express great hope for the future. They say secessionists are in great trepidation. Some are leaving the country, others expressing anxiety to be assured that they will not be molested if they come in and take the oath.[70]

Later the same day, Grant sent a message to Halleck informing him that several hundred black slaves had been captured at Fort Donelson. He informed Halleck that he had already released some of the slaves to their masters who had come to the forts.[71]

For several weeks the Union officers did not seem to know the status of the captured slaves. Incidents between the soldiers and slaves were common. In general, Union soldiers did not want to be branded slave catchers. At Bellwood furnace near Dover a slave community was pillaged and disrupted by soldiers. During this period the Union commanders began to realize that an official policy had to be instituted concerning the captured slaves.[72]

Grant reported that he had taken a very large store of Confederate supplies at Fort Donelson and Dover, "sufficient probably, for twenty days for all my army."[73] For several days after the surrender, the official reports mentioned that the town of Dover had suffered considerable damage as a result of the battle. Nearly every building had been damaged or destroyed and the civilians who had been wounded were in need of medical attention, but medical personnel and supplies were not available. Trees had been cut down, fences burned, windows broken, and a number of the buildings that had been left standing after the battle were razed and used as fuel against the bitter cold.[74]

As soon as the Union soldiers marched into the town, they had begun to plunder, pilfer, and demolish private and public property. The citizens were helpless and fell prey to the

---

[69]No exact tally of the number of men captured and then shipped out of the fortification was ever made. Halleck expressed great concern because he was never given the number.

[70]O. R. Series II, vol. III, 267.

[71]Ibid.

[72]O. R. Series I, vol. XX, 397-98; vol. XXIII, 37-41.

[73]O. R. Series I, vol. III, 286.

[74]Ibid. O. R. Series II, vol. IV, 129.

intractable soldiers. On the day of the surrender, federal soldiers were seen "luxuriating like children in hogsheads of sugar." Many soldiers were observed as they filled their canteens with molasses and their pockets with brown sugar. Soldiers looted the stores and homes taking anything of value. One soldier was seen walking down the street with a looking glass under his arm, and another soldier with him was loaded down with brass candlesticks and wearing a woman's bonnet.[75]

Grant did not appear to be concerned with the looting and pillaging. At least six days after the first reports, Halleck, who had then learned of the conduct of the soldiers, began to send messages to Grant about the reprehensible situation. He asked Grant several questions about the conduct of his men in Dover and the land between the rivers. A report had reached Halleck that the Union soldiers at Fort Henry and Fort Donelson were stealing, plundering, and committing atrocities against the people. The people had accused the soldiers of brutal beatings, rape, and murder, and Halleck requested clarification on these reports. There is no record of a response by Grant to Halleck's request.[76]

In the meantime, Grant had ordered General McClernand to organize a number of patrols to prevent any further flight of Confederate soldiers from the fortification. Grant sent Foote and the "Cairo" and "Conestoga" up the Cumberland River to Clarksville. Enroute to Clarksville, Foote destroyed the Cumberland Iron Works. D. H. Lewis, one of the owners of the furnace, was captured by Foote's men. Lewis claimed to be a Unionist, but Foote did not believe him and accused him of supplying iron to the Confederacy. Lewis argued that he had been forced to keep his furnace in operation even though he had not wanted to assist the Confederacy. Foote took the man to Fort Donelson and later Lewis swore allegiance to the Union and was released.[77]

On February 19, the people watched the smoke and fire up the river from Dover when the Union forces burned buildings around the iron furnaces and the Rolling Mills.[78] Floyd was in Nashville, when he learned that Foote was moving toward Clarksville. An attempt had been made to burn the railroad bridge in Clarksville, but the wet wood would not burn. The Union sailors arrived in time to take the bridge before it was destroyed and take possession of the spiked cannons at Fort Defiance.[79]

Foote's men marched into the town where they were met by Mayor George Smith and a former congressman, Cave Johnson. Johnson knew Foote's father and they spoke amicably for a time. Mayor Smith and Johnson requested that Foote make a formal statement to calm the civilians who were in a frantic state. Foote hesitated because he did not want to make a statement of policy. He was finally convinced by the men that some reassurance would help the situation. He finally stated that to all "peaceably disposed persons that neither in their person

---

[75]O. R. Series II, vol. III, 271-79.

[76]Ibid.

[77]Ibid., 279. Cooling, Forts, 129.

[78]Ibid.

[79]Ibid., 190.

nor in their property shall they suffer molestation by me or the naval forces under my command."[80]

Grant ordered General Charles Smith to garrison Clarksville. Grant went to Clarksville and moved his headquarters into a house on Second Cross Street to begin reconstruction of the city. The mostly deserted city did not bring joy to the invaders. The people were hostile and flaunted their allegiance to the Confederacy. An order to remove Confederate flags was made, but people were slow in compliance.[81]   There are conflicting reports from Grant and his officers about the attitude of the people in Clarksville. Grant in his messages to Halleck leaves the impression that many civilians declared themselves to be Unionist and were willing to support the Union forces.   Other reports indicate that very few men came to Grant's headquarters professing loyalty. Reporters from the northern newspapers said that few citizens of Clarksville would admit to being a Unionist.[82]

By February 20, 1862, some of the Confederate prisoners had been sent from Fort Donelson to prisons and hospitals in Illinois. No preparation had been made for handling the prisoners. At the prison in Chicago, a reporter for Harper's Weekly drew scenes at the camp and described the prisoners.

A more woebegone appearing set of men it would be difficult for the reader to imagine. Compared with the laborers we are in the habit of seeing upon our public roads, they would suffer somewhat, being less hardy and healthy in build and complexion. It may have been from exposure and low diet, but they were all sallow faced, sunken eyed and apparently famishing. The uniforms of the Confederate prisoners are just no uniforms at all, being wholly ununified in color, cut, fashion, and manufacture.[83]

Sending the captured Confederate soldiers out of the region did not alleviate Grant's problems. Hundreds of civilians and thousands of Union soldiers were contained within a small area with no viable authority maintaining control. Martial law was technically in effect, but Grant had waited until February 22 to issue General Order No. VII which declared martial law in Stewart County and in West Tennessee. The order stipulated that organized patrols were to be sent out daily by division commanders to maintain law and order. The patrols were ordered to check all soldiers who were found outside the fieldworks of Fort Donelson, and any soldier found outside the fieldworks without a pass approved by the division commander was to be brought into camp and punished by his regimental commander. In spite of the order, Union soldiers continued to wander at will throughout the entire area. They demonstrated no regard for the lives and property of the people. Grant and his officers seemed unable or unwilling to control the actions of the men. The commander at Camp Porter at Paris, Tennessee reported that there were "terrible depredations committed on the citizens between Fort Henry and

---

[80]O. R. Series I, vol. VII, 316-21. Thomas L. Connelly, The Army of the Heartland: The Army of Tennessee 1861-1862, (Baton Rouge: Louisiana State University Press, 1967), 1-360. It was apparent that Foote was not speaking for the army.

[81]Cooling, Forts, 190.

[82]O. R. Series I, vol. XVI, 862-70.

[83]Fletcher Pratt, Civil War (Garden City, New York: Doubleday, 1955), 33.

Concord," after the fall of Fort Donelson.[84]

No doubt, Grant had an enormous number of problems to solve at the time. Not only did he have to control his own men, but he also had to expend days dealing with the problems of the dispersion of Confederate prisoners and attending to the civilians who were camped, without food and housing, around the Forts. Added to these conditions, Grant had to deal with about fifteen hundred slaves who had been captured at Fort Donelson. The numbers of blacks at the fortification dwindled as the days went by because many of them slipped away before their owners could claim them. They had been told that they could expect insufferable treatment from the Union soldiers and they feared for their lives. Other slaves left simply because they saw an opportunity to gain their freedom and headed toward the northern states.

For several days, Grant did not seem too concerned with the dispersion of the slaves. There is no record of any attempt to control the movement of the slaves, until Grant finally realized that the labor supply was insufficient. On February 28, General Order No. XIV said that permission was not to be granted to people to pass through the camp to look for fugitive slaves. The slaves were not to be released or permitted to return to their masters. Slaves were to be employed in the quartermaster's department for the benefit of the Federal Government. Before the order was issued many slave masters had petitioned the Union army for the release of their slaves.[85]

Some of the slave owners from Lyon and Trigg Counties in Kentucky demanded the return of their slaves because the Union army in Tennessee could not confiscate slaves from Kentucky. They argued that they needed their slaves on the farms and in the iron industry. Exact records were not kept of the number of slaves who were returned to their owners in Kentucky before or after the General Order No. XIV was issued, but several hundred slaves left the Fort Donelson area before February.[86]

The difficulties between the Federal soldiers and the people in the land between the rivers seemed to worsen during February. Grant issued a stronger order to his officers about soldiers leaving the camp without passes. Officers had posted sentinels on the edge of the entrenchments to stop any soldier from leaving the area, but this precaution had not kept the men in the camp. Soldiers had left the area in large numbers and continued to steal and destroy the property around the countryside. In the land between the rivers, the soldiers did not try to determine if they were in Tennessee or Kentucky. They seemed to consider the whole area as enemy territory and they felt that they had the right to punish their enemies.[87]

Residents of the land between the rivers besieged the army headquarters demanding the return of dry goods, buggies, mail coaches, household and business property which had been confiscated by the Union forces after the fall of the forts. None of the records indicate that Grant's men made any attempt to find or return property. In a matter of a few days, the attitude

---

[84]O. R. Series II, vol. III, 272.

[85]Ibid.

[86]Ibid.

[87]O. R. Series I, vol. VII, 625.

of the people seemed to shift toward taking what they needed from the Union army.[88]

General Halleck became more and more distraught at what he considered Grant's failure to follow orders and control the men under his command. Halleck had received numerous reports on the activities of the soldiers from civilians, but he had not received a report from Grant even though he had sent numerous requests.

On February 19, a very brief message was received from General Grant which stated that he had taken from twelve thousand to fifteen thousand prisoners at Fort Donelson, including Generals Buckner and Bushrod Johnson. The supplies taken included twenty thousand stands of arms, forty-eight pieces of artillery, seventeen heavy guns, from two thousand to four thousand horses, and large quantities of commissary stores. Grant's report did not specify what was included in the commissary stores, but Confederate records indicated that there were hogsheads of sugar, barrels of rice, barrels of flour, bacon and soap.[89]

General Halleck became irate when he did not receive detailed reports from Grant, and on March 3, 1862, he wrote to General George B. McClelland and expressed his anger. He explained that he was infuriated because he had not heard from Grant for more than a week. He had learned, he wrote, that Grant had disobeyed a direct command and without authorization had gone to Nashville, Tennessee. Indeed Grant had gone to Nashville which technically came under the command of General Buell. Halleck and Grant had been at odds since the beginning of the invasion, and at least two other problems had caused Halleck to worry. He had been receiving unceasing reports of general disorder and illegal actions by Grant's men, and he believed that Grant was not submitting reports because he was usually drunk. Halleck concluded that the army seemed to be "demoralized by the victory of Fort Donelson."[90]

On March 4 and 5, 1862, Halleck sent orders to Grant to dismount water batteries at both forts and remove all the men and stores from Fort Donelson. His plan was to keep a small garrison at Fort Donelson. Grant was ordered not to allow his men to interfere with the movement of the people who were going up the Cumberland River toward Nashville. Civilian river traffic would be allowed, but no civilians should be allowed into either Fort Henry or Fort Donelson.[91]

At the time, it appeared that Halleck was prepared to relieve Grant of his command. In a message to Grant dated March 6, 1862, Halleck wrote that the lack of order and discipline and the many irregularities in Grant's command since the capture of Fort Donelson had become matters of general notoriety and people in Washington D.C. were asking questions. Halleck completed his message by writing, "Unless these things are immediately corrected I am directed to relieve you of your command."[92]

---

[88]Cooling, Forts, 199.

[89]Ibid.

[90]Ibid., 679.

[91]O. R. Series I, Part II, vol. VII, 680-681.

[92]Ibid., 12.

Halleck's threat must be considered carefully because the records do not indicate that he had been given instructions by his superiors to relieve Grant of his command. Also, it should be noted that if Grant was having difficulty in communicating with Halleck, his messages were being received by General William Sherman.

On March 6, General Sherman sent a message to Halleck and informed him that Captain Rawlins, Grant's adjutant-general, had reported that Grant was at Fort Henry with about 12,000 men and there were four broken regiments at Fort Donelson, two regiments at Clarksville, and Grant would remain at Fort Henry for at least one day. The report included an appraisal of the number of boats at the disposal of the Federal forces and an estimate of the number of soldiers expected to arrive at Fort Donelson within two days. On the same day, Halleck sent a message to Grant and informed him that General McClellan had directed him to order Grant to report to him daily on the number and position of the forces under Grant's command. In the same message, Halleck reprimanded Grant for his trip up the Cumberland to Nashville. He advised Grant that his superiors were upset and that there was a strong possibility that Grant would be arrested if he did not comply with all orders.[93]

The records show that Grant tried to enforce some of the orders that he had received from Halleck. He did, in fact, order Colonel R. J. Oglesby to dismount the guns at Fort Donelson and to ship them to Cairo. He informed Colonel Oglesby that all men, with the exception of one regiment, would be withdrawn from Fort Donelson in a few days. Grant was disturbed by the messages he received almost daily from Halleck. He insisted that he had reported his every move to Halleck's headquarters. Grant maintained that he had not disobeyed orders and that in fact, he had complied with each order promptly. After several days of trying to defend himself, General Grant sent a report to Halleck with the request that he be relieved from any further duty in Halleck's department. Halleck did not respond to Grant's request immediately, and other events occurred which delayed any further confrontation between the two men for a time.[94]

On March 7, 1862 Grant sent a detailed report to Halleck concerning the troop build-up at Fort Henry and Fort Donelson. He stated that at least 35,000 infantry men were in place and they were prepared for duty. A force of 3,168 cavalrymen was present and awaiting orders. A total of 1,231 artillery men was present with about fifty-four aggregated numbers of pieces of artillery. An infantry troop of more than 25,000 men had left Fort Donelson on March 6. They were in position at the landing above Fort Henry. At the time, at least 5,740 men were waiting for orders to move to Fort Henry. The men would remain at Fort Henry until detailed orders were received. There were 2,328 men at Fort Donelson and about 1,216 of these men were on alert to march to Fort Henry. Grant also stated that he had two broken regiments at Fort Donelson and one regiment, poorly equipped, at Fort Henry. Halleck replied to the report immediately and ordered Grant to garrison Fort Henry and Fort Donelson with the fragmentary regiments. The remaining force was to be sent without delay to Cairo.[95]

---

[93]Ibid., 8-9, 15.

[94]Ibid., 15, 16-17.

[95]Ibid., 15.

The people were astounded at the massive augmentation of soldiers in the area. The activity of the soldiers frightened some of the people, but others soon realized that if they had goods to sell, the Union soldiers had money to buy. People tried to barter and trade with the men, but the major problem was the lack of products, including food, available for sale. Life was extremely difficult for civilians and soldiers. Civilians sought protection near the forts, living with the terrible odor from dead and rotting mules, horses, and cattle around the forts. The water was bad and many people lived on salt meat and hard crackers. Diseases ran rampant, including camp fever, colds, dysentery, and lumbago. Housing was not available and people were often wet and uncomfortable.[96]

Later, when Grant was questioned about the procedures he followed with respect to the citizens, he denied that his men had looted the entire area, but an unsigned letter sent to Senator M. S. Latham of the United States Senate dated March 10, 1862, questioned the procedures used by an invading army to confiscate all civilian property in the area. The letter specifically referred to the battles at Fort Henry and Fort Donelson as examples of how the army seized property and no record of the disposal of that property was made. A portion of the letter stated:

> As an example of the effect of the present system, I will refer to the capture of Fort Donelson. As no one was interested in the property captured or caused to be accountable for it, large quantities were destroyed or carried away. This army was for some days as much demoralized by this plundering as was that of Bull Run by the defeat.[97]

By March 1862, numerous politicians were asking questions about what had happened to goods seized or confiscated by the Union army when they invaded any area. The events at Fort Henry and Fort Donelson and the actions of the soldiers during the weeks after the surrender had been the catalyst that brought the questions into public discussion. For example, David Davis, who was serving on a U. S. Senate committee investigating irregularities in army contracts, received an anonymous letter about the activities of the Union forces at Fort Henry and Fort Donelson.[98]

Senator Davis sent a copy of the letter to Grant. The letter outlined the chronology of events as they occurred at Fort Henry. The letter said:

> Dear Sir: As you are engaged in the business of investigating army contracts and frauds practiced on the Government, it may not be out of place for me to state a few facts as they have been told to me, and that by parties most interested. At the taking of Fort Henry there was a large amount of sugar, coffee, and rice captured, besides a lot of horses, jacks, mules, wagons, and other property. Now I would like to know who is to take charge of the property. . . .[99]

The letter continued with a lengthy explanation of the way the army managed to acquire control

---

[96]Cooling, Forts, 252.

[97]Ibid., 26.

[98]Ibid., 13.

[99]Ibid., 14.

of all the captured property. The profits in the operation amounted to at least $6,000 in the case of Fort Henry, and up to $8,000 at Fort Donelson. The illegal transactions were handled so expertly that the captains on the merchant vessels were unaware of the complicity.[100]

Grant responded to Senator Davis and the charges in the anonymous letters with a flat denial of any knowledge of the affair. He insisted that he had issued orders to prevent marauding and his orders had been carried out. Grant restated his position in several messages and then replied to the last inquiry, "There is such a disposition to find fault with me that I again ask to be relieved from further duty. . . ." Grant was not removed from duty, but the controversy continued.[101]

On March 15, Halleck tried to define and recapitulate the problems he felt he had with a recalcitrant Grant. In a message to General Lorenzo Thomas, Adjutant-General of the Army, Halleck wrote that while it was true that Grant had gone to Nashville after the fall of Fort Donelson, Grant had done so with the best of intentions, and the many irregularities that had occurred after the surrender of the forts had happened when Grant was away from the fortifications. Halleck had, for some reason, decided that he was not going to push his accusations against Grant. Halleck made no recommendations to General Thomas about how to handle the many complaints that had been made about the alleged illegal military and civilian operations at the forts. Halleck wanted to replace Grant, but he decided instead to take the credit for the victories at Fort Henry and Fort Donelson. His scheme worked and he was made commander of all the western theater.[102]

In March of 1862, the area between the Tennessee and Cumberland had the appearance of a large and very busy depot as Federal soldiers passed through the area on their way to Cairo. The immediate effects on the entire area were catastrophic because they intensified the existing problems. The situation worsened when thousands of soldiers, who were often traveling with short rations, confiscated whatever they needed or wanted from the civilians in the area. Quite literally, the citizens were constrained by the Union forces to relinquish almost every possession they owned. Reverend Robert Collyer of Chicago came to the area with a Christian commission in late March. He was awed by the devastation caused by the battles at Fort Henry and Fort Donelson. He found that most of the civilians were sick and very afraid of everyone. It was difficult to reach those people who needed help because they were suspicious of the motives of every stranger they saw.[103]

Federal operations were the most serious problem, but even the Confederate forces made life more difficult for the civilians. Frequently the Confederates from points below Paris, Tennessee raided the area looking for supplies. The Union forces responded to the Confederate raids with even harsher treatment of the civilians. It was impossible for citizens to determine which army was going to sack their home and property. The inhabitants were absolutely

---

[100]Ibid.

[101]Ibid., 30.

[102]O. R. Series I, vol. VII, 683.

[103]Cooling, Forts, 251.

138

convinced that they must not trust outsiders.[104]   Confederate forces in Paris and points west were busy complying with the orders from Governor Harris to enroll all eligible men in the area in the Army of Tennessee. General Grant, aware of the activity of these Confederate operatives, was determined to keep them out of the land between the rivers and other areas under Union control. No matter how resolute General Grant was, however, it was impossible to keep Confederates out of the area. Confederate soldiers wore Union uniforms and moved through the country with relative ease. Union troop movement was erratic and there was an insufficient force assigned to patrol the area. Orders given to Union forces were often equivocal or imprecise, and rampant confusion reigned throughout the countryside.[105]

Union soldiers were being sent back and forth from the forts to Cairo without any semblance of order. The soldiers, never sure of their assignment and inadequately supervised, wandered over the countryside and harassed the citizens. By this time, both the Confederate and Union armies had initiated a policy of impressing civilians, and the men who were left in the area hid whenever they sighted a stranger.[106]

One step that General Grant took to try to bring some sense of order was General Order No. XXI which was issued on March 15, 1862. Duties were assigned to individuals and great care was taken to see that proper records were kept and dispatched to the proper authorities. Captain Clark B. Lagow, aide-de-camp to General Grant, and Colonel John Riggins were appointed to supervise the procedure of allowing people, both military and civilian, to supervise the movement of property. Federal soldiers investigated all merchandise and people that entered the area. Greater care was taken to notify all officers that they must enforce all previous orders concerning the discipline of men under their command. Again, the officers warned all military personnel that they were accountable for any infractions of the orders from that day forward.[107]

As Grant began the reorganization of his army, preparing to leave the forts, he received orders to dismantle the garrison at Clarksville and assume command of the Union forces on the Tennessee River near Shiloh. General Grant removed the force at Clarksville, left 700 men at Fort Donelson, and placed the Fifty-second Indiana Regiment at Fort Henry. Colonel W. W. Lowe was placed in command at Fort Henry and Fort Donelson.[108]

Without realizing it, the citizens had just survived the first stage of their hardships. The big battles were over and the massive Union force had left, and only a few Union soldiers remained. The change did not radically alter the difficult circumstances the people had to endure. The rudimentary problems were still present. The area was a conquered territory occupied by the enemy and the people's lives and economic circumstance depended upon the judgment, or whims, of the military. The acts of destruction, physical attacks, and looting

---

[104]O. R. Series I, vol. X, 25.

[105]Ibid.

[106]Cooling, Forts, 93.

[107]Ibid., 41.

[108]O. R. Series I, vol. X, 25.

decreased, but they did not end.

The more optimistic citizens were confident that they could now resume a more normal existence. Farmers were anxious to plant their crops before the season ended, but the weather was unfavorable. Money was scarce and seeds and plants were unavailable. Farm animals had disappeared while the army was in the area and replacement costs were exorbitant. Even if a farmer had the money to purchase a mule or horse, it was not likely that one was available. The land owners suffered from an insufficient labor supply because many slave owners had lost their slaves, and day laborers were impossible to find because they were either in the army or they were hiding out. Farmers, who were determined to plant crops, harnessed a person to a plow to till the soil. In March and April of 1862, the farmers bartered with other farmers and merchants for seed corn, tobacco seeds, wheat, and other grains. The barter method was unsatisfactory, and many farmers were unable to plant crops that season. Thus, survival during the coming winter was going to be arduous. People were on the verge of starvation.[109]

A few farmers who had been successful in hiding goods and animals after the surrender of the forts found that they could not obtain a proper permit or authorization from the Federal authorities to allow them to ship their goods to markets. Federal authorities controlled the Cumberland and Tennessee and troops supervised all the goods that were sold. Union authorities hesitated to grant travel passes to individuals. Licenses were required before people could sell to an outside market.

Guerrilla Bands

Some of the people who had left the land between the rivers began to return after the troop withdrawals. They were not necessarily supportive of the Union occupation. Often, they assumed that since the fate of the forts was settled they could return to their homes and farms in safety. They seemed confident that the violence that had plagued them earlier had dissipated, but before the people could exhale sighs of relief, other adversities began to trouble the region. Guerrilla bands roamed the area pillaging and destroying at random. The more destructive bands operated out of Eddyville and Hopkinsville, Kentucky. The men moved about the area in search of men and supplies. They often operated under the guise of agents of the Confederate or Federal government recruiting men for the army. In fact, they were impressing individuals into their guerrilla operations. These men were not interested in the outcome of the war; they were using the war as a cover for their criminal activities.[110]

When men refused to join any of the guerilla groups, they were threatened and in some instances were beaten or killed. Some of the guerrillas took delight in burning the houses and tormenting the people. Citizens turned to Federal authorities for assistance and protection, but the number of troops stationed in the area was too small to control the guerilla operations. The major problem was the mobility of the guerrillas, and their strike and run strategy was a safeguard against capture. The perilous situation was exacerbated when the guerrillas realized

---

[109]Ibid.

[110]Ibid., 34-40.

that they could hide in a wilderness, and the soldiers, who were not familiar with the terrain, could not locate their camps. The intimidated citizens would not for fear of their lives disclose the whereabouts of the guerrillas.[111]

The problem became so extreme that many people asked for permission to move to camping areas adjacent to Fort Henry and Fort Donelson. At first permission was granted, but the Union forces, faced with the problems of occupying a conquered area, soon realized that they did not have the provisions or capability to care for the people. To add to the general chaos, many people were sick and needed medical attention. Those who moved into the camps suffered from the many communicable diseases which ran unchecked among the people. The living conditions were appalling. Sanitation was disregarded and the people suffered from parasites such as lice and fleas. Also, several hundred slaves, under the care of the soldiers at Fort Donelson, were suffering from sickness and other disabilities. The army could not supply the food or medical supplies which the people needed, and all people except the slaves were told that they must leave. The Union troops forced the people out of the camps and warned them that they must provide for their own protection because the army would not assume the responsibility. Once again, the people saw the Federal authorities as the enemy.[112]

For these people, the primary objective was survival. The social fabric of the region had been torn apart by war, fear, hunger, and criminal activities. The martial law, which was never effectively enforced, rendered excessive power to the military but did not protect the people. Abominable criminal behavior had increased because the rules set under the conditions of martial law made it illegal for the civilians to go armed. The people were in danger and they wanted the right to protect themselves. In some cases, the Union soldiers, who were responsible for the welfare of the people, were the greatest immediate danger to the lives and property of the people. Threats and beatings by the soldiers were as pervasive as the degradation suffered at the hands of the guerrillas. Yet, the soldiers were responsible for law and order, and to the people that included the welfare of the citizens. Those people who wanted to leave the region and seek sanctuary elsewhere were often unable to move because they could not get permission from the military authorities.[113]

During 1863, guerrilla activity and vigilante action were a constant problem. The bands were interested in attacking river traffic and thereby disrupting Federal communications and supply lines, but little distinction was made as to what supplies belonged to the government and what was owned by citizens in the area. Estimates of the size of the guerrilla bands varied, and in reports from the garrisons at Fort Henry and Fort Donelson, the numbers were from fifty to eight hundred men in several raids which occurred in 1863 and 1864. The situation worsened until citizens were afraid to be seen talking to a Union soldier because they would be branded Union supporters and visited in the night by a group of vigilantes and punished. It became

---

[111]Ibid.

[112]Ibid.

[113]Letters of Sara A. Kennedy, Civil War Collection, Box 10, Tennessee State Library and Archives, Nashville, Tennessee; Letters by Charles C. Nott, J. Milton Henry Collection, Tennessee State Library and Archives, Nashville, Tennessee.

impossible for the garrisons at Fort Henry and Fort Donelson to remain in telegraph communication with each other or with Nashville. The telegraph lines were cut daily even though Union patrols were sent to check and repair the lines each day. The guerrillas would often cut a telegraph line and set an ambush for the repair crew.[114]

A legend grew up around the activities of a man named Joshua Hinson who owned a farm near Tharpe in Stewart County.[115] Hinson had lost his sons in the Union invasion, and he was determined to avenge them. He formed an outlaw band and roamed the area looking for any man wearing a Union uniform or any person who agreed with the Union cause. When he found any of these people, he shot them. He hid on the banks of the Cumberland and shot at any Union uniform sighted on the boats. The reports from Fort Henry often mentioned that Hinson and his group were responsible for deaths and the destruction of substantial amounts of Federal and private property. It is said that by the end of the Civil War, Hinson had killed at least fifty Union soldiers. The legend claims he had the proof because he notched his gun each time he killed a soldier.[116]

The Golden Pond area suffered from the guerrilla activity and violence. Two of the worst of the guerrillas were Bill and Taylor Bogard. Citizens who were even suspected of being disloyal to the Confederate cause could expect a visit from the bands led by the Bogard brothers. The band confiscated property, and the men were not adverse to torture and hanging if they did not find all the money they expected to find.[117]

Survival from 1862 to 1865 was extremely difficult for most people. The Union authorities in Washington were aware of the difficulty, and in April of 1862 Colonel Rodney Mason, Commander of the Seventy-first Ohio Volunteers, was ordered to take command at Fort Donelson. He was specifically instructed to prevent any further marauding and destruction of private property in the area, and Colonel Mason was ordered to supervise his men and stop any assaults the soldiers were making on the people in the region. The authorities were aware of the treatment of the civilians but it was difficult to discipline the soldiers.[118]

The conditions had worsened, and in September, 1862 Colonel W. W. Lowe was ordered to patrol the region and find those people who were suspected of supporting the Confederate cause. The Union authorities seemed to think that the guerrilla activity was directed by Confederate leaders. These people were thought to be part of an organized network, spying and sending important information to Richmond. Colonel Lowe and his men, including some 200 blacks, were ordered to check the area toward Clarksville and then move into the land between

---

[114]Ibid., 347, 353, 354: Ibid., 215, 220-25, 239, 771-72; for more supporting information see O. R. Series I, vol. XXIII, pt. 2, 54-56.

[115]Joshua Hinson is sometimes listed as Josiah. It is not clear if the man used both names or the name was spelled incorrectly by county officials.

[116]O. R. Series I. vol. XXIV, 24.

[117]Notes found at the Land Between the Lakes Library at Golden Pond. Letters from people living in Eddyville, Kentucky from 1861 to 1865 had been copied in the notes.

[118]O. R. Series I. vol. VIII, 370: Series I, vol. X, 178.

the rivers.[119]   As the Union troops marched to Clarksville, Tennessee, a distance of about thirty miles, they destroyed most of the property in their path.   The soldiers were ordered to determine if the people they met were Union or Confederate sympathizers, and if they found Confederates, their property was to be destroyed.[120]

The whole area fell under the onslaught of these soldiers.   Houses and fences were burned or destroyed.   Cattle, hogs, and other farm animals were either stolen or shot where they stood.   All provisions and supplies were confiscated or destroyed on the spot.   Little food or household furnishings were left behind.   Slaves and freedmen were taken enroute and immediately sworn into Union service.   When the forces moved into Montgomery County about 200 blacks were impressed into Union service from the area.[121]   One citizen described the treatment as follows:

> The soldiers under Lowe committed outrages, spoilation, robberies, and insults upon the citizens of the area, without regard to sex or condition.   Citizens were visited by inflamed and drunken soldiers.   Demands of every scription were made upon them. Negroes were enticed from their masters, threats of pollution were freely made to ladies to enforce compliance with unlawful demands, and the most disgusting obscenity and shocking profanity freely indulged in.[122]

Colonel Lowe announced his plans for control by placing the entire area around the forts under strict military jurisdiction.   He stated that Fort Henry and Fort Donelson were important links in the Union line of communication and he was determined that the Confederate agents and supporters would not disrupt the communication lines or interfere with the Federal control of contraband trade on the Tennessee and Cumberland.   At the time, the garrisons at both forts were strengthened with several hundred men.   The number of patrols increased and were spread through a much larger area around the fortifications.   People were apprehensive because they soon learned that even a suspicion of any sympathy with the Confederate cause could result in a visit from the Union patrols.   The citizens were caught between the guerrillas and soldiers.[123]

---

[119]By this time, the slaves taken at Fort Henry and Fort Donelson were assigned to the army. Before Grant left, he had ordered that owners could not reclaim their slaves. From the communications, it appears that the Union army assigned the slaves to patrols commanded by white officers. No information about the number of slaves assigned to each patrol is given.

[120]O. R. Series I, vol. VIII, 371.

[121]Ibid.

[122]Letter to Grant, Civil War Collection, Manuscript Division, Tennessee State Library and Archives, Nashville, Tennessee.

[123]O. R. Series I, vol. XXIV, pt. 3, 9; O. R. Series I, vol. XXIII, pt. 2, 93.; Letters by Mary Walker Meriweather Bell, Civil War Collection, Manuscript Division, Tennessee State Library and Archives, Nashville, Tennessee. (The official records listed 111 officers and 2,187 men at Fort Donelson in 1863. At that time no mention was made of any black soldiers at either Fort Henry or Fort Donelson.) It is likely that the Union rosters did not include the black soldiers. See Cooling, Forts, 16, 72, 76, 241, 248-49, 268.

Survival

To determine how the people lived from day to day is a difficult task because so little information about the time has survived. A few letters and notes have been collected by families and these items reveal some of the events and attitudes. Letters written by Cordelia Lewis Scales to Loulie W. Irby were collected by Martha Neville Lumpkin. The letters were of family interest and were privately printed in a journal entitled "Dear Darling Loulie."[124] Cordelia Lewis Scales and Loulie W. Irby were classmates at the State Female Institute in Memphis, Tennessee when the Civil War began. Both girls were from Mississippi, but Loulie W. Irby remained in Tennessee when Cordelia Scales returned to Mississippi in January 1861. The girls were sixteen years old at the time, and their correspondence from 1861 to 1865 is dominated by references to the war. The girls were impassioned supporters of the Confederacy, and their fathers and brothers fought in the army. The war changed their lives, but they continued to interest themselves in the more mundane affairs of daily living. They spoke of clothes, boys, and parties. Since both girls came from large families with dozens of aunts, uncles, nieces, nephews, and cousins, their homes were always crowded during the war years with relatives who had come to visit. The usual visit lasted from two weeks to several months. They had relatives in Kentucky, and visits back and forth were common. They wrote to one another about the people and the countryside they had seen. The trips were usually by horse and buggy or by railroad. On several of these trips, they came through Tennessee and passed by Stewart and Montgomery Counties. They wrote about death and disease in most of their letters. Epidemics of smallpox occurred every year. People died from typhoid fever and from a malady called congested chest disease. They discussed the horrible wounds suffered by soldiers in the Confederate Army. Unlike the stereotypical southern belles of this period, Cordelia and Loulie were expert at training horses. They broke horses for men in the community and rode the horses throughout the countryside. On one occasion, Cordelia was badly bruised when she was thrown from a horse she was breaking. The women went armed and declared that they were unafraid of Union soldiers. They were confident that they could outshoot any man from the North.[125]

Even in the midst of war and occupation, the people attended parties. One particular type of gathering was called a bran dance. Wet bran was used to cover the ground and the people removed their shoes and danced. Another popular pastime was to write plays and have members of the family act out the parts. The war was often the theme of the plays and both females and males acted the parts of the soldiers. Of course, the Confederate soldiers were always the heroes. The Union soldiers were the blue devils.[126]

Both young women had musical backgrounds and they played the guitar and piano. They were interested in the new patriotic songs that had been written about the South. The rebel

---

[124]Martha Neville Lumpkin, ed., "Dear Darling Loulie," Privately Published by the family in 1959. (in the hands of the author)

[125]Ibid.

[126]Ibid.

songs were "My Maryland," "Mississippi Camp Song," "Cheer Boys Cheer," "Life on the Tented Field," and "Dixie." One song, entitled "Bonnie Blue Flag," was written in Jackson, Mississippi in 1861. It was the story of an incident that happened when Mississippi left the Union. C. R. Dickinson entered the capitol building, after the ordinance of secession was adopted, bearing a beautiful silk banner with a single star. He presented the banner to William S. Barry as a gift from Mrs. H. H. Smyth of Jackson, Mississippi. Mrs. Smyth had commissioned Miss Em Lou Cadwallader to design and make the flag. William Barry remarked that it was the first banner unfurled in the young republic. The people cheered and shouted.[127]

If we can take the events which these girls witnessed as a partial view of the lives of the people, then it is obvious that neither war nor occupation could keep people from attempting to relieve the horrors they faced. Many citizens tried to maintain a life as similar to the one they had before the war as possible.

Deprivation was a fact of life, and they faced death almost every day, but they tried to preserve a sense of normalcy.

A feeling of crisis could not be ignored when Union solders were placed on alert. Whenever a report came that Confederate forces were in the area, Union forces acted immediately. Almost every week rumors spread about a possible Confederate attack against the forts. Since control of the Cumberland and Tennessee was vital to the Confederacy, it was assumed that the Confederate army would try to liberate the area. Union leaders were sensitive to the rumors because they expected civilians to assist the Confederate soldiers even though many of the people had sworn an oath of allegiance to the Union.

Confederate Armies Return

Confederate invasion was a danger to the small Union force in Stewart County. In February 1863, General Joseph Wheeler sent Nathan Bedford Forrest with 800 men to the Cumberland River area. Their headquarters was at Palmyra, Tennessee, approximately thirty miles from the forts. The Confederate plan was to disrupt all traffic on the Cumberland River. As soon as the Federal forces at the forts learned of the activity, Colonel A. C. Harding ordered a company of men under the command of Major E. C. Bratt to take a steamer, the "Wildcat," up the Cumberland and remove the Confederate threat, but before the men could leave the dock at Dover, they were ordered ashore. A Confederate force was at that moment advancing overland toward Fort Donelson.[128]

Colonel Forrest, reinforced by General Wheeler, was in a line of march toward Fort Donelson when the Confederate troops met a small party of Union soldiers commanded by Lieutenant D. Lone, of Company B. Fifth Iowa Cavalry, who had been sent to arrest a family living near the Cumberland Iron Works. When the Confederate troop came within sight of the Union soldiers shots were exchanged. A civilian witnessed the assault and rode to Fort

---

[127]Notes found in Civil War Collection, Tennessee State Library and Archives, Nashville, Tennessee.

[128]O. R. Series I, vol. XVII, pt. 2, 436.

Donelson to sound the alarm. Colonel Harding sounded the long-roll and dispatched men all along the road leading from Dover to Fort Donelson. By this time, the Confederate force had advanced to within one mile of the Union picket lines and had sent a force around Fort Donelson to secure the road leading to Fort Henry.[129]

Colonel Harding, with 750 men, positioned his troops in the ravines, gullies, ridges around Dover and Fort Donelson. The Union soldiers were in an excellent position to stop the attack. The Confederate force moved quickly into position and made plans for the assault. Colonel Forrest stationed his men on a ridge overlooking the town. His men quickly mounted four guns and were ready to open fire on the Union gun batteries. Wheeler and Forrest had agreed upon an exact time to begin the assault, and while Forrest was waiting for Wheeler to get into position, he saw a number of Union soldiers marching in plain view in the direction of the Cumberland River. Mistaking the movement for an evacuation, Colonel Forrest ordered his men to mount their horses and capture the soldiers. Obeying the order, the men rode at full speed straight into deadly enemy fire from the Union trenches and the gun batteries. A thirty-two pound siege gun was in position. The heavy guns in the battery had been loaded to the muzzle with grape and canister shot. The deadly missiles ripped the Confederate cavalry line apart. Colonel Forrest had his horse shot from under him and when the horse fell, the men thought that Forrest had been killed, and they retreated. Colonel Forrest had not been injured. He grabbed another horse and rallied his men. This time, Forrest organized the men for an assault on foot. The line moved forward slowly in a solid mass toward the jail house in Dover, and then southward up the street toward the enemy trenches. The Union siege guns, double loaded with canister, were discharged at pointblank range into the Confederate ranks. Men and horses were torn into bloody fragments. The Confederate line was forced back through Dover and near sundown the Confederate firing ceased.[130]

For more than two hours, Colonel Harding's men waited for another assault. They were sure that Forrest would try again, but at eight o'clock, General Wheeler sent in a flag of truce and demanded a surrender, which Colonel Harding refused. At a Confederate staff meeting, a messenger arrived to warn them that Union reinforcements were on their way to Fort Donelson from Fort Henry. The Confederate soldiers were low on ammunition and realized that they could not defeat the larger Union force. General Wheeler gave the order to withdraw. The Confederates gathered up the wounded and all the supplies they could use. Anything left behind was destroyed including buildings and boats loaded with supplies. The little town of Dover lay in smoldering ruins.[131]

The short battle proved very costly to the Confederate army. Two hundred and seventeen men were killed, 60 wounded, and 8 missing. The Union casualty list was 13 killed, 51 wounded, and 46 missing. Once again the ravages of war had struck the people. Dover was turned into rubble; not a single building stood undamaged. Horses and mules had been taken by the retreating Confederate force. Even supplies which the citizens needed had been burned.

---

[129]Ibid.

[130]O. R. Series I, vol. XXIII, 34; O. R. Series I, vol. XXIII, 34-39.

[131]Ibid.

Wild rumors spread over the area that Colonel Forrest intended to return to destroy anything the Federal army might use. The Union officers, who were afraid of the possibility of further attacks, responded by ordering that work begin immediately to strengthen the defensive positions of both forts. All male civilians able to work were compelled to assist in the construction. In the meantime, six gunboats and a supply fleet arrived at Fort Donelson from Nashville.[132]

Effects of War

Typically any civil war divides families and disrupts friendships. The land between the rivers suffered the classic horrors of a civil rebellion when former close friends and members of the same family joined different armies. An incident at Eddyville in 1864 demonstrated the emotional effects of this situation. General Harlan B. Lyon, a native of the area, led a Confederate force into Hopkinsville and Cadiz, burning public buildings and generally disrupting the area. Since General Lyon was near his home in Eddyville, he made arrangements to bring his men close to the town so that he could slip into Eddyville to visit his wife. While he was in his home, a Union officer entered the house and demanded that Lyon surrender. Lyon killed the man and escaped. Lyon was convinced that some neighbor had betrayed him to the Federal authorities. He brought his men into the town and burned the court house and tried to find the neighbors who had betrayed him. General Lyon narrowly escaped being caught by a large Union force which had just moved to Eddyville. The incident caused the Union army to place the town under martial law for the duration of the war.[133] This incident and many others are examples of how all the land between the rivers was actually under military subjugation even though Kentucky had not left the Union.

By the winter of 1864, Federal soldiers were sent out periodically with a quota of materials which they must take, not buy from the citizens. An example of the practice was Colonel Streight's march from Nashville to Fort Henry then to Alabama and Georgia. He was sent to destroy rebel property and railroads found in the area. Before he left Nashville, Colonel Streight was allowed to draw half the number of mules and horses which he would need for his expedition. He was to seize the additional animals along the way. He and his men left Nashville by steamer and landed at Palmyra. When he arrived, he wrote that his men were dismayed at the condition of the mules and horses he found. He described them as nothing more than "poor, wild and unbroken colts." He worried that many of the animals were suffering from distemper and were too sick to ride.[134]

On his march to Stewart County, Colonel Streight had his men gather all horses and mules they could find along the way. After his first raid in Montgomery County, farmers in the whole area tried to hide their animals, but they were usually unsuccessful. Streight described the difficulty he had in finding the 1,250 animals he now had with his force. The animals were

---

[132]Ibid.

[133]Ibid.

[134]O. R. Series I, vol. XXIII, 285-293.

reported to be in good condition except "they were nearly all barefooted."[135] He noted in the report that he had found several hundred horses and mules in the Fort Henry region. It appears that some of the mules came from Trigg and Lyon Counties. Streight's expedition, and others like it, removed most of the work animals from the land between the rivers' region.

Starting Over

On July 5, 1865, the people of Stewart County accepted the end of military occupation and made plans to hold local elections. After elections were held on July 15, 1865, Isaac Williams, chairman of the County Court, began the task of rebuilding the economic and political operations of the county. The county court assumed the duties of levying and collecting taxes, receiving petitions, appropriating funds, appointing the overseer of roads, receiving letters of administration, accepting bonds, and receiving the inventories for the sale of property.[136]

The activities of these people in 1865 were almost a perfect re-enactment of what the first settlers did in 1804. Stewart County and those portions of Trigg and Lyon Counties included in the land between the rivers had moved backward from a prosperous economy to an impoverished area. From this time until the twentieth century, the area suffered overwhelming economic problems. An additional difficulty was that the people began the new era with the painful emotional burdens of the war still very clear in their minds. The physical effects of the war were apparent; the barren land was a constant reminder of what had happened over the past five years. Many of the male citizens had been killed or wounded in the war. In the face of all of these circumstances, however, the people had the determination to survive. They began to rebuild their lives and affirm their traditions. The war had taught the people that many of their beliefs had been valid; governments, especially the national government, could not be trusted. They had to watch outsiders, all of whom were suspect until they had become well known. The family unit had to be protected. An individual had to be as good as his word. Honesty was a virtue, but money usually corrupted. They believed that their poverty was a temporary condition.

One of the immediate and more conspicuous effects of the war was the decline in land prices and farm rental contracts. Trigg and Lyon Counties as well as Stewart County had to adjust to the free labor system now that slavery was ended. Even though land prices were slightly better in both Trigg and Lyon Counties, most of the land sold for a low price. A large farm on the river that had rented for over eight hundred dollars in 1862, now in 1865 rented for fifty-eight dollars.[137]

As the practices of tenant farming and share cropping were being shaped from 1865 to

---

[135]Colonel Streight was either misquoted by the telegraph operator or he had little expertise in handling these animals. He actually should have reported that the animals were unshod.

[136]1865, Stewart County Court records, Book I, 1-39.

[137]A comparison was made of the records in the county courts, circuit courts, tax assessors offices, and deed books for Lyon, Trigg, and Stewart Counties. See Lyon County, County Court records, Book 71, 12-19; Trigg County Court records, Book, 80, 11-19; Stewart County Tax Assessor records, 10-D, 19, 56, 57.

1875, the situation in the area became a microcosm of the difficulties inherent in the southern economic system. The people with land usually did not have the capital to hire workers to tend the crops. At the same time, people without land wanted to work, but they could not find jobs because land owners had no money. Land owners were afraid of assuming any financial responsibility for those people who wanted to work the lands and share in the proceeds of the harvest. For three or four years, the people were often unable to agree on the contracts for share cropping or tenant farming.[138]

Land values showed an obvious decline in the period between 1865 and 1868. Land that had sold for a dollar an acre in 1862 and even more before 1860, fell to a low of twenty to twenty-five cents per acre in 1868. Money was scarce and it was extremely difficult for many people to obtain loans to purchase land. The inflated prices of farm animals and equipment discouraged prospective farmers. Many people who wanted to farm were unable to buy more than a few acres. The size of an average farm decreased from a hundred acres in 1850 to forty or fifty acres in 1869.[139]

The iron industry was never able to recover from the effects of the Civil War. Most of the iron furnaces had ceased production during the war and new processes in the manufacture of crude iron doomed the industry. Several attempts were made to rebuild and repair the old furnaces, but the efforts were not successful.

After a decade, the lumber industry was revitalized in the area, but the sawmill operators were handicapped by the lack of labor and the expensive transportation costs. The industry was usually a family enterprise and the mills remained small with a limited production quota each year from 1865 to 1872.[140]

The Thirteenth Amendment to the Constitution did not change the people's attitude toward the freedmen. Accommodation seemed to be the general feeling. Some of the people blamed their economic plight on the former slaves, and others felt that the abolitionists had caused the war. The traditional beliefs of white superiority were very strong, but this did not mean that people would ignore the needs of the freedmen.

In January 1866, a smallpox epidemic broke out with the first cases of the disease reported in the black community that had grown up at the edge of Fort Donelson during the war. The slaves captured when the fort surrendered and others that had been brought in as workers by the Union army tended to remain in their crude huts and cabins when the war ended. The cabins were near Dover, and when the smallpox epidemic broke out there and spread into the county, the officials realized that the former slaves had little medical service available to them. After an extended debate, the county officials assumed full responsibility for the care of the black population. This decision was not very popular, but it set a precedent for the area. Blacks were recognized as a part of the community, and when they needed care the taxpayers

---

[138]Ibid. Stewart County Court records, Book 3, 12, 35, 56. Mention is made in the minutes of fair rental values.

[139]Stewart County records, Tax Assessment records, Book 1-A, 1-29; Book I-C, 1-40; Book 3-A, 1-59.

[140]The absence of railroads had always handicapped the economy of the area. It was never economically feasible to link the area with railroad lines across the rivers.

would assume the responsibility. Altruism was only a minor component of the whole decision. The court records indicate quite clearly that the fear that the epidemic would spread throughout the entire region was uppermost in the minds of the officials. The blacks were isolated in their quarters, and Isaac Williams, George Dougherty and James Ralls were appointed to a committee to aid the smallpox victims. They were asked to investigate the black community and ascertain the living conditions and needs of the people. They were requested to provide the best means in their power to stop the spread of the disease. The county court authorized the County Trustee to pay any expenses which would be incurred in fighting the epidemic. The committee visited the people and ordered that food, clothing, and medical supplies be given them at once.[141] The homes of the victims of the disease were burned.[142] No mention is made of attempts to aid family members who were forced out of their home. Mr. G. M. Stewart, who lived in Dover, assumed the responsibility of taking the provisions to those who were too ill to come to him, and he arranged for burial for those who had died from the disease. In January of 1867, a year after the disease was first reported, the county court paid G. M. Stewart the sum of $200.00 for his services, and the total amount spent on the care of the black citizens was over $500.00, a substantial amount for that time.[143] It was during this time that most of the black families in the land between the rivers were moved to the black community near Dover. For reasons that are not clear, these people did not leave the black community when the epidemic ended. They stayed near Dover or later moved to other villages outside the land between the rivers.[144]

Rebuilding and Repairing

Economic conditions from 1866 to 1875 seemed especially bleak for the majority of the people. The pauper rolls continued to rise. A majority of these people were widows and children of men who had been killed in the Civil War. Also, it was extremely difficult to find employment. There was no currency available; neither paper money, nor specie was in circulation. People tried to use barter, but the county governments needed money. The tax problem seemed insurmountable, and the leaders tried to organize a method of allowing the citizens to pay their taxes with goods instead of money. Difficulties arose over the method of determining the amount of goods for the equivalent tax dollar.[145]

---

[141]June through August, 1865. Stewart County court records, Book I, 49, 51.

[142]The practice of burning the houses of anyone who had died from smallpox was a common practice at the time. It was thought that the practice would stop the spread of the disease.

[143]1867, Stewart County Court records, Book 2-A, 12-14.

[144]Comparison of U. S. Population Census Records for 1860 and 1870.

[145]The practice was mentioned in 1865 and 1866 in all three counties in the land between the rivers. After 1866, Stewart County was the only county which had to continue the method, and it was continued until 1868. See Stewart County Court records, Book I, 22-25; Tax Assessor records, Book I-C, 11-39.

The cash problem became so acute that the county courts ordered the clerks and revenue collectors to accept properly authenticated county specie as legal currency for the payment of any revenue or wages for the counties. The county currency was used as good vouchers in most business transactions conducted by the county and all legally authorized agents of the county. The vouchers were generally accepted as cash by the people and merchants who lived in the surrounding areas. As soon as the counties realized that people accepted the vouchers as legal tender, they began to use them as well as U. S. dollars to transact business anywhere they were accepted.[146]

Stewart county began in 1865 to rebuild the public buildings that had been destroyed during the conflict. Because of limited funds, the jail was not completed until 1870, and construction on the courthouse was not complete until 1879. The people simply could not afford the luxury of replacing the buildings.[147]

One of the most perplexing problems was the structuring of a school system. All of the schools around the forts had closed during the fighting and had not reopened in 1865. For a decade before the war, the belief that every child in the area needed at least an elementary education had been taking hold. By 1865 the people, in general, accepted the view that basic education should be provided by using tax money. In 1867, the Tennessee legislature enacted the first laws to organize common schools, but within a few months the laws were repealed and the counties were responsible for all education.

It was the responsibility of the county court to find the revenue to furnish the school buildings, provide equipment, and hire teachers. For some time, each individual community worked to open some type of school because county funds were not available. Teachers taught classes in churches or any building available, and they lived with families in the community and their salary was supplemented with goods.[148]

Also, poor or pauper houses had to be re-established. Widows and orphans of the veterans of the Civil War made up the largest number of the impoverished. The trend was to hire a family in the area to care for indigent people and a small allowance was provided by the taxpayers for their care. One of the apparent cultural attitudes of the time was that anyone who had to live in the poor house was a social pariah. Such people were described as lazy, as sinners, or insane if they failed to provide for themselves and turned to public charity for care.[149]

Roads had to be rebuilt and ferries had to be re-established before the people could travel and transport their goods. It soon became apparent that more tax money had to be found to meet the cost of reconstruction. The dilemma was that people did not have the money to pay the taxes and if the counties seized land for delinquent taxes, the problem simply worsened. For

---

[146]County Court records in Lyon, Trigg, and Stewart Counties. See Stewart County Court records, Book 7, 12, 13, 16, 18, 19.

[147]Stewart County Court records, Book 1, 27-32; Book 6. 22-23; Book 15, 19-27.

[148]Even though Lyon and Trigg Counties had more revenue than Stewart County, the schools in the land between the rivers were much the same. See Stewart County Court records, Book 9, 12-14. Corlew, Tennessee, 396.

[149]The attitude toward the poor seemed prevalent throughout the region.

example, in 1865, the county court had levied a tax of five cents on each one hundred dollars of taxable property and a one dollar tax on each poll. The roster of delinquent taxpayers was quite long. The estimated value of all land had decreased by 1865. The figures for property in Trigg and Lyon Counties that was within the land between the rivers indicated the same decline. The property in the two Kentucky counties outside the area showed no reduction.[150]

Trigg, Lyon and Stewart Counties had declined in the estimates of property value when the slaves were freed, but in the land between the rivers, the reduction was also in livestock, buggies, coaches, and other personal property. The total tax revenue that Stewart County had been able to collect in 1865 and 1866 did not pay the interest on the debts that the county owed, much less for the many new expenses that the county had to assume.[151]

All social institutions suffered from the lack of funding. People resented the taxes, and a revival of the attitude that taxation by the government should be strictly limited became evident. It was felt that the local governments were trying to meet too many demands including education, law enforcement, road construction, and aid for the poor. The general attitude was that the government should leave some of those responsibilities to the community. Education, paupers, and roads could be handled by the families in the community. Inherent in the argument was the concept that they did not want to assume the tax burden of building facilities outside their own community.[152]

The task of raising revenue became critical in Stewart County about 1870. In a report submitted to the county court by Richard Ledbetter, Chairman of the Court, in 1874, the county had been spending about $600.00 a year more than the revenue received. Ledbetter advised the county officials that no funds were available to pay jurors, bailiffs, or election officials, and the justices of the peace had not received their payment in more than a year. He advised the people that the $600.00 annual deficits were only a small part of the total indebtedness that the county was facing at the time. The officials could not determine the exact amount of money that was owed by the county in the fiscal year 1874-1875. Yet, the county court continued to issue vouchers and increased the indebtedness each session of the court.[153]

The people became more hesitant to accept the vouchers as money for their services and labor when businessmen who lived outside the land between the rivers in Trigg and Lyon Counties hesitated or refused to accept them. As the confidence in the value of vouchers declined, the Stewart County officials found it increasingly difficult to operate. As late as 1878, the county court issued a report that told of the critical financial difficulties and warned of new taxes which would be collected.[154] When the Stewart county vouchers became

---

[150]Comparisons of Tax Assessor lists in 1860 to those in 1865 and 1866 show a marked decline in amount of personal property in the area.

[151]Ibid., Stewart County Court records, Book 7, 12.

[152]Ibid.

[153]Stewart County court records 1865 to 1875. Book 1, 34-36, Book 3, 23-27; Book 5, 24-35; Book 6, 12-19; Book 8, 32-34; Book 9, 45-49; Book 10, 22-28.

[154]Ibid. Book 11, 19-22.

unacceptable, the people turned to a system of barter. This type of exchange made it difficult to transact business, but in that critical period it was the only method the people had. Merchants accepted tobacco, livestock, and other farm produce for articles sold in the stores. Tobacco was the preferred barter item because merchants could ship the hogsheads of tobacco by boat to markets more easily than they could sell livestock and perishable farm produce. Merchant records, although incomplete, indicate that companies tried to import goods for sale, and had set up the practice of sending company wagons loaded with merchandise and medicine to the more isolated communities.[155]

These peddlers, as they were called, took goods for merchandise; then the merchants sold the goods outside the region for cash and in turn purchased goods for sale in the area. The practice proved profitable enough that independent peddlers began operations in the region in the two decades following 1870.

When economic conditions allowed, the merchants acted as commission agents and purchased the goods from the people for cash and then sold the goods to merchants. The commission agents made money in the transactions. Farmers would negotiate with the agents before the harvest period and borrow money toward the harvest. Quite often, the farmers ended the season in debt to the agents.[156]

The abundant natural resources of the region allowed a gradual change in economic conditions. By 1872, the second growth of timber had matured on the lands that had been cut for the early iron industry. Again, the area was well timbered with white and black oak which supplied material for staves and boards. Approximately 200,000 staves were shipped out of the area annually. Wooden shingles used for roofs and siding were sold at home and shipped to foreign ports. Wood was sold to fuel the steamboats still using the Tennessee and Cumberland Rivers. Shipping and transportation on the rivers, however, never regained the profits they had enjoyed before the Civil War. The area had a wealth of walnut, cherry, poplar, cedar, chestnut, cottonwood, ash, gum, linden, beech, maple, locust, sycamore, mulberry, pine, elm, and sassafras trees. The wooded land was selling for three to ten dollars per acre. The wild dogwood and redbud trees were so abundant that in the spring, the area seemed to turn into a red and white bouquet.[157]

The old coaling lands were gradually reclaimed and sold for one to three dollars per acre. The coaling land, at first thought to be sterile, was found to be productive, and farmers planted grasses including timothy, clover, millet, hay grasses and herds-grass. Four tons of hay per acre was the average yield. Farmers used these lands for cattle, sheep, goats, horses, mules, and

---

[155]Walters and Scarborough merchant records were found in the Court House in Dover, Tennessee. These loose records were found in County Court records, Book 13 and covered the period from 1866 to 1878. The records were incomplete for 1875 and 1877.

[156]Lyon, Trigg, and Stewart County records 1866 to 1879. See Stewart County Court records, Book 2, 13, 24. An example of permits to agents to purchase goods is in the Walters and Scarborough records; peddlers made periodic trips into the land between the rivers until World War II. Because some of the communities did not have grocery or hardware stores, the peddlers took merchandise to the people first in covered wagons and later in trucks. The peddler kept a schedule and many stories are told of children waiting for peddler-day so they could swap an egg for a stick of candy.

[157]Walters and Scarborough Merchant records.

oxen. Burley tobacco proved to be an excellent crop for the high rolling lands between the rivers and soon became the major tobacco crop.[158]

Farmers who were trying to increase profits introduced sheep herds in the area by 1880. They had experimented with the Cotswold, Leicester and Southdown breeds and were satisfied with the wool production. Because grazing lands were plentiful, sheep raising had the potential of becoming one of the most profitable enterprises, but the farmers were plagued with dogs which killed approximately ten per cent of their sheep annually. Attempts were made to require citizens to restrain their dogs, but the actions failed and provoked discord and some violence among the farmers. Sheep owners were eventually forced to admit that they could not compel the local governments to enact restraint laws or any other controls over the dogs. The general sentiment was that a people had the right to own as many dogs as they wished, and those dogs were free to roam at will. There was similarity between an attitude toward allowing dogs to roam free and a disdain for fences to control the movement of livestock.[159]

From 1875 to 1890, a number of Swiss and German families moved into the region. They were excellent farmers and recognized the need to reclaim the worn out farmland and showed by example how the land could be replenished. Manure was used as fertilizer and their farms flourished. They increased their cattle herds, and the Swiss developed prosperous dairy farms. They introduced Durham cattle to the area. The dairy farmers sold milk and cheese to their neighbors, but the lack of adequate transportation facilities handicapped the sales outside the region. The German settlers, already familiar with growing grapes and wine production, planted vineyards. Wine production was a flourishing enterprise and they had no problem selling all they produced in the area.[160]

The bottom land on both sides of the Tennessee and Cumberland Rivers comprised some of the richest farm land in the United States. The lands produced abundant yields of corn, oats, wheat, tobacco, and hemp. The farmers could produce seventy-five or more bushels of corn per acre. The low lands on either side of the many creeks, which drained the water into the Tennessee and Cumberland Rivers, was only slightly less fertile than the river bottom lands. The farms produced good average yields of the same crops. The river bottom land sold for ten to fifteen dollars per acre and the creek bottom land sold for an average of five dollars per acre.[161]

Land was abundant and cheap, but the cost of clearing the land, approximately ten dollars per acre, was often prohibitive. The injudicious destruction of forest land abated to some degree because the larger farms with cleared land were partitioned and sold to outsiders. The lucrative

---

[158]Tax Assessor records, Book 18-A, 33-47.

[159]Interviews with residents in 1959, and former residents in 1989. Interviews in the hands of the author.

[160]The names of these settlers were found in the U. S. Population Census Records, 1870 to 1890. The family names were traced to Tax Assessor lists in the counties.

[161]Tax Assessor lists in the counties. Estate Sales in the period in the counties.

lumber enterprises were the major hindrance to the reforestation of the region.[162]   Land was selling for much less than the price it had brought in 1859, and those farmers who had been able to preserve their large acreage adopted more modern methods for cultivation. To try to escape the constriction of tight money, land was rented for one-third of the crop. Tobacco land was rented for six to eight dollars per acre. Wheat land rented for one-third of the yield. When the land owners furnished tools and teams, they expected to receive one half of the crop. Farm hands were scarce and farmers paid, on the average, fifteen to twenty dollars per month for laborers.[163]   Because the farmers did not have a stable or reliable labor supply, they were forced to reduce the amount they produced or rent the land to small farmers. By 1880, a few farmers depended upon recruitment of workers from outside the region to tend the crops. These workers lived on the farm for a specific period of time and were housed, fed, and paid a wage by the land owner. This system was often costly, and the sharecropping and tenant farming superseded the imported labor system.[164]

The effects of the Civil War would linger in the region for generations. The immediate economic effects could be observed in the increasing number of landless and unemployed. These people often moved out of the region to find employment. The population decreased during the Civil War and the trend continued until just before World War II.[165]

The Civil War's greatest effect on the population was the numbers of men killed and wounded in the war. The widows and orphans of the veterans soon made up the most impoverished group in the area. Widows were forced to find employment because the public assistance was not enough to keep the family together. These women were without skills and soon became the working poor. They were often employed as domestics or in agriculture. For more than two decades, numbers of women tried to survive as heads of households, working in jobs which paid the lowest wages .[166]   It was extremely difficult to educate children or even provide the basic needs. One of the results of this change in the status of women was that the lines of the gender related jobs were often changed. Jobs that had at one time been considered male jobs were now done by women. Social reaction to those women who existed at the poverty level was negative. Even women who came from middle class families who could not find jobs to support themselves were often denigrated by the community.

---

[162]Ibid. Records of Deeds show that people from states outside the south bought some of the land. Approximately three families came from Pennsylvania during this period. People from Maryland and Kentucky also bought land.

[163]Advertisements for rental and tenant farmers appeared in the newspapers of the period. Eddyville Journal, January 29, 1881.

[164]Ibid.

[165]Survey of U. S. Population Census indicates a decline in the population for 1870 to 1920.

[166]A rough estimate from the U. S. Population Census is that about 30% of the households were directed by women. In interviews with the residents of the area, the author found that women looked upon domestic workers as one of the lowest ranking jobs in the community. Women who were forced, by whatever circumstance, to enter that job were looked upon with pity.

CHAPTER VIII

LIFE FROM 1890 TO WORLD WAR I

The countryside and people were changed by the Civil War and its aftermath, but by 1880 the people had made adjustments to the changes and re-established many of the old traditions and values. The survivors wanted to preserve as much of their old life as possible. The immigrants who entered the area just after the Civil War were the last large group of outsiders to enter the area. These people seemed to assimilate into the culture without difficulty, but the locals would not continue to welcome outsiders. Surprisingly, the population was similar to the early settlement period. The black families had moved to the periphery of the region and lived near Dover, Twin Rivers, and Cadiz.[1] The reclaimed traditions included an antipathy toward powerful government, a strong belief in self-sufficiency, and clannish behavior. Self-preservation was the motive in many of their actions. They had no other way of overcoming the trauma and upheaval of the Civil War. Memories of the conflict formed a romantic attachment to the Civil War, a strong bias against outsiders, and a growing opposition to the Republican party.

Politics

The opposition to the Republican party was seen in local politics. When politicians ran for office, either they described themselves as Democrats or they did not divulge their political affiliations. The pervasive notion was that everyone should be a Democrat, and if you were not, you kept your mouth shut in political discussions.[2]

In 1880 the Democratic presidential candidate received over 60% of the vote in Lyon and Trigg County and nearly 70% of the vote in Stewart County.[3] The Democratic party was not threatened by the Greenback or Prohibition parties during the era, even though parts of their platform appealed to some.

Between 1880 and 1888 the Prohibition Party, championed by the Protestant churches, was catching fire in other states. Only a few voters in the three counties supported the Prohibition candidate. One explanation for the difference between the vocal support for

---

[1]Interviews with residents of Lyon, Trigg, and Stewart Counties in 1959 and former residents in 1989 held by the author present evidence that the residents had by 1880 begun a long history of wanting to exclude outsiders, including blacks. According to these people it was just understood that certain people were not welcome so they didn't come into the area. The author interviewed fifty residents outside the region in 1960 to determine if they were aware of the attitude toward outsiders in the region and all of them explained it the same way; no strangers, especially blacks, were welcome in the area.

[2]Interviews with citizens of the area in 1959 and former residents in 1988. Interviews in the hands of the author.

[3]Original returns are in the Archives of Kentucky Historical Society, Frankfort, Kentucky, and Tennessee State Library and Archives, Nashville, Tennessee.

prohibition and the small number of people who actually voted for the candidates could be that women constituted the majority of the church congregations. Women, the faithful foundation of the church, were not allowed to vote. Also, it must be recalled that the whiskey industry was one of the most profitable businesses in the region. They felt that it would not be in their best interest to outlaw the sale of alcohol.

Tariff issues pulled many of the voters to the Democratic Party, even while the Populist movement was successful in making some inroads into the Democratic vote in the election of 1892.[4] Even though the Democratic candidate, Grover Cleveland, carried both Kentucky and Tennessee, a significant number of voters supported the Populist movement and wanted changes in the Democratic Party. The strongly agrarian areas of both states were the most receptive to the Populist demands.[5]

Certain salient facts stand out in the tremendous voter turnout in 1896. William J. Bryan aroused the old Jacksonian Democratic counties with his appeal to the farmers and the small towns. Bryan was popular in the rural areas of Tennessee and Kentucky, but could not sway voters in other parts of the states. Sound money was one of the issues which affected the old agrarian elite, and they did not look kindly on the "Cross of Gold" candidate.[6]

From 1896 to 1900 the Democratic Party was torn by bitter dissension growing out of the Populist revolt. The newly elected governor of Kentucky, a Republican, was assassinated. Tennesseeans were demanding changes. In general, politics in both states were unsettled. In the land between the rivers the fall-out from the strife was a larger victory for the Democratic candidate, William J. Bryan.[7]

During the early years of the twentieth century, progressive impulses struck the South. A series of movements unfolded as politicians, educators, and other professionals became reformers. They posed questions about public education, welfare systems, and more efficient methods of farming. People wanted to solve the social problems of the time. Temperance, prohibition, and women's suffrage were some of the issues which concerned the people. The reformers believed that economic development and material progress could be achieved if the regulatory powers of the government were expanded. Social controls were necessary to preserve moral values. Men and women had to be protected from themselves, and laws would force them to control their weaknesses.[8]

For these people, some of the progressive spirit was not hard to assimilate into their

---

[4]Ibid.

[5]Ibid. Populists were advocates of the People's Party (1891-1904) favoring free coinage of gold and silver, public ownership of utilities, an income tax, and support of labor and agriculture.

[6]William Jennings Bryan became famous at the Democratic national convention in July, 1896 when he challenged the conservative wing of the party with a chilling speech on the gold standard. His closing words were: "You shall not press down upon the brow of labor this cross of thorns, you shall not crucify mankind upon a cross of gold." He carried the counties in the area.

[7]Bryan ran again on the Democratic ticket in 1900 and 1908.

[8]For an excellent survey of the progressive spirit in the South see Dewey W. Grantham's Southern Progressivism: The Reconciliation of Progress and Tradition. (Knoxville: The University of Tennessee Press, 1983).

157

political beliefs. The most difficult problem was to accept the concept that governmental regulatory powers were the solution. They accepted the ideas of economic advancement and support for public education. Suffrage for women did not divide the communities because individual rights for white Americans was acceptable, but Prohibition caused the people to question the reformers. They could not accept the theory that social controls were necessary to preserve moral values. The very idea that laws should be passed to tell them what was right and wrong was unacceptable. For generations these people had guarded their sense of individuality and independence, and regulatory laws were the antitheses to their right of choice.[9]

The progressive programs, during the period from 1900 through 1920, had a limited success in the land between the rivers. In the election of 1904, the Democrats were able to gain strength in Kentucky and Tennessee, but as in the past, the counties in the area continued to support the Democratic Party. The people did not seem to respond to the Teddy Roosevelt "brand of politics."[10] In all the counties, the more progressive candidates saw an increased vote when the Democrats ran a conservative candidate such as Alton B. Parker, who was too much like a Republican to suit the voters. The personal and populist appeal of William J. Bryan brought voters in all of Kentucky and Tennessee to the polls in larger numbers in 1908 than in 1904. Once again they supported the Democratic candidate.[11]

The presidential election of 1912 was an exciting one for the people. The split in the Republican Party between Taft and Roosevelt offered a topic for discussion in most households and at the country stores; however, fewer men felt that they must vote in the election. The number of voters in all the counties declined in 1912. Wilson carried all the counties, but the number of votes was lower than it had been for Bryan in 1908. One of the reasons was many people thought Roosevelt would win the election. Residents expressed surprise when Wilson won the election.[12]

The atmosphere was different in 1916 when Woodrow Wilson ran for re-election. This was the first time a Democratic president had run for re-election since 1888.[13] The issue of war and peace was before the voters, and Wilson had been successful in pushing Congress for labor legislation. Discussion about the Prohibition and Suffrage movements grabbed the imagination of many voters. Whatever the reason, voters went to the polls, and seemed eager to cast their ballot for Wilson.

---

[9]Interviews by the author with citizens in 1959. The people were asked to comment on how they and their parents had reacted to Prohibition.

[10]The term meant that Roosevelt was saying some good things about reform but after all, he was a Republican. They thought he was trying to put a new face on an old party. His brand on the party was not enough to make it palatable.

[11]Tennessee and Kentucky Archives. Some of the populists joined the People's party (1891-1904).

[12]Theodore Roosevelt left the Republican Party and ran on the Progressive Party ticket to oppose his former friend William Howard Taft. Woodrow Wilson was the Democratic nominee. In interviews with the older residents many of them talked about the amazement the people felt when they learned that Wilson had won the election. Interviews in the hands of the author.

[13]Grover Cleveland was elected in 1884 and ran for re-election in 1888. He was defeated by Benjamin Harrison. Cleveland ran again in 1892 and was elected for a second term. He served two non-consecutive terms.

Economic and Social Conditions

In the early twentieth century, the unfavorable economic conditions of the region did not make life dismal or disconsolate for the people. It is true that they worked hard and there was very little time left for recreation. They had a background of making do with what was available to them. Most of the people raised all, or some, of their food. They devised their own forms of entertainment. Their social events were reminiscent of the frontier and settlement era.

Men formed literary societies, such as the Rushing Creek Literary Society which met near Dilday's Landing. They announced a topic for discussion at monthly meetings. Everyone was encouraged to study the topic and be ready to discuss it at the next session, held in churches and homes. Often, the literary societies conducted debates on contemporary topics. Lectures were formed around issues which drew the attention of the people, and often the whole community would attend. Politics and religion afforded the most popular topics for conversation. Large crowds gathered and local politicians took the opportunity to make their views known.[14]

Much of the entertainment was centered around the home and family. People enjoyed talking to one another and telling stories about their lives and the things their ancestors had done. Of course, they did not realize that they were oral historians; they wanted their children to remember their heritage. Genealogy was an extremely significant facet of a child's education. Families gathered in the evenings and told tales which they called "yarns." These stories were told as truth, and the teller vouched for the authenticity of his story by claiming that he had witnessed the event or he had heard it from a reliable witness. Whether a yarn was true or not, it was in all likelihood embellished.[15]

People took great delight in their ability to hold the audience spellbound with their stories and songs. The master story teller held a special place in the community, and each community seemed to have at least one man and woman who held the honor. Men told stories about the exploits of other men. Women told stories about the family and community.

Ghost stories appealed to the children. Frequently, these stories were interpretations of events which the people could not logically explain. The supernatural interpretations were accepted, and often included sightings of family members or friends who had died. The ghost had returned to portend the future. Apparitions were either good or evil depending upon the message they brought. Poltergeists were blamed for mishaps or unexplained accidents. Elderly women were often thought to be conduits of the supernatural. These women had a familiar most often in the form of a cat or wild animal. The people who were believed to have supernatural powers did not become outcasts and were not described as witches. They were thought to be

---

[14]Lyon, Trigg, and Stewart County court records, 1880 to 1916.

[15]Yarns were defined by some of the people as tall tales. The word was used to describe a story that was slightly unbelievable. Since the story could have happened just the way it was told, it was not labeled a lie. Interviews with people in the area. Interviews in the hands of the author.

159

different but not evil.[16]

Postulates and aphorisms were an important part of life, and sayings containing these beliefs were passed down from one generation to another.[17] A large body of the beliefs centered around superstitions about the death of babies. This circumstance could be understood given the high death rate of young children. Individuals were warned not to cut a baby's hair until he was a year old, or he would die. Babies were not allowed to see themselves in a mirror before they reached their first birthday. An exceptionally brilliant child would die before reaching adulthood. A baby who talked before it walked would die. Parents were told not to love their child too much or it would die young.[18] Dreams warned people that death was near. Anyone who dreamed of falling and hit bottom was going to die. A dream of a wedding was a sign of death. If a person dreamed of a birth it is a sign of death, and a dream of a storm meant a relative was going to die.[19]

Certain beliefs associated with the human body warned people of an event. It was said for example: if you had a ringing sound in the ears, you would hear of a death in three days. If you had your hair cut during the month of March, you would die before the year was out. If you stepped over somebody who was lying on the floor, you had to step back across him before he got up, or he would die. If shingles went all around the body, the person having them would die. Shivers indicated that someone was walking over the spot that would soon be your grave. Children were not allowed to sing after they went to bed; it would bring bad luck.[20]

Certain actions in the home were taboo because they could bring on death or bad luck. It was believed that if you swept under a person's feet with a broom that person would never get married. If you swept under someone's bed while he was sick he would die. To break a mirror was a sign of death or very bad luck. It is a sign of death to spin a chair on one leg. If you left a rocking chair rocking, it would cause a death in the family. If a hoe was brought into the house, that hoe would dig your grave. If you left the house and realized that you had forgotten something, you could not re-enter the house until you had made a cross in the dirt and then spit in it.[21]

Sayings about certain days, holidays, or special events were common. A green Christmas indicated that the graveyard was going to be filled. A white Christmas indicated that

---

[16]The author was able to collect a number of the ghost stories in 1959 from the residents. The stories are quite varied and interesting. The people who were thought to have supernatural powers were allowed to be different. Descriptions of their behavior made the author wonder if perhaps they suffered from minor emotional disorders. Interviews are in the hands of the author.

[17]A collection of the adages and beliefs was made from 1956 to 1962. When the people were asked whether they followed the saying, most of those questioned said yes. They agreed it was better to be safe than sorry.

[18]From the author's collection.

[19]One saying was: dream of a death and you will attend a wedding.

[20]From the author's collection.

[21]Ibid. There were ways to deflect evil. A black cat crossing your path was bad luck, but if you turned your cap around the bad luck would be behind you.

there were not going to be many deaths in the community. A light or mild Christmas denoted a good crop year and a fat graveyard. If you carried ashes out of the house between Christmas and New Year's there would be a death in the family. If you took anything out of the house on New Year's day, all the family's money would be lost. If you started a project on Friday and didn't finish it, you would die before the year was out. Any miscreants who sewed on Sunday would have to remove the stitches with their teeth after judgement day.[22]

Many beliefs centered around flowers and trees. Superstitions about cedar trees were common. It was believed transplanting a cedar tree would cause your death when it grew large enough to shadow a grave. It was also believed that most older people died when the sap was going up or down in trees. If a person dreamed of flowers, that person was going to die.[23]

The actions of animals and birds were believed to be predictions of the future. Howling dogs, bawling cows, and a rooster crowing at night warned of death. If a rooster came to the front steps and crowed, someone was coming to visit. It was bad luck to hear a hen crow, and the only way to stop the bad luck was to kill the hen. If a bird got into the house, it was a sign that someone was going to die. A mockingbird singing at night was a sign of death. One of the most repeated sayings was: "A whistling woman and a crowing hen always come to some bad end."[24]

Before telephone service was available, it was difficult to communicate, even with the nearest neighbor. To keep in touch people rang the dinner bells or hollered. Three rings of the bell meant "help," and everyone within hearing distance immediately rushed to aid the neighbor. Hollering or yelling was used to communicate over shorter distances. Messages were sent from farm to farm in this manner. Reminiscent of techniques of yodeling, the people would holler back and forth to the neighbors, and certain tones of the yell were the message.[25]

Burial customs had not changed since the settlement period. Neighbors and family members prepared the bodies for burial. The neighbors would gather, wash the corpse, and choose or even make the clothing for the dead. The dress for burial was usually very simple clothing or a shroud. The shrouds were made of white, gray, or black material. The woman's shroud was full length, pleated in the front, with lace stitched on the pleats for adornment. All the shrouds were opened in the back. A man's shroud resembled a suit of clothes with full length trousers and a regular shirt. Babies were buried in white gowns. Coffins were generally made by the community cabinetmaker, carpenter, or a member of the family, according to individual need or size.[26] The coffins were unadorned and were kept covered until after the

---

[22]The interviews in 1959 and 1960 indicated that a general concern about who visited the home first on New Year's morning was important. The ideal visitor was a female with dark hair. The author tried to determine the origin of that particular superstition, but no clues could be found.

[23]Ibid.

[24]Ibid.

[25]Ibid.

[26]Ibid. Funeral homes were not in common use until after WWII.

funeral service. The corpse was usually kept in the home until the burial ceremony. Several people sat with the body throughout the night; someone was always in attendance. The principal reason given was that it showed respect and affection for the deceased; however, the practice was used in Ireland for hundreds of years, and these and many other burial customs can be traced to Ireland, Scotland, and Wales.[27]

From the time of the death until the funeral, neighbors brought food to the home of the deceased. The food was for the family, as well as for the neighbors who came to console the bereaved and sit with the body. Neighbors took care of all the chores until the funeral.[28]

Until well into the twentieth century, it was considered proper for wives to wear mourning clothes for a period of twelve months after the death of a husband. The usual practice was to wear black for a period of six months and black and white clothing for the rest of the year.[29] It was expected that both men and women wait at least a year before remarriage. The expectations were often ignored, especially for men. Practicalities forced men with small children to marry quickly after the death of a wife.[30]

The people were not obsessed with or despondent about thoughts of death and bad luck. They were optimistic, and found enjoyment in their associations with family and friends. They learned how to cope with life quite effectively. They had a deep faith in their religious teaching and they trusted their family, neighbors and friend. They took great delight in one another when they gathered on Saturday nights to sing, dance, and talk. Stories about the exploits of family members and friends captivated the older audiences.[31]

The era of the Civil War continued to affect the people, and the tendency seemed to be to blame most of the economic problems on the North and the United States government. The families of the veterans of the Civil War maintained a lingering distrust and even hatred of people in the North. These families related stores of mistreatment and claims that Confederate prisoners were deliberately starved by the prison guards. They ate rats and dogs in order to stay

---

[27]See Kevin Danaher, In Ireland Long Ago, (Hatboro, Pa.: Folklore Association, 1967), 172; Sean O'Suilleabhain, Folktales of Ireland, (Chicago: University of Chicago Press, 1966), 166-74.

[28]Collections of interviews by the author include many customs about attending funerals. Funerals were social occasions for the community. To show respect for the living, people visited the family before the funeral and viewed the corpse. The visitors talked with one another and discussed community events. Men usually gathered outside and drank, while the women soothed the grief-stricken family. Afterwards, comments were made about how "natural" the corpse looked in the casket. Individual family members were judged on how they "took" the death. People who did not lament out loud were judged uncaring by the onlookers, and those who mourned the loudest were most affected by the death.

[29]Ibid. No specific mourning time was set for men.

[30]People gossiped about these marriages. The comment was often made that the man did not wait until his wife's tracks were out of the yard before he had remarried.

[31]Many of the stories were accounts of people in the Civil War. As the stories were told over and over again, many of the privates became generals in the Confederate army. A mythos developed about family life before the Civil War. They remembered that their families had large farms and a corresponding complement of slaves before the invasion from the north.

alive, and the guards were cruel.[32]

The people were experts on the genealogy of the families. The concern about kinship was significant for several reasons. The geographical isolation of the sector led to intermarriage between families. As fewer people moved into the region to live, it was important to know who was related by blood and marriage because marriage was not allowed between close relatives. Also, the familial ties bound all blood relatives as part of the immediate family. Those people who moved into the area soon realized that they were outsiders. A person unfamiliar with the culture could easily alienate a whole community if negative comments were made about one person because that individual was connected either by blood or marriage to almost everyone around.[33]

The custom was to address individuals in terms of their family connections to the speaker. One would greet a "Cousin Sam" or an "Aunt Fannie," always with those titles, because to omit the family relationship was considered bad deportment. Older people in the community were often addressed as "aunt" or "uncle" even though they might not be kin to the speaker. "Miz" or "Mr." was the proper address to show deference or respect for an individual who was not a relative. The elderly, no matter their station in life, were treated with courtesy. Children were schooled in the proper way to address their elders. A child's conduct was a reflection on the family. Adults and children were expected to be gracious and generous toward all people.[34]

Violence, a characteristic in the culture since the settlement period, was still a viable part of the patterns of behavior. Honor was important to these people and they did not hesitate to defend themselves and their family against any defamation, real or implied. Court records show numerous accounts of violence between men when one dared to humiliate the other by implying that he was dishonest or unprincipled. Men were quick to defend the honor of women in their families, and duels, although illegal at the time, were fought. The survivor (there was usually only one) was often arrested, but just as often he was acquitted on charges of murder by a trial jury. The juries acted on the axiom that a man had the right to kill anyone who insulted him or any member of his family.[35]

Men and women often went armed, and children learned to use firearms at an early age. Males and females who were good marksmen earned status in the community. The proficiency with guns was often necessary for hunting wild game as well as personal protection. Most

---

[32]Among the interviews conducted by the author, about 10% of those people who claimed to have relatives in the Civil War expressed a strong antipathy toward the North. A total of 97 people interviewed had evidence that their ancestors had been held in Union prisons. An interesting analysis of the attitudes of the Confederate veterans in Tennessee toward the North is found in Fred Arthur Bailey's Class and Tennessee's Confederate Generation (Chapel Hill: The University of North Carolina Press, 1987).

[33]Interviews with the people in 1959. Materials in the hands of the author.

[34]Ibid.

[35]Survey of trial records in Lyon, Trigg, and Stewart Counties from 1880 to 1945. See Stewart County Circuit Court records, Book 101, 24-39.

people took pride in their guns and it was unusual for an individual not to have at least one.[36]

Hunting parties were an integral part of the masculine camaraderie. Hunters killed coons (raccoons), foxes, beavers, skunks, and other wild animals for the pelts. If for some reason, the environment allowed some of the animals to multiply too rapidly, the counties often offered bounties for the heads of the animals. Bounty hunters formed groups and killed the animals. Wild game was a part of the food supply, including squirrels, rabbits, geese, ducks, and quail. A superstition protected the doves from the hunters. It was bad luck to kill a dove and most hunters would not dare kill one. Good hunting dogs, trained to detect particular animals, were prized by their owners. Dog trainers could earn extra money by training their neighbor's dogs.[37]

Although some women did join the hunting parties, most of them did not take much interest in hunting animals. Women did not brag about their shooting expertise. Community standards often demanded that women learn to shoot, but they were not allowed to flaunt their achievements. It would be "unladylike" for a female to outshoot a man.[38]

Customs and traditions determined the dignity of jobs and even chores at home. To have status in the community, the family had to own a home and land. Sharecroppers and tenant farmers were of a lower status than day laborers who owned a house. Land owners, businessmen, and professionals, such as ministers and teachers, were among the elite. Education continued to be the element which crossed the land-ownership barriers. A person with an education was given a certain social standing whether he owned land or not.[39]

Women, regardless of the social or economic status, still had the responsibility of maintaining the home, caring for the children, and tending the sick. Since the Civil War, women had outnumbered the men, but there is no evidence to indicate that the numerical superiority changed their status. A number of the households were headed by women, but that did not change the types of jobs available to them. Few families were able to afford servants, and women from the middle class tried to earn money to supplement the family income. Women kept chickens and sold the extra eggs, or butter might be sold to neighbors. It was unacceptable for married women to leave the home to earn extra income. Outside employment was a negative reflection on the husband. Single women were allowed to work in specified jobs in the community, including dressmakers, clerks, and teachers.[40]

The majority of the women worked with the family in the fields. The one job that women did not want to perform outside the home was domestic work, especially washing

---

[36]Interviews with residents of the land between the rivers in 1956. Interviews in the hands of the author.

[37]Ibid.

[38]Ibid. Rules for women varied somewhat in different communities, but most women were supposed to refrain from involvement in activities such as hunting because it was reserved for men. The term "lady" was important because it denoted someone who followed the prescribed rules of behavior in the community.

[39]Ibid.

[40]Ibid. For a survey of the status of women in the United States see Louis W. Banner's Women in Modern America: A Brief History (New York: Harcourt Brace Jovanovich, Publishers, 1974).

clothes. A stigma was attached to cleaning the houses and washing the clothes for other families. The attitude was that this was a demeaning job and only the very poor women would do such tasks. It was a matter of social status for a woman to have someone to come in to do her washing.[41]

Religion, because it served a multiple function as a social as well as spiritual activity, fulfilled an increasing need in the lives of the people. After the Civil War, the numbers of churches steadily increased, and in the period from 1870 to 1890, the Baptist churches had the largest congregations. Other denominations, including the Methodist, Christian Church, and the Christian Union Church, established congregations in the area. The Catholic Church established the St. Joseph's Parish led by Father Charles Halsey in 1882. The churches gradually adopted more and more activities which provided a social outlet for the people. Pie suppers, play parties, and other social activities were held weekly.[42]

For the women in the community, the churches were an important social institution which allowed them to meet with other women with similar interests. Traditionally, women had formed their gatherings around projects which aided the church or the community. They met to make quilts or cook suppers to raise money. These fund-raising projects were still the only function that some farm women could rely upon for acceptable social interaction with their peers. Women did not have the luxury of joining in the political discussions or equally participating in the literary societies. Their own churches often did not allow them to participate in church ceremonies. Their church societies allowed them the opportunity for socializing under the guise of providing financial assistance for their church.[43]

The missionary societies took the lead in organizing groups of women for membership in the temperance organizations. The organizational skills learned in the missionary societies were used later in social reform associations in the area. A few of these women championed the generally unpopular movement for women's suffrage.[44]

Even though the lifestyle of these people would have been considered monotonous and orthodox by the more urbane people, their lives were rich with tradition and an historic commonalty. The old values which had led the people to economic prosperity before the Civil War were still present. The work ethic was a part of the culture and parents expected their children to achieve more than they had accomplished. Social status was based, in large part, on economic prosperity, yet there was more involved. Even though economic success was measured by the amount of land and money a family was able to accrue, respectability was based on family name and background. As one man said, "A man could be as poor as Jobe's

---

[41]By 1880, the women did not work in the fields if the family could afford hired help. A lady worked inside the home, and women tried to maintain a white skin by covering the head and arms when they were in the sun. A suntan was a giveaway that she did outside chores.

[42]County records 1880 to 1900.

[43]Most of the churches had missionary societies which were led by women. At this time there were no women who served in an official capacity in any of the churches.

[44]Records of the older Baptist and Methodist Churches in the region indicate that almost every congregation in the land between the rivers had a missionary society. There were at least three temperance societies in the area by 1890.

turkey, but if he came from a good family, he was respected."[45]

The prosperous people used their money to buy land and farm machinery, or they extended their business operations by investing in non-agricultural pursuits. They bought stock in banks, lumber mills, grist mills, and the iron industry. The goal was to fit into the generally accepted standards of the community. The wealthiest citizens did not spend excessive amounts of money on expensive clothing and other superfluous goods. A conspicuous display of wealth led to ridicule and made the person a laughingstock.[46]

From 1890 to the early 1900s, the productive power of the area appeared to be increasing. Industrialists and investors banded together and tried to revive the iron industry in the region. The population increased by approximately five hundred people.[47] By 1873, the Bear Springs Furnace owned by the Cumberland Iron Works Company, by then based in Nashville, rebuilt the operation. The new furnace was steam powered and used a cold waste gas and produced between 12 and 15 tons per day. The furnace was shut down in 1890, but an English company, the Cumberland River Lands Limited, acquired the property and began operations in 1894. Production continued until the 1920s.[48]

The Clark Furnace, owned by the LaGrange Iron Works, reopened in 1872, and by 1880 was scheduled for alterations to increase the stack height from 36 feet to 42 feet. Its specialty at the time was car wheel pig iron. The furnace burned in 1881, and was abandoned by 1883.[49] The LaGrange Iron Works owned the LaGrange Furnace which was rebuilt in 1880 and 1884. The furnace stack was increased to 65 feet which allowed the productivity to increase to 18,000 gross tons annually. James C. Warner had organized the LaGrange Iron Works, and the company was consolidated into the Southern Iron Company around 1890; it continued production until 1900.[50]

The Rough and Ready Furnace, one of the most productive at the time of the Civil War, closed around 1856 and did not begin operations again until 1868. Just before it closed the Cobb, Bradley, and Company owned about 16,000 acres of land. The furnace had a brick and stone stack standing twenty-eight feet high and used 150 bushels of coal to a ton of iron, producing some ten tons per day. When the Rough and Ready Iron Works reopened the furnace in 1868, it was rebuilt and stood 45 feet in height and nine feet across the bosh. The I. Westheimer Company of Pittsburg purchased the furnace in 1880 and discontinued production

---

[45]1957 quote from Mr. Leonard Riggins.

[46]Interviews with individuals indicated that this attitude was an important part of the cultural standard. Most of the men made an effort to conceal their wealth. It was an inside joke that an outsider would mistake them for very poor uneducated individuals. "Some of them had enough money to burn a wet mule." (quote from Mr. Lexie Wallace)

[47]Federal census records.

[48]Samuel D. Smith, Charles P. Stripling, and James M. Brannon, A Cultural Resource Survey of Tennessee's Western Highland Rim Iron Industry, 1790s-1930s (Nashville, Tennessee: Department of Conservation, Division of Archaeology, 1988). 105-107.

[49]Ibid, 109.

[50]Ibid, 110.

in 1888.[51]

The Dover Furnace closed during the Civil War and was rebuilt in 1873. Operations were sporadic from 1880 until after WWI. It was the last blast furnace in operation in Stewart County. The regional iron industry could not remain competitive because of the changes in furnace technology, including the use of coke, produced from coal, for fuel.

By the turn of the century most people had become concerned about a good quality education for all children in the area. Gradually since 1870 when the Tennessee General Assembly assumed the responsibility for providing a state public school system, people had come to accept the idea of public schools. The state did not provide the necessary funds and schools made little progress. By 1880, Stewart County had levied a local tax for education and had made an unsuccessful attempt to provide some education of the children. Organization and funding were two of the most important problems at the time. Stewart, Trigg, and Lyon counties were attempting to hire teachers for a two to three month school term. Teachers of good moral character were employed if they passed a satisfactory examination administered by the county court. The examination included questions on orthography, reading, writing, mental arithmetic, written arithmetic, grammar, geography, and U. S. history.[52]

Advances in Education

The Tennessee Four Mile law was implemented in Stewart County in 1881 with the establishment of schools in Cumberland City and Indian Mound. Within the next five years schools were established in Bumpus Mills and at the LaGrange Iron Works. The law mandated that a student would not have to travel more than four miles to reach a school.[53] By 1885 Stewart county had 3,770 white students and 884 black students attending the public schools. Fifty-eight teachers were employed to teach a four-month school term.[54]

In 1891 the Tennessee General Assembly passed legislation to provide high schools in the state. The first public high school in Stewart County was established in Model in 1914, and Dover opened a school in 1917. For several years, the school at Model was considered the most progressive school in the area. In 1921 Big Rock and Indian Mound established their high schools.[55]

By 1900, most citizens had accepted the view that a thorough public education was the

---

[51]Goodspeed, Histories, 895; Killebrew, Resources of Tennessee, 931; Smith, Stripling, and Brannon, Resource Survey, 111.

[52]The change in attitude toward education can be seen in the discussion over taxes and education in the county court records from 1880 to 1900. See example Stewart County Court records, Book 89, 14. A copy of a blank certificate was found in the Court House in Dover.

[53]Stewart County court records 1881, Book 90, 47.

[54]Stewart County Court records 1885, Book 94, 43-44; Book 95, 34-39.

[55]Stewart County court records 1880, Book 82, 12-15; Book 91, 24-29; Book 102, 34-37, 44; Book 105, 12-16.

responsibility of all of the people. The people had come to accept the view that an education was necessary to provide the tools for economic success for the country. Traditionally, the better educated individuals had been looked upon as the potential leaders in the community, but paradoxically, these same people were expected to acquire substantial property and become productive members of the community. Thus, education, just for the sake of acquiring knowledge, was not the objective. Education was expected to provide the individual with the knowledge which would enable him to succeed financially.[56]

The schools were primitive by national standards. The school buildings had only one or two rooms for all the grades. In many cases the classes were held in church buildings. Water came from either wells, creeks, or cisterns, and the teachers and children shared a common water bucket and dipper. The rooms were heated with a wood or coal burning stove. In the better school settings, the children had an outhouse or privy. The community schools usually had fewer than fifty children in regular attendance.[57]

Attitudes toward education were consistent in the three counties, but the procedures for regulating the school systems varied because of state laws. In Stewart County, three school directors in each of the twelve districts supervised the schools. These directors had considerable autonomy and the schools varied from district to district. One of the standard practices was for the school directors to hire the teachers in their district. It was entirely up to them if the teacher passed the examination to qualify. These men often gave an oral examination to the prospective teacher. Whatever question they might deem important was asked, and the accuracy of the answer was entirely up to the director.[58]

In 1907, the Tennessee state legislature decreed that a Board of Education had to be created for each county. Each county was required to provide a minimum school term of six months. If teachers did not have a high school diploma, they were required to pass a certification examination. Teachers earned from $25.00 to $35.00 per month. Salaries were based upon experience, gender, and the attitude of the school board members.[59]

In Kentucky, a school board operated the schools, and the teachers were not required to have a high school diploma or take an examination for certification. Four years of teaching experience was equivalent to a high school diploma. The pay for teachers was comparable to the salaries of teachers in Tennessee. From 1890 to 1900 the school districts in the land between the rivers showed a small decline in the school enrollment. The problem of finances

---

[56]The view that education was a tool for economic success had not been a part of the attitudes before 1900. The argument that children had to be educated to get a job resulted in more tax money for education and movements to establish local elementary and high schools. The primary emphasis was on education of the males. Females were expected to learn to read and write, but they were not expected to train themselves to earn a living. For the most part, women were still expected to fill the traditional role of wife and mother.

[57] Study of County Court records in Lyon, Trigg, and Stewart Counties from 1880 to 1910. The annual school budgets are included in the records.

[58]Interviews with former teachers. Interview with Mrs. Lorena Bagwell was especially informative.

[59]Stewart County school records found in the Stewart County Court records Books 100-107 for the period from 1900 to 1907.

and the increased cost of maintaining the small, one-room community school was a problem which escalated during the twentieth century.[60]

Twentieth Century Life

The first two decades of the new century brought very few changes in the lives of the people in the land between the rivers. Transportation was still limited principally to the Tennessee and Cumberland Rivers, and ferries were used to cross the rivers. Mail came by river boats and roads were still paths along creek beds or crude trails which followed the valleys. Many of the roads were impassable during wet weather. The view of the outside world was limited to three or four newspapers including the Memphis Weekly Commercial Appeal, the Stewart Breeze, and the Louisville Weekly Courier-Journal which were delivered by river boats to the region. Visitors from the outside came in with stories of the big cities and the new inventions which reduced work, but it was several years before the people in the land between the rivers had real contact with these changes.

In 1914, several new school buildings were planned for the land between the rivers. The plan was to construct school buildings and discontinue the use of church facilities. County funds were not sufficient to begin construction in all the communities, and the citizens, demonstrating their own ingenuity, took matters into their own hands. The community of Model wanted a high school because it was difficult for the students to attend the academy in Dover. Also, Model wanted to have the distinction of having the first public high school in the county. The people in Model decided to handle the costs themselves. They solicited donations, either money or produce, and held barbecue suppers to raise funds. They raised the money and built the school.[61]

During the period, fund-raising schemes became a fashionable social event. School and churches used "auction suppers" to sell ice cream, pies, cakes, and box suppers to raise money. People attended the auctions to socialize as well as eat. It was one of the few opportunities for young men and women to get to know one another. People traveled great distances to school or churches to watch and become involved in the auctions. Women prepared the delicacies, and men were encouraged to bid on the items made by their wives or girlfriends. The man felt obligated to outbid anyone who might want to purchase the item brought by his woman. The excitement of the bidding and the rivalry among the bidders were incentives to attend the auction.[62]

The box suppers were the most prevalent fund raiser. The woman prepared a dinner for two, enclosing it in an extravagantly decorated box, to be sold at auction. The box, usually made of cardboard, was decorated with bright cloth and ribbons or any decoration which would

---

[60]School records in Lyon, Trigg, and Stewart Counties. Lyon County Court records, Book 114, 24-27; Trigg County Court records, Book 121, 39-42; Lyon Court records, Book 119, 35-39.

[61]Stewart County Court records 1914, Book 112, 34-39. Interviews with citizens in the hands of the author.

[62]These auctions were held in the land between the rivers until about 1950.

win the prize at the supper. The boxes were auctioned off to the highest bidder, and the woman was obligated to eat supper with the man who bought her box. The preferred box always belonged to the most popular young woman, regardless of how it looked or what it contained. The men did not always give the highest bid to the best cook. Many courtships began or ended at these suppers.[63]

Cake walks were events for both the old and young, single or married. A circle with numbered blocks was placed on the floor and the people paid a fee to walk around the circle. When the walk began someone was ready to draw a winning number. The walking continued until the lucky number was called and the person standing on that number won the cake. In this event at least, the people wanted to win the cakes that came from the kitchens of the best cooks.[64]

An unusual type of beauty contest was also used to raise money. Young women were chosen from the community gathering and a bidding was held. The woman who received the highest bid was declared the beauty winner and the money went to the school or the organization holding the event. The custom was for the man making the bid to escort the young woman home at the end of the evening. An interesting variety of a beauty contest was also held at events called play parties. These parties were usually held in private homes and included music, dancing, and games. At these parties, the young men could bid on their favorite young women. It was expected that the young man who made the highest bid would be the young woman's companion for the rest of the party. The money from the contest went to the people who hosted the event. It appears that rivalry for the companionship of the most popular women could result in tumultuous behavior from a disappointed suitor. This rather strange social activity was very commonplace during the depression years when families hosted the party in order to make money.[65]

A game called passing the thimble was a popular activity for young unmarried people at parties. The people were seated in a large circle and one person passed the thimble through the cupped hands of all the people participating in the game. The judge then had to guess the individual who held the thimble at the end of the game. If he were correct, he would win a prize, and the thimble was passed again. The judge had to keep playing the game until he or she guessed correctly. Obviously, the excitement of the game was the limited physical contact between the sexes, not the prize.[66]

---

[63]Interviews with citizens in the land between the rivers. Copies of the interviews are held by the author.

[64]Ibid.

[65]Ibid.

[66]Ibid.

170

Promoters and Dreamers

People worked long hours on the farm or business, and it proved difficult at times to provide for their families, but as always, there were a few individuals who were dreamers and promoters. They often tried to create a utopia by merging futuristic dreams with the contemporary.

One example of such a dreamer was Tom Lawson who lived on the northern edge of the land between the rivers. Tom Lawson dreamed of building a city that would encompass the entire area from the Tennessee to the Cumberland river. He planned a canal that would join the two rivers at their nearest juncture.[67]

As early as 1890, he began an operation which he hoped would turn his dream into a reality. He spent ten years trying to convince investors that his city could be built and it would evolve into an industrial and shipping center in the South. He formed The Grand Rivers Land Company and capitalized the company at three million dollars. The company bought land and advertised it for sale to people who wanted to live in the new city of Grand Junction. The company began its operation by cutting and selling timber. Very soon thereafter, the company sold lumber, staves, barrels, and wagons to settlers in Grand Rivers and to other markets.

Plans were made to build roads and railroads to provide access to domestic markets. The planned iron furnaces, glass factories, and grain mills would bring laborers into the region. Tom Lawson envisioned an industrial complex including cotton compresses, grain elevators, foundries, forges, shops, tanneries, water works, and gas works which would provide jobs for all the people in the area. The city would include a variety of retail stores. Natural gas and electricity would be made available.

Tom Lawson's plan was not an impossible dream but it was never realized. The Grand Rivers Company encountered various economic problems, but the most difficult task was convincing the potential settlers that the scheme would work. People were not easily convinced that the city with all of the modern conveniences was the environment in which they wanted to live. The company might have eventually succeeded in creating the city, but the economic difficulties which began in the region in 1918 doomed the project.[68]

The small village of Grand Rivers was developed and survived, but the industrial complex was never completed. The canal was built, not by the people in The Grand Rivers Company, but by the federal government. Growth and development would come, but not as dramatically as Tom Lawson had envisioned.

When the first automobile came to Stewart County in 1903, some people in the land between the rivers used the ferry to go to Dover to see the car. They began to realize that the world was changing, and it would be many years before they could purchase such an invention, but they could dream. The automobile would be practical if they had roads. For the first time, people seemed willing to pay taxes to build roads and bridges. But the desire did not produce

---

[67]The activities of Mr. Lawson are recorded in Lyon and Trigg County records for 1890 to 1920. See Lyon County Court records, Book 92, 27-32; Book 94, 34, 39; Book 102, 23, 29; and Trigg County Court records, Book 98, 34-39; Book 101, 43, 44; Book 103, 56, 59, 62.

[68]Ibid.

the funds, and twenty-five years elapsed before the first road, linking Model to Dover, was completed in the area.[69]

Need of Change

In the early twentieth century, people were still plagued with communicable diseases. Typhoid fever, small pox, and other diseases occurred throughout the countryside. Most of the physicians lived in the towns and villages surrounding the land between the rivers, but they were often too far away to be reached in the event of an accident. For many people, the doctor's fee, usually one dollar for each visit, was considered prohibitive. Many individuals still relied upon folk medicine to treat accident victims and diseases.[70]

In the period from 1890 to 1900 the houses and farm buildings had not changed considerably since the 1870s. The frame or log homes were enlarged by adding additional rooms or they may have been painted or whitewashed, but by and large they were the same. A few brick homes had been built, but most of the new homes were of frame construction and duplicated the older style of architecture in the area.

Farmers continued to cultivate their land in much the same manner as their ancestors. They had learned more about crop rotation and fertilizers, but they still followed the practice of planting their crops by the signs of the moon and the stars. Almanacs were an important tool in the home because they contained the astrological information and tips for planting crops.[71]

The biggest changes were in the use of labor-saving farm machines such as the reapers, cultivators, tractors, and combines, even though most were still too expensive for the average farmer. A farmer who could purchase one of these machines realized that he could pay for the machine by harvesting his neighbor's crops. Farmers would often pay for the use of the machine in goods. When the first combines came into the area, a new holiday grew up around the threshing of wheat.[72]

Economic Conditions in Early Twentieth Century

The growth and prosperity in the land between the rivers seemed to reach a peak from 1900 to 1910. After that time, a steady decline began to occur. The change was so gradual that people did not seem to take notice, but the population decline was slow and steady. This

---

[69]Stewart County Court records 1913 to 1925. From Book 99, 23-29; Book 102, 39-43; Book 104, 43; Book 114, 21; Book 115, 23-35.

[70]Interviews with citizens of the land between the rivers 1956 to 1960.

[71]Ibid.

[72]In the interviews with the people, mention was made of how the farmers in the community worked together to use the machines to plant and harvest crops. Farmers would help each other, moving from farm to farm, until all the crops were planted or harvested. The women cooked the food and served the meals to the workers.

decrease in population would result in a lack of growth in years to come.[73]

Several economic factors were coming into play. The lumber industry was beginning to feel the impact of the competition with coal as a source of power for the river boats. By 1918, the lumber industry, already showing signs of failure, was crippled even further when the cost of shipping freight by water increased. Railroads would have helped to alleviate transportation problems, but investors were unwilling to bring the railroads into the area because of the prohibitive cost of railroad bridges across the rivers and streams.[74]

Museling or fishing for mussel shells was an important economic enterprise during the period. Fresh water mussel shells were plentiful in the Tennessee and Cumberland. They were harvested with metal bails with lines and hooks. The contraption was dragged along the river bed and snagged the mussels. Museling was profitable if the operation had the use of gas powered boats. The more efficient operators earned as much as $36.00 per day.[75]

After the mussels were collected, they were cooked in big pots or vats to remove the mussel from the shell. The shells were graded into two categories--sand shells or washboard shells. The sand shells were preferred because they brought a better price on the market. When the shells were classified, they were shipped by boat to factories and made into buttons.[76] The meat from the mussels was fed to hogs.

A few individuals realized that the mussel pearl or fresh water pearl might be of some value. But at the time, these people did not have the capital to develop the industry. The Japanese had already engaged in the development of the cultured pearl, using ground mussel shells to seed for the cultured pearl. The cost of labor reduced the profits in the business and it was not until after World War II, when the Japanese began to make larger purchases that the mussel industry prospered.[77]

Some of the secondary enterprises which provided additional demands for labor included the manufacture of gun powder, coffins, ice, bricks, maple syrup and sugar, sorghum molasses, and pottery. The blacksmiths had a lucrative business making horseshoes and farm implements. Sulphur was mined and processed into sulfuric acid.[78]

Printing was done at Eddyville and Model. James M. Thomas published the "Model Star" and a number of other papers and tracts. Mr. Thomas became well known through his activity with the Christian Unity Church, and two of his papers, "The Gospel Light" and "The Zero Star," made him an internationally known writer. A movie was made of his life in 1950.

---

[73]Federal Population Census records 1890 to 1950.

[74]The closest railroad to the land between the rivers ran from Clarksville to Paris. Bridges across the Cumberland and Tennessee would have to be built to put a spur line to the railroad.

[75]Interviews with people in the land between the rivers.

[76]Ibid.

[77]Several men in the area harvested mussels for sale in Japan. Records are limited mostly to newspaper accounts of the growing industry.

[78]The lists of taxable property showed that these business were found in Lyon, Trigg, and Stewart Counties.

The printing industry remained small because of the economy of the region. The circulation of the newspapers was affected both by the anemic economy and the declining population.[79]

A combination of many economic factors caused the land between the rivers to prosper and conquer the devastation of the Civil War. Yet, these same factors were somehow changed after 1910 and the area began to decline.

---

[79]Ibid. The movie about James M. Thomas was not shown in the land between the rivers because there was not a movie theater in the area.

CHAPTER IX

WORLD WAR I
AND THE DEPRESSION YEARS

By 1914, the decline in the price of agricultural goods and the deterioration of the iron industry helped to produce an economic recession. According to many, the property taxes were oppressive, and county officials, who were usually farmers, resisted any increase. As a result, tax revenues declined, and the shortage of money affected the quality and number of services the local governments provided. The people realized little difference in the way they conducted their lives.[1]

The outbreak of World War I in Europe had little immediate, perceivable effect on the people of the region. The people seemed to give little notice to the war news. When world trade was affected, they began to pay attention to the events. In typical fashion the war was discussed at the local stores and courthouses, but it made little differences in the lives of people. The farmers blamed the capitalistic powers, mostly the industrial tycoons, for their economic problems, not leaders in Europe. They formed The Farmers Educational and Co-operative Union to develop programs, hoping to solve their economic problems. The Union was unable to enlist the support of the majority of the farmers. The rhetoric was centered on organization for power.[2] Traditionally, these people had been individualistic; they were not joiners. They had to be convinced that a union could deliver on its promises. True, they wanted the higher market price, but they could not agree on ways of accomplishing the goal. Absorbed with their own problems, people went about their daily lives without much concern about events in Europe until the United States entered the war.[3]

When the U. S. entered the war, the news received a mixed reception. It was good when they were asked to produce more goods and supplies for the war effort. Land was cleared, including the land that had been cut over by the lumber industry, and put under cultivation. With more products to sell, the future looked bright. Even The Farmers Educational and Co-operative Union of America reacted to the war by disbanding.[4] The Co-operative members, like other economic analysts, assumed that the problems were now solved. It was not good when young men were asked to volunteer to fight in Europe. Men volunteered, but the enthusiasm was lackluster. A few men left the area to work in the war industries. On the whole, the people did not seem to be affected by the powerful propaganda campaign waged by the administration of Woodrow Wilson. The strong anti-German sentiment which influenced other

---

[1]County records in Lyon, Trigg, and Stewart Counties, 1913 to 1915. Lyon County Tax Assessor records, Book 210, 34-45; Trigg County Court records, Book 159, 23-34.

[2]One book of minutes from The Farmers Educational and Co-operative Union can be found in the Court House in Dover, Tennessee.

[3]Ibid.

[4]Ibid.

parts of the country did not catch on in the area. The region was still too isolated to react to the early events of the war; it seemed too far away to concern them.[5]

The war became more controversial when it was learned that young men would be drafted. The general attitude was that the U. S. government should not force men to fight, especially in Europe. People argued that it was unconstitutional to draft. When the law was passed, it was easily evaded by some of the young men. Since most of the children were born at home, the birth records were usually found in the family Bible. In many cases, the records at the county seats were incomplete or non-existent. It was a simple matter to change dates on birth certificates or in the family Bible to make young men ineligible for the draft. Local authorities did not seem to check state records against the records presented by the individuals.[6] Other men accepted the draft and went off to war.

When the war ended, most of the men returned home and tried to take up their life as they had left it. The same was true of the people who had left the area to work in the war industries. The economy looked good and farmers, expecting good prices, increased their production of tobacco, corn, and livestock, accordingly. The sawmill owners had responded to the war demands by increasing production and further depleting the forests. The iron furnaces were losing money and gradually went out of production. By 1919 a general economic recession was hitting the area, but it seemed mild, and the prognosis was that a boom period was coming. The general economic depression came gradually, while the country was talking about prosperity and progress. The people heard about the rapid technological changes in the rest of the country, and they heard news about Ford and Chevrolet cars which they wanted to own.[7]

Recession will Lead to Depression

Farm prices began their steady decline in 1919 and plunged in 1929. During the period, the farm population decreased by 27.3 percent, and a number of farms went out of operation. Farmers and merchants who were not in debt were able to survive, but those who had expanded their holdings during the war years were in trouble. Farmers met the problem of lower prices the only way they knew; they put more land under cultivation.[8]

As prices continued to decline, farmers sold off parcels of land. With the decline in corn

---

[5]Interviews with the people in the land between the rivers, 1956-1960. Interviews in the hands of the author. World War I was described as a conflict which the country should not have entered. The people viewed the involvement of the U. S. as a mistake. There was no sense of aroused patriotism about the war.

[6]In interviews several men admitted that they had evaded the draft in World War I.

[7]Interviews with residents. Interviews in the hands of the author.

[8]County records in Lyon, Trigg, and Stewart Counties indicate that approximately twenty farms in the land between the rivers were sold in the period from 1919 to 1929. Most of the sales were either because of delinquent payments on the property or bankruptcy. The number of foreclosure and bankruptcy sales for the period of 1890 to 1918 was twelve. There were no foreclosure or bankruptcy sales recorded in 1900.

prices, the farmers turned their corn into whiskey.[9] Families reverted to the old practices of producing everything they needed on their land. Cotton, which had been replaced by tobacco as the money crop, was raised again. Cotton prices dropped but the farmers continued to raise a small crop to provide cloth for family needs. In 1924, the Southern Trust Company of Clarksville became one of the largest land holders in the area when they foreclosed on mortgages.[10]

The tradition of voting the Democratic ticket did not change even with poor economic times. The people continued to support the party that was blamed for their economic woes. The sentiment was that one did not change religion or political party affiliation. A few voters might have turned away from the party, but on the whole, economics was not enough to change the historical aversion to the Republican Party.

Suffrage Movement

One of the more interesting political controversies during the period was the suffrage movement, which did arouse much interest in the area. The Nineteenth Amendment was proposed and caused considerable political controversy outside the region. Many women in the land between the rivers seemed to agree that women should vote, but no organization was formed to push the ratification vote. Women all over the country faced the same dilemma; they had been conditioned to believe that they should not vote. Since the Civil War, women had been forced by economics to enter the labor force. They had suffered under restrictive laws, customs and the disparity in wages. Suffrage leaders had proclaimed the Nineteenth Amendment as the solution to all these problems. Women who studied the issues of the day could relate to some of the solutions proposed by the suffragists. A difficulty was the doctrine of the churches. The churches prescribed the role of women and did not allow them to involve themselves in the activities of men. Politics had certainly been a male dominated and controlled activity. To suggest that women should enter politics engendered a discussion of how God expected women to behave, thus a discussion of sin. Ministers preached against women's suffrage, and when the Church of Christ and Baptist congregations faced the issue, the resulting controversy split congregations.[11] Here, as well as in the rest of the country, the church leaders voiced some of the strongest opposition to suffrage rights for women.

On the whole, the issue of suffrage did not seem to cause organized resistance from local political leaders. One of the traditions of the region was that men were expected to exercise

---

[9]The Eighteenth Amendment put Prohibition into effect, but farmers continued to produce and sell whiskey. Until 1921, they were open in their violation of the Volstead Act. Representative Andrew Volstead sponsored the act which became law in 1919. It would not be accurate to call these people bootleggers because they did not smuggle or hide their traffic in whiskey.

[10]It appears that the Southern Trust Company took control of seven of the farms sold in the land between the rivers from 1919 to 1924. That number is indicated by Deed Records.

[11]Existing records for the First Baptist Church in Dover, Tennessee and The First Church of Christ in Eddyville, Kentucky indicate that those ministers did not favor the right to vote for women.

their right of franchise, and those men seemed to accept the idea that women had that right as well. One rather unique factor in the society was the tendency of the individuals to take a positive stand on many social reform issues. These people placed an emphasis on equality for all white, enterprising people in the communities. The prospect of women becoming voters did not pose a threat. This progressive attitude continued throughout the history of the region.

When women got the right to vote in 1920, they sought local county offices in Lyon, Trigg, and Stewart Counties. The amazing result was that men voted for these female candidates, and they were elected to office. Females were elected over male opponents in two offices for County Court Clerk in Stewart and Lyon Counties, and Trigg County elected a female sheriff.[12]

In each of these elections, males seeking the offices tried to defeat the females by declaring that women were not qualified by gender to hold the job. The voters did not believe the charge.[13] It is quite amazing how an area that appeared to be socially conservative on the role of women elected them to office at this time. It is possible that many of the conclusions about the status and role of women in the area have been erroneous. Perhaps the gender barriers in the region did not exist to the same degree as they did in other parts of the country.

An example of a woman who defied the traditional role was Lurline Humphries, a petite, pretty, young woman who became a deputy sheriff in Trigg County in 1920. She was the epitome of a genteel southern lady, who had chosen not to marry. Always outspoken, she was respected throughout the county, and people were not surprised when she chose to take the job. No one doubted her when she said she could be as efficient in handling lawbreakers as any man. In 1933, she was elected sheriff of Trigg County, and even though her opponent made references to her gender and said that he would be a better sheriff because he was a man, the voters elected her to the office. She chose not to wear a uniform, and usually attended to her duties without weapons. Perhaps she did not need to carry her gun because everyone knew that she was an expert sharpshooter with her 38 Smith and Wesson. When she was asked about the difficulty of handling law enforcement during Prohibition, she responded that she was never forced to use a gun because men obeyed her orders. They acted like gentlemen and not a single lawbreaker refused to obey her commands.[14]

Prohibition

Around 1921, Prohibition caused hardships and controversy when agents were sent to arrest the whiskey producers. Earlier arguments about the Eighteenth Amendment had gone unnoticed, and the people paid little attention to laws restricting what they viewed as their god-given right.

---

[12]A survey of the election returns from 1900 to 1960 shows that the people voted for the liberal candidates in each of the elections. A study of the names of the local officials shows that women could get elected quite easily in certain jobs. It was not so easy to get elected as a county judge, tax assessor, or school superintendent.

[13]Lyon, Trigg, and Stewart County records for 1920 to 1940. There were at least two women in the county governments in each of these years.

[14]Material about Lurline Humphries can be found in the Land Between the Lakes Library at Golden Pond, Kentucky. Her story also shows the attitude that chivalry was alive and an accepted rule of behavior among the men.

Prohibition was not, in their opinion, a reform movement at all; it was governmental obstruction and abuse.[15]

From time to time, community pressures from the temperance forces had required the consumers to restrict public consumption of whiskey. The attitude seemed to be that drinkers must be prudent in the amount of alcohol they consumed, but they could not be expected to abstain completely. Temperance groups, mostly women and ministers, had asked for voluntary moderation in consumption, and the people agreed. Even though some of the churches advocated total abstinence, the membership usually disregarded the doctrine in the privacy of their homes. The paradox was that deacons in the churches which advocated total abstention were producing very good whiskey and selling it to their neighbors. Whether they drank their brew is not known. Public drunkenness was not tolerated, and anyone who could not control his drinking was ostracized.[16]

As the arguments over the violation of the Volstead Act entered politics, ministers used the pulpit to denounce the sale and consumption of whiskey. They were careful in their condemnation because the men who were the financial benefactors of the church might bootleg, and they controlled the minister's salary. At this time, active congregations as well as the total church membership were comprised mostly of women. Ministers and churchwomen continued to support Prohibition, but local traditions of making whiskey and the monetary necessity of continued production tended to blunt the effectiveness of the Prohibitionists.[17]

The Volstead Act could not be enforced because most of the people refused to obey the law. The law violated their individual rights. They would agree that certain controls over the sale of whiskey were acceptable. Yes, they would agree naturally that they should regulate the amount they drank in public because decorum was important. But in their homes, they would make the determination of what and how much they consumed. The whole concept of prohibition as prescribed in the Volstead act was an affront to their rights, and the law was considered ludicrous. Even though the people did not talk in terms of the violation of their civil liberties, they simply denied the right of any government to tell them what they could or could not manufacture and consume.[18] They did not openly oppose the law. They seemed to acquiesce, but instead they moved their stills to isolated areas and continued the production of some of the best whiskey in the nation.[19]

Tucked away between the rivers, the wooded, sparsely populated countryside was an ideal area for the production of illegal whiskey. The only way to enter the area was by one major road and the river ferries. Sentries, usually on horseback, were posted at the ferry landings and

---

[15]Interviews with residents in the hands of the author.

[16]Interviews with residents held by the author.

[17]From interviews with people who remember this period, the conclusion is that there was never a viable temperance or Prohibition organization in the region. Church congregations often approved of temperance, but they never formed an organization to work for the Eighteenth Amendment.

[18]Traditionally these people quietly disregarded any law which they did not wish to obey.

[19]Interviews with citizens. Interviews in the hands of the author.

the road to spread the word when strangers entered the region.[20] When outsiders entered the area, sentries rode to the nearest farm house and rang the dinner bell. The signal was four bell tolls and a delay to the count of twenty and then two tolls of the bell. The alarm was acknowledged at the nearest farmhouse, and then conveyed from farm to farm until the entire area echoed to the slow, metallic clang of the bells.[21]

Once the danger was past or the stranger had been identified, the all clear signal was sounded with three blasts from a shotgun. Travelers were stopped and asked what their business was in the area. If the individual's business was verifiable, the greeting was courteous. If his reason for being in the area sounded implausible, the individual was warned to leave the area. If the verbal warning was not heeded, the person was in danger. Travelers reported that they had been shot at as they traveled through the area. It was known by all the inhabitants, law enforcement people included, that if a stranger had not been killed, he was just being warned. The shooters did not waste ammunition, and they seldom missed their targets. If they had wanted to kill the person, it would have taken only one shot.[22]

In a very short time, word spread throughout the United States that excellent whiskey could be bought in the land between the rivers if one knew the right person to contact. Regardless of the law, people wanted alcohol and these individuals could supply the goods. Agents sought out those men who had the reputation of producing the best drinking whiskey and arranged for the transportation to cities outside the region. The whiskey went to Chicago, Cleveland, Detroit and other areas.   Caravans of trucks, often protected by armed guards, came in from the metropolitan centers to transport the whiskey. Law enforcement officials were completely ineffective because they did not have the manpower to handle the situation.[23]

Many times, the local law enforcement did not really bother to find the stills. They knew that if they destroyed a still, it only took a few days for the men to rebuild their operation. It did not take long for both the federal and state authorities to realize that they were fighting a losing battle against these producers.[24]   The legislation was not enforced because a large number of people disobeyed the law, and they were supported in their communities. The local law enforcement tended to ignore the violations. As it turned out there was not enough money in the state and national treasuries to hire and train outside law enforcement officers to control the whiskey production.

When the Great Depression hit in 1929, the people depended even more on the illegal sale

---

[20]Ibid.

[21]Ibid.

[22]Ibid.

[23]Item in The Nashville Tennessean, July 26, 1931. The article reported that Golden Pond, Kentucky had become the illegal whiskey production center in the country. For a decade these comments had been made in the newspapers. Yet, only a small number of people were arrested. Reporters concluded that law enforcement officials were either in agreement with the illegal actions or they were too afraid to interfere.

[24]Notes made in the County Court records in Lyon, Trigg, and Stewart Counties indicate that the county officials knew that the attempt to control the production of whiskey was a failure. It appears that the county officials noted their attempts at control and then let the matter drop until the next session of court.

of whiskey to supplement their income. It was common knowledge, although no one spoke openly of the matter, that whiskey was available at all times. Local legend has it that Al Capone had agents throughout the countryside, especially around Golden Pond, to purchase whiskey for his organization. These men came in by trucks, cars, and airplanes, using an air strip built near Golden Pond so they could fly in, buy whiskey, and leave again in just a few minutes.[25]

By 1930 the whiskey producers became quite open in their illegal operations. One operator printed his own labels, reading "Genuine Golden Pond Kentucky Whiskey," and pasted them on the jars and jugs used for bottling. A huge sign, which read, "Whiskey Ridge Distilling Co.--No Trespassing," stood along a hillside trail east of Golden Pond.[26]

Whiskey was the real money crop for many people during the depression years. People often mentioned that Golden Pond might have gotten its name because the early settlers found small gold fish in the pond, but after 1919, the name represented a liquid that could be purchased there, and after a few sips of the brew, everything took on a golden hue.

Because of their religion, sense of propriety, or for whatever reason, some people did not want to be seen buying or selling the illegal whiskey. Of course, there was always an outside chance that they could be arrested, and some of the bootleggers did not want their name associated with illegal activities because they were respected members of the church who donated to the poor and in public supported prohibition. These people developed elaborate and surreptitious schemes to protect their anonymity. One such strategy was to sell the whiskey only at night, and only to those people whom they trusted. They had special rooms in their homes, with double walls. Whenever a regular customer knocked at the door, he was invited in and stayed for a short visit. After a time, the person was handed a small bottle, package, or large bag and the visitor would leave. The package appeared to be a jar of jam, a cake or some other food, and the bag could contain anything from vegetables to a covered dish. But hidden in the package was a jar of whiskey. The transaction was so casual that other visitors in the house might not be aware that a purchase of alcohol had been made.[27]

The Prohibition era expanded an existing deportment among these people. Traditionally, as we have noted, they were selective about welcoming outsiders. Visitors to the area were welcome if they did not involve themselves with the personal affairs of the citizens. The people could be generous and hospitable if they chose to be, but they were not usually gregarious. When federal agents found that it was almost impossible to gather information from the people about the illegal stills operating in the area, they stereotyped all the people as criminal who disregarded the law. Word spread that the people were poor, uncultured, and insolent individuals who took great delight in assaulting strangers. When the people heard these descriptions of themselves, they became even more selective about accepting strangers. They

---

[25]Interviews with local residents indicated that Al Capone's men were in the area all the time. This conclusion is supported by newspaper articles which report that the region, especially Golden Pond, Kentucky was known for its whiskey production.

[26]The Nashville Tennessean, April 12, 1931. The article reported that men such as Al Capone did business in the illegal whiskey trade in the land between the rivers.

[27]Interviews with citizens included eye witness accounts of these activities. One was given by Mr. Roy P. Wallace and Mrs. Rees L. Wallace.

intended to protect themselves and their way of life by not divulging anything about themselves. Personal questions simply were not answered.[28]

This characterization of the people was both fallacious and undeserved. The Celtic heritage did contribute to a strong sense of family loyalty and clannish behavior. Outsiders had to earn respect and acceptance. Strangers had been treated with courtesy until they were deemed to be worthy or not. In reaction to how they were described, the people became even more selective about accepting people who moved into the area. Resentment developed among the locals when they were described as lawless. They believed in supporting all beneficial laws, but they would resort to civil disobedience if the law was an obvious violation of their individual rights. They felt that they, as individuals, had the right to determine which laws they would support and those they would ignore.[29]

Outsiders often commented on the cultural attitudes of the region and concluded that people who were not born in the area or had not married someone born there were destined to be outsiders as long as they lived. These outsiders would never be trusted completely nor would they be privy to confidential information about their neighbors.[30]

Depression

In 1928, the voters supported Alfred E. Smith even though he was described as urban and Catholic, and of course they liked the fact that he was "wet."[31] The candidate did not seem to represent the agrarian, protestant, and individualistic people in the region. Nonetheless, Smith was a Democrat, and the tradition of voting the Democratic Party ticket was too ingrained for the people to vote against him. The election returns for 1928 showed the people did not follow their sister counties. Hoover carried Tennessee and won one of the greatest victories ever in Kentucky when he carried 93 of the 120 counties in the state.[32]

By the 1930s the Great Depression had further reduced the standard of living for a majority of people, and very little money was in circulation. Farm prices were low, and farmers tried to find other jobs to supplement their income, but few jobs were available. During the period from 1930 to 1934 all the people felt the depression, and as the economic situation worsened, human suffering increased. The rising number of jobless in Tennessee and Kentucky was the highest in the history of both states. Leaders were without plans and a financial paralysis hit

---

[28]Two articles in the Louisville Courier Journal December 4, 1930 and July 22, 1931, reported that the land between the rivers was an unsavory area to visit. The same articles described the attitudes of the people.

[29]Ibid.

[30]Ibid.

[31]A wet candidate supported the repeal of Prohibition. It should be noted that the whiskey producers in the area were often undecided about whether they wanted the repeal of Prohibition. They realized that legal alcohol could hurt their business.

[32]Secretary of State, manuscript records of elections, Office of Secretary of State, Frankfort, Kentucky.

the area. Comparatively, because the region was agricultural, the people suffered less than did the urban wage earners, but they suffered nonetheless. To add to their woes, a severe drought in 1930 plagued the region. The parched fields reduced the crop yields and forced farmers to sell livestock for a fraction of their value. Grain was so scarce that farmers were warned not to sell outside the area because their winter feed would be at a premium. Farmers made silage from the stripped and dried stalks, trying to provide feed for their remaining livestock.[33] By early 1932 farmers, unable to maintain their losses and pay mortgages and property taxes, were selling their land by choice or forced sales. People left the area to find work in the industries in Detroit, Michigan and Granite City, Illinois. Newspaper articles announced that recruiters were looking for employees to work in the rolling mills and automobile industries in northern cities. These articles implied that there were many job opportunities available to honest, industrious applicants.[34]

When Franklin Roosevelt promised a New Deal, the people were ready to follow his lead for almost any experiments which would change the existing conditions. In the election of 1932, voters went to the polls in record numbers. Democrats won a resounding victory in both Tennessee and Kentucky. Even in the traditionally Democratic counties, a higher percentage of the people voted for Roosevelt.[35]

Only a small number of farmers, with farms of over a hundred acres and no outstanding debts, had been able to make profits during the depression. These people voted against Roosevelt. Their profits had been made by taking advantage of the very cheap labor supply. A worker who had earned $20.00 a month in 1919 could be hired in 1932 for $4,00 to $6.00 per month.[36]

For the average person, one of the most beneficial programs of the New Deal was the Farm Credit Administration. Headed by Henry Morgenthau, Jr., the FCA consolidated several existing farm agencies and provided a central clearinghouse to assist rural homeowners. The most immediate problem was farm foreclosures. Congress granted emergency funds to the FCA to provide immediate assistance. The Emergency Farm Mortgage Act and the Farm Credit Act put into motion federal machinery that allowed refinancing of farm mortgages with longer terms and lower rates of interest. The loans were made to farmers through private institutions such as co-ops and Federal Land Banks. Farmers rushed to apply for the low interest rates at 5

---

[33]George T. Blakey, Hard Times and New Deal in Kentucky 1929-1939 (Lexington, Ky: The University Press of Kentucky), 1-39; Stewart County Times, January 5, 1930; July 25, 1930; November 20, 1930; January 12, 1931; June 16, 1931. People interviewed told of instances of hunger among the poor. People often shared with neighbors, but the conditions were insufferable.

[34]Ibid.

[35]Ibid. Tennessee voting records for 1932 found in the Tennessee State Library and Archives Nashville, Tennessee. Republicans voted for Roosevelt. Residents of the area told the author that Roosevelt soon earned a matchless reputation because he championed the poor, and he was revered second only to Jesus Christ.

[36]Interviews with citizens. Interviews in the hands of the author.

percent or less.[37]

The Tennessee Valley Authority

The Tennessee Valley Authority had the most long-lived effect on the people. Employment was one of the immediate major goals of the agency, but in part the agency itself was a product of the growing concern in America about the management of natural resources. These resources had been depleted at a rapid rate, and concerned citizens hoped the trend could be halted through the governmental intervention. As early as the administration of Theodore Roosevelt, people were trying to convince the American public that the only way to protect the nation's natural resources was to force the federal government into an active role in preservation. At that time, the proposal was for the state and federal governments to unify resource development. This ideology provided the cornerstone for the formation of TVA more than two decades later.

The chain of events which led to the formation of TVA began with the early conservationists and World War I. In 1916, as Americans prepared for World War I, the nation needed synthetic nitrates to make munitions for ourselves and our allies. A treacherous thirty-seven mile stretch of water on the Tennessee River at Muscle Shoals, Alabama was chosen by President Woodrow Wilson as the site for two nitrate plants and a hydroelectric dam. The dam was designed to provide the power for the nitrate plants.[38] The U. S. military, especially concerned with the activity of the German submarines, was afraid that the nitrates from Chile could not be imported in sufficient quantities to build weapons needed for war.

Just after the nitrate plants at Muscle Shoals were completed, the United States negotiated the end to World War I. President Wilson, who was conscientiously working to involve the United States in forming an alliance of world powers to limit arms production, did not see the need to expand nitrate production at Muscle Shoals.

In 1921, Congress began a four-year debate about the sale of these plants to private developers. Henry Ford, who had already become a successful businessman, was interested in the project. He made a bid of five million dollars for the properties at Muscle Shoals. It had cost the American people at least one hundred and thirty million dollars to build the plants. Congressmen and the public were bothered at the obvious profits that Ford would amass from the sale; it was said the sale amounted to an outright gift.[39]

A group of dedicated conservationists in Congress and the public sector were dubious about the outcome of such a sale, and an informal coalition began to investigate the matter.

---

[37]Commonwealth of Kentucky, Agricultural and Industrial Development Board, Deskbook of Kentucky Economic Statistics, 1952, Table I, 2.

[38]For a detailed history of the beginning of the Tennessee Valley Authority see Preston J. Hubbard's Origins of the TVA: The Muscle Shoals Controversy (Nashville, Tennessee: Vanderbilt University Press, 1961); Judson King, Conservation Fight from Theodore Roosevelt to the Tennessee Valley Authority (Washington, D.C.: Public Affairs Press, 1959). For development of the programs see Tennessee Valley Authority, TVA--the First Twenty Years: A Staff Report (Knoxville: University of Tennessee Press, 1956).

[39]Ibid.

Members of the group argued that the plants should continue the production of fertilizers which were badly needed in the country, and conservationists expressed fear that private developers would destroy the resources of the area.[40]

Ford's purchase bid came before the Senate Committee on Agriculture and Forestry, headed by Senator George Norris of Nebraska. Senator Norris, a Progressive Republican, was strongly opposed to the sale. Not only did he consider it a disgrace to sell the project for such a small sum, but he was opposed to selling the facility to an industrialist who would use the resources and make tremendous profits. American taxpayers would be subsidizing a business which could be contrary to their concerns about preservation of natural resources.

While Congress was debating the merits of the sale, the residents of northwest Alabama were actively supporting the action. Ford had been quoted as saying that he intended to build a city near the plants, and the people, eager for jobs, were ready to support his plans. When it was learned that Ford had talked about a plan to employ a million workers in his plants, the residents of the area were captivated. Local businessmen who wanted to take advantage of the prospective sale began to develop the area around the nitrate plants. They knew that developed properties would sell for more money once the sale was complete. Roads were built and building sites were purchased in anticipation of a boom time at Muscle Shoals.[41]

The sale was stalled in committee debates in Congress, and three years later, Congress had still not voted on the issue. Ford was exasperated with the delay and withdrew his bid. The issue of what to do with the property continued to cause problems among politicians. As it turned out, the Great Depression resulted in new plans for the area. Earlier, Senator George Norris had developed a plan to ease some of the problems that Americans faced in 1929. His plan was to develop depressed areas through the production of cheap electricity, promotion of soil conservation, and planned use of the natural resources. When Norris presented his plan to President Herbert Hoover, he received no support.

By 1932, the American dream had all but vanished in the minds of many citizens. Some thirteen million people were unemployed, and the gross national product had dropped to about one half of its former rate. Farm prices had plunged to an all-time low. Marriages and birthrates were lower. The somber mood of the nation was evident, and extraordinary measures were needed.[42]

By 1933, Senator George Norris had proposed seven bills for the creation of a regional federal agency in the Tennessee Valley, and when these proposals were called to Roosevelt's attention he gave his support to them. The cornerstone of the development was the federal properties at Muscle Shoals. Senator Norris had researched his proposals and showed the Tennessee Valley area was an excellent region to test the hypothesis that a basic harmony existed

---

[40]King, Conservation, 217-230.

[41]Ibid.

[42]The literature on the New Deal is extensive. A representative sample is as follows: James McGregor Burns, F. D. R.: The Lion and the Fox (New York: Harcourt, Brace, 1956), Paul K. Conkin, The New Deal (New York: Crowell, 1967), William E. Leuchtenburg, Franklin D. Roosevelt and the New Deal (New York: Harper and Row, 1963), Arthur Schlesinger, Age of Roosevelt (Boston: Houghton Mifflin, 1951), and Rexford Tugwell, The Democratic Roosevelt (Garden City, N. Y.: Doubleday, 1957).

between man and nature. A river could be controlled to reduce flooding while furnishing dependable transportation and electricity. Depleted soil could be restored. Eroded soil could be restored, and forests could be rejuvenated. The people would have jobs, and the economy would be stimulated.[43]

Senator Norris produced statistics which demonstrated that the Tennessee River area was one of the more economically depressed regions of the nation. By 1933, the residents were demoralized and destitute. The annual per capita income was less than $168.00. The birthrate was above the national average, and the literacy rate was low and the labor force was generally unskilled. More than half of the people lived on farms, and only three farms in 100 had electricity.[44]

In his address to Congress on April 10, 1933, President Roosevelt remarked that the Muscle Shoals development was but a part of the conceivable public usefulness of the Tennessee River. He predicted that the development would be more than ordinary power production. He suggested that congressmen pass legislation to create the Tennessee Valley Authority which would serve as a corporation with the powers of government but with the flexibility and initiative of private enterprise. The agency was to plan for the proper use, conservation, and development of the natural resources of the Tennessee River drainage basin and its adjoining territory for the general social and economic welfare of the country. Congress quickly responded and the bill was signed on May 18, 1933.[45]

It must be mentioned that there were many opponents of the whole concept of TVA. When the Tennessee Valley Authority promised cheap electrical power and the government was ready to subsidize rural electrification, the private utility companies prepared to do battle. Court battles initiated by these companies delayed all of the promised benefits until 1938.

The Tennessee Valley Authority provided immediate and protracted benefits, and of all the New Deal Programs, TVA created the most obvious changes in the physical and social environment. One could speculate that the agency might never have come into being if the country had not been facing the appalling economic conditions of the time. Political leaders feared the worst possible outcome to the depressed economy, conceivably an insurrection. The communist revolution which had recently occurred in Russia was still fresh in the minds of the leaders. Fear of drastic actions from the unemployed resulted in the willingness to experiment with the economy. But the issue which has continued to linger centers on the conflict between private enterprise and TVA.

The destiny of the Tennessee Valley Authority rested, to a great degree, on its early leadership. Roosevelt appointed a three-member Board of Directors, and the operations for the agency were divided into three major areas. Chairman Arthur E. Morgan was responsible for engineering and construction. Board member David E. Lilienthal took charge of organizing the power system, and Harcourt A. Morgan headed the fertilizer and agriculture program. In a relatively short time, differences occurred among the TVA directors. The basic disagreement

---

[43]Marguerite Owen, The Tennessee Valley Authority (New York: Praeger Publishers, 1973), 39.

[44]Ibid.,42.

[45]Ibid., 98.

was about offering low-cost electrical power to the public. Chairman Arthur E. Morgan proposed entering into an agreement with the private utilities to distribute TVA power. Directors David Lilienthal and Harcourt A. Morgan openly opposed the policy. The whole agency was almost discredited by the public argument which ensued.[46]

People who disagreed with the ideological concepts of TVA were gleeful that the Directors of the agency were in open disagreement. Former Republican presidential candidate, Wendell Willkie, was among the first to voice his opposition to the whole concept of TVA. Willkie was president of Commonwealth and Southern Corporations, a utility holding company with major interests in the Tennessee Valley. Willkie and others argued that TVA could not legally compete with private enterprise. They maintained that the TVA rates were too low and would force private utilities out of business, and there was no market for TVA power because the region had enough power production from private companies.[47] This issue has brought TVA to the attention of the nation since 1933.

After months of arguments, President Roosevelt entered the fray and ordered the TVA Board members to offer evidence to support their positions. The President and his staff studied the situation and removed Arthur E. Morgan from office. The policies espoused by Harcourt A. Morgan were adopted and TVA moved ahead to offer cheap electric power to the people. It appears that the leadership of Harcourt A. Morgan, and to a lesser degree, David Lilienthal saved TVA in the 1930s and expanded the horizons of the agency for the future.[48]

Only a few hundred people in the land between the rivers had electrical power because the private power companies did not consider it profitable to run their lines into rural areas.[49] TVA worked with the Public Works Administration to build power plants and string lines to provide enough electrical power for the area. Both agencies hired workers from the region, and these jobs kept many people fed and clothed during the worst months of the depression.[50]

The Rural Electrification Administration, one of Franklin Roosevelt's priority programs, had to fight private companies when it attempted to make electricity available to the rural areas. Court cases brought against the REA program delayed its implementation for several years, but by 1938, almost five years after it was proposed, the government assisted in the development of rural electric co-operatives. The co-operatives purchased the power provided by TVA and sold it to their members. In the land between the rivers, when agents from the private companies tried to delay, or perhaps stop, the REA workers from setting the poles and stringing the electrical wires, they faced angry citizens with shotguns who ordered them off their property and away from the roads which passed their homes. The agents hired by private companies did

---

[46]Thomas K. McCraw, TVA and the Power Fight 1933-1939 (New York: J. B. Lippincott Company, 1971), 29-78.

[47]Ibid., 129-178.

[48]Ibid.

[49]Only those people who lived in the towns on the edge of the region had electricity. Even in towns such as Dover, Cadiz, and Eddyville, which had the largest populations, many of the people could not afford the rates. Interviews with residents in 1957. Interviews in the hands of the author.

[50]Interviews with citizens of the area in 1957. Interviews in the hands of the author.

187

not dare interfere with these people; their reputation was known.[51]

If the people could afford to wire their homes and pay the electrical rates, they joined the co-operative. Families saved money and skimped on other expenses in order to afford electricity. The first expense was wiring the house, and money was saved for that purpose. Then, the access fee was paid to the co-operative. At first most homes had only electric lights. It was not unusual to see a farm home with the visible electrical wiring running along the interior walls and a naked light bulb hanging from the ceiling. In many of these homes, economics forced a gradual purchase plan for electrical appliances. Most people did not want to use installment purchasing plans. In order of priority, the people wanted refrigerators, washing machines, and radios. By 1950, eighty-five percent of the homes had electricity.[52]

In 1938, currency was not circulating, and people who could find jobs were earning twenty-five to fifty cents a day as laborers. Merchants in the area often accepted barter as a means of exchanging goods. For example, an individual could trade a young pig for a radio. The first family in the community to own a radio invited all the neighbors to the house to hear the programs.[53]

In the evenings, the house was filled with neighbors who wanted to listen to the programs. People soon chose their favorites and were avid, loyal listeners. Surely, the visitors became a nuisance when they came every night to listen to their favorite programs. Yet, the rules of hospitality would not allow the host to tell his guests that they were not welcome to come at any time.

Gradually, other electrical appliances were purchased. Refrigerators were needed because very few people owned ice boxes. Often, the refrigerator was placed on a porch because the kitchen was not large enough to accommodate the bulky appliance. When affordable, electric washing machines were purchased, but most of the homes did not have indoor plumbing. The washing machine did not save much time or labor for the housewife because the water had to be carried to the machine from the well or cistern. Whenever possible, the family bought an electric pump for the cistern or well and brought the water inside the home. Electric irons replaced the sadirons, but again, the cost of the item was prohibitive.[54]

One of the promises made by TVA was that cheap electrical power would eliminate most of the drudgery faced by the homemaker. Appliance companies had used this advertising theme for some years and based their claims on the promise that women could expect much more leisure time. It was advertised that the extra time would place the women in the lap of luxury, and appliances would eliminate all the drudgery and hard work for the housewife.

In reality, the electrical appliances provided some amenities for all members of the family, but the drudge work was not eradicated, only modified. Farm women still had to spend hours cleaning and cooking. The advertised labor-saving appliances provided very little extra time,

---

[51]Ibid.

[52]Ibid.

[53]Ibid. WSM radio in Nashville was one of the most popular stations. The people liked country music, especially the Grand Ole Opry, and religious sermons.

[54]Sadirons or flatirons were heavy irons heated on a stove, or the hollow ones were filled with hot coals.

certainly not leisure time. For example, the wood burning cook stove was replaced by the electric stove and in the summer, the electric stove made the kitchen cooler. But, it took approximately the same amount of time to cook meals on the electric stove as it did with the wood burning stove. In fact, the old stove was usually kept in the kitchen and used in the winter because it did provide needed heat. Throughout the house, the old appliances and new stood side by side and both were used for many years.[55]

When TVA built dams to produce electrical power, an added benefit was that dams reduced the problem of flooding. Caught between the Tennessee and Cumberland, the people were well aware of the damages caused by floods. Every year, farmers gambled that they would not lose their crops and homes to the flood waters. In the midst of the depression, flooding was an especially severe problem. In 1928, the rivers had risen out of their banks five times, and in 1937, one of the worst floods in the region's history struck the area. Farmers who could ill-afford the loss of crops, livestock, and homes felt the impact. The people welcomed the activities of TVA even more when they realized that TVA dams would control flooding. Also, farmers were told that they could purchase the fertilizers produced by TVA to increase the productivity of their soil.[56]

The Work Project Administration benefited the region in several ways. The most immediate assistance was associated with the projects to build roads and public buildings. Men were employed because the programs stipulated that the majority of the work force must come from the residents of the area. In 1933, reclamation projects were started on Honker Lake, Hematite Lake, and the Empire Lake. Gravel roads replaced the trails and paths in the area. For the first time in the history of the region, people could easily travel from one community to the other during the entire year without worry about the conditions of the roads.[57]

The repeal of Prohibition in 1933 placed the people in the area in a rather unique situation. When state laws once again controlled the sale of alcohol, the legislatures of both Kentucky and Tennessee, sensitive to the political power of the temperance movement, passed legislation regulating the production and sale of alcohol by allowing the counties to determine whether they would allow the sale of beer, wine, and whiskey. Lyon, Trigg, and Stewart counties voted to maintain a dry region.[58] The whiskey makers saw no difference in prohibition whether by the county or federal government. Either way, they could not legally sell their whiskey.

The people learned that the repeal of prohibition had affected them in one way; legal distilleries supplied most of their former markets outside the region. The only way to keep their

---

[55]"Women and TVA," a paper written by the author for Clarksville-Montgomery County TVA display.

[56]A flood in 1927 was bad, but the flooding of 1937 was even worse. The rains began in January 1937 and the expected rainfall was two inches for the month, but the area received more than twenty inches. When the waters began to recede in February the whole area was devastated. See Blakey, Hard Times, 191-97.

[57]Marguerite Owen, The Tennessee Valley Authority, 199. From the interviews with the residents, it was noted that many people felt that the administration of the federal work programs was not fairly applied. Some of the people stated that men had to pay county officials for their jobs. Even though the statement was made by several people, no proof of the charge could be found by the author.

[58]These local returns are noted in the County records in Lyon, Trigg, and Stewart Counties.

189

whiskey industry in operation was to lower the price so that people would choose it over the legal, taxed alcohol. Money from the sale of whiskey had kept people off the dole and they intended to stay that way. They increased their production and lowered their prices and did not enroll in the welfare program. To these people, any of the government programs which provided free food and other commodities was charity, and they were too proud to take it.[59]

But the picture was not as bleak as it first appeared. When the price on the illegal alcohol was lowered, the domestic market grew and the illegal industry remained profitable. Some people preferred the whiskey made in the area and continued the practice of buying it for sale in other parts of the country. It appears that the whiskey had developed a large following and these customers wanted it whether it was legal or not.[60]

The Agricultural Adjustment Act helped farmers in the area. If over-production was the cause of farmers' problems then the government could help by encouraging farmers to grow fewer crops. Under the domestic allotment plan the government would pay subsidies to farmers to reduce their acreage or plow under crops already in the fields. Farmers would receive payments based on parity, a system of regulated prices for corn, cotton, wheat, rice, hogs, and dairy products that would allow them the same purchasing power they had during the prosperous period of 1909 through 1914. In effect, the government was making up the difference between the actual market value of farm products and the income farmers needed to make a profit. The funds for the subsidies would come from taxes levied on the processors of agricultural commodities.[61]

It was not until 1936 that the people in the region began to take advantage of the public works program in the New Deal. In 1935 Congress passed and Roosevelt signed the Emergency Relief Appropriation Act which authorized the president to issue executive orders establishing massive public works programs for jobless, including the Work Progress Administration. Later renamed the Work Projects Administration, the WPA employed people to built highways, streets, and roads. Construction and renovation of public buildings provided jobs. Construction of bridges, airports, and other structures changed the appearance of the countryside. Through The Federal Theater Project and The Federal Music Project entertainment was brought into the land between the rivers.[62]

When President Roosevelt announced that he was going to provide relief by initiating a work project called the Civilian Conservation Corps, young men in the area were very interested. The philosophy of the CCC was already integrated into the culture of the region. People believed that they must earn what they needed. They were opposed to charity, and the CCC program allowed the young men between the ages of eighteen and twenty-five to work to support themselves and their families. They worked planting trees, clearing camping grounds, cleaning beaches, and in other projects such as building bridges, dams, reservoirs, fish ponds,

[59]Interviews with citizens of the land between the rivers.

[60]Ibid.

[61]John D. Minton, The New Deal in Tennessee, 1933-1938, (New York: Garland, 1979), 49-52.

[62]Blakey, Hard Times, 45-76.

and fire towers.[63]

As impressive as the CCC was, it did not meet the need of the jobless youth. Roosevelt was obviously mindful of these problems and issued an executive order establishing the National Youth Administration. A part of the WPA but an autonomous administrative unit, the NYA was to help schools find jobs for students so they could remain in school. The project served a much larger group than the CCC, and it included females in the program. For some reason, the program never captured the public imagination as did the CCC.[64]

In 1935, as a part of the conservation project, the federal government took control of the Kentucky Woodlands Natural Wildlife Refuge, land formerly owned by the Hillman and Company iron industry. The national refuge was intended to provide and maintain an environment conducive to the proliferation of native small game and waterfowls.[65] Conservationists were concerned about the possibility of the extinction of some of the species, and at that time, the region was the only one in Kentucky where wild turkeys could be found, and one of the few places in the South where deer could be sighted. All the turkeys and most of the deer that went into the Kentucky restocking programs were trapped at the refuge and resettled in such places as Mammoth Cave, Beaver Creek Refuge, Pennnyrile Forest and other areas. In 1938, the wild turkey was so rare that each bird was worth one thousand dollars in trade for species of wildlife with other states. The state government had been unable to control illegal hunting in the area and the issue had caused considerable controversy in the politics of the state. The political argument centered on paying game wardens to protect the wildlife.[66]

In 1935, the U.S. Resettlement Administration purchased more land and brought the amount of land federally owned to approximately 65,000 acres. In 1938, Franklin Roosevelt declared all federal lands between the Cumberland and Tennessee Rivers from Moss ferry to the Turkey Creek road a national wildlife refuge.[67] Various governmental agencies hired workers in the area to provide detailed maps of the region, and to propose ways to combat soil erosion and implement reforestation programs. The first step in the program was the construction of several roads to make the whole area accessible. On June 13, 1940, title to the entire area was turned over to the U. S. Bureau of Biological Survey. The Bureau began an extensive wildlife development program. Special interest was shown in increasing the waterfowl population. The Bureau was successful in bringing geese and ducks to the area. Within a twenty year period,

---

[63]Although the records are scattered, approximately 200 young men from the area spent time with the CCC program. This information was gathered from interviews with people, and John Salmond, The Civilian Conservation Corps, 1933-1942: A New Deal Case Study (Durham: Duke University Press, 1967), 30-32; Perry H. Merrill, Roosevelt's Forest Army: A History of the Civilian Conservation Corps (Montpelier, Vt.: privately printed, 1981), 196-199; CCC Annual Reports, 1934-1941, 4, 20, 28,33, 67,71-77, 104.

[64]Many of the youth in the area were involved at one time or another with the NYA. The program ran from 1935 to 1943.

[65]Marguerite Owen, The Tennessee Valley Authority, 200.

[66]Some politicians argued that the state revenue was needed in other areas and it should not spend additional revenue for salaries for game wardens.

[67]Owen, The Tennessee Valley Authority, 210.

it was estimated that 25,000 geese and 60,000 ducks wintered there.[68]

Even though the Tennessee Valley Authority was created in May, 1933, firm plans for harnessing the Tennessee River were not initiated until 1937. Late in 1937, TVA announced plans for the construction of dams, including the Kentucky Dam, on the Tennessee River. Before all the plans had been publicized, TVA had started to purchase land at Aurora, Kentucky. A private company had already planned the construction of a dam in the area and had purchased most of the land on the Tennessee River. When the Tennessee Valley Authority realized that it would appear to be in direct competition with a private company, it halted the plans to purchase more land. After careful consideration, the directors of TVA decided that the Aurora site was not the prime location, and decided to build the dam about twenty miles down stream.[69]

The Kentucky Dam was 206 feet high and over one and one-half miles long. It backed up the water of the Tennessee River to form Kentucky Lake, reaching as far as 184 miles up the river from the dam. The reservoir included a total of 134,000 acres of land plus an easement of 100,000 acres for flood control.

The proponents of the New Deal had been successful in convincing the people that the proposed programs would release them from the clutches of the Great Depression. It was true that the New Deal had been able to deliver only a part of the relief it had promised, but the people did not blame Franklin Roosevelt and the Democrats for the delay. The Great Depression had eased slightly in 1936. The people blamed the capitalists, or tycoons as they were called, who had delayed the plans the Democrats had made. In the minds of many people, the Republican party had to take total responsibility for the poor economy. The people were united in their opposition to the very wealthy industrialists and large companies who, they felt, exploited the worker. In their minds the wealthy industrialists controlled the Republican Party.[70]

Following their tradition of concern for the welfare of all their neighbors, people were ready to allow the federal government to intervene in economic and social affairs if that was necessary for economic relief. It was an interesting phenomenon that a society which had so jealously guarded its individual rights and abhorred the view that a government could tax or restrict its production of whiskey or force it to fence in its animals was unopposed to the intervention of the federal government in determining jobs and even the types of crops that would be planted. Nonetheless, the people supported Roosevelt and the New Deal almost to a person.

---

[68]Ibid.

[69]Ibid.

[70]Interviews with citizens of the land between the rivers.

CHAPTER X

WORLD WAR II AND CHANGES

When the United States entered World War II, the people in the land between the rivers immediately joined the war effort. Unlike the conditions which existed with World War I, the United States had been openly attacked by an enemy, the Japanese. The people were united in their desire to defend their country and to retaliate against all her enemies.[1]

The radio played an important role in arousing the emotional responses of the people toward the war. Now, the people had almost immediate access to current events and they joined in the war effort with vigor. Men did not wait for their draft notices but volunteered for service and received a rousing send off from their friends and neighbors. Men who volunteered or were drafted were considered heroes. School children were urged by their teachers to adopt local servicemen as pen pals. Classroom assignments included instructions on how to write to these men each week to tell them about local events. Children and adults were aware of the war news and discussion about the battles and other war related topics replaced the old topics of politics and religion.[2]

A few families left the farms because they could make more money in industrial jobs, expecting to return when the war ended. Some people simply wanted to escape and left never to return. During the early months of 1942, many families felt the effects when these men and women made decisions to leave home. Without realizing it, people were experiencing a permanent change in the area.

During the war, those people who remained at home felt a gradual change in their lives. Money was still hard to make and families had to save for months for large purchases, but more people were able to save to buy automobiles and farm machinery, using installment payment plans. Accepting installment purchases was a significant change. Up to that time, the general sentiment was against any debts. The attitude was that a person who made payments on property or machinery was not the owner until he had paid all indebtedness. A social stigma usually followed debtors, but attitudes changed during the war years.[3]

In less than a decade, the New Deal and the beginning of World War II had changed lives and attitudes. The people were less opposed to allowing outside investors to bring industry to the area. A few politicians were already suggesting that incentives should be offered in order to attract more industry. Their speeches always included the promise that new revenue from industry would lead to better schools and lower property taxes. The people were still very interested in preserving their traditions, but they were willing to concede that the world had

---

[1]The people interviewed in 1957 expressed their strong belief that there was no way the U.S. could have avoided the Japanese attack in 1941. To a person, the sentiment was that everyone had to support the war effort. It would have been totally unacceptable to evade the draft.

[2]Ibid.

[3]Interviews with citizens in 1957. Interviews in the hands of the author.

changed around them and if their children wanted to remain in the area, new jobs most be developed for them.[4]

The problems connected to rationing and sacrificing for the war effort seemed to have little effect. People owned few cars or trucks and were not concerned with the rationed gasoline and tires. Farmers were provided with special rationing coupons for farm machinery. A few whiskey producers had trouble getting enough sugar for their operations, but they could use the more traditional way of making whiskey without sugar. People did the best they could with what they had and life continued.[5]

People relied upon the old methods of entertainment. They attended their parties and socials and more people bought radios. The church was still an important focus in their religious and social life. If they did not have a car to take them to church, they could always use a wagon. Young people did not seem to feel deprived if they had to stay home instead of going to a movie. Usually the movies were too far away to attend, and television sounded much like science fiction. The whole concept was too crazy for words.[6]

Development of Fort Campbell

In 1942, Camp Campbell, near the border of the land between the rivers, was established as a training camp for the military. Approximately 106,000 acres of land was purchased from people in Christian and Trigg Counties, Kentucky and Montgomery and Stewart Counties in Tennessee. The federal government paid an average of $39.94 per acre for the land. Since 69,000 acres of the land came from Tennessee, it was decided that the camp should be named for a Tennessean, General William Bowen Campbell. General Campbell had fought in the Creek and Seminole Wars and in the Mexican War. In 1857, he was elected governor in Tennessee.[7]

From 1942 to 1945, some 100,000 soldiers were trained annually at Camp Campbell. The construction of the facility and the numbers of soldiers training at the installation had an enormous effect on the people in the region. Local men were hired to build and maintain the camp. Later, women were hired in the offices and other civilian service jobs. The employment

---

[4]Newspaper articles in the local press discussed the need for more industry. See The Nashville Tennessean, January 19, 1944; June 7, 1945; August 19, 1945; Stewart County Times, February 24, 1943; March 19, 1944; July 16, 1945.

[5]People said that rationing was not a real problem because they seemed to have enough coupons for the amount of money they had to spend. Family members were able to swap coupons if they had difficulty and it all seemed to work quite well.

[6]Enterprising individuals obtained films and showed them at the schools on Friday and Saturday nights. Some of the people saw their first movies in this setting.

[7]After protracted debate, it was decided that the address for the installation would be Kentucky since the post office was located on that state's side of the installation. This decision bothered Tennesseans because more of the reservation land came from Tennessee.

opportunities helped the economy and affected attitudes.[8]

For some time, the soldiers who came from all parts of the country to Camp Campbell found an interesting reception in the area. People were proud of them for protecting the country, yet these men often had different attitudes and customs. The traditional reservations about outsiders resulted in a certain aloofness toward the soldiers. The soldiers misunderstood the reaction and voiced negative opinions about the people in Tennessee and Kentucky. They described the natives as old-fashioned, illiterate, and uncultured. The people reacted with hostility and even anger. Soon, the soldiers were not welcome at social events or the homes of the natives, and parents would not allow young women to attend the social functions if soldiers were present. Daughters were told they could not associate with the men, and women who refused to listen to the warning found they had earned a dishonorable reputation after dating soldiers. Of course, young men and women found ways of meeting and women married servicemen, but many years elapsed before these anti-military attitudes changed.[9]

Military spending helped the economy of the region. Until 1945 most of the benefits, except jobs, were limited to the areas immediately surrounding the camp. Because they liked the countryside and property was cheap, a few of the servicemen decided to purchase land in the region and return when they had completed their tour of duty. Land purchases continued after the war.

From 1943 to 1945, German prisoners were kept at the installation. The men were housed in two compounds--one for the Nazis and one for the anti-Nazis. Under heavy military guard the prisoners were taken to jobs on surrounding farms each day. It became a common sight to see the military trucks and guards transporting the prisoners to and from work. In 1946, the last German prisoner left Camp Campbell.[10]

The Tennessee Valley Authority and the Tennessee River

The people learned in 1941 that TVA was interested in buying their land along the Tennessee River. They had not paid much attention to news items when President Roosevelt had said as early as 1941 that there was an urgent need for more power for national defense.[11] From time to time, it was mentioned in newspapers that TVA had ten dams under construction,

---

[8]To this day, the installation is the single largest employer in the area.

[9]By 1943, to identify someone as a soldier brought a strong reaction. For whatever reason, these people were not acceptable. These men were described as untrustworthy. It was said that they would take advantage of women because they knew that they would be leaving the area in a few months. Women were thought to have lowered their moral standards if they dated soldiers.

[10]In 1951, Camp Campbell became Fort Campbell, a permanent military reservation. In the same year, it became the home of the 11th Airborne Division. In 1956, the 101st Airborne Division was permanently placed at the fort.

[11]In 1941 President Roosevelt asked Congress for funding for Douglas Dam in east Tennessee. Senator Kenneth McKellar from Tennessee, who had supported previous dam projects, tried to block the Douglas project. When the Japanese bombed Pearl Harbor, the President's defense program, including the Douglas dam, got quick approval in Congress.

but the demand for electricity was increasing faster than TVA could provide it. The idea of flooding the Tennessee with a high dam, providing electricity and flood control, had not occurred to the people. Yet, the agency announced that it was acquiring approximately 158,000 acres of land for development of the Tennessee to form Kentucky Lake. In 1942, 234,000 acres were impounded. The Authority announced that some 3,500 families would be moved to make way for the lake. The citizens learned that the towns of Birmingham and Newburg were to be obliterated and villages and communities would be covered by water. These events did not transpire as easily as it might appear.[12]

When TVA agents entered the area and made offers for the farms and woodlands, people living on the western side of the land between the rivers were the first to be affected. Their response was that they would sell if the government offered them what their land was worth. The offers were too low according to the owners, and opposition mounted. Land owners were severely distressed when they realized that the government could condemn the land and buy it even if they refused to sell. The TVA officials promised that the whole region would benefit from the production of cheaper electrical power, the tourist trade, and industry which would come to the area to take advantage of the cheap power. These promises destroyed public support for those people who would be forced to move.[13]

Some of the people felt it was inevitable that TVA would acquire their land, and they negotiated and reached an acceptable price.[14] Other people refused to sell and condemnation proceedings followed. Public opinion was usually in favor of those who wanted better prices for their land, but little effort was made to bring public pressure on TVA to lower the acreage it wanted.[15]

One example of those who resisted TVA offers was the owners of the Tishel farm. For several generations the Eagle Hill Farm, as it was named, had included some six hundred acres of land including about four hundred acres of valuable timber land. TVA offered $15,765.78 for the four hundred and fifty-three acres it needed. The family refused the offer and demanded at least $26,740.00 for the property. The case went to the Federal District Court and finally on appeal to the U. S. Circuit Court of Appeals, but TVA lost the decision. People who had already sold their land to TVA felt betrayed by the agency. They spoke of the Tishel case as an example of how TVA deliberately under-valued their land.[16]

Undeniably, the removal of the people from their land produced a crisis in their lives. The older people were the most resistant to being moved, but there were also conspicuous effects on

---

[12]Marguerite Owen, The Tennessee Valley Authority, 200. The people argued that the dam was not needed. The dams on the upper Tennessee could control the flooding, or at least a series of low dams would not flood so much of their land.

[13]Ibid.

[14]One former resident explained the feeling as, "You can't fight the government." Interviews in 1957 with Lon Dilday who had moved at the time to Trenton, Kentucky.

[15]Ibid.

[16]Stewart County Times, August 12, 1947. The Tennessee Valley Authority had to pay the higher rate for the land.

all the people. Stewart County lost 28,965 acres of land to the dam and its easement, and the loss included people and tax revenue which in turn affected all the political and social institutions in the county. Many of the people were forced to relocate outside Stewart County because they were unable to find comparable farm land in the area.[17]

Within a short time, people were bitterly complaining that TVA's promise to bring industry into the area had not been fulfilled. Once again, they accused the agency of deliberately misrepresenting their intentions. TVA had advanced the theory that cheap electrical power would lure many industries into the region, but these theorists did not take into account the lack of cheap, reliable transportation in the region. Cheap power and a sufficient labor supply did not offset the lack of roads and railroads.

Development of the Cumberland River

By 1949, the people were aware that plans for the development of the Cumberland River valley had been discussed among political leaders in both Tennessee and Kentucky. It seemed unbelievable that TVA needed to flood the Cumberland for sources of power; surely the Tennessee was sufficient. If the rumors were true, they would be even more affected than they had been by the development of the Tennessee River. Congressman Percy Priest of Nashville introduced a bill that would enable TVA to extend its development into the Cumberland Valley. The people joined together to protest the plan and the bill was eventually defeated.[18]

Groups of businessmen who lived outside the area in Lyon, Trigg, and Stewart Counties mounted a campaign in 1950 to generate support for the construction of a high dam on the Cumberland to prevent flooding at Eddyville and Kuttawa and other communities in the area. Unquestionably, the frequent flooding of the Cumberland brought economic distress to the residents along the river, and the danger could be alleviated with the construction of a high dam. It was also evident that many of the same people did not fully comprehend the consequences of a high dam.[19]

By July 1953, the general public knew that the House Public Works Committee had approved an appropriation providing for a high dam on the lower Cumberland, costing an estimated $155,000,000.00. In August, they learned that Congress had passed the bill and a road was to be built to connect U.S. Highway 68 east of Kentucky Lake with Grand Rivers.[20]

Senator Erle Clements of Kentucky had included in the bill an appropriation to spend $748,000.00 to purchase lands on the lower Cumberland to replace the Woodlands Wildlife Refuge that would be lost when it was inundated by the waters resulting from the new dam.

---

[17]Census Records and County Court records indicate approximately 110 families left the area.

[18]The Nashville Tennessean, April 22, 1949.

[19]Louisville Courier Journal, Louisville, Kentucky, June 17, 1950; Sun Democrat, Paducah, Kentucky, June 29, 1950.

[20]Ibid., July 10, 1953; The Commercial Appeal, Memphis, Tennessee, July 10, 1953; Banner, Nashville, Tennessee, July 11, 1952 and August 1, 1953; Sun Democrat, Paducah, Kentucky, August 3, 1953.

Newspapers in Cadiz and Eddyville supported the activities of the politicians. Other papers remained neutral or silent on the subject. Their reports were restricted to an announcement of the proposals.[21]

For two years the discussion of the proposed dam seemed to result in more support outside the region. Because economic conditions remained stagnant in the region and people were anxious to encourage almost any new economic development, it was often mentioned that the construction of the dam would energize the economy. At least people could look forward to new job opportunities.

People in Lyon County who lived in the land between the rivers blamed the Democrats for the proposals to buy more of their land, and in the elections of 1955 they supported the Republican candidate for governor. The vote was very unusual because the county had always voted the Democratic ticket even if the party had made poor proposals. Regional and national coverage of the election noted that the people living between the rivers were not in favor of the dam even though it would prevent floods and bring new jobs.[22]

The media reports appeared to denigrate the people by describing them as poor, uneducated, and uninterested in the development of the region. The people were prompt in their reaction to these characterizations. They wrote numerous letters to newspapers and journals informing the editors that they were descendants of famous Americans and that among the citizens were many who were nationally known. They listed the accomplishments of families in the region. The names of such families as Smith, Bleidt, Wallace, Earhart, Lane, Stone, Jefferson, Spiceland, Luton, Ryan, and Brandon were examples of the upstanding members of the community.[23]

At this point, the natives felt a sense of alienation from people who lived just outside the region. Friends were among the outsiders who had formed organizations which demanded immediate construction of the high dam. Four hundred people joined the Lower Cumberland Development Association and petitioned the government for the early construction of the dam. The major argument in support of the dam was the control of annual flood waters. Farmers near the river were quoted in news releases as saying that the dam would prevent the crop damage and destruction which occurred almost every year.[24]

The people who were the most vocal in their support of the dam seemed to envision a dam which would keep the Cumberland River within its banks. They did not understand that the project would result in extensive flooding of croplands on either side of the river. Not once in all the comments did the supporters of the project mention that easement lands would have to be taken along both sides of the Cumberland. The supporters of the project did not discuss the fact that some of the land which they were trying to keep from flooding would be within the

---

[21]Record, Cadiz, Kentucky, July 22, 1953; Lyon County Herald, Eddyville, Kentucky, July 22, 1953.

[22]Lyon County Herald, Eddyville, Kentucky, August, 1955.

[23]Lyon County Herald, Eddyville, Kentucky, September 19, 1953; Stewart County Times, Dover, Tennessee, September 12, 1953; Louisville Courier Journal, Louisville, Kentucky, September 20, 1953; Record, Cadiz, Kentucky, September 20, 1953.

[24]Record, Cadiz, Kentucky, November 19, 1953; Sun-Democrat, Paducah, Kentucky, November 14, 1953; Democrat, Murray, Kentucky, November 15, 1953.

easent limits.

As the news media gave more detailed explanations of what the construction of the high dam would entail, residents realized that their land would be taken if the plan were implemented. They realized that the dam project would affect many more farms and homes than they had anticipated. Some of the early supporters of the dam changed their minds as soon as they learned that they would lose land. For the first time since its inception, many people began to perceive The Tennessee Valley Authority as an enemy instead of a benefactor. Daily, people wrote to politicians or newspaper editors expressing their concern over the magnitude of the Barkley Dam project.[25] The opposition groups began to describe TVA as a giant corporation feeding on privately owned lands in order to become more powerful. They argued that TVA could produce enough electricity to supply the whole region by using its present power sites. Flooding the Cumberland, they said, was unnecessary, because flood control could be augmented by more low dams on the river. The low dams would not affect the farms along the river.

The people expressed amazement that TVA would initiate a project which would destroy some of the best farm land in the United States. Not only would approximately 57,000 acres of the most fertile soil be forced out of use, the property tax revenue would be critically affected. Since the property tax remained the major source of revenue for the counties, the tax money could not meet the needs of the local governments. Citizens and officials of Trigg, Lyon, and Stewart Counties expressed concern, not only about the loss of revenue, but about the effect the project would have on the citizenry. If several hundred of the prominent citizens were forced out of the region, those people who remained would be affected both socially and politically.

Perhaps the major failing on the part of the leadership of TVA at the time was its inability to understand the culture of the region. These people did not understand the purpose, as explained by TVA, for taking the land. Certainly, better communication with the people would have eased some of the difficulties. For the first time, TVA failed to do an adequate job in public relations, and as a result it found itself faced with a host of opponents.

The hardest task for the people was to accept the fact that they could not stop the project. Barkley Dam was going to be constructed regardless of how they felt about the matter. Agents from the Corps of Engineers were already on the scene and had started a survey of the area. Now, the people were faced with the problem of establishing the market value of their property. It was a genuine dilemma to separate the emotional value attached to the land from the actual market price. Almost to a person, the people were unable to separate the two. None of the people were satisfied with the prices they were offered. After several months of anguish and heated arguments the people began to accept the inevitable. They received, on the average, $200.00 per acre for their land.[26]

---

[25]Alben Barkley was a Democrat from Kentucky who served seven terms as Representative (1912-1927), four consecutive terms as Senator (1927-1948), and vice-president with Harry Truman. After leaving the vice-presidency in 1943, he was elected to his old Senate seat in 1954. He died suddenly on April 30, 1956, while making a speech in Virginia. Barkley Dam was named for him.

[26]Barkley Dam Report, Tennessee Valley Authority, Knoxville, Tennessee, 1956. Depending on whether the land was riverbasin (natives referred to the land as riverbottoms) or hill lands the price seemed to correspond with the open market value of the land. On the open market land in the area sold from $50.00 to $300.00 per acre. See Stewart

Even though the opposition was convincing and well articulated, the people received little support from their political leaders. Letters were written describing their losses, but the dam project stayed on schedule. Surveys found that twenty-four churches and fifteen cemeteries were affected. The churches and cemeteries were slated for removal as soon as suitable locations could be found for them.

The Trigg County Association of the Lower Cumberland led by J. R. Vinson, Jr. met to formulate a united action against the acquisition program of the Corps of Engineers. The proceedings of the organization indicate that even though most of the people had accepted the fact that they would be forced to sell their land, they were concerned with keeping the total acquisition to a minimum and demanding a more just consideration from the agents of the Corps of Engineers.[27]

At the meetings, the people expressed the view that the agents for TVA had no feelings for the people. The Corps of Engineers employees were described as arrogant, brash, and disdainful. They were characterized as men who had no concern about the rights of the people. The citizens demanded that the federal employees treat them with civility and respect the sanctity of their homes. They felt that no one, especially an agent of the government, could enter a person's home without an invitation.[28]

It was soon apparent that the Corps of Engineers had not schooled their agents on the techniques of how to develop a reasonable rapport with the people in the area. This oversight resulted in acrimony and pain for the citizens and costly delays for the Barkley Dam project.

The most difficult situation for the Trigg County Association was its inability to bring all the citizens in the area into a workable, united organization. Even though the group sent a representative to Washington to carry their concerns to Representatives and Senators, their requests made a lesser impact because of the limited number of citizens in their organization. The only accomplishment of the organization was that it did force the members of the Corps of Engineers to change some of its policies. The Corps sent a directive to all of its agents in the land between the rivers, ordering them to treat the citizens with respect. They were told not to enter a home unless they were invited.[29]

The Barkley Reservoir Project was on schedule and the completion date was moved forward to 1961. It was decided that a 7,000 foot canal should be constructed to join Kentucky Lake with Barkley Lake. The dream that had driven Tom Lawson into bankruptcy was now a reality. The completion date for the canal was set for 1966. By the time the canal project was accepted and funded, the Corps of Engineers was nearing the completion of Barkley Dam, and the construction of the canal took top priority.

When the plans for the canal were made public, the people learned that it would be located a little more than two miles south of the Kentucky Dam. The landowners realized that

---

County Times, July 12, 1952.

[27]Notes found in the Trigg County Court House, Cadiz, Kentucky. A notebook contains some of the minutes of the organization.

[28]Ibid.

[29]Ibid.

they were surrounded by water on three sides. Delighted with these plans, they began efforts to take advantage of the opportunities that the new shore lines offered in prospective tourist trade. The area could be developed into a recreational gold mine and they intended to take advantage of the situation. The Tennessee Valley Authority had promised that tourists would come to the area; now they had the perfect opportunity to capitalize on the tourist trade. Boating, swimming, and hunting would draw the tourists. The area included from 50,000 to 70,000 acres of land with excellent harbors for boat docks, restaurants, and camping facilities. The capital to develop the land into recreational facilities was readily available, and some developers made plans to begin construction immediately.

While the residents came to terms with the changes in their lives, agencies of the federal government were reviewing the land acquisitions in Kentucky and Tennessee. Someone, nobody seems to know who, noticed that the region that had been left in the land between the rivers was composed of a hilly spine between the two giant reservoirs. The land was not rated as productive farm land and the population of the area was sparse. It was determined that the government had created a problem when it removed the productive land from the area. Perhaps the government could resolve the problem by purchasing all the remaining property.[30]   As early as 1959, TVA expressed interest in the area which they called the land between the lakes.[31]   TVA made tentative recommendations about using the land for recreational development, but the agency was unsure of the actual procedures to follow in order to initiate the project. From 1959 until 1961, TVA did not take any action, but discussions were held with other agencies about the feasibility of a recreational area between the lakes. The problem had been one of how to propose the program in a way that would appeal to the Congress. As it turned out, the election of John F. Kennedy in 1960 opened the way for the proposal.

---

[30]Owen, Tennessee Valley Authority, 40. According to this source a technician flying back to his office in Knoxville from Paducah noticed the outline which the peninsula would follow once the Cumberland was flooded.

[31]Origins of Land Between the Lakes, "Document Origins," (Knoxville, Tennessee: Tennessee Valley Authority), 1-5.

CHAPTER XI

CREATION OF THE LAND
BETWEEN THE LAKES

In February 1961, President John F. Kennedy spoke to the country about its natural resources, expressing interest in the establishment of a comprehensive federal recreational lands program. The President instructed the Secretary of the Interior to cooperate with the Secretary of Agriculture and other appropriate federal, state, and local officials along with private leaders in the recreation field, to formulate a comprehensive federal recreational lands program and conduct a survey to determine where additional national parks, forests, and seashore areas should be proposed.[1]

Obviously taking a cue from former conservationist presidents such as Theodore Roosevelt, President Kennedy expressed his interest in reclamation of lands. More significantly, he was concerned with the preservation of wilderness areas in the United States. Even though his remarks were vague, the tone implied that he was mainly concerned with preservation of lands so that future generations of Americans could appreciate the past.[2]

As soon as President Kennedy made the announcement about his interest in conservation, the Tennessee Valley Authority took action. By March, the Board of Directors was ready to present a preliminary study of the area which they referred to as the Land Between the Lakes. Herbert Vogel, Chairman of the Board of Directors of TVA, submitted a report entitled "A Proposal for a National Recreational Area Between the Lakes formed by Kentucky and Barkley Dams.[3] In a cover letter dated June 23, 1961, Vogel reported to the President that TVA had developed a proposal and had already received endorsements for the proposal from Governor Burt Combs of Kentucky and Governor Buford Ellington of Tennessee. Vogel proposed that the TVA develop the area under Section 22 of the TVA Act and Executive Order No. 6161 issued on June 8, 1933.

He proposed that 140,000 acres, later changed to 170,000 acres, of land between the Cumberland and Tennessee be set aside as a national recreational area. The area would include about 300 miles of shoreline fronting the two reservoirs. One third of the land was in Trigg County and another third was in Lyon County; Stewart County held the remaining lands. The federal government had approximately $300 million already invested in the Lakes project.[4]

Vogel reported that the Land Between The Lakes was within 300 miles of 70,000,000

---

[1]See President Kennedy's speech The Nashville Tennessean, Nashville, Tennessee, February 3, 1961.

[2]Involved in the discussion was the nature and goals of the LBL development. The area was usually referred to as a protected wilderness area with regulated recreational facilities. Beginning in 1964, TVA officials began to substitute other terms for wilderness.

[3]Land Between The Lakes, Tennessee Valley Authority, 8.

[4]Ibid.

people or approximately 38.5 percent of the population of the United States. The land, according to Vogel, should be appraised at $100.00 to $150.00 dollars per acre. Vogel assured the President that the project would be supported by the public officials in the states of Kentucky and Tennessee and the tourists in the region. To support the plan, Vogel included several demographic maps and data that showed that a large segment of the nation's population was concentrated around the area of the Land Between The Lakes. Almost all of the national parks and forest lands were from Colorado and New Mexico, westward. Therefore, millions of Americans did not have access to national parks. As justification for choosing the site, the interior region of the Land Between The Lakes was described as having few natural resources for economic development, other than recreation, and very few residents lived there. The land was not conducive to industrial development because of the rugged topography, largely forested with scrub timber that would not prove profitable to the lumber industries. Farming was confined to narrow creek bottoms between ridges which rose to 300 feet above the lakes. The area had no mineral deposits which could be exploited. It was estimated that 5,000 people lived within the area and many of the farm dwellings had already been abandoned. A considerable amount of land, including the Kentucky Woodlands Wildlife Refuge with 63,000 acres and 2,000 acres owned by TVA along Kentucky Lake, was already out of use. The Corps of Engineers was in the process of acquiring about 2,000 acres along Barkley Lake.[5] The implication was clear: the public already owned a substantial portion of the area and it would be feasible to purchase the remaining land for the proposed park. The principal asset, according to the report, was the cove-studded shoreline resulting from the federal investment of nearly $300 million in Barkley and Kentucky Lakes Projects. A national recreation area could be established to serve all the people in the eastern United States. An overview included in the report suggested that the park should be about 40 miles long and from 6 to 12 miles wide. The project would provide economic stimulus to the area and the construction of access roads, campgrounds, picnic areas, and other public facilities could begin immediately in the area already under public ownership. The area was ideally suited to many of the outdoor recreational sports and activities that people enjoyed. Camping, boating, fishing, hiking, and water skiing would be available to families seeking these types of recreation as a way of relieving modern stress. The President was assured that TVA would be glad to cooperate in any way it could to see that the plan was implemented.[6]

Included with the proposal and letter from Vogel was a message from Governors Combs and Ellington, supporting the TVA proposal. Vogel had contacted the men securing their support before submitting the TVA recommendations. Both Combs and Ellington assured Vogel that they were in full agreement with his recreational proposal. Governor Combs, expressing delight at the idea, said that he would support fully any actions necessary to convince President

---

[5]The activity of the Corps of Engineers with the Barkley Lake Project had an indirect effect on the people when they responded to the LBL project. During the entire acquisition period, the people watched the activity and blamed all of their negative responses on the federal government which included TVA.

[6]Ibid., 28-35. Records of Land Between The Lakes indicate some 600 plus households were affected by the acquisition of land. The 1960 Federal Population Census show that approximately 5000 people lived in the area.

Kennedy that a part of his state should be established as a national recreation area.[7]

Problems for the Citizens

Citizens in Trigg, Lyon and Stewart Counties learned of the proposed park when they read newspaper accounts of the recommendations. The response was one of disbelief and confusion. They wanted to know what was going on in Washington. When it was announced that the President had referred the matter to the Secretary of the Interior for further study, the people tried to obtain specific information about the plan.[8] In the meantime, Pierre Salinger, White House press secretary, announced that congressional representatives from Tennessee and Kentucky had been discussing the matter with the Department of the Interior and all had agreed that the park would be an asset to the states involved.[9]

In July, 1961, Governors Combs and Ellington told the press that they had discussed the park proposal with TVA officials before it was submitted to President Kennedy. When reporters asked why the matter had not been discussed more openly with the people of both states, the response was that they were in the process of planning a meeting with the citizens of the counties involved in the park project.[10]

Area newspapers began to speculate on the size and function of the new park and added to the confusion. It was reported that there were only about 1,300 homes and 5,000 people affected by the proposed park. The land value was estimated at $100.00 to $150.00 per acre and it would not cost too much to purchase the land for a park or recreation area, and it would be ideal for the region.

On July 7, 1961, the White House released details on the plan. President Kennedy officially endorsed a study of the area to determine if the park proposals were feasible. The proposed park would be the only one of its kind east of the Rocky Mountains, and the area was ideally suited to outdoor recreation. It was estimated that the land for the park would cost approximately $10 million and would become an extension of an area that the federal government had developed at a cost of $300 million.[11] The report led the readers to believe that the project was a bargain because of the money which had already been spent.

---

[7]Land Between The Lakes, TVA, 8.

[8]Banner, Nashville, Tennessee, June 20, 1961; The Tennessean, Nashville, Tennessee, June 22, 1971; Courier-Journal, Louisville, Kentucky, June 15, 1961; Press-Scimitar, Memphis, Tennessee, June 27, 1961; News-Sentinel, Knoxville, Tennessee, June 27, 1961; News-Free Press, Chattanooga, Tennessee, June 27, 1961; Sun-Democrat, Paducah, Kentucky, June 27,1961; Messenger & Inquirer, Owensboro, Kentucky, June 28, 1961.

[9]The Tennessean, Nashville, Tennessee, July 6, 1961; Sun, Jackson, Tennessee, July 6, 1961; News-Sentinel, Knoxville, Tennessee, July 6, 1961; Sun-Democrat, Paducah, Kentucky, July 6, 1961.

[10]The Tennessean, Nashville, Tennessee, July 7, 1961; Courier Journal, Louisville, Kentucky, July 7, 1961. The newspaper accounts do not mention any meetings with the people to discuss the matter.

[11]The Tennessean, Nashville, Tennessee, July 7, 1961; Commercial Appeal, Memphis, Tennessee, July 7, 1961; Oak Ridge, Oak Ridge, Tennessee, July 7, 1961; Courier-Journal, Louisville, Kentucky, July 7, 1961; News-Sentinel, Knoxville, Tennessee, July 7, 1961.

In the same news release, Pierre Salinger said that the Secretary of the Interior, Stewart Udall, would soon make a suggestion to the President, and if both agreed, the next step would be a recommendation to Congress for the creation of the park. When asked why TVA had submitted the proposal, Salinger said TVA had been encouraged by a number of agencies to study the area with a proposed park in mind. All the agencies had agreed that the TVA proposal was a good one.[12]

TVA Director Vogel had spoken to the press about the urgency of moving to develop the park in order to keep private developers from building recreational facilities before the federal government had a chance to purchase the land. If private developers came into the area, the price of the property would increase and it would cost the federal government even more money to develop the area. Citizens interpreted Vogel's statements to mean that TVA would condemn all the land and no privately owned facilities would be allowed.[13]

When on August 2, 1961, Conrad Wirt, Director of the National Park Service, endorsed the recreational park project, it was only a matter of funding and a decision on which agency which would develop the park.[14] Wirt proposed that 140,000 acres of land should be purchased and turned into a national park. He estimated that at least 4,000,000 people would visit the park each year. He speculated that within eight years, tourists would be described as the new money crop for the region. With Wirt's public endorsement, it appeared that indeed this would be a national park under his direction. It was expected that the Park Service would take a portion of the area, and citizens would develop the remaining land.[15]

On August 13, 1961, Hall Allen, night editor of the Paducah Sun Democrat, reported that the recreational park would be named the Between the Rivers National Recreational Area and would extend from a point two miles south of the canal connecting Kentucky and Barkley Lakes to Paris Landing and Dover. The new plan was advanced by the National Park Service and would increase the original proposal made by TVA from 140,000 to 167,000 acres of land. The TVA plan called for the southern border to run a few miles south of Model and split the land between the lakes area. The Park Service planned to retain the Kentucky Woodlands National Wildlife Refuge which included 58,000 acres and the Refuge would continue to operate under the control of the United States Fish and Wildlife Service. The Park Service was interested in extending the southern boundary because it would be able to include areas that had interesting historical features which would not only add to the interest of the park, but would preserve the old landmarks for future generations.[16] The Park Service wanted to take in all that

---

[12]Ibid. No specific agencies were mentioned.

[13]Sun-Democrat, Paducah, Kentucky, August 23, 1961; The Tennessean, Nashville, Tennessee, August 23, 1961.

[14]Many people supported the Park Service as the agency best qualified to operate a recreational park.

[15]The Tennessean, Nashville, Tennessee, August, 20, 1961; Courier-Journal, Louisville, Kentucky, August 20, 1961. For some time the people believed that Wirt's proposal was a sure sign that the Park Service would take charge of the project.

[16]Sun-Democrat, Paducah, Kentucky, August 13, 1961. People were interested in preserving the historical name of Between the Rivers for the area.

was left of Fort Henry and the two roads over which General Ulysses S. Grant's army had advanced from Fort Henry to Fort Donelson.[17]

Wirt announced that his proposal was tentative and certain parts of the plan could be modified. The Park Service was already considering excluding some areas. They intended to exclude: Fort Donelson Military National Park, Fort Donelson Military Cemetery, the town of Dover and the Pumpkin Ridge section in Stewart County, the town of Golden Pond and an adjacent corridor along U.S. Highway 68, and the town of Fenton in Kentucky. Wirt said that there were several boat docks, fishing facilities and motels in the area that would not be included in the Park Service's proposal. Also, along Highway 68 there were several places which had been developed by private investors that might be left out of the final proposal. Further study, said Wirt, could indicate further exclusions. He pointed out that the Park Service was considering a plan to permit continued agricultural use of some of the land. These areas would be considered open places in the park, allowing private ownership. In some instances the government could purchase the farms and allow the people to remain on the land for a specific number of years or for the duration of their lives.[18]

Major newspapers in Tennessee were in favor of the park, and as one account stated, "This rose by any name will smell sweet." The park would be an economic asset to Tennessee and Kentucky especially to those people who lived on the land. Residents would find "legitimate employment" serving the sportsmen and tourists who visit the park.[19] The media did not understand that the use of the word park did have meaning for the citizens. They had liked the proposals from the Park Service, but Vogel's statements had bothered them. Most of all, they were angry with the implication that they were not already involved in "legitimate" pursuits.

During this time, all the public discussions seemed to include some commercial recreational development to flourish side by side with public development. Development was the key word in the discussion. The people wanted to know who would develop the project and how much land it would involve. Several Kentucky newspapers included articles and editorials which pointed out that it had taken a little more than a month for the park proposal to receive the endorsement of the President and plans were ready for submission to Congress.[20]

At least one of the newspapers expressed concern that the exact plans had not been made public and the people living in the land between the lakes could be hurt if they were forced to sell all their land to the government. Some people suggested that no one could stop the development because the projections were that the area could expect an annual gross income of

[17]Fort Henry had been covered by the waters of Kentucky Lake.

[18]Sun-Democrat, August 20, 1961; The Tennessean, August 20, 1961.

[19]The Tennessean, Nashville, Tennessee, August 27, 1961; By the end of August, 1961, other newspapers including the Sun-Democrat, News-Sentinel, and the Courier Journal had announced support for the park proposal.

[20]Sun-Democrat, August 29, 30 1961; Courier Journal, August 13, 29, 33, 1961, and Messenger & Inquirer, August 29, 1961.

$25 million, and a few individuals must not stand in the way of prosperity for the whole region.[21]

Reactions from the Citizens

On July 7, 1961 the people learned that Representatives Ross Bass of Tennessee and Frank Stubblefield of Kentucky planned to introduce a bill which would provide the funding for the park.[22] A group of citizens from all three counties met with representatives of other counties in the areas and formed the Between the Lakes Development Association. At its first meeting in Cadiz on August 2, 1961, Smith Broadbent, Jr. from Trigg County, was elected President of the organization and Ira Atkins, from Stewart County, was elected vice-president. When the meeting was opened for discussion, George Bleidt, acting as spokesman for a group from the Golden Pond area, said, "We have the hottest spot in the United States," and the people should be allowed to develop their own lands. The representatives from Stewart County expressed concern over the loss of their lands and said that they felt that their county had already lost too much land to the federal government.[23]

The Between The Lakes Development Association held a meeting at Kenlake Hotel to design a set of specific proposals to submit to federal and state officials. The group attempted to list proposals which would set the park boundaries and limit the amount of land taken. The group wanted the proposals ready for the visit of Secretary Udall, who had just announced that he planned to visit the area in the near future. The visit was planned for August 28 and 29, 1961.[24] The Association did not plan any strategies to halt the park project. The major concern was the amount of land that would be involved. At this point, the Association was trying to suggest viable proposals for the operation of the park.

The Association supported the plan to make the area into an outstanding recreation center, but they wanted to develop private business enterprises in the area, thus limiting the amount of land for the park. They submitted an eleven point plan which the Association would support. Item eight in the plan was to promote a close working relationship between state and national agencies in promoting a state park on the eastern side of Lake Barkley and allowing private development on the western side. The Association leaders directed John H. O'Bryan,

---

[21]Commercial Appeal, Memphis, Tennessee, August 25, 1961.

[22]Sun-Democrat, Paducah, Kentucky, July 10, 1961; The Tennessean, Nashville, Tennessee, July 10, 1961.

[23]Sun-Democrat, Paducah, Kentucky, August 16, 1961. Judge Atkins and the Stewart County citizens were appropriately concerned with the circumstances facing the county. Stewart County had been riddled by federal and state land acquisitions since World War II. Geographically, it had been one of the largest counties in the state until 25,000 acres was taken by Fort Campbell; 14,000 acres to Kentucky Lake; 23,500 acres to Barkley Lake; 500 acres to Fort Donelson National Park; 1,250 acres to Cumberland Steam Plant, and 4,000 acres for the Stewart State Forest. The population had been reduced by thirty per cent. See Stewart County Times, July 16, 1964.

[24]Sun-Democrat, Paducah, Kentucky, August 16, 1961; The Tennessean, Nashville, Tennessee, August 16, 1961.

Johnson, and Frank Ashley to begin procedures for incorporating the group.[25]

As soon as the Between the Lakes Development Association was formed, it was obvious that a considerable number of people was opposed to total federal control and the formation of a wilderness area. These people envisioned working with the government in the development of a recreational area. George Bleidt and others expressed their concern over the agency which would control the park.

By August, 1961, too many unanswered questions and a multitude of rumors caused a reaction among the people in and around the proposed park area. When it was officially announced that Secretary Udall planned to tour the site of the proposed park on August 28, the people in the area called a meeting to organize a group of citizens who would act as representatives to ask the Secretary specific questions. The people learned of the visit via newspapers that Chairman Vogel had extended the invitation to Udall, and when he accepted the invitation, Vogel had then invited Under-secretary of the Interior John Carver as well.[26]

Governors Burt Combs and Buford Ellington informed the press that they would attend the meetings which were to be held at Kentucky Dam Village State Park. The first meeting would include a speech by Director Wirt, and the next day, a meeting would be held at Paris Landing State Park where Governor Ellington would preside at a noon luncheon, and after a press conference the group would tour the area by car and by plane.[27]

As details of the meeting were arranged it was decided that Udall would fly from Washington to Fort Campbell then go to Paris Landing for the opening session followed by a press conference that afternoon. All the state officials involved in the parks and recreational services in Kentucky and Tennessee would be invited to the meetings. Local civic leaders were extended an invitation to attend the press conferences and the general meetings that would be arranged in Tennessee and Kentucky.

Several members of the Between the Lakes National Recreational Association had already gone to Washington to discuss the proposed park with their congressional delegations and Secretary Udall. At one of these meetings, Ira Atkins, County Judge of Stewart County, had expressed opposition to the proposal which would remove 70,000 acres from his county's tax rolls. He had told Secretary Udall that Stewart County had already lost forty-five percent of its population and its assessed valuation on property had decreased by fifty percent because federal installations had already taken thousands of acres from the county. If another 70,000 acres were removed, he feared that the county would dissolve. Although no public announcement was made at the time, a compromise agreement was reached on the line that was to mark the southern boundary of the park area.[28]

---

[25]Ibid.

[26]News-Sentinel, Knoxville, Tennessee, August 27, 2961; Sun, Jackson, Tennessee, August 28, 1961.

[27]Sun-Democrat, Paducah, Kentucky, August 23, 1961; The Tennessean, Nashville, Tennessee, August 24, 1961.

[28]Sun-Democrat, Paducah, Kentucky, August 25, 1961. The meeting was held on April 6, 1961, before much of the discussion about the park. Judge Atkins was very concerned with the future of Dover. He worked diligently to save the town.

Confusion about the Proposal

Everyone seemed confused over the exact plans the federal government intended to follow. Governor Ellington, when questioned, admitted he was confused over whether the facility was to be a park or a recreation area, and he was waiting for the meeting with Udall to find out what the federal government intended to do. Ellington went on to say that he was not aware that any exact plans had been made for the park, and it was possible that the federal government would not develop the park at all.[29]

Even as the governor was expressing doubt that a park would be created, Secretary Udall was announcing to the press that he had no doubt that the proposed park would be developed because there was a pressing need to establish such a facility. He reiterated the need for national parks in the eastern and central portions of the country, and the proposed park was in an ideal location to serve a major portion of the population. Secretary Udall said that his meeting with people in the Tennessee and Kentucky delegations scheduled for August 28, was to determine the exact nature of the proposal.[30]

Looking back on the speeches, interviews, and discussions in August 1961, it now seems apparent that TVA officials understood President Kennedy when he talked in terms of obtaining land for preservation of natural resources and the protection of the beauties of nature. President Kennedy had made it clear that he was not concerned with creating resort areas or playgrounds, but establishing several protected areas. Officials seemed to have had difficulties with the President's goals because they kept tripping over terminology. What was the difference between a park and a recreational area? What was a recreational park? The local leaders had obviously taken the view that a park would exclude most commercial enterprises and all private enterprises. A recreational park would allow private enterprise and a park to co-exist. Confusion ran rampant.

On August 28, Udall promised that the Kennedy administration would present concrete recommendations for the park at the next session of Congress. He did not clarify the administration's definition of a park, but he had hastened to say that every means would be taken to soften the effect on landowners. When questioned about his description of the park, Udall would only say that he would recommend that the development be turned over to the National Park Service and certain standards had to be observed and they must guard against "honky-tonk type of private development."[31] Secretary Udall was politely vague about the plans that were being developed, but it was clear that he did not intend to recommend the development of certain types of recreational facilities in the park area. No one questioned him on the meaning of

---

[29]The Tennessean, Nashville, Tennessee, August 25, 1961.

[30]Sun Democrat, Paducah, Kentucky, August 27, 1961; The Tennessean, Nashville, Tennessee, August 27, 1961

[31]Sun-Democrat, Paducah, Kentucky, August 28, 1961; Courier Journal, Louisville, Kentucky, August 29, 1961; Commercial Appeal, Memphis, Tennessee, August 29, 1961; Messenger, Madisonville, Kentucky, August 29, 1961; Sun, Jackson, Tennessee, August 29, 1961; Times, Kingsport, Tennessee, August 29, 1961; Oak Ridger, Oak Ridge, Tennessee, August 29, 1961. Everyone present knew what Udall meant by "honky tonk." He used the slang expression for a low class club. In the area it meant a cheap, disreputable beer joint.

"honky-tonk," but the tenor of the newspaper accounts makes it obvious that strict regulations would be applied to the recreational facilities. Smith Broadbent, Jr. questioned Udall about the extent of private development within the park and what plan the government intended to follow in allowing land owners to remain in the park area. Udall said that the general tenor of the questions was "good and constructive" and he saw nothing in the Association's policy of protecting the people in the land between the rivers that would pose a stumbling block to the development of the park. He indicated that there would be few problems involved in the dislocation of residents and the development of private enterprise.[32]

When Udall was questioned further about farmers in the area, he pointed out that plans had been submitted to allow farmers to remain on their farms, and he did not have any trouble with the concept.[33] The people seemed to believe that Udall spoke for the Kennedy administration and they could expect to remain on their land, but it was clear from the answers that he gave that he had not made any explicit promises. His remarks were vague and those who listened carefully realized that he had not provided answers to their questions. One cannot be sure that the Secretary had an understanding of the details of the proposal in August, 1961.

On September 15, 1961, the Advisory Board of the National Park Service recommended the establishment of a national recreational project to be known as the Between the Rivers National Recreational Area. The board wanted to retain the historical name for the region, and they planned to include approximately 140,000 acres of land located in Kentucky and Tennessee.[34] The next step was to draft and submit the proper legislation to the next session of Congress in January, 1962.

Representatives Bass and Stubblefield met with some of the citizens in the land between the rivers, and the main problem was an obvious lack of communication. The people wanted to know the exact boundary lines that had been proposed for the park, and they wanted to know what provisions had been made to allow the residents of the area to remain on their land. The people were told that the towns of Grand Rivers, Golden Pond, Model and Dover were to be excluded from the park and roads leading to these towns would be exempted as well.[35] For several months, the people were confident that they understood the plans for the park and only a few families would be affected by the proposal. The speculation was that Congress would consider the park proposal in February 1962.[36]

C. A. Jeffers, park planner for the Park Service, in a meeting with local officials, said that in his opinion the proposed excluded areas should be left in the park. "We are trying to set up an area of national significance," he said. "We don't want just another area surrounded by

---

[32]Ibid.

[33]Ibid.

[34]News -Sentinel, Knoxville, Tennessee, October 9, 1961; Oak Ridger, Oak Ridge, Tennessee, October 9, 1961; Sun-Democrat, Paducah, Kentucky, October 9, 1961; Journal, Knoxville, Tennessee, October 9, 1961; The Tennessean, Nashville, Tennessee, October 9, 1961; News, Birmingham, Alabama, October 9, 1961.

[35]Ibid.

[36]Courier Journal, January 31, 1961.

honky tonks."[37] His statements bothered the people because they thought the open places were a part of the final proposal.

In May, 1962, the news media began to speculate that the bill to establish the park would not get through Congress during the regular session. This news caused an immediate reaction among the people--grunts of anger and tears of joy. Editorials lamented the great loss to the economy if the government did not develop the project. These outcries for the immediate establishment of the park later came back to haunt some of the people.[38]

True to predictions, the necessary legislation did not get through Congress during its regular session, but on January 3, 1963, Representative Bass announced that TVA would take over the development of the park. The Park Service would step aside, allowing TVA to assume the responsibility because TVA did not have to wait for Congress to pass the legislation. Under the existing law, TVA could establish the park and begin development and wait to ask Congress for the necessary funding to complete the project.[39]

On January 3, spokesmen for TVA said they had not been informed of the proposal, but they were eager to develop the park if given the responsibility. Paul Evans, Director of Information for TVA, said that the agency was waiting for authorization to take control, and even though that authorization had not been received, TVA had already planned to submit a request to Congress for necessary funding to complete the project.[40] Reaction from most people was a sigh of relief. The park had been saved! A few people still wanted the Park Service to control the project, and they expressed concerns that TVA had not released any information about its plans for the project.

Confusion about TVA's Plan

Representative Stubblefield was one of the first to question TVA about the compromises to establish the boundaries for the park. His concern was that TVA had not agreed to allow private development in the area, nor had they met with citizens to determine who could remain and who would be forced to leave the area. He wanted to know what procedures would be followed for relocation and settlement of the people. He wanted a definite statement about the fate of the Kentucky Woodlands Wildlife Refuge.[41] Stubblefield's questions were the ones the people wanted answered.

The Chairman of the Board of Directors for TVA, Aubrey J. Wagner, announced on January 9, 1963, that the agency would be glad to undertake the development of the proposed

---

[37]Ibid.

[38]Sun-Democrat, Paducah, Kentucky, May 5, 1962; The Tennessean, Nashville, Tennessee, May 10, 1962; News-Sentinel, Knoxville, Tennessee, May 10, 1962.

[39]Park City News, Bowling Green, Kentucky, January 3, 1963; Sun, Jackson, Tennessee, January 3, 1963; Press-Scimitar, Memphis, Tennessee, January 3, 1963; The Tennessean, Nashville, Tennessee, January 3, 1963.

[40]Ibid.

[41]Courier Journal, Louisville, Kentucky, January 5, 1963.

park, but he would not comment on any plans which they had made. He said the plans had not been agreed upon.[42]

A group of citizens who represented residents of the area sent a message to Kentucky congressmen asking them to halt any plans for the purchase of land for a national recreational area. The citizens had concluded that TVA would take all the land and they intended to question its right to take land for recreational purposes. Their argument seemed to have been based on the premise that TVA did not have the authorization to develop recreational facilities.[43] They expressed their concerns about just compensation for the loss of their land. The implications were that if TVA became the agency in charge of the development, they would not receive fair compensation. They had just witnessed the difficulties of their neighbors who had been displaced by the construction of Barkley Dam, and they were not satisfied that they would be offered a fair price by TVA. They also knew that it would be difficult to finance a court battle over the price. Some of these people had bought land when they were forced out by Barkley Lake and once again they would be forced to move.[44]

Wagner spoke to the Kiwanis Club in Clarksville on April 3, 1963, and outlined numerous positive effects that TVA had achieved in the Tennessee Valley. He said that the proposed park was an excellent opportunity to demonstrate the essence of an industry which was new and unique, not only in this area but in the United States. He was speaking of tourism as a national industry.[45]

As early as January, 1963, TVA officials had tried to explain that TVA had always had a singular goal of total resource development. The development of the Land Between The Lakes would convert a resource-poor area into a camping and boating vacation spot. Also the area would become a "conservation classroom." It would provide an ideal environment for millions of Americans in a part of the country where "few acres have been set aside for outdoor recreation."[46]

Tennessee Senator Estes Kefauver was representative of a group which seemed worried that the federal government might decide against the project. On March 27, 1963, he wrote a letter to President Kennedy and Interior Secretary Stuart Udall urging prompt transfer of authority for the development of the Land Between The Lakes recreation area to the Tennessee Valley Authority.[47]

---

[42]Sun-Democrat, Paducah, Kentucky, January 9, 1963. Mr. Wagner had replaced Herbert Vogel as Chairman of the Board of Directors. On January 9, he was speaking before the Paducah Rotary Club, and from his comments, it was clear that he was not ready to discuss details of the park proposal.

[43]Sun-Democrat, January 20, 1963. The group sent a petition with signatures from residents of the land between the rivers.

[44]Ibid. Once again the people did not seem to designate the difference between the Corps of Engineers and TVA.

[45]Leaf Chronicle, Clarksville, Tennessee, April 3, 1963.

[46]Ibid. From this time on, the area was referred to by TVA as the Land Between the Lakes.

[47]News Sentinel, Knoxville, Tennessee, March 27, 1963.

Finally in April 1963, TVA officials began to explain in detail their view of the scope of the project. TVA proposed to create a unique recreational facility that was described as an industry. Recreation would draw millions of people into the area, and the whole region would benefit economically.[48]

As soon as the media carried interviews with citizens in the area, they argued that TVA did not have the authority to take their land for a recreational facility. Politicians were alerted to the possibility of general negative sentiment. People would not react kindly to having themselves removed from their farms, businesses, and homes in order to provide a place to have fun; private developers could do that.[49]

On June 14, 1963, President Kennedy informed several people including Representative Stubblefield and Senator John Sherman Cooper, of Kentucky, that TVA had been directed to take control of the Between The Lakes project. Kennedy outlined the general policy TVA would follow: it would develop a national recreational area as a demonstration in resource development. It was an extension of area preservation, one result of which would be economic development of a region.[50] Reporters rushed to question the TVA officials about specific parts of the plan. The response was that at the present time, planning was too general and too tentative, and TVA would not be able to discuss specific plans until Congress had appropriated the necessary funds for the project.[51]

The citizens were weary and distressed. They had been unable to keep TVA out of the project and they had to keep waiting to find out how their lives would be changed. They waited with a strong sense of foreboding; they, only about 5,000 strong, could not fight the federal government. They felt betrayed by their government.[52] They heard on June 19, 1963, that the Bureau of the Budget had added $4 million to its recommendations for funds for the Tennessee Valley Authority. TVA had announced that it would use the money to begin the acquisition of land in the new Land Between The Lakes Recreational Area.[53]

TVA announced four basic steps would be taken to organize the project: the land would be mapped; property ownership would be established; a policy of land acquisition for the 170,000 acres would be determined, and some development would be started on Barkley Lake before all the land in the land between the rivers had been acquired. TVA estimated that it would take about six months to get organized, but even before that time, they intended to have

[48]Sun-Democrat, Paducah, Kentucky, April 12, 1963; The Tennessean, Nashville, Tennessee, April 12, 1963.

[49]Sun-Democrat, Paducah, Kentucky, May 19, 1963; The Tennessean, Nashville, Tennessee, May 19, 1963.

[50]Sun-Democrat, Paducah, Kentucky, June 14, 1963; Press-Scimitar, Memphis, Tennessee, June 14, 1963; Times, Chattanooga, Tennessee, June 14, 1963; Leaf Chronicle, Clarksville, Tennessee, June 15, 1963; Courier Journal, Louisville, Kentucky, June 15, 1963.

[51]Ibid., June 16, 1963.

[52]Interview with Ira Atkins in Dover, Tennessee on July 26, 1989.

[53]Courier Journal, Louisville, Kentucky, June 20, 1963.

some of the boat dock facilities ready for use.[54]

With a new burst of energy, the citizens in the area tried to convince the TVA officials that they should be allowed to remain in certain sections of the area. The more optimistic citizens seemed to feel that their arguments would have an effect on TVA policies. In July, they wrote to TVA asking that they not be forced to sell their land to the agency. They proposed that TVA purchase the land which the people wanted to sell but not force all the people to sell. They reminded TVA that the government had, already in its possession, ample land for the development of an outstanding recreational area. TVA could zone the land to control the types of facilities which were constructed in the future.[55] They refuted the material circulated by TVA which said the land was unfit for farming, and they pointed out their most valuable land was along the shoreline of the lakes. They urged TVA to evaluate the potential development of the land. They informed TVA that the land was not owned by absentee landlords, which they understood TVA had claimed earlier. Most of the people who lived in the area could prove that their land had been owned for generations. The citizens expressed their anxiety about how TVA intended to develop the area and its effect on the growth of the counties involved.[56]

TVA Reveals Its Plan

The people had been waiting for two years when on July 13, 1963, TVA announced that even though detailed plans for the development of the project had not been completed, the agency had tentatively agreed that they would not permit the operation of any type of lodging, restaurant, or resort facilities within the boundaries of the area. TVA was interested in the development of a variety of camp grounds, picnic areas, and other outdoor facilities in the woodlands, in the fields, and along the shoreline of the park. A five year plan for the area was in the developmental stage, and it would cost an estimated $32 to $35 million.[57]

Recreation, according to TVA's new definition, would be only those activities that could be pursued by tourists who wanted to visit a protected area. If the people wanted lodging, food, drink or supplies, they would have to leave the facility to buy what they wanted. They could then return to the camping areas, but the managed environment would be protected.[58]

Wagner announced that the agency had worked with a number of universities to conduct a survey of industries to determine what they looked for most in a local government when they were trying to decide whether or not to move into the region. Since TVA was involved in trying

---

[54]Ibid.

[55]Atkins interview in the hands of the author.

[56]Ibid.

[57]The Tennessean, Nashville, Tennessee, July 13, 1963; Sun-Democrat, Paducah, Kentucky, July 14, 1963 and July 17, 1963; Times, Huntsville, Alabama, July 17, 1963; News, Birmingham, Alabama, July 18, 1963. The newspaper account used "wilderness environment" and "recreational camping area" interchangeably.

[58]Ibid.

to get industries to enter the regions surrounding the project, they had concluded that the counties needed to perform well in the regular functions of government which included a well-run school system, an adequate law enforcement operation, and an area which guaranteed their workers a quality lifestyle. He complimented the counties for grasping the boundless potential which would be realized from the recreational business.[59]

The officials of the counties said they were too stunned to grasp anything. They wanted an explanation of how the Land Between The Lakes project would help them provide better government when a large portion of their population and property tax would be lost. The logic of their argument was that counties needed funding for services and TVA was reducing the funding. The TVA officials argued that the land taken could be expected to generate larger tax revenues because industry would move in. County officials argued that it was only a promise that industry and tourism would move in and bring in more revenue.[60]

Michael Avedision, a Paducah attorney who represented a group of citizens in the Twin Lakes area, appeared before the Senate Appropriations subcommittee and asked that TVA be barred from acquiring about 4,000 acres of land in the Twin Lakes region. In his testimony, Avedision said that TVA would have some 170,000 acres in the development and the 4,000 acres along the canal connecting the two lakes were not needed. The land included farms, businesses and subdivisions and the people wanted the land excluded from the park.[61]

Avedision's argument was based upon the premise that the land had been developed before and after the Barkley Lake program, and the people had been careful to build their establishments to meet any guidelines which the government or TVA might impose. The community would not detract, in any way, from the Land Between The Lakes proposals. As a matter of fact, the private business establishments would be an attraction to tourists, because of their close proximity to the park.[62]

Congress was in a budget cutting mood in November, 1963, but TVA's $4 million dollar proposal for the Land Between The Lakes survived the cuts.[63] TVA was ready to move and on January 3, 1964, it was announced that the property acquisition would begin in the early spring, probably in February or March. Plans were to hire employees from the area to begin the construction of the harbors and other water front facilities. The project would be completed before the adjacent Barkley Lake was impounded. It was estimated that it would take at least five years to complete the project at a cost of $33 million. A personnel office would be located near

---

[59]Sun-Democrat, Paducah, Kentucky, September 1, 1963; Times, Chattanooga, Tennessee, September 1, 1963; Times, Kingsport, Tennessee, September 2, 1963.

[60]Atkins interview.

[61]Sun-Democrat, Paducah, Kentucky, November 20, 1963.

[62]Messenger, Madisonville, Kentucky, November 20, 1962.

[63]The Tennessean, Nashville, Tennessee, November 20, 1963.

the project, and applications would be taken for the employment of about 250 men.[64]

On March 1, 1964, TVA commenced its acquisition of land between Kentucky Lake and the yet-to-be-filled Barkley reservoir near Grand Rivers, Kentucky to the southern boundary, generally along U. S. Highway 79. The recreational area included approximately 103,000 acres which were privately owned and another 67,000 acres already owned by the federal government, an area with some 300 miles of shoreline. January 1, 1968 was the target date to acquire the land. Land owners were promised that TVA would help in their relocation, and the labor force would be drawn, as much as possible, from counties adjacent to the Land Between the Lakes.[65]

The project was officially launched when President Johnson announced his unqualified support and the project would receive $6 million from the recommended $50,915,000 appropriated for TVA projects. President Johnson had recommended an increase in the total TVA appropriation of some three million dollars. On January 23, when TVA officials mentioned again their policy of not allowing private commercial developments in the area, it was questioned why the plan was necessary. The official response was that the project was designed for maximum public use and private establishments would be a deterrent to the design. The commercial facilities would present serious problems in administration and control of the area.[66] This was the first time, under public works appropriations, that the federal government had proposed to develop an area of this size to provide an environment for outdoor recreations. TVA stressed that the area of rolling acres and scenic shorelines would be linked with roads and trails. The people would have easy access to beaches, campgrounds, picnic areas, and other facilities. In January the Paducah, Sun-Democrat conducted a study of the types of home and businesses affected by the project. It reported that Golden Pond and Model would be obliterated. Twin Lakes on Kentucky Lake and a large Negro settlement sometimes called "Little Chicago" would also be demolished. On Highway 68, a total of three motels, six service stations, one hundred and forty-eight homes, two churches, thirteen stores and restaurants, eleven house trailers, and a school would be destroyed. In the immediate area of Twin Lakes, two motels, three service stations, ninety-one homes and six stores and restaurants would be affected.[67]

On January 28, 1964, TVA opened a field office at the Blue Castle Motel on U.S. Highway 68. Sherril Milliken was assigned to the office to answer any and all questions with respect to the agency's plans. Herman C. Kemmer was assigned to the office to take applications for employment on the project.

In February, the land acquisition office was established, and I. N. Pitts was made district manager. He was responsible for the purchase of 103,000 acres of land which still remained under private ownership. The remaining 67,000 acres belonged to other federal agencies and

[64]Sun-Democrat, Paducah, Kentucky, January 3, 1964; Record, Cadiz, Kentucky, January 3, 1964; The Tennessean, Nashville, Tennessee, January 3, 1964 and January 9, 1964.

[65]Record, Cadiz, Kentucky, January 16, 1964; Commercial Appeal, Memphis, Tennessee, January 16, 1964; Times, Kingsport, Tennessee, January 16, 1964; Sun-Democrat, Paducah, Kentucky, January 16, 1964.

[66]The Tennessean, Nashville, Tennessee, January 23, 1964.

[67]Sun-Democrat, Paducah, Kentucky, January 22, 1964.

that land would be transferred to TVA.[68] Landowners in the area were informed that they would usually be given the option of removing any structures on their properties; buildings not removed by the seller or used by TVA would be offered for sale at public auction or by sealed bids and must be removed from the area.[69]

Information about the exact southern and northern boundary lines of the project was released on January 17, 1964. The southern boundary line would run from the Scott Fitzhugh Bridge on Kentucky Lake eastward along the north side of U. S. Highway 79 to Bear Creek, about four miles west of Dover. At that point, the boundary would leave the highway and extend generally northeast along the southern slope of the ridges south of Bear Creek to reach Barkley Lake at about mile 86 on the Cumberland River. The northern boundary line would follow the canal which would link the Tennessee and Cumberland Rivers. Highway 68 would be maintained free of commercial development as a protected road through the project. The people had their worst fears confirmed; the land that they had fought to keep was now lost.

TVA assigned four officials in the Division of Reservoir Properties as supervisors for the area. R. M. Howes, the Division Director, W. R. Holden, Assistant Director, Harold Van Morgan, Director of Recreation Staff, and W. Sherril Milliken, Resource Development Officer, were to begin work immediately. Milliken was to serve as liaison officer between TVA and the people and organizations in the area.[70]

The People React

In January 1964, when it became clear exactly what TVA planned to do with the land, the people were mystified. They read and heard all the talk about thousands of tourists rushing to the wilderness area. They would come for camping, picnicking, hunting, hiking, and nature study. One farmer made a grim face and said, "They'll have to put a bounty on rattlesnakes first." He could not believe that people would camp with snakes crawling around them.[71]

Other people were pessimistic about the estimated numbers of tourists. They commented that they had visited state parks in the region and they had never seen the parks full of people. Another question was asked, "Why would people drive from St. Louis to be chased off by snakes and bugs?" The most widespread comments were that TVA had failed to adequately inform people about their plans for the region.[72]

The Cadiz-Trigg County Chamber of Commerce met at the Court House in Cadiz on January 21, 1964. The organization led by A. T. McCarley, President of the Chamber of Commerce, reaffirmed its policy of urging TVA not to force landowners to sell property for recreational use. The organization was primarily concerned about 1,500 people in Trigg County

---

[68]Sun-Democrat, Paducah, Kentucky, February 5, 1964.

[69]Ibid.

[70]Ibid.

[71]Record, Cadiz, Kentucky, January 22, 1964.

[72]Ibid.

who would be forced out if the current plans were followed.[73] Most of the residents were angry and bitter. They felt they had been betrayed by the National Park Service, the Congress, and especially TVA. They felt that if the bill to establish the park had been sent through regular channels in Congress, as it should have been, TVA would not have been involved in the program. In their view, when TVA stepped into the picture, the people had no voice at all in determining the type of park that was to be created.[74] People questioned the right of TVA to get involved in the recreational business in the first place. TVA was supposed to be concerned with electrical power, fertilizer, and flood control, and it was not organized to develop a playground.[75]

TVA officials learned of the people's reactions and expected trouble when they sent agents into the area to determine the property lines. When the TVA employees came into each community, they were amazed that the people were polite and some even appeared friendly. What the TVA officials did not realize was that these people were bound by their culture and traditions to be courteous to these workers. It was inappropriate to direct their anger and frustration at them because they had not made the decision to remove them from the land. They were angry with the directors of TVA.

Once again, these officials demonstrated their lack of understanding of the people, when they reported to the media that 5,000 or so citizens would be glad to sell their land. They commented that the offers of $100.00 to $200.00 per acre was more than fair and would be acceptable to the people.[76] Repeatedly, as in the procurement policies for Barkley Lake by the Corps of Engineers, TVA official made no attempts to acquaint themselves with the attitudes of the people. This failure led to unnecessary problems, inviting antagonism. The people said again and again that they could not trust any agency of the federal government. The controversy over the project was soon to become a political weapon for all the opponents of TVA.

In January Bob White, Publicity Chairman for the Chamber of Commerce of Cadiz, said that the next move was to try to arrange a three way meeting of the Directors of TVA and the county officials of Lyon, Trigg and Stewart Counties in the hope that they could forge a statement of joint objectives.[77] Consequently, a joint meeting was held on January 29, 1964, to discuss their strategy and the methods of protest which they would use to stop TVA. The mass-protest meeting was held at the Golden Pond School, and the school and tax officials outlined what effects they estimated the loss of population in the counties would have on the

---

[73]Record, Cadiz, Kentucky, January 22, 1964. The people seized upon the wilderness concept to criticize the activities of TVA.

[74]Ibid.

[75]Ibid. Even though TVA had not used the term wilderness as the only descriptive term for the area. The people noticed the descriptive term "recreational facility" and called it a "playground."

[76]See comments of the TVA officials in Courier Journal article March 1, 1964.

[77]Record, Cadiz, Kentucky, January 23, 1964.

schools and the county governments.[78] It was estimated that the schools would suffer not only a loss of students and teachers but the loss of revenue from the state and federal government.[79]

The group listened as Michael Avedision spoke to them about how he had tried to argue the case for his clients before the Senate subcommittee. He advised the group that TVA might not have the legal authority to take their property. He said TVA knew that the property might have enhanced prices in the near future, thus to take the land would be illegal. In the general discussion, the people agreed that in the past TVA had been an asset to the region and they would not be opposed to selling their land if it served the general welfare of the people; however, they also agreed that TVA had sufficient land at the present time to provide a playground for the eastern United States.[80]

J. H. Wiseman, Lyon County Court Clerk, speaking as a county official and private citizen, wrote several letters to Congressman Stubblefield, in which he pointed out very clearly that his view that Lyon County would be forced to close down the county government if TVA took all the land in the area. Wiseman said that he had been told by the Corps of Engineers in 1958 that Barkley Dam was needed for progress and perhaps that was true, but he asked the question, "Was the construction of camp grounds and camping sites progress?" It seemed absurd, according to Wiseman, for people to lose their homes, businesses, schools, churches and farms to provide a place for people to come and be bitten by rattlesnakes and mosquitoes.[81]

Wiseman asked Stubblefield to force TVA to prove to Congress that all the land in the area was needed for the park. His most effective point was when he related the details of some 8,076 acres of land purchased by TVA for the Kentucky Dam. Wiseman said that TVA bought the land for as little as five dollars per acre and later they made two subdivisions, graveled some roads through it and resold two hundred and seventeen acres to individuals at auction. The price ran from two hundred dollars to two thousand and twenty-five dollars per lot.[82] Wiseman said this was a case of profiteering by a government agency, and the same situation, he said, could occur in the Land Between The Lakes. The land would become more valuable as time went by, and TVA could hold the land until prices increased and then sell it.[83]

An inauspicious TVA news release on February 2 about the procedure that TVA employees would use in appraising property reached the people. Robert J. Coker, TVA Land Branch Chief, said the first step would be for an appraiser to visit and inspect the land and buildings of each individual property and set a price.[84] A few days later, a supervising

---

[78]Record, Cadiz, Kentucky, January 30, 1964.

[79]Ibid.

[80]Ibid.

[81]Lakeside Ledger, Eddyville, Kentucky, January 30, 1964.

[82]Ibid.

[83]Ibid.

[84]Sun-Democrat, Paducah, Kentucky, February 2, 1964.

appraiser would inspect the property and review the first appraiser's report. Then, a TVA land buyer would call upon the owner and offer a purchase contract at the price fixed by the appraisers. Coker stressed that this price would be a firm offer, and the land buyers could not make the purchase at a higher or lower price. If the owner did not consider the TVA offer satisfactory, he could refuse it and require condemnation of the property. Coker explained that in such condemnations the Federal Court would appoint a commission of three disinterested men who would establish the amounts to be paid after inspecting the property and hearing evidence presented by both sides.[85] Coker reiterated that as soon as the property had been purchased, owners would be told when they must relocate. Some properties would be needed immediately because construction was to begin on needed facilities. TVA intended to offer prices for land that would be fair and equitable, and the agency would assist anyone who needed help in relocation.[86]

The people were disconcerted at what they considered the "high-handed" tone of the announcement. They knew that TVA had the right to set prices, and they also knew that they could go to court if they did not agree with the set price. What they didn't like was the way TVA seemed to threaten them with immediate eviction.[87]

The stark realities for the future were vividly demonstrated in February, 1964. Bulldozers and demolition crews began the removal of homes and public buildings in Eddyville as the last stage was completed for the Barkley Lake reservoir by the Corps of Engineers. With a sense of great loss, the people watched as the buildings were razed and the foundation stones of historic sites were torn from the ground. It did not seem possible that the historic LaClede Hotel, a reproduction of an old English Inn built by Chittenden Lyon, was being destroyed. The hotel had hosted many famous guests including Andrew Jackson, Henry Clay, Peter Cartwright, and others. Jenny Lind had sung to the people of Eddyville from the doorway of the Inn. Eddyville had been one of the first towns in the state to have a newspaper. Matthew Lyon and his son James had purchased a printing press from Benjamin Franklin and brought it to Kentucky. The Lyon family had even manufactured the newsprint that they needed for the paper from linden trees growing along the banks of the Cumberland. The old press was removed and the building destroyed.[88]

A public meeting at a school in Trigg County was held on February 3, 1964. The mood of the people had changed. They dropped their conciliatory attitude and talked in terms of using open warfare and violence of any kind to protect their property. The people were very emotional, and their statements were filled with outrage against TVA. People accused TVA of using political take-over policies, and they were ready to take their grievances to the Supreme

---

[85]Ibid. It would have been prudent for TVA to follow a practice it had used in the past of asking the owner how much he wanted for the land, listen and then present a much smaller offer. Give the land owner time to think and then settle on a compromise between the two amounts.

[86]Ibid.

[87]Record, Cadiz, Kentucky, February 4, 1964.

[88]Workmen saved some of the bricks from the older buildings which were used in the construction of the Visitor Center Museum.

Court before they would allow their land to be taken. The people said they were embittered because TVA and the newspapers had made fun of them and their "stingy lands." They had been described as poor people unable to make a living on the land. They agreed that none of them would allow any TVA employee on their property.[89]

The shift in attitude was linked to the progress of the Barkley Lake development. As the people who were displaced from their homes and businesses left the area, the people in the land between the lakes identified with them. Homes were moved or demolished. Historical sites were lost as construction crews came into the area. The realities of the changes which would come with the Between the Lakes development became clear to the people, and they responded with hostility.

Congressman Stubblefield realized that many of his constituents were furious with him for not speaking out against the amount of land that TVA intended to take. The pressures were so strong that on February 7, 1964, he sent a strong protest to Wagner, accusing him of misleading statements about Golden Pond, Twin Lakes and a corridor four miles wide along Highway 289 running north from Highway 68. Stubblefield said he had been told that land would not be taken. He said he was "shocked" when he learned that these areas were to be taken along with the rest of the land.[90] Stubblefield sent a copy of his letter to Judge Francis Utley and urged him to encourage the citizens of Trigg, Lyon and Stewart Counties to continue their protest.

The citizens took Congressman Stubblefield's suggestion and organized another meeting at Golden Pond on February 16. They met and developed plans for the organization of a tri-county protest. The major concern expressed at the meeting was that TVA had deliberately deceived the residents. They were led to believe that the recreational area would be limited to the 67,000 acres the government already owned. The tri-county organization planned ways to delay the appraisal of the land so they could find legal avenues to stop TVA.[89]

The Tennessee Valley Authority proceeded with its plan to acquire the land and seemed to disregard the concerns of the people when a meeting was not called with the residents. The first workers were employed and began work on February 19, 1964, planting 600,000 pine seedlings on a 600 acre tract in the Kentucky Woodlands Wildlife Refuge. Other individuals who were seeking employment were told that they would be employed immediately on other projects.[90]

The tri-county organization held meetings and wrote letters to public officials. Judge Utley went on WPSD-TV to discuss the concerns of the citizens in Lyon, Trigg and Stewart

---

[89]Ibid.

[90] Sun Democrat, Paducah, Kentucky, February 7, 1964. The same issue of the newspaper carried an open letter from Stubblefield to the President and Congress. He requested that the current appropriation bill for the Tennessee Valley Authority delete the funding for the Land Between the Lakes project. He compared the people in the land between the rivers to the Cherokees who faced a "Trail of Tears."

[89]Ledger & Times, Murray, Kentucky, February 17, 1964; Democrat, Murray, Kentucky, February 17, 1964; Courier Journal, Louisville, Kentucky, February 17, 1964.

[90]Sun-Democrat, Paducah, Kentucky, February 20, 1964.

Counties.[91] By February 20, TVA officials began to comprehend the growing resistance to their actions. At that time, the TVA Board of Directors announced that the three counties affected by the project would not suffer financial loss. They promised that any tax revenue lost to the counties would be offset by tax replacement arrangements made with the individual counties. The counties were informed that TVA had already completed a detailed analysis of the county tax rolls and had studied the assessed valuation of property to be purchased and the records indicated that TVA purchases represented about eight percent of the county's total revenue in Trigg County, ten percent in Lyon County and twelve percent in Stewart County. However, the taxes on that property provided only about two to three percent of the total revenue for the counties.[92]

The TVA Board made it clear that TVA paid five percent of its revenues from non-federal power sales to states and counties in lieu of taxes, and much of the payments to states was shared in turn with county governments. TVA would seek to have the state share at least half the revenue with the counties most affected by the loss of land.[93]

It was announced on February 21, 1964, that President Johnson had been asked by Kentucky Senators Cooper and Morton to halt the purchase of any land by TVA until the residents of the area had time to protest the move. Both Senators agreed that TVA was taking more land than was needed for a recreational project.[94]

While the people waited to see what President Johnson might do about the request, Judge Utley, speaking for the tri-county organization, informed TVA that the people were not ready to accept promises from them. "The road to Hades is paved with good intentions," said Judge Utley. He said TVA was not known for keeping promises made in the past, and the county governments were near bankruptcy. He noted that TVA had paid Lyon County $384.00 in lieu of taxes in 1963. That amount was received in payment for approximately 11,000 acres of fertile Tennessee River bottom land purchased for the Kentucky Dam reservoir.[95]

In response to a statement made by TVA which said that the counties would save money when they no longer had to provide services to the people in the land between the rivers, Judge Utley said that the statement was an insult "to the intelligence of a moron." He continued his response by saying, "Why not justify it [acquiring the LBL land] by destroying the three entire counties and thereby save 100 percent of operating costs?" Judge Utley refuted the TVA report that the land was thinly populated. He maintained that the land that was held by private

---

[91]Sun-Democrat, Paducah, Kentucky, February 19, 1964.

[92]Lyon County Herald, Eddyville, Kentucky, February 20, 1964; Courier Journal, Louisville, Kentucky, February 20, 1964; Sun-Democrat, Paducah, Kentucky, February 20, 1964; The Tennessean, Nashville, Tennessee, February 20, 1964.

[93]Ibid.

[94]News-Free Press, Chattanooga, Tennessee, February 22, 1964; New Sentinel, Knoxville, Tennessee, February 23, 1964; Sun-Democrat, Paducah, Kentucky, February 23, 1964.

[95]Courier Journal, Louisville, Kentucky, February 24, 1964.

individuals was rather densely populated, but TVA was including approximately 100,000 acres of land owned by the government where people were not allowed to live. Thus, TVA was deliberately distorting the population figures of the area.[96]

In March, TVA began a program of releasing news items and sending speakers to meetings of civic organizations to inform the public about the projects that had already commenced in the LBL program. The response was positive outside the area. People saw the merits of the proposals and spoke in favor of more funding for the projects.[97]

The TVA spokesmen still did not seem to understand that the people who lived in the land between the rivers were being insulted by comments made by the agency. When the spokesmen visited area civic organizations to discuss the LBL project, they continued to make statements that the land was selected because the country could no longer support the people and that the land was so poor it had not really supported the people since the Indians left. These comments continued to exasperate the citizens. They felt even more betrayed because they realized that they were losing support on the outside.[98]

The TVA officials announced that the agency was already involved in planting pine trees so that the area would have some winter cover. Hunters would be able to use the area for both large and small game hunting. Because TVA was involved in planning an unusual park, the emphasis would be placed on recreation, rather than on the preservation of a particular scenic area. The plans included 5,000 camping sites which could care for 20,000 campers each night. More camping sites would be added after TVA had time to develop the plans. A model farm was planned to demonstrate farming activities as they had existed in the past. Marine biology laboratories were planned and a herd of buffalo would be brought to the park.[99]

When the TVA agents arrived in Twin Lakes to discuss the procedures for purchasing the land, they were met by a group of women carrying picket signs. These women marched with signs which read: "TVA GO HOME," "WE WEEP FOR OUR HOMES." "LEAVE US OUR LAND AND TEND TO YOUR OWN DAM BUSINESS," and "WE WANT TO BE FREE OF TVA." The women picketed the area for about an hour and then left. It had taken the TVA officials several months, but they were finally getting the message. The agency did not look good with this type of publicity.[100]

In an editorial in the Paducah Sun-Democrat, Otho Stone Holland compared the fight of the people in the land between the rivers to the Spartans that held the pass at Thermopylae against the Persians and the handful of Americans at the Alamo who were butchered by Santa Anna's army of 20,000. He challenged all his readers to pay attention to the situation because

---

[96]Ibid.

[97]Beginning in March 1964, all of the newspapers in this study carried news items relating to events where TVA officials met with civic groups. On each of these occasions they mentioned the need to move quickly with the LBL project.

[98]Ibid.

[99]Ibid.

[100]Sun-Democrat, Paducah, Kentucky, February 4, 1964.

it was a fight of American citizens for their rights. He accused TVA of having a tradition of deliberately publicizing the backwardness of people when the agency wanted their land. He characterized TVA as greedy and an expanding octopus that wanted everything in the area.[101]

Wagner delivered a speech in Memphis in March and ignored the adverse publicity. He broached a new plan when he tied recreation to the goals of TVA. He said, "Recreation has become a very real business in the Tennessee Valley Authority's region in Western Kentucky and Tennessee." He went on to say that there was a total public and private investment of more than $150 million in recreational facilities along TVA reservoirs and hundreds of millions of tourist dollars were attracted to the area every year. TVA was involved in developing a new recreational attraction which would bring in even greater benefits to the area and to the nation. He described the Land Between The Lakes as an outdoor recreation facility of a type which did not exist anywhere in the United States.[102]

For the first time, Wagner explained why the Tennessee Valley Authority felt it had to acquire all of the 170,000 acres of land. He explained that TVA had chosen the natural boundaries for the area by following the rivers and the canal. It was almost entirely surrounded by water, with some three hundred miles of shoreline. With the use of these natural boundaries, TVA could set this unique area apart for complete development of the woodland environment, and TVA could protect the back-to-nature atmosphere. If any land were allowed to remain in the hands of the present owners, the inevitable souvenir shops and commercialism would destroy the character of the land which TVA was trying to protect.[103]

Wagner asserted that the project was especially needed at this time in the United States because of the pressures of urban-industrial living. People faced with these pressures needed a place for quiet relaxation and the necessary time and money to enjoy the site. Men, he said, have always turned to the lakes and to the woods for replenishment. The Land Between The Lakes was within a day's drive of a fourth of the nation's population.[104]

He promised at least 5,000 camp spaces of various types. The sites would accommodate a minimum of 20,000 overnight campers. People who wanted a more primitive setting would be able to find all the places they wanted. The parking and sanitary facilities would be set up to fill the minimum need. Some of the areas would accommodate house trailers and provide water, sewerage, and power outlets. One of the most appealing characteristics of the new project was that it would be unlike parks with air-conditioned lodges, cabins, and restaurants. Visitors could enter and enjoy the beauty of nature. People would be encouraged to experience the pristine beauties of the natural environment. TVA would encourage people to utilize the area during the entire year by providing facilities for group camps which would enable school groups, among others, to visit the area as an outdoor educational experience.[105]

---

[101]Ibid.,March 1, 1964.

[102]Press-Scimitar, Memphis, Tennessee, March 3, 1964.

[103]Ibid.

[104]Ibid.

[105]Ibid.

In March, the Tri-County Organization for Constitutional Rights, a reorganized part of the tri-county citizens group, petitioned President Johnson to relieve the TVA of the responsibility for the development of the area. The petition requested that the project be turned over to the National Park Service and the Fish and Wildlife Service because TVA had ignored agreements made about the amount of land to be included in the project.[106]

Another group of residents formed the Between the Rivers Research Association. The group led by Mrs. G. J. Marler set up committees to research mineral rights, oil leases, land grants, old churches, cemeteries, rights of way, and historical land marks in the area. These people wanted to document as much historical information as possible before they were forced to leave the area.[107]

A group of nine women and one man picketed the TVA headquarters building on Highway 68. They carried signs denouncing the land acquisition, but they did not interfere with traffic entering or leaving the buildings. From this time until TVA removed the people from the area, picketing groups were present at most of the meetings where TVA representatives were present. The demonstrators were mostly women who peacefully marched to protest the loss of their homes.[108]

Officials of TVA and Kentucky officials worked in February and March to design an agreement on the acquisition of land. On March 18, an announcement was made that the agreement had been completed and signed for assistance to the states in their program of planning and development in the five counties surrounding the recreation area.[109] The Authority agreed to provide financial assistance to the Department of Commerce and its divisions of planning and zoning in working on area development plans with officials and citizens of Trigg, Lyon, Livingston, Marshall, and Calloway Counties, Kentucky. A sum of $9,240 was provided for immediate assistance to Lyon and Trigg counties and the town of Grand Rivers.[110]

Planning groups, made up of local citizens and TVA officials, were organized to study the possible opportunities for industry, public and private recreation, and residential and business development. Also, TVA agreed to pay for the reproduction of maps and reports and other expenses. The agency agreed to provide consultative services and materials.[111]

On March 5, 1964, A. R. Jones, Vice-Chairman of the Board of Directors of the Tennessee Valley Authority, made the first of a series of speeches to Chambers of Commerce

---

[106]Sun-Democrat, Paducah, Kentucky, March 3, 1964.

[107]Record, Cadiz, Kentucky, March 5, 1964.

[108]From time to time, newspaper reporters would interview these people. The pickets appeared each day and marched in silence.

[109]Democrat, Paris, Tennessee, March 18, 1964; Messenger, Madisonville, Kentucky, March 18, 1964; Sun-Democrat, Paducah, Kentucky, March 18, 1964; Lakeside Ledger, Eddyville, Kentucky, March 18, 1964.

[110]Ibid.

[111]Ibid.

in Kentucky and Tennessee. All of the speeches followed the stratagem of outlining the accomplishments of TVA during its thirty year history, and then a significant amount of data pertaining to the LBL project. Mr. Jones described the project as a new combination of recreation and resource preservation not available anywhere else in the country. He said that TVA had requested $448 million for operation in 1965. He explained that power production supported itself, and in 1963 the Tennessee Valley Authority paid back 2.7 million dollars more than it borrowed for operation. He challenged his listeners to study the advantages of TVA's low-cost wholesale power since 1942. He pointed out that beginning in 1951 there had been periodic decreases in the cost of electricity. He gave TVA credit for bringing industry into the states of Kentucky and Tennessee.[112]

The response to the new style of presenting the goals for TVA was positive. The continuing protests by the citizens of LBL were generally ignored by the larger newspapers. Gene S. Graham, staff writer for Nashville's The Tennessean was one of the few reporters to take note of the feelings and activities of the people. He wrote on March 8, 1964 that TVA, which by now should be an authority on dealing with displaced persons because it had been involved in that business for thirty years, was having serious trouble in the Land Between the Lakes. He said that poor diplomacy, fuzzy policies, and lack of liaison with elected officials were the major factors provoking the angry resistance in the area. Graham along with Nat Caldwell, another reporter for the newspaper, had spent several days in the area talking to the people, after which he commented on the fact that almost all the people had no quarrel with the recreation proposal. He quoted Mr. Joe Dill, owner of a general store in Model, as saying that he had a profitable business and he certainly did not want to leave. It would break his heart to see the town of Model disappear, but if the recreational area was developed correctly, it would benefit the region and he was willing to sacrifice his feeling for the good of all the people. His concern was with the proposals TVA had about how to develop the area.

Graham found that TVA's severest critic was Lyon County Judge Francis Utley who said that he had always supported the concept of the recreational area, but he was not going to allow the TVA people to come into the area and push people around. He said he was going to borrow heavily from a quote from Winston Churchill when he said that he was not elected to preside over the dismantling of Lyon County. Judge Utley accused TVA of bad faith. He charged that the agency had promised that it would consult with local officials and collaborate with them before making basic developmental decisions, but TVA had not done this. Instead, he said, TVA took the upper end of Lyon County where the people had expected to create a $50 million development along the lake front. The basic resentment which the reporters found stemmed from the belief that TVA would take the land, pay a cheap price for it, wait a few years, and then re-sell it at a considerable profit to outside commercial interests. Also, people were angry because TVA had not hired residents for the available jobs. Of some forty-one men hired to plant trees, only seven lived in the area. The surveyors were all outsiders. The reporters could see the blazed trees, painted white, and hundreds of rags knotted to twigs along the roads throughout the area. One citizen near tears, said that a surveyor went right into a churchyard and started surveying. When one of the deacons told him to leave, he was rude.

---

[112]The speech delivered by Mr. Jones was typical of at least 30 speeches given by TVA employees to civic groups in Tennessee and Kentucky in 1964 and 1965.

The deacon told him that if he expected to survey church property he would have to return with a court order.[113]

During the time that reporters were in the area talking to the people, the Tennessee Valley Authority made good on its promise to hire workers in the area. As the new construction began, TVA made a special effort to recruit and hire workers from the area.[114] In April the citizen protest continued. A picket of eight elderly women marched around the Ken-Bar Motel where TVA officials were conducting a meeting with local officials. Mrs. Ruby Petty and Mrs. Ola Jones carried signs to protest a meeting of local officials and TVA representatives which was held at Cadiz, Kentucky.[115]

On April 5, 1964, many people were surprised when Senator Vance Hartke, Democrat from Indiana, called for public hearings on the Land Between The Lakes project. Hartke asked for a hearing before the House Appropriations Committee when it considered funds for the project. He issued a news release which said that he had learned that the Committee would discuss the funding for the Land Between The Lakes project in late April or on May 6. He requested that all people interested in the issue prepare statements, and he would present them to the Committee. The Senator said that he was not opposed to the concept of the project, but he was concerned about the excessive area of land which was to be included in the park.[116]

Evidence indicates that by April 1964, most of the people in the groups opposing the Land Between The Lakes project were convinced that they could not stop or gain a delay in the acquisition of the land for the first step of the development, but they still hoped that they could organize enough political opposition to limit the amount of land which TVA could acquire. They had also concluded that TVA would manage the project, regardless of their demand that another agency assume control. About 2,000 people had already made plans to leave the area. Approximately 3,000 people were still trying to decide where they would go.

Judge Atkins and Judge Cosey had announced their support of the project.[117] Judge Utley was the only dissenter left in the tri-county leadership group. After a meeting with Wagner on April, 21, 1964, Utley made it clear that he would continue to oppose the amount of land which TVA intended to acquire.[118]

An invitation was sent by Wagner to the local county officials to meet with him to discuss the project. It was an attempt to convince the leaders that TVA had the best interests of the

---

[113]See The Tennessean, Nashville, Tennessee, March 21, 1964; April 25, 1964; June 23, 1964.

[114]Lakeside Ledger, Eddyville, Kentucky, March 31, 1964.

[115]Lyon County Herald, Eddyville, Kentucky, April 19, 1964. Judge Utley is very vocal during the entire period. He was quoted in the Courier Journal on April 21 as saying that people ought not to be asked to give up their birthright to make way for a bunch of opossums, raccoons, rattlesnakes, and mangy buffalo.

[116]News-Sentinel, Knoxville, Tennessee, April 6, 1964; Times, Chattanooga, Tennessee, April 6, 1964; Journal, Knoxville, Tennessee, April 6, 1964; Banner, Nashville, Tennessee, April 6,1964.

[117]Ira Atkins, one of the leaders of the protest groups,made a speech to the Paris, Tennessee Kiwanis Club on April 8, and he praised TVA for acquiring property to develop the national park.

[118]Messenger, Mayfield, Kentucky, April 24, 1964.

region in mind. The invitation stipulated that no representatives of the news media or property owners from the affected area could be present at the meeting. Once again, the good intentions of TVA were obliterated by the wording of the invitation. Wagner and his assistants did not seem to understand that one of the major problems in this situation was the feeling that the people had been betrayed. Any meeting to discuss their land to which they were not welcome was clearly a meeting to betray their best interests.

On the day of the meeting, a crowd of concerned citizens and members of the news media gathered outside the Kenlake Hotel where the meeting was to be held. When the county officials and TVA representatives gathered, Judge Utley voiced his opposition to the restrictions that had been imposed on the meeting. He demanded that at least two property holders and two representatives of the press attend the session. He wanted the activities of the meeting recorded on tape so that no mistakes could be made about what was said.[119]

After a prolonged discussion and a considerable delay, the TVA delegation agreed to a compromise. It was agreed that all discussion of the recreation area would be omitted during the luncheon, and a conference with the judges, property owners, and the press would be held after the meal.[120]

At the conference, Wagner stressed the importance of the recreation area as a way of allowing people the opportunity of getting back to nature. Judge Utley and others questioned Wagner about the need for the amount of land which TVA planned to acquire. Wagner restated the TVA policy. George Bleidt, Secretary of the Tri-County Organization, asked Wagner why he had refused to speak to the crowd of concerned citizens who were waiting outside the hotel. Wagner replied that he did not think it was necessary.[121]

After the meeting, the concerned citizens questioned the local officials and the news media about what had transpired in the meeting. They wanted to know if TVA officials had discussed the possibility of reducing the amount of land. They learned that was not the case. Judge Utley described the meeting as completely fruitless.[122]

During the last week of April two incidents brought the Federal Bureau of Investigation into The Land Between The Lakes. A shot from a high powered rifle went through the front of the Tennessee Valley Authority's land acquisition office in Trigg County, and another bullet was fired into the hubcap of a TVA car parked in the lot outside the building. Federal officials were called into the case because TVA officials were convinced that the rifle shots were connected to the group of picketers who had been marching in front of the office for fifteen days.[123] Judge Utley, speaking for the demonstrators, denied that they had any knowledge of the shooting incidents. The FBI and local law enforcement officers were never able to find the person or persons who fired the shots.

---

[119]Sun-Democrat, Paducah, Kentucky, April 19, 1964.

[120]Ibid.

[121]Ibid.

[122]Lyon County Herald, Eddyville, Kentucky, April 23, 1964.

[123]Kentucky New Era, Hopkinsville, Kentucky, May 1, 1964; The Tennessean, Nashville, Tennessee, May 1, 1964.

The Tennessee Valley Authority announced on April 27, 1964, that Dr. Milton Gabrielson of New York University, a nationally recognized authority in the field of outdoor recreation, had been hired as a consultant in the Land Between The Lakes project. Dr. Gabrielson had been quoted as saying that the Land Between The Lakes Project was potentially the most significant single development of outdoor recreation that had happened in this century.[124]

Dr. Gabrielson had held the title of Director of Recreation and Camping Education at New York University, and it appeared that he was going to assist in the planning of camping sites in the LBL project. He had just assumed his new position when the budget appropriations for TVA ran into difficulty in the U. S. Senate in 1964. Gabrielson began to talk about the LBL as the place where formal and informal opportunities would be provided for education. TVA planned to provide the opportunity for the development of a vast outdoor classroom in conservation and related subjects.[125]

TVA's Problems Spread

In May, officials of Trigg and Lyon Counties appeared before the House Appropriations subcommittee to testify against the request for six million dollars requested by TVA for the development of the LBL project. Stewart County was not represented in the delegation led by Corinne Whitehead of Lyon County and Judge Zelner Cosey of Trigg County. The delegation requested that the project be turned over to the Department of the Interior. Their request was based on the accusation that TVA had used methods that generated fear, confusion, and anger among the residents of the area. They denounced TVA officials whom they described as conquerors who demonstrated no concern for the misery and unhappiness the people were facing in the loss of their homes and land.[126]

Senator Hartke joined the protest and said that he had received many letters opposing the actions of TVA. Hartke told the subcommittee that he believed that TVA had the legal foundation to build the recreational area but the methods used to acquire the land left much to be desired. Hartke said that the TVA officials had not held enough public hearings. They had seemed to ignore the residents of the area. By ignoring the people, according to Hartke, TVA had engendered a feeling of helplessness among the residents. He joined with the other opponents of the project and requested that TVA be denied its funding request.[127]

After the subcommittee hearings, several national leaders expressed concern over the

---

[124]Sun-Democrat, Paducah, Kentucky, April 27, 1964.

[125]Ibid. Dr. Gabrielson was quite successful in his discussion of the educational opportunities which could be made available in LBL. The response to his speeches was positive and the emphasis on education would help TVA in its funding requests.

[126]Sun-Democrat, Paducah, Kentucky, May 5, 1964; Courier Journal, Louisville, Kentucky, May 5, 1964; The Tennessean, Nashville, Tennessee, May 5, 1964.

[127]Ibid.

future of the project. Representative Joe L. Evins from Tennessee, a subcommittee member, was quoted as saying that the project was in deep trouble because the TVA Board had demonstrated poor public relations tactics. Representative Evins was especially concerned with the accusation that TVA representatives had gained information by questioning residents about their neighbors' business affairs.[128] He said that he had lectured the TVA Board on its poor public relations policies when they had appeared before the subcommittee in April. In his opinion, he said, TVA officials did not know how to work with people.[129]

The Citizens for the Tennessee Valley Authority, an organization that had been formed twelve years earlier, held a meeting to speak in support of TVA. The organization expressed its confidence in the fairness of the methods used for acquiring land. They pointed out that TVA had a thirty year record of acquisition practices that were fair and just. They were concerned about the criticism at the time because Republican presidential candidate, Barry Goldwater had been quoted as saying he would favor the sale of TVA to private interests.[130]

Now another element had been added to the controversy. Those people who were speaking out about the acquisition practices of TVA might join forces with those people who wanted to sell TVA. The citizens of LBL had never advocated that TVA be disbanded. They were concerned that such a plan could somehow be linked to their proposal of restricting the amount of land TVA could take for one project. Many individuals now felt that it was better to contain their criticism of TVA and not give weapons to its enemies.

In June and July, the Tennessee Valley Authority took steps to assure the nation that TVA was conscious of the concerns of the people. The agency hired ten teachers on a temporary basis to assist people who were trying to relocate. These teachers from Trigg and Lyon Counties worked with the people to find comparable homes and farms.[131] TVA and the Kentucky Department of Public Information invited thirty-five travel editors and photographers to tour the Land Between The Lakesproject. The agency took the opportunity to announce that cemeteries in the area would be kept open and accessible for visiting and maintenance by relatives and friends. The cemeteries, some two hundred and twenty, dating back to the earliest settlements, would remain open for additional burials up to the limits of available space. TVA would assume the responsibility of fencing the cemeteries and maintaining access roads. If families wished to remove relatives from the cemeteries, TVA would assist in the removal.[132]

The Tennessee Valley Authority learned in June that their request for six million dollars for funding the LBL project had been cut by one million dollars by the House Appropriations subcommittee. The cut did not harm the TVA project. As a matter of fact, when the subcommittee appropriated five million dollars to fund the LBL project, it had given TVA the

---

[128]The Tennessean, Nashville, Tennessee, May 7, 1964.

[129]Ibid.

[130]The Tennessean, Nashville, Tennessee, April 12, 1964.

[131]Sun-Democrat, July 1, 1964.

[132]Courier Journal, Louisville, Kentucky, July 8, 1964.

authority to continue the plans for the 170,000 acre project.[133] Apparently, the TVA program that would remove all the people had won the approval of the subcommittee. When the House Appropriations Committee approved the subcommittee's request on July 10, 1964, the completion of the project seemed a certainty.

Suddenly, without warning the project seemed in jeopardy. It was learned that the Senate Public Works Appropriation subcommittee meeting on July 29, had some serious concerns with the TVA appropriations. Tennessee Senator Albert Gore attended the closed meeting as an ex-officio member of the subcommittee. After some discussion, the subcommittee voted the five million dollars to continue the project, but the subcommittee voted to include language in its report reserving judgement on who should operate the park.[134] It was learned that Senator Allen J. Ellender, Democrat from Louisiana, Chairman of the Senate full committee had waged a fight against the appropriation. Ellender had pledged to block further appropriations for the LBL project.[135] On August 6, 1964, the Senate Appropriations Committee took under consideration the TVA request for $47,915,000 which did not include three million dollars which had been cut from the budget by the House of Representatives. It was pointed out that some five million dollars had been included in the appropriation request by TVA and that money was to go to the LBL project. The original request for the project had been six million dollars.[136]

At that time, two Senators expressed concern over TVA's involvement in an extensive recreational project. Senator Hartke of Indiana and Senator Ellender of Louisiana expressed the opinion that TVA might not have the authority to take land for recreational purposes. Senator Ellender, Chairman of the Senate Appropriations Public Works subcommittee, vigorously questioned the activities of TVA in acquiring land solely for recreational purposes. When TVA officials submitted their budget request in 1964, they had titled their project The Land Between The Lakes Demonstration Program even though the original title of the Land Between The Lakes Recreational Area was still used in most of their communications. Senator Ellender was quoted as saying that TVA knew it did not have the authority to get into recreation.[137] Senator Ellender said he felt that there was a substantial question whether any of the present development was authorized. If the development was to be a simple study, an experiment or demonstration necessary and suitable to the making of plans which were useful to Congress and the several States under section 22 of the Tennessee Valley Authority Act of 1933, then TVA would be authorized to request funding. Senator Ellender then posed the question of whether or not TVA was developing the project to provide recreation. If, in fact, that was the end result of the development, then in his opinion, TVA did not have the authority to continue the development.

---

[133]Courier Journal, Louisville, Kentucky, June 11, 1964.

[134]The Tennessean, Nashville, Tennessee, July 30, 1964.

[135]Ibid.

[136]News Sentinel, Knoxville, Tennessee, August 6, 1964; Commercial Appeal, Memphis, Tennessee August 6, 1964; The Tennessean, Nashville, Tennessee, August 6, 1964.

[137]Ibid.

He said he believed that their own testimony convicted them on this score.[138]

Senator Ellender wanted the project under the control of the National Park Service, not the Tennessee Valley Authority. He was concerned TVA had acquired land by condemnation and then sold it to private developers, from which the agency made profits. It was not the intent of Congress, said Senator Ellender, to acquiesce in the condemnation of private lands for subsequent disposal to private interests according to the whims of a bureaucrat. The Tennessee Valley Authority was accused of trying to enter into a new sphere of operation. According to Senator Ellender, TVA had the authority to provide for studies in reforestation, the best use of fertilizer, and things of that kind, but TVA's purpose was not to embark on a new program to purchase land for the development of a national recreational area.[139]

After a lengthy debate, Section 22 of the Tennessee Valley Authority Act of 1933 was read into the record. An outline of the historical background for TVA's involvement in the Land Between The Lakes project was discussed and several letters from citizens in the area were read into the record.[140] The letters contained complaints about how the TVA officials handled the surveys of land before a purchase offer had been made. The people said they had been threatened and surveyors had sneaked onto the land before they had asked the owner's permission. The letters included a list of the real property owned by the United States in the states of Kentucky and Tennessee as of June 30, 1963. It was shown that the federal government owned 4.225 percent of the land in Kentucky and 5.814 percent of the land in Tennessee, totaling 441,296.4 acres. Tennessee ranked third and Kentucky twelfth in the United States in the cost of federally owned real property.[141]

After further debate, the appropriation bill was passed, but TVA had gotten a clear message: the programs that had been designed for the LBL Recreational Area needed to be reevaluated, the directors of TVA needed to come to a common agreement about the goals for the project, and they needed a common language with which to communicate those goals. Some of the Senator's expressed concerns alerted various people to the precarious position that TVA might be facing. If other opponents of TVA joined in the debate on whether the agency had in fact entered into a new area of development, the agency could be abolished, or certainly curtailed by Congress.

People Unite to Protect TVA

From the editorials in the newspapers, it became apparent that supporters of TVA were concerned, and many of the editorials supported the immediate acquisition of all the LBL land. Editorials warned the people that if they did not stand up and fight for the development of LBL,

---

[138]Ibid.

[139]Ibid.

[140]Ibid.

[141]Ibid.

they were going to lose TVA. If Kentucky and Tennessee lost the development associated with the LBL, millions of dollars in tourist trade would be lost, not counting the extra money industry would bring into the region. The mood of the people outside the area had shifted to one of blaming LBL citizens for damaging TVA. They were accused of standing in the way of progress and prosperity for the whole region.[142] The people who considered themselves victims were now being blamed for a crime which they did not commit. Suddenly, they were told they were trying to destroy TVA. It was a dispiriting and frustrating time for these people.

The larger newspapers in Kentucky and Tennessee called upon the senators from both states to support the LBL Park. The senators were accused of sitting there tranquilized while the enemies of TVA tried to destroy the agency. They were warned to wake up and support the development of the park or the citizens would hold them accountable. They responded immediately by sending messages back to their respective states saying they had talked with Senator Ellender and were sure that he now understood that the people of Tennessee and Kentucky supported the Land Between The Lakesproject.[143]

Officials in Kentucky and Tennessee began a time of competing for the benefits of the LBL project. Kentucky newspapers gloated over the fact that their state had started early to develop highways which would funnel tourists into the area. Tennessee had been outmaneuvered and had not developed a realistic highway program that would use the Land Between The Lakesto their advantage. Judge Atkins was quoted as saying that because Tennessee had not planned roads into Stewart County so that visitors to LBL would come through the county to reach the recreational facilities, the county would lose a great deal of the tourist trade to Kentucky.[144]

A protected recreation area posed an interesting concept. In July 1964, Bob Howes, manager of the LBL project, gave Harold Van Morgan, who was at that time director of the planning staff for the project, credit for the concept.[145] In 1959, as a staff member for TVA, he began a study of large-scale national recreation possibilities and recognized the unique prospects of the area. When President Kennedy mentioned his interest in such developments, TVA already had the germ of the idea on the planning board. This revelation did not please the citizens of LBL. They accused TVA of a conspiracy or at least a sub rosa plan to take their land long before the President suggested new parks. Renewed controversy broke out in August and September, but it had little impact on TVA's implementation of its plans.[146] The Chairman of the Board for TVA, ignored the new charges against TVA and tried to eliminate the criticism about the agency's dealings with the people: that TVA officials did not meet face to face with

[142]Courier Journal, August 10, 1964; Sun Democrat, Paducah, Kentucky, August 10, 1964; Post Intelligence, Paris, Tennessee, August 12, 1964; Kentucky New Era, Hopkinsville, Kentucky, August 15, 1964; The Marshall Courier, Benton, Kentucky, August 26, 1964.

[143]The Tennessean, August 29, 1964; Courier Journal, Louisville, Kentucky, August 30, 1964.

[144]The Tennessean, Nashville, Tennessee, August 2, 1964.

[145]Messenger, Mayfield, Kentucky, July 30, 1964.

[146]Ibid.

the citizens of the area. He arranged to meet with large groups in Cadiz in September 1964. Wagner, described as a folksy type, with great intelligence, was meeting a challenge with the emotional crowds. He handled the situation with aplomb. Skillfully and with sincerity, Wagner answered the questions asked by people. He described the project as the most important one in the United States and he assured the people that one day they would feel the same way. Appealing to the emotions of his listeners, Wagner said they had a moral responsibility to provide a protected area for future generations. America, he said, had to provide now for people of the future. The people did not leave the meeting feeling better about their plight, but they did admit that Wagner was willing to try to answer all their questions and he was certainly a good speaker.[147]

Wagner went away from the meeting aware that he was facing a tough audience. They asked probing questions, and they were quick to tear his responses to shreds. He conceded that people were willing to listen to him if he treated them as worthy, intelligent citizens. Wagner would not characterize his questioners as ignorant and backward people. They had let him know that they especially resented comments which implied that all the people were comic moonshiners.[148] Reporters described Mr. Wagner's demeanor as truly compassionate. They could hear the tears in the voices of the people who asked questions. Bill Powell, reporter for the Paducah Sun Democrat, was especially moved by the demeanor of the people asking questions. He commented that these were people with high standards, who were unusually honest and demonstrated great consideration for their fellow man. He wrote several articles about the frustration these people felt when they were treated as inferior people.[149]

Soon, the houses were moved out of LBL--some on dollies, some on barges, towed across the lakes. George Bleidt, postmaster at Golden Pond, continued to oppose the project. He described the people as scared to death over the prospect of leaving the area. He had two parcels of land which TVA was taking, and he complained that he was being paid farm land prices for resort land.[150]

Pollard White, a 79 year old resident, was an example of those citizens who were in favor of the project. Pollard was head of the Trigg County Trading Company, and he responded to questions about the project by saying:

The Land Between The Lakes used to be a bootlegger's paradise, a hideout for outlaws, and forsaken. You could only reach it on a ferry. They even had a brand of moonshine called Golden Pond whisky. There was a settlement of infidels there. Development of the area for recreation will turn this entire section into a commercial gold mine. This area will boom. Everybody is for it now.[151]

---

[147]Commercial Appeal, August 12 and August 29, 1964; Sun-Democrat, Paducah, Kentucky, August 27, 1964; Ledger & Times, Murray, Kentucky, August 29, 1964; Courier Journal, Louisville, Kentucky, August 29, 1964.

[148]Ibid.

[149]Sun-Democrat, Paducah, Kentucky, September 12, 1964.

[150]Press-Scimitar, Memphis, Tennessee, September 21, 1964.

[151]Ibid.

White's opinions reflected an attitude which many long-time residents despised. They argued that a person who would describe the land between the rivers in such a manner was not aware of the real history of the region. They were not embarrassed about making whiskey because the historical background of making it was important. True, present-day bootleggers should probably stop selling whiskey, but that in no way explained the reasons why people had taken pride in what they had done in the past.

When TVA officials came into contact with the people, they formed new opinions about them. Many colorful stories were discussed by TVA officials who were working in the area in the 1960s. W. Sherrill Milliken, a resources development officer in the area, noted that he had found some deeds to be land grants from the King of England in 1769, and some of the families had claimed the land from that time. When he expressed surprise about the grants, the response from the families involved was, "We told you that fact. Now do you believe us?"[152] Numerous incidents were told about how generous the people were. The one thing that they would not tolerate was any suggestion that they would have a better life living outside LBL. Many of these incidents were clear indications of the pride the people took in their culture and traditions.

As 1964 was coming to an end, TVA attempted to devise a peace formula. They wanted to end the bitter opposition about the LBL project. Members of the TVA board, Governor Edward Breathitt of Kentucky, and representatives of the business interests and land owners met in Nashville and arrived at some compromises. As a result of the meeting, private firms who wanted to operate real estate or commercial developments at Barkley Lake were urged to have their plans in order by September 1965.[153]

In January 1965, TVA released a progress report on its achievements during the previous fiscal year. It had set a new record in the sale of electric power and the net income of 58.2 million dollars was a new high. The agency had paid more than twenty-two million dollars to state and local governments in tax equivalents. The power revenue was over $286 million.

TVA had made a repayment of $10 million in appropriated funds.[154] Included in the report was a broad outline of the goals for the LBL project. TVA officials emphasized the outdoor activities, conservation programs, wildlife management, and erosion control goals of the project. It was noted that the land acquisition had begun in the spring of 1964 and was continuing. Already, the camping areas had provided facilities for over four hundred campers, and approximately 12 thousand campers had used the area during the first months of operation even though most Americans were not yet aware of the existence of the area.[155]

State officials in Kentucky were actively involved in promoting the facility. Meetings were held to coordinate plans for the development of tourist attractions outside the project. A five-county area study had been completed by the Spindletop Research Center, and the report

---

[152]Ibid.

[153]Courier Journal, Louisville, Kentucky, December 30, 1964.

[154]Tennessee Valley Documents, "Progress Report on the Land Between the Lakes," January 1965. Available in Knoxville, Tennessee.

[155]Ibid.

concentrated on the development of facilities in all the Kentucky counties near the project.[156]

At that time it was announced that TVA had acquired approximately 70,000 acres of the total 170,000 in the project. Sixty percent of the remaining 100,000 acres was in Stewart County and eleven percent in Lyon County, and the remainder was in Trigg County. The target date for the removal of all the people was set for January 1, 1968.[157]

In January 1964, the people understood that one of the major arguments against LBL had been removed in November 1964 when a ruling was handed down by the Department of Health, Education, and Welfare under Public Law 874. The ruling said that the school systems affected by the LBL project were entitled to federal aid to replace school tax losses caused by the project. Under the same ruling, the school systems also received undiminished federal payments to help educate children who lived on or whose parents were employed on the federal property acquired for Fort Campbell, Barkley Reservoir, and the U. S. Fish and Wildlife Refuge. Previously, these payments had been reduced by amounts equal to what the school systems were receiving from TVA payments in lieu of taxes, both directly and through redistribution of the TVA payments by the state governments.[158]

People knew that their schools would receive support from the federal government, and at the same time citizens became involved in a proposal to straighten and widen Highway 79, originally known as the Austin Peay Memorial Highway. The people in Stewart and Henry counties wanted the state to replace the Scott Fitzhugh bridge spanning the Tennessee River and the Sidney Lewis bridge over the Cumberland. The officials of the two counties explained that Highway 79 was the only southern entrance to LBL and the state must concern itself with the fact that people would enter the area through Kentucky if Tennessee did not provide adequate roadways.[159]

In March of 1965, Douglas Crockarell, J. M. Atkins, Frazier Riggins, and Eugene Raylor from Stewart County wrote an open letter to Frank G. Clement, Governor of Tennessee, expressing their concern that Tennessee had fallen behind in its highways, especially U. S. Highway 79. They warned the governor that Tennessee stood to lose millions of dollars in tourist trade because people would not travel the highways. The men pleaded with the governor to work with the state legislature to appropriate funds for the construction of roads at the southern entrance to LBL.[160] It became apparent that state officials in Tennessee were not going to take action. The Tennessee State Legislature waited almost two decades before money was appropriated to rebuild the road. Finally in 1987-88, construction was begun to replace the Sidney Lewis bridge and construction began on a new Tennessee River bridge.

---

[156]Courier Journal, Louisville, Kentucky, December 31, 1964; Sun-Democrat, Paducah, Kentucky, February 12, 1965.

[157]Ibid.

[158]Democrat, Murray, Kentucky, November 11, 1964; Lyon County Herald, Eddyville, Kentucky, November 26, 1964.

[159]The Tennessean, Nashville, Tennessee, March 12, 1965.

[160]Ibid. March 3, 1965; Stewart-Houston Times, Dover, Tennessee, March 3, 1965.

In March, 1965, the Kentucky Woodlands National Wildlife Refuge, a 58,000 acre tract, was transferred to TVA. Paul Sturm, manager of the Refuge since 1959, was hired by TVA to join the staff of LBL. Camping facilities would be located in the Refuge and a conservation education center was planned near the historic ruins of Center Iron Furnace. It was announced that the major portion of the Refuge would remain a protected area for wildlife and TVA intended to double its size, making additional feeding grounds and shelters available.[161]

News of proposed programs at LBL caused excitement in 1965. As soon as funding was available the development would include: a marine science center, a nature craft center, a fish management demonstration center, a natural sciences museum, camp craft demonstrations, reforestation and soil conservation demonstrations, hiking trails, trails for disabled persons, a weather station and other facilities. Gabrielson suggested that it was possible to include a national leadership training center for outdoor education. People, including conservation teachers, planners, and administrators could come to the park with facilities for learning. Approximately two hundred camping centers for small groups, as well as for larger organizations such as the Scouts and YMCA, would be available.[162]

From the beginning of the LBL project, TVA had tried to bring the goals of the project in line with its legal objectives. In 1965, TVA began to define the goals. TVA spokesmen said they agreed with the 1962 report by the Outdoor Recreation Resources Review Commission. The Commission reported that the chief reason for providing outdoor recreation was the broad social and individual benefits it produced. Recreation could bring about desirable economic effects. TVA had touched the right cord when it brought the long range goals of national recreation in line with the economic benefits it could provide for the people.[163]

The Recreational Development Project was now within the guidelines of Section 22 of the TVA Act which said that TVA had the authority to further the proper use, conservation, and development of natural resources and to provide for the general welfare of the citizens in the area. All that was needed was for the President to request funding and if Congress provided the resources, TVA could use its authority to foster an orderly and proper physical, economic, and social development in the area. TVA then could make studies, experiments, or demonstrations as it might deem necessary and suitable to enhance the general welfare.[164]

More importantly, the new approach needed to counteract much of the criticism had been found. TVA made recreation an economic goal, but education was the ultimate achievement. LBL would become a learning laboratory. Plans were made, and construction began on a Conservation Education Center. It was described as an adult and youth activities center which provided housing, meeting, and study facilities for students and teachers in conservation education. It was designed to benefit schools from elementary through graduate level. Henry S. Mosby, an expert on Forestry and Wildlife, and Dr. Leslie L. Glasgow, a noted author on

---

[161]Democrat, Murray, Kentucky, February 10, 1965.

[162]Ibid.

[163]Ibid.

[164]Lakeside Ledger, Eddyville, Kentucky, April 1, 1965.

wildlife and Director of the Louisiana Wildlife and Fisheries Commission, were hired as consultants to develop an extensive wildlife program. TVA announced a two year deadline for the project.[165]

A 4,500 acre tract of land was set aside for the Conservation Education Center and classes were organized to teach the ways of nature and methods of conserving soil and wildlife. Visitors would be taken along trails which led to points of historical, natural, and wildlife interest. Stations were set up to provide comparable demonstrations of good and poor conservation practices.[166]

The last protests from the citizens of LBL were mere whimpers. Howard Barnett, who had been born in the land between the rivers, wrote to the Murray Lakeside Ledger about a meeting which was held at Ray's Garage. About forty people had gathered for the last time before they left their homes. They brought boxes and baskets of country ham, roast turkey with trimmings, fried chicken, salads, cole slaw, baked beans, cakes, and pies. They held their social to remember the times they had met together in the past. The people were continuing a social function which had been practiced in the region for hundreds of years.[167]

Charles L. Baccus, a life-long resident, wrote to the newspaper to comment on a television show he had seen. The show had been filmed by TVA on the Land Between the Lakes. Baccus said that as he watched the show, he wondered if the visitors to the Land Between The Lakeswould even enjoy the region the way the citizens had. He questioned whether these visitors would ever feel a part of the land. He concluded that they would never have a kinship with the wild, lonely hills and hollows because they would never know their history. He remembered the names of landmarks that would soon fade away. He felt that names of such places as Wildcat Hollow, Hal's Patch, Race Track, White Oak, Devil's Pocket, Curry, Sullivan, Travis, and others would soon be forgotten. The roots of his people had been pulled up forcibly without compassion, in the name of progress, and exposed to the sun to die. "And die they will because no transplant is possible."[168] All of the last letters were filled with pathos, and it was easy to see the trauma and sorrow these people were facing.

One citizen, Homer Ray, wrote an open letter to the newspapers and said that his worst problem, even worse than moving, was that the news media and TVA had degraded the citizens of the area and gotten away with it. The reports had described the people as "inbred," and people who had never traveled outside their own backyards. He agreed that he and his neighbors were simple people, but they had built their own homes and were content with their friends and neighbors. He questioned TVA's relationship with the news media. In his opinion, TVA had a strange definition for progress. How could it be progress to buy valuable, productive land and then flood it? What was the value of land if people did not tend it?[169]

---

[165]Ledger & Times, Murray, Kentucky, March 24, 1964.

[166]Ibid.

[167]Lakeside Ledger, Eddyville, Kentucky, January 21, 1965.

[168]Lakeside Ledger, Eddyville, Kentucky, January 21, 1965.

[169]Lakeside Ledger, Eddyville, Kentucky, February 4, 1965.

Another citizen, William D. Travis filed suit in July 1965 charging that TVA and the Pennyrile Rural Electric Cooperative had conspired to depress the value of some real estate in LBL. His complaint stated he had sought electrical service from the cooperative for his residence which TVA was trying to buy, and that an excess construction charge of $219 was set by the cooperative to discourage his application.[170] When it was finally determined that Travis did not have to pay the fee, his winning was not a victory; it was final proof to some people that you can't fight the government and win.

In early 1965, TVA approached colleges and universities in the area and proposed joint programs to encourage the use of the learning facilities in LBL. Churches and religious groups were encouraged to form inter-denominational working groups to plan how to best serve the tourists. Mental health groups were asked to develop plans to provide emergency mental health service for the tourists. This group was encouraged to study the skills of retired residents and involve them in the life of the area. Civil defense organizations were asked to develop plans for shelters for residents and tourists. Hospitals and local health departments were encouraged to submit proposals for expanded health facilities and first aid stations in the area.[171]

In July 1965, Joe Morgan, President of Austin Peay State College in Clarksville announced that the school had signed a $42,744 contract with TVA for the study of certain plants and animals in the Land Between The Lakes and he had chosen Dr. Haskell Phillips, Chairman of the Department of Biology, as Director of the study. Dr. Phillips would study lichens and ferns, Dr. William H. Ellis would study the higher vascular plants, David Snyder would investigate the reptiles and amphibians, and Alfred Clibsch would conduct a study of mosses and liverworts. This comprehensive study of the area would result in an extensive collection which would be housed at Austin Peay. Results of the research would be published in scientific journals, and several illustrated booklets would be prepared for publication by TVA.[172]

To appeal to visitors, a unique overlook was built around a silo which had been left on a farm. People could see deer, wild turkeys, and other animals and birds from the observation point. School systems throughout the region were invited to bring classes to the Youth Activities Station, and many elementary school children were brought. Work was started on an educational farm and an Arts and Crafts building was constructed. Highway 453, known as The Trace, was rebuilt and a number of access roads were constructed to allow visitors to travel to the more remote areas of the park. Plans were proposed to allow hunters to kill deer, doves, squirrels, rabbits, turkeys, and quail.

Once again, when the subcommittee hearings on appropriations were held in Washington in July 1965, debate developed around the legalities of TVA's activity in the Land Between the Lakes. Senator Allen J. Ellender, a Louisiana Democrat, led a bitter, scathing denunciation of TVA. The proposed appropriations for LBL provoked a debate between Ellender and Wagner. TVA had asked for 9.9 million dollars for the fiscal 1966 budget. Wagner said that the total

---

[170]Herald Leader, Lexington, Kentucky, July 4, 1965.

[171]Post-Intelligence, Paris, Tennessee, July 8, 1965.

[172]Ibid.

cost of the land had increased from twelve million dollars to twenty-four million dollars. The twelve million dollars had been an estimate; the increase was needed because the initial assessments had been too low. Ellender accused TVA of deliberately setting the cost at a low level in order to get the first appropriations for the project.[173]

Senator Ellender, who had learned his politics as Huey Long's floor leader in the Louisiana Legislature, was an able orator. He took the LBL as the key item to launch his criticism of all of the programs under TVA control. He asserted that more than seventy percent of the power generated by TVA came from steam in coal-burning plants, and not from water power through dams. He accused TVA of taking tax money from states outside the TVA area and using the money to build an industrial empire. He maintained that TVA received too much federal funding.[174]

A. R. Jones, Vice-chairman of the TVA Board, refuted Ellender's charges with statistics. The federal government had spent 2.2 billion dollars in TVA appropriations and received in return, assets of 2.6 billion dollars. TVA had paid back $300 million in dividends. Ellender said that TVA was again clouding the issue because the money they called dividends should be labeled interest on the money it had received from the federal taxpayers. He asserted that TVA had the facilities to generate the money it needed to operate if it would stop its expansion program, specifically the Land Between The Lakesproject.[175]

Representatives, speaking for the citizens of the Land Between the Lakes, Corinne R. Whitehead, George W. Bleidt, and Juanita L. Snipe, who were in Washington to present their concerns about TVA before the committee, criticized TVA on its land purchasing policies. They continued to argue against the amount of land which TVA planned to purchase. They asked for a detailed outline of TVA plans for spending money on the project.[176]

Debates continued, tempers flared, and senators and congressmen disagreed, but in August, 1965, a Senate-House Conference Committee agreed that an appropriation of $10.4 million should be made to the LBL. TVA officials announced that they intended to act immediately to purchase the remaining land in the area.[177]

In September 1965, Barkley Dam was near completion. TVA disclosed that the University of Louisville had received a $17,000 contract to study the fate of animals when the Barkley Dam flood-waters entered the Land Between the Lakes. Dr. Thane S. Robinson would direct the study of approximately one hundred and sixty animal species in the area for three years. The three hundred and twenty square mile area would be reduced to two hundred and forty square miles after the flooding in December. The study would include animal reproductive

---

[173]Courier Journal, Louisville, Kentucky, July 17, 1965; Sun-Democrat, Paducah, Kentucky, July 18, 1965; Democrat, Murray, Kentucky, July 19, 1965; Messenger & Inquirer, Ownesboro, Kentucky, July 21, 1965.

[174]Ibid.

[175]Ibid.

[176]Ibid.

[177]Sun-Democrat, Paducah, Kentucky, August 8, 1965.

status, their movement within the area, and diseases.[178]

In the fall of 1965, citizens in Tennessee were even more distraught when newspapers presented evidence that the state was lagging behind in development of facilities which would bring tourists into the Land Between The Lakes. Tennessee was losing at least eight million dollars a year in potential tourist trade.

Larry Doughtrey, staff writer for The Tennessean, investigated the activities of tourist promoters in Kentucky and compared them with their counterparts in Tennessee. He concluded that Kentucky had been much more successful in using the attraction of LBL to bring money into the state. He found that investments had tripled in the state in less than a year.[179] Doughtrey placed the responsibility for the status of Tennessee at the feet of Governor Clement. Two years earlier, Clement had agreed to let Interstate 24 be changed from Stewart County to a route north of Kentucky and Barkley Dams. Interstate 24 allowed investors to purchase land and build facilities for the ten million tourists who were funneled into the Kentucky end of LBL.[180]

It was good news when TVA announced that its goals for LBL had been met more effectually than projected. It had been estimated that approximately 75,000 to 100,000 visitors would come to the Land Between The Lakesin 1965. The actual number was 300,000 or more. TVA was still essentially involved in the construction of the project, and it had not turned its full attention to promulgating the attraction of the facility, but it had, as promised, made the project something unique in the nation. The area offered recreational facilities, nature studies and conservation information. In this park-like atmosphere hunters were allowed, actually encouraged, to hunt.

TVA demonstrated that it could accommodate public use of a vast area without destroying the natural beauty. When TVA made public other goals, the project captured the imagination of the public. A considerable amount of work had been done to eliminate breeding places of the malaria mosquito. Plans also included the paving of the underwater portions of eight launching camps for small craft and deepening of two future boat harbors to depths satisfactory for year-round use by pleasure craft of all sizes. A half-million trees were planted to enhance the appearance of the area. Trees were selected for their value as wildlife food and habitat and to test superior strains of the most valuable forest species, using forest management techniques. In the process of applying these techniques, TVA planned to harvest up to three million board feet of cull timber annually during the demonstration period.

Ecologists and economists were pleased to learn that TVA had two basic concerns which affected the environment outside the project boundaries. First, there was the desire to protect the project's values by preventing air and stream pollution, roadside slums, and other visitor deterrents, and a concern in aiding the people to take full advantage of the economic potential that would be generated by the project.[181]

---

[178]Sun-Democrat, Paducah, Kentucky, September 21, 1965.

[179]The Tennessean, Nashville, Tennessee, November 12, 1965.

[180]Ibid.

[181]Report in Sun-Democrat, November 13, 1965.

After some confusion over the interpretation of the Land and Water Conservation Fund Act of 1965, TVA had reached the decision that they would charge an entrance fee for LBL. TVA had proposed to charge a user's fee at some of the sites, but after due consideration it was decided that the fees would not be put into effect in 1966. It was expected that certain fees would be charged at locations which were primarily designed as an experiment in recreation, as well as wildlife and woodland conservation.[182] Those campsites which had a user's fee charged travel and camping trailers with sanitary holding tanks one dollar and fifty cents per night. A campsite with electrical outlets designed for tents cost one dollar and twenty-five cents per night. Boat launching facilities cost fifty cents per day. Other sites without electrical facilities were available for one dollar per night.[183]

Beginning in 1966, tourists were provided with church services each Sunday. Nine churches had formed an inter-denominational program to conduct services on a rotating basis at Hillman Ferry, Rushing Creek, Kenlake, Kentucky Dam Village and at other sites as the facilities were opened to the public.[184]

June 13, 1966 became an historic day when the Corps of Engineers allowed waters of the Tennessee River to mingle with the waters of the Cumberland River. The press, of course, used the new names, Kentucky Lake joined Barkley Lake, but the residents of the area still considered the enlarged streams as rivers. At 8 a. m. a hugh cutterhead of the dredge "Alabama" ate through a red-clay strip of earth across the canal which separated the two lakes. Onlookers watched as the opening was completed and a canal 1.75 miles long, 400 feet wide at its base and 600 feet across the top was nearly completed. By July 10, the canal, costing $3,540,000, would be opened for traffic.[185]

In the summer of 1966, The Resource Development officer, Milliken, was concerned with a situation which could pose problems for the project. He noted that businesses were needed along the edge of LBL because people had to travel from twenty to thirty miles to buy supplies, and the drive was inconvenient. At that time, Milliken suggested that TVA might be forced to offer vending machines which sold bread, milk, ice, and cigarettes. He said that he would prefer a rolling store, much like the old peddlers who traveled the area in the early twentieth century, which would come to the campsites daily. He suggested that a floating store might serve the same purpose.[186]

In July, officials announced that President Johnson and members of his family were coming to Fort Campbell to review the 101st Airborne Division and tour LBL. Major General Ben Sternberg, Commander of the 101st, issued an open invitation to the public to attend the

[182]Courier Journal, Louisville, Kentucky, November 22, 1965. The confusion was over which areas could charge usage fees.

[183]Ibid.

[184]Sun-Democrat, Paducah, Kentucky, January 9, 1966.

[185]Courier Journal, Louisville, Kentucky, July 13, 1966; Banner, Nashville, Tennessee, July 16, 1966.

[186]Ibid.

ceremonies at Fort Campbell.[187] As expected, the President and his entourage arrived at Fort Campbell on July 23, and hundreds of citizens attended the welcome ceremonies. Later that day Johnson took an aerial tour of LBL and expressed his support of the project.[188] He mentioned that the Vice President, Hubert Humphrey, would represent him at the official dedication of the Barkley Lake Lock and Dam project on August 20, 1966.[189]

In August, at the dedication ceremonies, Humphrey recalled the contributions which had been made by Alben W. Barkley as governor of Kentucky and Vice President of the United States. He said he was honored to name the area for the man.[190] In a brief commentary on the cost and purposes of the Barkley Lake project, he mentioned that the impoundment for the Lake had included a 57,000 acre area, and a dam had been constructed at a cost of approximately 142 million dollars. The Lake had covered land in parts of Livingston, Lyon, Caldwell, and Trigg Counties in Kentucky, as well as lands in Stewart, Montgomery, Houston, Cheatham, and Dickson Counties in Tennessee. Approximately 1,500 miles of shoreline was now available on the Cumberland River.[191]

The dedication ceremonies were considered a success, but even in the preparations for the event, it became quite apparent that private enterprise was not keeping pace with the governmental construction along Barkley Lake and along the perimeter of LBL. Newspapers reported that this was the first time in the history of an official Corps of Engineers dedication ceremony in the Nashville District that no commercial docks or resort installations had been completed. The lack of such enterprises had resulted in a number of problems for the Corps of Engineers. Fuel for the hundreds of boats which were scheduled to travel on the Cumberland and Tennessee for the dedication ceremonies was not available. There were no privately owned stations to provide for the sale of gasoline, and the Corps finally arranged to locate a gas barge at Mile 88, at the site of old Lock and Dam D, just north of Dover, near the mouth of Hickman Creek. Gas was made available at Clarksville and at Ken Bar Resort.[192]

During the summer of 1966, accounts appeared in the newspapers about the protests and pickets by people who were still unwilling to accept the fact that TVA was going to remove them from their land. But for the first time, reporters tried to present the attitudes of those people. At the time, more than 1,300 parcels of land had been purchased and some of the people were willing to talk to reporters. The general sentiment was that they had not wanted to sell their land, but they realized that they would have the money from the sale to start life

---

[187]Leaf Chronicle, Clarksville, Tennessee, July 20, 1966.

[188]Ibid. July 31, 1966; Sun-Democrat, Paducah, Kentucky, July 31, 1966.

[189]Ibid.

[190]The Tennessean, Nashville, Tennessee, August 16, 1966.

[191]Ibid.

[192]Ibid., September 1, 1966.

243

over in other areas.[193]

The official TVA versions of the sales were more positive. An example was a couple who lived in a tar-paper shack, on a meager veteran's pension. TVA saw the couple early and moved quickly to buy them a two-room house and lot. As it turned out, the couple was eligible for a larger Veterans Administration pension but wouldn't apply because they had heard a rumor that they could lose hospital privileges of the original pension.[194] Since the couple had no relatives to help them relocate, TVA sent an agent to assist the couple and provided transportation to a VA representative to discuss the pension. The hospital rights were preserved and the couple received $29 more a month.[195]

Another couple, who lived six miles from the nearest grocery store when they sold their land, was helped to relocate in a modern house with a garden plot only one block from a highway that had a bus service.[196]

An elderly woman lived on an estate which had to be divided among her and five children. When TVA purchased the land, her share was not enough to allow her to relocate. TVA's family assistance workers came to her assistance and the children helped her to take an option on a modern home.[197]

Without doubt, TVA officials did work to assist any individual who contacted them about relocation. Several problems made the relocation process difficult for both the individuals concerned and the TVA workers. Many of the people were convinced that TVA would not work in their best interests. Too much adverse publicity had occurred concerning the condemnation of the Barkley Lake lands by the Corps of Engineers and the actions of the first group of TVA surveyors who came into the area.

In August 1966, TVA received an appropriation of $63.7 million and $11 million of the fund was for the continuation of the LBL project. TVA would spend $10.7 million dollars for the purchase of land which would complete the land purchases.[198]

Most of the people who had sold their land were resettling in areas outside their home counties. Of the one hundred and thirty-four Trigg County citizens who had already sold their land, forty-six remained in Trigg County. Most of the others had moved to Calloway County.

During the entire time that TVA was in the process of acquiring land, officials were aware of the moonshine activities in the region. To make the matter more difficult, or amusing as the case might be, some of the whiskey was made on land that TVA had bought. In February, 1967, agents for the Internal Revenue Service tried to apprehend the moonshiners. All things considered, they were not too successful. After months of investigation, they arrested

---

[193]Courier Journal, Louisville, Kentucky, September 23, 1966.

[194]Sun-Democrat, Paducah, Kentucky, September 13, 1966.

[195]Ibid.

[196]Ibid.

[197]Ibid.

[198]Courier Journal, Louisville, Kentucky, August 19, 1966.

one man and confiscated his still. Not far from the still, a rough sign nailed to a TVA sign read, "Get that thing out of Here." Federal agents surmised that authorities had discovered the still and had warned the man to discontinue his production, but he had ignored the warning.[199] The agents destroyed six wooden fifty-gallon barrels of mash and a number of glass jugs. The whiskey was ready to be run off and the man was at the still when the officers arrived. The agents would not comment on the numbers of moonshiners still operating in the area. Kentucky officials guessed that the production was less now than it had been earlier. The comments were amusing because at least half of the citizens had moved out of the area by that time.[200]

As recorded earler, the Tennessee Valley Authority had hired two nationally recognized authorities in the field of wildlife management, Dr. Henry S. Mosby and Leslie L. Glasgow, to study the program that TVA had used and to make recommendations for a new program. They found the turkey population sufficient for a hunting season. A plan was implemented which included the rental of farm land for crops and wildlife management. Farmers rented the land under strict guidelines, and land was to be planted in corn and hay with a share of the crop left for wildlife food. Farmers had to agree to fertilize the soil according to soil test recommendations. Wildlife management allowed eight hunts for the season. Hunters were to kill certain limits of deer, doves, quails, rabbits, raccoons and turkey gobblers. Hunting was limited as to season, weapons, and numbers of animals allowed in the kill. [201]

In May, President Johnson's Citizens Advisory Committee on Recreation and Natural Beauty met at the Kentucky Dam Village Park and made a thorough study of LBL. The committee, headed by Laurence S. Rockefeller, made several tours of the project and Rockefeller said he considered the region as a pioneering area in the educational aspects of the project.[202]

During the time the President's committee was in the area, the Lyon County Fiscal Court unanimously endorsed congressional measures, introduced by Tennessee's Republican Senator Howard Baker and Republican Representative William Brock, permitting jury trials in land condemnation cases brought by TVA. Under the existing law, a landowner who was dissatisfied with a TVA offer for his or her property could appeal to a federal judicial panel for redress of their grievances.[203]

The Lyon County Fiscal Court sent letters to all Kentucky congressional members requesting support for the Baker and Brock proposals. The Court announced that the county was losing more than $25,000 a year because of the land which TVA had taken from the tax rolls. In 1966, the Court reported that the county had received only $4,771 from TVA in lieu of

[199]Sun-Democrat, February 3, 1967.

[200]Ibid.

[201]Cadiz Record, Cadiz, Kentucky, February 9, 1967.

[202]Sun-Democrat, Paducah, Kentucky, May 5, 1967.

[203]Ibid., May 6, 1967.

taxes.[204] The county, according to the study, had suffered a misalignment of the tax base because they had lost about one-half of their population since 1960. Retail prices decreased about 13 per cent from the previous year, yet the state had showed an increase of 23 per cent. As of June 1, 1967, TVA had purchased 8,673 acres of land in the County and had paid the property owners $5,361,025. According to the County Fiscal court, the price had been, in some instances, less than half the assessed valuation of the property as made for tax purposes by the county. Based on a then current tax rate of 4.84 dollars per thousand, the land acquisition of the 8,673 acres reflected a tax loss of more than $25 million for the county.[205] The Fiscal Court claimed that 663 families or 2,850 people had sold their land and only 70 families had remained in Lyon County. Nearby Livingston County had been able to lure most of the people who had to resettle. These former citizens of the county no longer were able to purchase goods and retailers had been forced out of business.[206]

The Tennessee Valley Authority denied that Lyon, Trigg or Stewart counties had lost money because of the land purchases. TVA said the figures used in the Lyon County report were inaccurate. TVA showed that the County received more money in lieu of taxes than it would have on the same land before TVA acquired it. As it turned out the County received $31,611 from TVA in 1967.[207]

While the press continued to carry reports of the tremendous success of the project during 1967, a small number of citizens continued their protest. A group met in July at the home of Mrs. Corinne Whitehead. They had an old-fashioned meeting called a dinner-on-the-ground and singing. Approximately thirty-five members of what was often referred to as the hard-core resistance to TVA, talked to people who attended the party. The hard-core group pledged not to move out of their homes no matter what TVA planned to do. The group had been successful in keeping appraisers off their land.[208] When this group alleged that TVA was not giving a fair market price for their land, TVA officials, once again, tried to explain their acquisition policy. TVA based its policy on the premise that owners of land acquired by TVA would be compensated fully. The price offered for each parcel of land was established by determining the price of comparable land in the area and the value of property in surrounding areas where the people wanted to relocate.[209] TVA officials explained that the non-price-trading policy afforded fair treatment to all owners, including those landowners of limited means who might not be able to contest the taking of their property. TVA officials said that their policy had always been to check the assessed price if landowners objected to the price they were offered because they did not want to make a mistake. If they found an error, they offered to readjust

---

[204]Ibid.

[205]Sun-Democrat, Paducah, Kentucky, July 14, 1967.

[206]Ibid. According to TVA estimates the $25 million was a highly inflated figure.

[207]Ibid.

[208]Courier Journal, Louisville, Kentucky, July 9, 1967.

[209]Ibid., July 13, 1967.

the price.[210]

No matter how logical the TVA officials were in their acquisition policy, there were some people who were too emotionally involved to accept the reasoning. Of course, these people were expressing real feelings and doubts about their future. One example of the complexity of the problem was discussed by Corinne Whitehead. Her family had lived on the same farm for a century and a half. She expressed her opposition to the LBL project by comparing what had happened to the people in the area to the injustices suffered by the Cherokee Indians when they were removed from their lands by the federal government. The few Indians who remained in the land between the rivers after the Indian removal policy had been implemented had been loaded on barges at old Birmingham Ferry and sent down the Tennessee River. She said that she could well appreciate the anguish and grief of the Cherokees. To her, the land between the rivers had always been an enchanted land and no one would ever love the hills, rocks, trees, and wildflowers as much as she did. No one would ever understand the moods of the land and its climate as much as the people who had lived there for generations. She pledged that TVA would not move her, but of course she did move in 1968.[211]

By 1967, many people were satisfied with their relocation. The Black community of "Little Chicago" had reestablished itself just outside LBL. The community kept its original name, and many merchants built new businesses nearby. Farmers had a more difficult time finding land. Often they had to move to one of the surrounding counties or to other states to find good farmland.

The last legal stand made by the people occurred on December 14, 1967, when Federal Judge Henry L. Brooks, in a lawsuit over 28.10 acres of land owned by Blondall Lilly Flood and Robert F. Flood, ruled that TVA did have the right to acquire the land. The lawsuit had charged that TVA's acquisition of the land was unnecessary, arbitrary, capricious and in bad faith. Judge Brooks denied the motion to stop TVA from acquiring the land. He ruled that the agency had not violated the rights of the people under its condemnation process. Also, TVA, unlike other federal agencies, did not have to go before a jury to justify the price it paid for land.[212]

The Judge took under advisement the legality of the acquisition of what the petitioners described as excess land in the development of LBL. In December, Judge Brooks stated that TVA had the right under the commerce clause and the general welfare clause of the Constitution and the TVA Act of 1933 to acquire land. TVA could exercise the right of eminent domain in the condemnation of land. Thus, even the antagonists had to agree that TVA did have the right to complete the LBL project.[213]

TVA reported that approximately 800,000 people had visited LBL in 1967, and the expectation was that even larger numbers of people would use the facilities in the future. With

---

[210]Ibid. Note this statement of policy is nothing like the original statements about what the citizens could expect from TVA.

[211]Courier Journal, Louisville, Kentucky, July 9, 1967.

[212]Courier Journal, Louisville, Kentucky, July 14, 1967.

[213]Ibid., December 18, 1967.

TVA's predictions ringing in their ears, the people gave up. They realized that it was only a matter of time until they would be forced to leave. In the final stages, TVA attempted to handle the negotiations with the people with more diplomacy than they had used in the past. They worked closely with those people who had resisted. They were willing to extend the time for people to make arrangements to move. Gradually during the summer of 1968, almost one by one, the last families moved out. Some people chose to move their houses to land they had bought in other counties. The houses that were not moved were razed by TVA. The land appeared more and more solitary and abandoned. It did not take many weeks, once the houses and other buildings were removed, for the land to seem to revert to the way it appeared in much earlier times. Bushes and small trees took over the farmland. The only way one could tell that homes had stood on sites was to take special care to notice the flowers and shade trees that were still there.

Only one person defied TVA and remained on his farm. Cleo Griffin, born near Model in 1923, refused to leave his home even though TVA officials informed him that he would be removed by force because the house was scheduled for immediate demolition. Griffin was attending Martin College when World War II began. He left school to volunteer to serve in the army. He fought in the battle of the Anzio Beachhead and was stationed in Italy after the battle. When he returned home, he enrolled at Murray State University, but the psychological effects of his battlefield experiences had taken their toll. Griffin, unable to cope with the demands placed on him, left school and came home to Model where he spent most of his time in seclusion. He had changed from a young man with a bright academic future to a person who did not want to meet strangers or be in a crowd. TVA officials were stymied when their threats of force made no impression on him.

His family, especially his sister Mrs. Christine Whitford, worried about what would happen. "In the middle of the night TVA officials came to my home and told me to remove my brother from the house right then," said Mrs. Whitford. My husband told them that he was not going to force Cleo out of the house. The Veterans Administrations had heard of what they were trying to do to Cleo and stopped them. Since then, Cleo was left alone and he continued to live on the home place.[214] About once a week his sister had someone drive her to her brother's home. She took him food and medicine and tried to make sure that he did not run out of supplies. Whitford's worst fear was that she would die before her brother, and he would have no one to care for him. Mr. Cleo Griffin was moved to a nursing home in Dover. Of all residents of the land between the rivers, one man who never said a word against TVA was able to defeat their attempts to remove him from his home.

The other people moved away and found new homes throughout the country, but many of them did not forget their birthplace. Each year a reunion is held by those people who feel that it is necessary to come back to the land that was settled by their ancestors. But each year, the number of people who come to the reunions grows smaller. As the older people die, their children and grandchildren do not feel the same impulses to keep in touch with their friends and former neighbors. They do not have the feel for the land and the old ways are slowly being forgotten. With each death, the memories of the good times and the bad times in the land

---

[214]Interview with Mrs. Whitford in 1988.

248

between the rivers are diminishing. In a few years, none of the former residents will be alive to tell the stories of adventure and struggle that were the fabric of their culture in the land between the rivers.

CHAPTER XII

TRIUMPH OF LBL

During the early months of 1969, the last stage of purchasing the land was completed. TVA was now in the position to develop the area into a unique facility. A herd of nineteen buffalo, once plentiful in the area, was introduced in a 200 acre compound. The fenced pasture, near the former site of Model, Tennessee was planned to enable visitors to watch the animals from sites along the road. Nineteen buffalo came from the Theodore Roosevelt National Memorial Park near Medora, North Dakota. The herd has thrived, and animal management supervisors have recently allowed the slaughter of certain animals to provide food for visitors to the Land Between The Lakes.[1]

As early as 1969, TVA was questioned about its contributions to economic development in the region. According to the agency's own objectives, the project had been designed to demonstrate how an area with limited natural resources for conventional forms of economic use could stimulate economic growth. TVA had touted public recreation as the answer. The policy was to encourage private enterprises to invest in motels, resorts, restaurants, and other commercial facilities on the opposite shores of both lakes and along approach highways leading to the area. Where were the signs of economic development? They had not appeared in 1969 and the people wanted to know why.

Once TVA came under scrutiny, other questions were asked about how the money provided in 1964 by the Public Works Appropriation Act had been spent. Four million dollars had been allocated to TVA to begin development of the camping and reforestation. TVA had done some work at Rushing Creek and opened camp sites. Tree seedlings had been planted, but visitors were not aware of the locations because of the vast area included in the development area.

New Alliance with the People

In 1979, TVA began an organized effort to inform the public of its activities. It was announced that the Golden Pond Visitor Center, located just off LBL's central highway--the Trace--near the main entrance on the Kentucky side, was serving as the primary information and orientation facility for visitors. To demonstrate the available facilities, the center would include: a domed multimedia theater and planetarium, an observatory, a library, and a gift shop featuring handmade local crafts and souvenirs. The Visitor Center was open throughout the year, except on certain holidays.

In the 1970s, people were encouraged to visit the Woodlands Nature Center, located in the Environmental Education Area, because it would serve as the natural resources interpretive center. The Center featured live animals and plant exhibits, a multimedia theater with programs available upon request, and a staff person available to lead activities. Daily activities varied with

---

[1]Sun-Democrat, July 9, 1969.

the seasons and featured demonstrations, field trips, and audiovisual presentations about plants, wildlife, and resource management activities. The visitors were encouraged to use the trails around the center. They were able to obtain maps and brochures of the trails. Wildlife observation stations were available. Exhibits, including the bald and golden eagles, fallow and white-tailed deer, coyote, alligator snapping turtle, owls and hawks, and hummingbird-butterfly gardens, were shown. This type of publicity helped the public to understand what the workers at LBL were trying to do.

Publicity about the Youth Station created interest. The Station provided a year-around, resident outdoor education facility designed for use by school groups, kindergarten through university level, seeking educational opportunities in the wilderness area. Other groups which were not affiliated with schools were encouraged to make use of the facilities. Environmental study sites provided opportunities for activities such as map and compass study and sites for the study of geology, fossils, forests, aquatic habitat studies, and other activities. TVA hired and trained staff members to assist group leaders in planning and activities. The Camp was designed to accommodate approximately seventy-two persons. Six dormitories, each with ten beds in the main room and a more private teacher-counselor room with two beds, were built near a dining hall which served at least ninety people.[2]

People were encouraged to visit Hillman Ferry Campground which provided twelve informal non-fee camping areas for campers. These camps, located in the northern portion of LBL, were quickly becoming the largest family campground in the development. While camping or visiting, people were encouraged to visit the Silo Overlook. Visitors were able to survey the Barkley Lake shores and inlets from the wooden platform on top of an old concrete farm silo.[3]

The ever vigilant opponents of TVA had watched the development of the project and by 1970 were ready to interject another criticism. From 1964 to 1970, the number of visitors had increased annually from 12,000 in 1964 to 1,514,000 in 1970. TVA had based its figures on a random count of the number of visitors who drove through the area. In 1970, TVA spent $1,175,000 in operations and construction. Opponents of the project were declaring that the cost of the project was too much. If there were ten million people who wanted to use the area for recreation and education, as TVA had estimated the demand in 1964, where were they? People were not coming to the area and the detractors wanted to know the reasons why.[4]

In 1970, the appropriations for the project decreased to $2,574,000, a drop of close to a million dollars, and the development reflected the decrease. Plans for new projects were deferred. The concern was that there was not enough money available to maintain, continue, or to complete the projects already in operation. Officials agreed that the only expansion would be in providing more camping sites, because they were relatively inexpensive to construct.

In 1971, the appropriations increased to $3,187,000, a minimum budget, and officials realized that only a few of the planned projects could be completed. One of the first

---

[2]The Tennessean, Nashville, Tennessee, August 6, 1969.

[3]Ibid.

[4]Ibid., August 30, 1970; Courier Journal, Louisville, Kentucky July 21, 1967.

undertakings was the completion of additions to the Piney Campgrounds. The first priority, for new construction, was the Long Creek Trail National Recreation, some two-tenths of a mile long, located in the Environmental Education Area. The Trail was designed especially for the physically handicapped. A paved trail, to serve those people using wheelchairs, was constructed.[5]

TVA Encounters Significant Problems

By this time in 1971, President Richard Nixon's policies of decentralizing the federal government through his New Federalism program in which power, funds, and responsibility would flow from the central government to state and local governments caused concern among the proponents of TVA. With its myriad programs, TVA would surely be affected. Nixon had proposed revenue-sharing-- where federal money was turned over in block grants to state and local governments. Instead of earmarking the funds for specific purposes, localities could decide which problems needed attention and how best to attack them.[6]

Coinciding with Nixon's plans was a worsening economy. In 1970 the nation had entered its first recession in a decade. Traditionally, a recession brought a decrease in demand for goods and a rise in unemployment. Manufacturers then cut wages and prices in order to preserve profit margins and encourage demand for goods. In the recession of 1970, while unemployment rose as expected, wage and prices were also rising in an inflationary spiral.[7] Nixon responded by cutting federal spending. He anticipated that inflation would slow down even if unemployment continued to rise. By December, 1970, unemployment had risen and so had inflation. Interest rates were at their highest point in a century, and Nixon decided that unemployment posed a greater threat than inflation. He recommended a deficit budget designed to stimulate the growth of jobs.[8]

In 1971, the President announced a surprising piece of news. In order to provide short-term relief for the economy, wages and prices would be frozen for ninety days. The dollar was devalued in order to reverse the foreign trade deficit. Cheaper dollars raised the price of imports and made American exports more competitive in foreign markets. By the fall of 1972, a short economic boom followed the deflation of the dollar. Spending for LBL reflected the change in the economy, and increased slightly. The appropriations, a total of $3,719,000, were somewhat larger than the allocation for the previous year, but the cost of operations had increased as well.[9]

With the limited funding in 1972, TVA was able to complete the U. S. Highway 68

---

[5]Tennessee Valley Authority Annual Report, July 1971, Knoxville, Tennessee, 12.

[6]Courier Journal, Louisville, Kentucky, May 18, 1972.

[7]Observations about the state of the economy were in all the newspapers during the period.

[8]Courier Journal, December 9, 1970.

[9]TVA Annual Report, 1972, 19.

overpass and Gatehouse Road connecting it to The Trace, and the Kentucky Lake Drive. The Drive, beginning near the northern entrance, followed the shoreline of Kentucky Lake for approximately two miles and looped back to The Trace just north of the North Welcome Station.[10]

At this time, the Turkey Bay Off-Road Vehicle area was readied for use by the public. The area, including 2,350 acres located near the central entrance, was planned to include campsites and unloading ramps. Operator's licenses would not be required when vehicles were used within the area, but all riders had to wear safety helmets. Enough money was available to complete an archery range. Both of these attractions proved to be popular sites.[11]

The outlook was bleak when it was learned that the appropriations for 1973 amounted to only $3,745,000. The yearly operations and maintenance costs had increased to $1,897.000; more threatening, however, was the realization that, despite all the expectations, visitors were not coming to the area. Creative approaches to draw visitors were uppermost in the minds of the directors. Yet, because of severely limited funds, the staff was unable to increase the offerings. New building construction was delayed, and plans were drafted to try to offer new areas of recreation which did not include buildings or large amounts of money spent to construct the site. The plans were to design areas which would pay their own costs through user fees.[12]

The Wranglers camp was an example of the type of facility which could be provided with minimal funds. Capitalising on the national interest in horseback riding, the Wranglers Camp was opened. Until that time, horses were not allowed on any of the hiking trails because of sanitation and maintenance problems. Hundreds of requests had been made by equestrians for riding trails. The Camp, located in the central portion of LBL, was readily accessible, and a riding trail, approximately twenty-three miles long, was provided. Three large barns and a building providing toilets and showers were constructed for use by the riders. The schedule allowed public use of the buildings and trails from March through October. One of the requirements was that all horses brought to the camp had to meet all the health requirements stipulated by the state of Kentucky, including the Coggins test. Health certificates showing that horses met these requirements had to be exhibited before horses were allowed in the area. Sick riders might enter the Camp, but unhealthy horses were not admitted. Horseback riding was once again a favorite recreational activity, and whole families dressed in their western gear and came to the site. [13]

The Fort Henry Trail System, a series of loops that range in length from two and nine-tenths miles to twenty-six miles, was designed to follow the route taken by General Grant's army during the Civil War. As noted earlier, Grant's army moved over the rough countryside from Fort Henry, located on the Tennessee River, to Fort Donelson on the Cumberland River. The trail could not begin at the site of Fort Henry because the Fort's earthenworks were now under

---

[10]Ibid.,22.

[11]Ibid.

[12]The Tennessee Valley Progress Report for the Land Between The Lakes, 1973, 24.

[13]The Tennessee Valley Progress Report for the Land Between The Lakes, 1974.

flood waters of Kentucky Lake. [14]

The Trail of These Hills, a loop of one and five-tenths miles, was completed in 1973, featuring the resource management techniques. The hikers are able to view the techniques and hear presentations on ways to improve the forest and the wildlife populations. People are instructed on the successful management of forests, allowing a program of selective cutting. Visitors were able to see the Missouri wild turkey which had been stocked earlier. [15]

In 1973 inflation was soaring and industries struggled against mounting competition from manufacturers in Europe and the Pacific rim (Japan, South Korea, Taiwan, Hong Kong, Singapore, and the Philippines). American-based multinational corporations began to establish their manufacturing centers overseas to take advantage of lower costs and cheap labor. American workers either lost their jobs or faced reduced hours. Less money could be used by families for recreation, especially if it meant that they had to travel long distances to reach the recreation site. And when it seemed matters could hardly become worse for recreation facilities, along came the Yom Kippur War and the OPEC oil boycott. On October 6, 1973, Syria and Egypt launched a devastating surprise attack against Israel. The Soviet Union airlifted supplies to the Arabs; the United States countered by resupplying its Israeli allies while pressing the two sides to accept a cease fire. The seven Arab members of OPEC backed Egypt and Syria and imposed a boycott of oil sales to countries seen as friendly to Israel. Since the 1920s the major multinational oil companies, known as the Seven Sisters (Exxon, Shell, Gulf, Mobil, British Petroleum, Socal, and Texaco) had dominated world marketing. Never before had the OPEC nations controlled the distribution of their oil, but the boycott from October 1973 until March 1974 severely affected most of those nations who relied upon the Middle East for oil. [16]

At this time, the United States recognized its dependency on Middle Eastern oil and realized that it was heading toward an acute energy shortage. The price of petroleum-based plastics soared. In some places motorists hoping to buy a few gallons of gasoline waited for hours in lines, miles long. Many tourists could not come to LBL because they could not find gasoline and the necessary funds to make the trip. [17]

With the slightly higher appropriation of $4,617,000 in 1974, the LBL staff was able to open the Brandon Spring Group Camp, which had been planned as early as 1970 but delayed because of funding. After the completion of the primary buildings, reservations could be made anytime by youth and adult groups interested in conducting programs in the quiet and beautiful surroundings of a wilderness area. By providing more programs and dormitory space, the camp could accommodate the interest in the wilderness program. [18] Officials of LBL sent invitations to individuals and community groups encouraging them to take advantage of the large activity building which provided facilities for large assemblies and small meetings. The Camp included

---

[14] Ibid.

[15] Ibid.

[16] Newspaper accounts of this situation are abundant.

[17] See annual reports by TVA for 1972, 1973, 1974.

[18] TVA, Annual Report 1974, 22.

a swimming pool, hiking trails, a large multipurpose play court, archery targets, campfire circle, play fields and amphitheater. Canoes, sailboats, and rowboats were available at a nominal cost. A user fee of eighteen dollars for youths and twenty-three dollars for adults was levied. An extra fee of two dollars was charged for linens. For those people who wanted to attend functions but who did not wish to stay in the dormitory, meals were available in the dining room. Breakfast and luncheon food rates were approximately three dollars and dinner was four dollars per person.[19]

In the same year, the Boy Scouts of America High Adventure Area opened near Shaw Branch. The Boy Scout Area was available for any boy scout function, and the news of the availability of the area was sent to the news agencies throughout the region. In accordance with the goal to provide more camping facilities, Hillman Ferry Campground was completed, adding thirty-six additional camping sites. The installation of a fishing pier at the Devil's Elbow site made that attraction even more appealing. At the same time, the Hillman Heritage Trail opened to visitors.[20]

The management of LBL had anticipated the need to cut trees in its forest management program. The site for the first long-term timber contract, was granted to the Averitt Lumber Company of Clarksville, Tennessee. The Company was awarded a five-year contract to harvest designated trees. Their renewable contract would be honored if the company followed all the rules which had been agreed upon by the forest management team. After designated trees were cut, trouble arose when the lumber company began to cut the trees and transport them out of the area. Citizens and visitors who witnessed the cutting were distraught and angry. The massive logs, filling the beds of the trucks and often extending several feet behind the vehicles, were an imposing sight. Viewers considered the trees as old and valuable. Rumors spread that the management of LBL, breaking the contract to preserve the forest areas, had allowed lumber companies to cut any and all the trees in the area. The concept of the preservation had apparently been violated, and indignant voices were raised in protest. Concerned citizens publicly denounced the management of LBL and accused them of deliberately and clandestinely breaking the regulations of the preservatiom agreement. The people seemed to feel that if the officials were not breaking laws, they were certainly guilty of dishonoring the concept of preservation.[21]

The forest management team realized that they had failed in their campaign to inform the public about their planned-cutting program. They tried to remedy the problem by responding to the accusations by issuing public statements including a detailed explanation of the scientific reasons for cutting some of the timber. They tried to inform the public that they were involved in a plan of forest management. The plan was to let nature reforest the area. The controversy continued for months, and some people were never convinced that the forest management program was an appropriate item in the preservation program. The controversy was indicative of the growing public awareness about the environment, and the constant suspicions toward

[19]The Tennessee Valley Authority Progress Report, 1975.

[20]Ibid.

[21]Sun-Democrat, August 9, 1974.

TVA.[22]

A New Era

An era in the history of LBL ended when Robert M. Howes, Director of LBL, retired in 1974. For some time, the Directors of TVA had been deliberating over how to reorganize LBL, but they were unable to agree on where the project should be located in the TVA organization. The LBL project did not coalesce completely with any of the departments or agencies. At the time of Howes' retirement, a decision to relocate the project resulted in a constant shifting from one division to another. When the Directors could not decide, their indecisiveness caused instability within the LBL program and resulted in rumors that the management goals of the project were being abandoned. Employees were distraught because they felt their jobs were endangered, and morale suffered more each time the project was moved.[23] The general attitude of the region was that the whole concept of a recreational program was in jeopardy, but the most disturbing rumor was that once again TVA intended to sell the project to private developers.[24]

People in Tennessee and Kentucky were quick to speculate that the program would not survive the economic woes besetting the country at the time. They felt sure that eventually the Tennessee Valley Authority would grow weary of the difficulties inherent in the combined program of preserving the wilderness and attracting tourists. If TVA divorced itself from the program, it was felt that the area would be changed to a recreational playground, and tourist attractions would be built to bring in enough money to make it a financially viable area. Since TVA had promised to protect the area from private developers, the people waited to see what would happen.[25]

The first move TVA made was to merge the LBL with the Division of Forestry, Fisheries, and Wildlife under the direction of Dr. Thomas H. Ripley. Dr. Frank Holland was selected as the Manager of LBL.[26] National attention was paid to the move because TVA was in a period of atomic energy expansion. The response was generally enthusiastic because people were interested in new, cheaper sources of energy. The only complication was the large expenditures involved in the program.[27]

Some people feared that as TVA spent more money on the construction of nuclear power plants, the available resources directed toward LBL projects would be less. The new energy

---

[22]Courier Journal, Louisville, Kentucky, August 20, 1974.

[23]Progress Report, 1975.

[24]Sun-Democrat, Paducah, Kentucky, August 10, 1974.

[25]Ibid.

[26]Progress Report, 1975.

[27]Items appeared in the newspapers throughout 1974.

expenditures and the difficult economic times were a serious complication. It was decided that each offering within the project might have to pay its own way. Each program had to become cost effective at the very time that it was trying to broaden its appeal to the public by adding as many new attractions as possible.

The TVA officials were troubled when they learned that the number of visitors had declined in 1974, a decline from 2,054,000 in 1973 to approximately 1,908,000 in 1974. This decrease occurred at the most inopportune time. Congress, not especially receptive to appropriating funds for TVA energy development, was hostile to requests for additional money to replace revenue lost when the number of tourists declined in LBL. The Tennessee Valley Authority had a serious financial problem.[28]

Since its inception, the promoters of LBL had worked under the assumption that the project could entice many millions of potential visitors into the area. They had asserted, time and time again, that the real merit of the project was its ability to provide recreational facilities to millions of people in its service area. If people were not interested in visiting the area, the facility was not meeting one of the most critical justifications for its existence.

The TVA officials had to ascertain why the recreational area was not appealing to tourists. It was simple enough to see that the economic recession and rising oil prices were part of the problem. The increased cost of travel, however, was only part of the problem. People were unaware that the facility existed.

Why were tourists refusing to come to the area? When people were asked to comment, they responded that the estimated tens of millions of people who made up the visitor pool were not interested in the rustic camping facilities which were available in LBL.[29] The ramifications of this view are that there was something intrinsically wrong with the project. When congressional leaders expressed the same view, it was obvious that funding was in jeopardy.

People who had argued that tourists wanted to relax and play in places which included all the modern amenities said we told you so.[30] TVA had insisted that tourists wanted to return to the managed area. The problem seemed to be that protecting the area had caused the failure of the recreation program. The detractors argued that the whole concept of LBL had failed and it should be abandoned. People who followed a conservative political philosophy and those who were concerned with the ever increasing federal spending were vocal in their condemnation of the TVA and its LBL project.[31]

Supporters of TVA mustered their forces to inform the populace that many of the programs in LBL were flourishing. They presented statistics which showed that an ever increasing number of hunters were buying permits to hunt the Whitetail and Fallow deer and turkey gobblers in the area. Hunters using bows had increased from 6,682 in 1973 to 8,345 in 1974, and the season had been extended by only one day--39 days in 1973 to 40 days in 1974.

---

[28]The problem becomes visible with the Progress Report, 1975.

[29]Courier Journal, Louisville, Kentucky, October 9, 1975.

[30]See the argument against the wilderness recreation idea in 1963 and 1964.

[31]Courier Journal, October 19, 1974.

A total of 202 deer had been killed in 1973 and the harvest had increased to 289 in 1974. Deer hunters using guns in the Kentucky portion were limited to a six-day season and had killed 842 deer in 1973 and 1,172 in 1974. Even though nearly ten thousand applicants wanted to hunt in 1973, only 5,426 permits were issued. The hunting area was not sufficient to meet the demands. In the Tennessee portion, hunters were limited to a four-day hunting season using guns, and of the 4,134 applicants in 1973, only 2,000 permits were issued. These hunters were able to kill 275 deer. In 1974, all of the 6,754 applicants received permits and killed 1,237 deer. Since the deer and turkey populations were growing, the indications were that more hunters would be allowed into the area.[32]

Help from the Environmentalists

The environmentalists came to the assistance of TVA at this crucial time. By 1970 the environmental movement had incorporated elements of both the conservationists and preservationists in its program, referring to themselves as ecologists. Ecologists were eager to point to LBL as an example of the possible success of using a preserved wilderness area as means of educating the public about the necessity of protecting the environment while they used the bounties of nature for recreation. For years these groups had warned the world that it was reaching the limits of abuse that the environment could take. Searing clouds of acid smog hung over cities. People were warned that radioactive fallout from nuclear bomb tests was detrimental to the environment. More and more people took notice of the drastic changes in the ozone layer. As early as 1962, Rachel Carson had enumerated the environmental hazards of the pesticide, DDT, and state legislatures had passed restrictive laws.[33] Certainly, no one could ignore the Cuyahoga River running through Cleveland, Ohio since it had become a major fire hazard. Smog, fallout, dangerous pesticides, hazardous consumer goods, and polluted rivers were all by-products of industrial technology. Americans began to recognize that a deteriorating environment was the not-so-hidden cost of unbridled economic growth, and those areas which remained mostly unaffected, such as the Land Between The Lakes, should be protected.

The environmental movement in 1970 was a departure from both the traditional conservation associated with Theodore Roosevelt, Gifford Pinchot, and Harold Ickes and preservationists like John Muir and the Sierra Club. Conservationists had always stressed the idea of proper use of both renewable and nonrenewable resources as a way to ensure the nation's future growth. Preservationists had the Romantics' vision of man's spiritual link to nature. They sought largely to save unique wilderness areas such as Yellowstone, Yosemite, and the Grand Canyon. Most Americans would agree that the LBL facility should be protected from development and commercial exploitation.

The new environmental movement incorporated elements of both conservationists and preservationists into the field of ecology, the biological science that since the early twentieth century had been demonstrating the linkage and dependencies of life processes. Barry

---

[32]Ibid., September 29, 30, and October 1, 4, 1975.

[33]Rachel Carson, Silent Spring, (Boston: Houghton Mifflin, 1962).

258

Commoner in his book The Closing Circle, published in 1971, argued that modern society lived under the illusion that it could improve on nature. In doing so it imposed a terrible price on the environment. Industry profited in the short run, but in the long run the environment might be bankrupt. An ecologically responsible society much transform its cultural values.[34]

Environmentalists organized to change society. They brought a lawsuit to block the plan of a consortium of oil companies to build a pipeline across Alaska. A coalition of environmental groups fought a proposed jet airport that threatened south Florida's water supply and the ecology of the Everglades National Park. Battles over the location of airports drew clear lines between the new ethic of environmental restraint and traditional champions of economic growth. The Nixon administration responded to the call for more stringent environmental regulations and supported the National Environmental Policy Act. Nixon also established the Environmental Protection Agency to enforce the law.[35]

During this period, the impact of the ecological view forced a more lenient attitude about the money that was needed to protect the LBL from obliteration. The threats of reduction of funds lessened and in public, at least, the acceptable party line was to praise the efforts to preserve the wilderness.[36]

Construction

From 1975 to 1979, several projects were completed including the Ginger Ridge Back-Country Camp, Administrative Office at Golden Pond, a Maintenance Complex, Camp Energy, and the Homeplace. Money from Title X funding had helped to complete some of these projects.[37]

At this time, a major reorganization within TVA led to the formation of the Office of Natural Resources. The LBL project was moved from the Division of Forestry, Fisheries, and Wildlife Development to a division-level organization in the Office of Natural Resources. The Division of Forestry, Fisheries, and Wildlife Development was eliminated.[38]

Another sharp decline in the number of visitors to the project began in 1979 with approximately 100,000 fewer people coming to the area. A slow decline in visitors continued until 1984 when a small increase began, but the total number of people who visited the area from 1964 to 1989 reached a peak in 1979. From 1980 to 1983, the funding was slightly more

---

[34]Barry Commner, The Closing Circle, (New York: Knopf, 1971).

[35]The National Environmental Policy Act was passed in 1969. The First Earth Day and the Environmental Protection Agency were created in 1970.

[36]Budget problems for the Tennessee Valley Authority for the Land Between The Lakes eased somewhat. See Annual Progress Reports for TVA, 1976-1979. In 1975 the total appropriation for LBL was $4,151,000; for 1976, $4,229,000; 1977, $5,626,000; 1978, $10,877,000, and in 1979, $7,692,000.

[37]Ibid.

[38]Ibid.

259

than seven million dollars each year. During 1980s, most of the money was needed to maintain the existing facilities. Fishing piers were installed in Lake Barkley at Cooked Creek and Neville Bay. An energy efficient underground building was completed at the Homeplace. Some of the programs suffered; for example, the Scouts of America closed their High Adventure Base and the Empire Farm was closed to the public.[39]

Unfavorable Publicity for TVA

In the meantime other forces were gathering which would combine with old problems to affect TVA. At first the weather and the continuing need for foreign oil resulted in a call from President Carter for voluntary conservation. Carter urged conservation as the cheapest and most environmentally desirable way to discourage dependency on foreign oil. The American way, however, was to produce more, not live with less. The oil industry insisted that deregulation of energy prices would stimulate sufficient production to meet the needs of the country. In 1978 the revolution against the Shah of Iran allowed OPEC prices to rise. Again, voluntary efforts to handle the problem were encouraged. People were asked to lower thermostats and curtail the use of the automobile. The drivers who were forced to use their cars were asked to observe the 55 mile per hour speed limit.

A stuck valve at the Three Mile Island nuclear power plant in Pennsylvania resulted in immediate and acute responses from the general public. People had flocked to see antinuclear activist Jane Fonda in the movie "China Syndrome," a tale of a faulty construction resulting in a meltdown of the core of a nuclear power plant. Then on March 28, 1979, the Three Mile Island plant released a cloud of radioactive gas into the atmosphere. It took nearly two weeks before the reactor was shut down. A hundred thousand nearby residents fled their homes. For twenty years public utilities and the Tennessee Valley Authority had promoted nuclear power as the answer to future energy needs. Nuclear plants were constructed before the technology to provide safeguards and solutions on how to handle nuclear waste had been developed. A backlash against the use of nuclear energy swept the nation. The people turned on TVA nuclear programs with a vengeance. Now, TVA faced the problem of deciding whether or not to continue the program of building nuclear power plants.[40]

Events in 1980 and 1981 reflected the old and new criticism of TVA. Solutions to the old problems of decreased funding and declining tourism had not been found. It was difficult to implement plans to attract more visitors to the area with very little money and no assurance that potential visitors would have the resources to visit the area. When The National Science Foundation and Institute of Ecology designated LBL and Murray State University's Hancock Biological Station as an Experimental Ecological Reserve composite site, leaders were hopeful that this added attention would result in more visitors.[41] At the same time, changes were made

---

[39]See Progress Reports from 1969 to 1989.

[40]Courier Journal, March 29, 1979. See any major newspapers for detailed coverage of the events.

[41]Progress Reports, 1980-1985.

in the management of the project. Dr. Frank R. Holland transferred to Knoxville to serve as Assistant General Manager for TVA. Elizabeth E. Thach was named Manager of LBL, and the facility was placed under the Division of Land and Forest Resources in the Office of Natural Resources, under the direction of John R. Paulk.[42] A project to determine how to increase the public awareness of the attractions was initiated. One of the negative factors was the lack of publicity. People were not coming to the area because they were not aware that it existed. Plans were made to establish an outside support organization. The goals of the organization would be to raise private funds and to disseminate information to various media sources about the existing facilities.[43]

Ameliorations Begin in 1983

Public concern about the future of LBL resulted in pressure on Congress to increase funding to the project and financial problems lessened in 1983. To supplement the $7,361,000 appropriated by Congress, the Jobs Bill Program that had just been approved by Congress to relieve the national problem of unemployment, with total budget of $11,225,000, enabled LBL to employ workers to build roads and bridges, add new sites at Piney Campgrounds, improve water and sewerage systems, and add energy conservation features to existing facilities. Also funded by the Jobs Bill Program was the reconstruction of the Tennessee portion of the Trace.[44]

The Empire Farm reopened for public visitation in 1984. The otter restoration project was funded. Citizens organized The Land Between The Lakes Association, an independent, nonprofit foundation whose goal was to support the development of LBL projects and activities. At its first meeting, the Association announced programs to recruit as many members as possible and solicit donations and private gifts. In an attempt to solve the problem of too few LBL workers, the Association pledged to recruit volunteers to assist with the activities.[45]

Again, LBL was moved about in the TVA structure. The Directors wanted a reorganization within the Office of Natural Resources and Economic Development (ONRED). The reorganization led to the merging of the Division of Land and Forestry Resources with the Division of Economic and Community Development. LBL was removed from the Division of Land and Forestry Resources and made a separate organization within ONRED.[46] The reorganization did not change the structure at the facility, but once again many employees were concerned about their jobs and changes in policy that could result from the reorganization. For

---

[42]Ibid.

[43]No new construction was possible in 1982. When the dogtrot cabin at the Homeplace was destroyed by fire, a replacement cabin was obtained from the U.S. Fish and Wildlife Service. River otters in the TVA's barge exhibit at the World's Fair in Knoxville were moved to LBL.

[44]Ibid.

[45]Progress Report, 1984.

[46]Ibid.

261

some time, the mood was one of negative anticipation. At the time, the good news was that the budget for the year, including the Jobs Bill funding, increased to $16,646,000.[47]

Officials suggested that outside contractors should be allowed to run some of the components programs. Protests came from people who lived near the area. This time, the protests centered on the loss of jobs. Also, people expressed concern about the possibility of allowing contractors to perform more and more of the jobs. Workers were already concerned about job security, and businessmen in the area were concerned about the possible loss of revenue from the salaries of workers. It was thought that contractors would bring in outside workers and the inhabitants of the area would not be employed. The news media reported on the concerns of the people, and speculated that in the future TVA would repeal its promise not to lease land to developers.[48] Even a hint that the land would not remain in the hands of the government caused angry outbursts.

In 1984 TVA and the United States Department of Agriculture agreed on a four-year cooperative research project. For some time, ticks had plagued many parts of the United States. The project was to study the pests and generate an integrated system of tick management. Included in the project was a series of feasibility studies on techniques of host management, vegetative management, and acaracide applications. The studies at LBL would result in information about pest control in high-use areas. The goal was to determine the economic feasibility of instituting a control system usable in all recreational areas.[49]

In order to expand the wildlife programs, LBL entered into an agreement with Eagle Trust International, a private foundation for the propagation of rare and endangered or unique birds of prey. The site became the headquarters for the Eagle Trust. The bald eagle was already in the area and people were anxious to include the bird in the expansion of the Wildlife Restoration Center. In 1984, a bald eagle's nest was discovered in the southern portion of the area, which was especially important to the Wildlife Management team. An eagle hacked there in 1981 had returned with a mate to nest and had raised an eaglet. An earlier announcement of the program to protect the eagles was welcomed by the general public; then the announcement of the wildlife program and the ensuing publicity about the sighting of the eagle attracted national attention.[50] Tourists began to arrive at the information stations with requests about where they could go to see the eagles.

Another shift in sentiment toward support of wilderness preservation began to occur in 1984 and 1985. People seemed less hostile to the idea of spending tax money to maintain wilderness programs. They were even more concerned about approaches which would protect endangered species. Several magazine articles cited the success of the wilderness programs in LBL as an example to be followed by the federal and state government programs. The publicity was positive, and it came at a time when the TVA needed to strengthen its image in the minds

---

[47]Courier Journal, Louisville, Kentucky, July 10, 1985. Rushing Creek Campgrounds reopened.

[48]Sun-Democrat, Paducah, Kentucky, April 7, 1986.

[49]Sun-Democrat, Paducah, Kentucky, April 8, 1986.

[50]Ibid. The term hack (hacking or hacked) probably originated with the term used for a board on which a falcon's meat or food was placed. The term came to mean a nesting or resident site for birds.

of the taxpayers and Congress.[51]

The project felt the impact when Congress cut the funds for the Jobs Bill Act in 1985. The total budget for the facility fell to $8,503,000. In order to stay within the budget, cuts were made in the proposed construction projects. The major project, an observatory at the Golden Pond Visitor Center, was in danger of delay, until funds were donated to the project through the Land Between the Lakes Association. The Center received a telescope for the observatory from a private donor. Because no money was available, the eagle-rearing facilities at the Wildlife Restoration Center were in danger of possible cancellation. Again, interested volunteer laborers, working with donated materials, came to the assistance of the Center and were able to complete the project.[52]

For the first time in the history of the facility, the majority of people who lived in the surrounding areas came to the realization that they were next door to one of the most valuable projects that had ever been initiated. These people were ready to extend financial assistance and volunteer their time and labor.

From the 1970s until 1985, the project had made progress under a program which insisted that an annual visitation level of approximately five million people had to be maintained. That number of people was needed in order to demonstrate to the taxpayers that the basic assumption--people would visit for recreation--was correct. Five million visitors seemed to be the magic number which would justify TVA's sponsorship of the plan. Remember, the original argument was that the area would draw visitors mainly from urban areas. The basic theory was that these visitors needed to see and experience a wilderness area. In the early summer of 1984, the management team reported that they needed a new, well-defined strategy to draw visitors. The new strategy should be the foundation for planning, development, and operations of the reservation. It was obvious that at the present time the goal of five million people was not realistic. If the project were to continue and to receive the necessary support from the people and adequate funding, new goals must be established.[53] At that time, a team of TVA employees, chosen from throughout the entire agency, was formed to help establish the new strategic goals.[54]

The TVA policy of allowing contractors to bid for the right to operate certain attractions within their agencies had proven to be cost effective. Taking note that other agencies of TVA had increased revenue with the use of contractors, the management of LBL hoped that the same procedure would prove effective for their programs. The personal services contractors offered bids and began taking over the operations of both the Piney and the Hillman Ferry Campgrounds. Research data showed that it was more cost effective to let the bids to personal

---

[51]"Artificial Lakes," Recreation and Park Yearbook, (Washington, D.C.: National Recreation and Park Association, 1984) 17-29.

[52]Progress Report, 1985.

[53]Progress Report, 1984.

[54]Ibid. The budget for 1986 was $8,578,000. To increase revenues, fees were charged at most of the attractions.

services contractors than to use LBL employees.[55]

Planning for the Future

The operating budget was cut to $8,299,000 in 1987. The cut had a debilitating effect on all the programs. Users fees were extended, but new policies had to be developed. The decision was to close some of the recreational sites.[56] The Rushing Creek Campground closed to the public and the entrance buildings and other structures were sold at auction. Information was needed on how to operate the facility without increasing user fees. To answer some of the questions, TVA hired the Economics Research Associates of Fort Lauderdale, Florida to conduct a study and present proposals for the future development and operations of the Land Between The Lakes. The company, with the help of LBL employees, conducted a study and completed a proposal entitled "A Concept Plan For The Development Of TVA's Land Between The Lakes Through The Year 1999."[57] After extensive study of the proposal, the TVA Board accepted all the items in the proposal.

The Economics Research Associates gathered data and surveyed the operations of all existing facilities. They mapped the existing viable facilities and listed them as follows:

Campgrounds located at Hillman Ferry, Piney, Rushing Creek, Energy Lake, and Wranglers; Group camps located at Colson Hollow, Brandon Spring, and at the Youth Station.

Interpretive and Recreation Facilities located at the Homeplace, Empire Farm, Woodland Nature Center, Golden Pond Visitor Center, the Multimedia Theater, and the Buffalo Range.

Information Centers located at the Golden Pond Visitor Center, North Welcome Station and the South Welcome Station.

The Infrastructures were throughout the facility and included 420 miles of roads, 200 miles of hiking trails, 24 miles of horseback trails, 10 miles of bicycle trails, 2,350 acres for off-road vehicles, picnic areas, lake access roads and sites.

Other facilities included: Administrative Office Building, a Central Entrance Control Station, the Bear Creek Waterfowl Management Unit, a Maintenance Center, a Patrol Headquarters Station, a North Entrance Control Station, a South Entrance Control Station, a Wildlife Restoration Center, and North and South Shops.[58]

The consultant team, which studied the interpretive centers and attractions, concluded that visitors were seeing only one or two sites when they toured the area. A visitor who entered at Golden Pond and traveled to the Homeplace and then went to the Woodlands Nature Center had to travel a distance of 21.5 miles. Tourists did not wish to travel the required distances to visit more than one attraction. Time and travel costs were parts of the same problem.

---

[55]Ibid. A mild protest over the use of these contractors could be found in the newspapers.

[56]Ibid.

[57]Ibid.

[58]"A Feasibility Analysis of the Land Between The Lakes Concept Plan," (Knoxville, Tennessee: Economics Research Associates, 1988), 1.

The consultants found that the Golden Pond Visitor Center was serving as the main orientation facility. The Golden Pond facility was popular because it also had a multimedia theater, wildlife displays, and a moonshine still. The presentation of displays of 19th century crafts at the center pleased the tourists. The consultants estimated that 126,742 people came to the Golden Pond center in 1987. This number constituted approximately ten percent of the total visitors to the area. The consultant team concluded that many people came to the Visitor's Center and then left the park without visiting any other attraction. One serious problem was that those people who visited the Center often did not even know that other attractions were in the park.

After some study, the team decided that the Woodlands Nature Center located 11.4 miles from the Golden Pond Center was the second most attractive facility. The Nature Center included a wildlife refuge and an animal display. The animal display, including the bald eagle, owls, coyotes, and fallow and white tailed deer, was important because in 1987 approximately 41,987 people came to the center but this was only 3.6 percent of the total number of visitors. The Nature Center needed to attract more of the visitors who drove in the park.

The Homeplace located 10.1 miles from the Golden Pond Center was concerned with the life of the 1850s. Sixteen original log buildings comprised the farm, and one of the major attributes of the farm was that the employees dressed in period costumes to reenact the life of an average farm family in the 19th century. Approximately 75,534 visitors came to the Homeplace in 1987. This number was approximately 6.5 percent of the visitors to the area.[59]

The Great Western Iron Furnace was roughly 11 miles from the Golden Pond Visitor Center. The Furnace stack was over one hundred years old and in excellent condition. Some 69,511 people, or 6 percent of the total number of visitors, came to the Furnace in 1987.[60]

The Buffalo Range about 10 miles from the Golden Pond Visitor Center had fifty buffalo available for public viewing. Around 114,692 people came to see the buffalo in 1987. This figure was about 9 percent of the total visitors.[61]

The consultants reported that the last of the most popular attractions was the Empire Farm about 13 miles from the Center. The Farm was an active farm program with livestock, vegetable and herb gardens, a greenhouse, and beehives. Approximately 35,287 people visited the Farm in 1987, about 3 percent of the total visitors.[62]

The consultants agreed that each of the major facilities was accessible by paved roads. They all had paved parking lots, and most of the facilities served the needs of the handicapped. Picnic facilities were close to each of the attraction areas.[63]

The Concept Plan stated that in recent years the visitation had stabilized at less than two million people each year, and research indicated that certain population trends in the eastern

---

[59]Ibid., 4.

[60]Ibid., 6.

[61]Ibid., 8-9.

[62]Ibid., 10.

[63]Ibid., 14-18.

United States would affect the future of the facility The population within a 25-mile ring around the facility was declining. The population within the radius of 50 miles was static. Even though the population was extensive, little or no growth could be expected in the next decade. The consultants agreed that these population trends would affect LBL because these people were the resident market.[64]

Surveys indicated that only 9 percent of the visitors came in from outside the resident area of 50 miles and this included the remainder of Tennessee and Kentucky. Thirteen percent of the people came from the Midwestern states, and 9 percent of the total number came from the rest of the United States.[65] The research teams determined that the facility did not attract younger people. Approximately 79 percent of the visitors were between the ages of 26 and 65. Their proposal was to develop attractions to appeal to younger people and family groups who lived within a one-to-four-hour drive time to the park. The researchers agreed that these potential visitors must be made aware of the activities already offered and new and more varied enticements must be developed. Activities and displays which would keep the visitors in the park longer must be developed.[66]

For several years the management at LBL had been concentrating on the maintenance of the existing attractions and programs rather than expending time and money in the development of new plans and programs. The fees had been the only major change in the operations. The consultants considered the fees as a way of raising revenue, but they were concerned that fees would reduce the number of visitors to the attraction. A study was made and data collected to determine if admission fees caused a decline in the number of visitors. Results showed that the fees did not seem to affect the numbers of visitors to any of the attractions except the Homeplace. Even though the Homeplace is considered the most popular attraction, it drew only 7.5 percent of the visitors. It was possible that even though the attraction was very popular some tourists did not visit because they did not wish to pay the entrance fee. The researchers did not elaborate on why they concluded that fees did not affect the total number of visitors, yet concluded that the popularity of the Homeplace was affected by the admission cost.

People who came to take advantage of campsites had 866 sites to consider, but only 504 of these sites were electrified. In a comparison with the Tennessee and Kentucky state park systems, the researchers found that LBL offered more campsites, but the sites did not provide the same amenities as the state park camping sites. The fees charged at the state sites were approximately the same, but the occupancy rates were lower in LBL. Obviously, campers wanted more than they were receiving in the Land Between The Lakes. The researchers advised the management team that campers wanted food supplies, gasoline, and other goods, and those supplies should be located near the camping sites.

In 1988, the planners realized that the project was at a turning point in its history. The preliminary findings by the researchers and consultants included a series of position statements

---

[64]Ibid. Resident market was defined as those individuals who would likely support activities on a day trip basis. These people constituted abut 70 percent of the visitors.

[65]Ibid., 22-30.

[66]Ibid.

concerning the development of the project. The number one policy agreement was that the facility should never lose sight of the fact that it was established to serve people. The second consensus was that the stewardship of the land and its resources was imperative in the overall plan. The third position statement was that environmental education should remain an important objective. Lastly, the teams agreed that the local and regional economy should benefit from the future development of the project.[67]

The policy statements indicated a slight change in the emphasis from the original objectives. The earlier policy had emphasized the concern with maintaining the protected area in conjunction with provisions for recreation. Those two plans had been the foundation for the development. Within this scheme it was assumed that millions of people would want to visit the primitive, rustic area. The attitude was that the ascetic character of the land necessitated placing the attractions in isolated areas. The attractions were placed so that they did not detract from the atmosphere or the appearance of being in a managed environment. Now, it was recognized that cost of travel and the public's demand for convenient supplies were factors which had to be taken into consideration.

When the planners focused on the cost effectiveness of each of the attractions, they realized that thousands of tourists would have to visit each attraction if it paid its way. Originally, the attractions were not developed to charge fees and they were not expected to supply even a fraction of their cost for operation. Those attractions which were the most popular also demanded more employees. Funding was critical; therefore, the original plan had to be modified.

The major problems in development of the project were identified by the consultants. They explained that although the original plan designated the project as a multiple land-use park, the typical visitor did not have a thorough understanding of what the park had to offer. In other words, the park had an identity problem, and that problem had to be overcome before growth could occur. They found that the identity crisis was linked to the size of the park and the many miles between attractions. The survey indicated that the facility was so decentralized that the visitors did not desire to take advantage of all the attractions. As a matter of fact, the visitors probably did not know what they were missing when they drove through the park. The researchers theorized that since the park suffered because of its size and decentralization, a concerted effort should be made to increase the visitor's length of stay. They wanted to make an effort to decrease the number of visitors who left the park prematurely as well as influence other visitors to enter the park. They suggested that measures should be devised to encourage visitors to return to the area. The weakest point in the efforts to draw people to the facility was that visitors did not have their demands met. Therefore, their recommendation was to expand the visitor-related services. They suggested that food and beverage services should be provided for the visitors. They recommended that food and drink be dispensed from a central location. If central locations were not feasible, the services should be provided wherever possible. Convenience groceries, baits, tackle, and other supplies were mentioned by the visitors when they were asked what they needed when they visited the area. The consultants urged that these provisions be made available at all the campgrounds. The consultants convincingly argued that

---

[67]Ibid., 27-30.

a service station should be located along the Trace.[68]

The interpretive centers were failing to accomplish their purposes, which were to educate and entertain the visitors. The centers were not drawing the young visitors even though an organized school program had been developed. The researchers felt that the centers lacked market attractiveness because they were too passive and did not have strong entertainment value. They suggested that explicit plans should be made to present programs which would inform as well and entertain all the visitors.[69]

Since it was agreed that the project had a serious identity problem and the facility centers were not attracting the visitors, the researchers suggested that the park capitalize on its two major assets--history and water. They suggested that the centers should develop their programs around the rich historical background of the area and include the visitor in the learning exercises. This particular proposal presented the management of the Land Between The Lakes with a profusion of possible events. The major problem would be the people who planned the events. They must know the detailed history of the region as well as understand the unique culture of the region. Most importantly, they must have the capabilities to develop programs which would challenge the visitors to participate in the exercises. The consultants agreed that the historical uniqueness of the area set it apart from other large public recreation and resource management areas in the world.

From 1986 to 1988, the administrators began their own study of the visitors to the area. They used surveys to ascertain what the visitors wanted and how they viewed the attractions in the park. Their findings agreed with the data collected by the consultants. The visitors wanted more services and activities. Several types of surveys, including the Public Area Recreation Visitor Survey, were used to determine what the visitors were thinking. Approximately 1,000 groups were interviewed and their responses were recorded. Studies by Central Michigan University and Southern Illinois University were conducted. The Land Between The Lakes Association conducted assessments on services desired by campers and Association members. TVA workers analyzed its internal records and initiated additional market surveys. The information gathered from these sources was given to the consultants.[70]

While the consultants were concluding their study of the project, TVA officials were concerned about resource management and educational fields. Consultants sent letters and conducted interviews to determine the professional needs of the facility. Six federal and fifteen state agencies were contacted regarding probable impacts of future developments in the area. TVA officials organized a panel of seventeen recreation experts from ten states to meet and make projections of changes in visitation. The members of the panel were selected on the basis of their knowledge about recreation and the resource management of public lands, including federal and state agency personnel and individuals from universities and professional organizations. The panel was concerned with three major questions. Specifically they were asked to predict changes in visitation that could be expected from the attractions, along with the

[68]Ibid.

[69]Ibid.

[70]Progress Reports, 1988 and 1989.

preliminary proposal which had been provided by the consultants. The panel predicted that the proposed increase in the campground services would result in a growth in the number of campers from between 8,000 to 26,000 people. They predicted an increase in the number of days the visitors would spend in the camp.[71]

In order to determine regional interests, thirteen community meetings and five general-public meetings were held during the period from January through April of 1987. Approximately 266 people participated in the public meetings. An attempt was made to determine the reaction of the people toward any possible changes in policy which might affect LBL. All the information was gathered and examined, and a common perception emerged from all the responses. They agreed that the project was and must remain a unique national treasure, and TVA should maintain its commitment to the original mission with emphasis on ensuring the natural character of the area for future generations to enjoy. The people were not in favor of any drastic changes in the operations of the project.[72]

A secondary theme which emerged from the information was that management should provide additional basic services for the visitors. The service could range from upgraded trails and campsites to expanded recreation and education facilities. They agreed that camp stores and visitor attractions related to the area were permissible. The regional surveys indicated that many of the people who lived near LBL were not in total agreement with all of the proposed expansion in the area. They agreed that the visitors were especially interested in conveniences which included basic groceries, first aid items, and camping supplies.

Some people were interested in alternative camp-style lodging. Other people wanted access to snacks, supplies, and improved washroom facilities. Professionals were interested in expanding the program capabilities for educational studies. A smaller number of people recommended the installation of full-service automotive centers, marinas, hotels and other facilities. The problem of convenience versus preservation of the wilderness was inherent in the establishment of goals. Some visitors were not anxious to camp in the area because of the so-called primitive accommodations. Because they wanted modern facilities, usually they visited the area for a day and then went to other recreational areas. Several thousand visitors came through and tried to view the area from their cars. Of course these people were unable to understand the concerns with protecting the undeveloped areas. One of their problems was that they were often unable to find suitable hotels or motels just outside the facility. They were frustrated when they had to drive thirty to forty miles to find accommodations, and often left the area after a short drive. Other visitors complained that there were not enough signs along the highways or on the Interstate which directed them to sites. A few visitors mentioned that they were unable to find maps or information about the area until they had entered the project.[73]

Overall, the greater response from the surveys indicated that the people were in favor of moderate development of services, and most of those people surveyed suggested that LBL should

---

[71]Ibid.

[72]Progress Report, 1987. Courier Journal, Louisville, Kentucky, June 22, 1987, July 29, 1987, August 27, 1987, November 3, 1987, December 30, 1987.

[73]Ibid.

be advertised throughout the country. People needed to be informed of the attractions and services which were already available in the area. The consensus was that publicity would increase the number of visitors.

After the study and revision of plans, TVA determined its course of action. The agency would remain totally committed to maintaining the natural character of the area. Resource conservation would ensure a quality outdoor recreation and environmental education area for future generations to enjoy. Subject to the availability of funding, the project would continue to provide additional services to its visitors. Some of the services would be provided by TVA employees, others by nonprofit organizations. Also, some of the services could be provided by private concessionaires. This plan would depend on who could provide the service most effectively and efficiently.[74]

A major factor to be considered in developing and evaluating proposed co-operative undertakings was the type of organization which would be considered. First consideration would be extended to private, public, nonprofit, small, or economically disadvantaged businesses in determining the suitable organization to provide the service. Even though TVA indicated that those businesses which would be allowed to provide services would be screened and strictly regulated, public opinion in the area was against allowing any businesses to operate in the facility. The people were quick to point out that the original owners of the land had wanted to provide the same services that TVA was now ready to allow others to perform. These people demanded that TVA adhere to its original plan and keep all business out of the area. Also, they argued, services which tourists needed should be provided by businesses in the fringe areas around the project. In fact, some argued that TVA supported businesses would be in direct competition with area businesses.[75]

TVA officials proposed that because its first obligation was to protect and maintain the area for the future as well as to support consummate use at all times, they had decided that services would be clustered in locations readily available to those groups which required them. The services would be limited to areas which had already been developed and new attractions added to the facility. A system of zoning would be developed for the service areas and in each zone the goods would be priced so that they would be compatible with the general prevailing prices in the immediate region. The plans, including the developmental proposal, would extend campground services, the day-use facilities, and other attractions.[76]

The Campground services would require work and planning to make them more attractive to visitors. Added sales, rental, and activity areas would attract more people to the sites. It was decided that the services would be for registered campers only and would not be made available to the public at large. The first stage of the plan would include the campgrounds at Hillman Ferry, Piney, Rushing Creek, Energy Lake, Wranglers, and the Turkey Bay area. As other sites were developed, the services would be provided as quickly as possible. The items for sale would vary, but the first stage of the plan would allow for the sale of ice, firewood, snack items,

---

[74]Progress Report, 1988.

[75]Ibid.

[76]Ibid.

newspapers, first aid supplies, and live bait. Snack items would include food and beverages from machines or over the counter items. It was decided that gasoline would not be sold. Rental items would include camping equipment. Tents, shelters, sleeping bags and hammocks would be made available and other items could be added to this list if the need arose. Recreation rentals could include bicycles and sporting equipment. Motorized boats and boat docking facilities could also be rented. The plan would specifically exclude all gas-powered boats. Individuals could rent washers and dryers from the service areas.[77]

In the activity areas in some of the camping sites, new facilities would include swimming pools and additional court games. Programming would be expanded to include more activities such as hayrides, cookouts, and enactment of historical events. Services at the existing day-use centers, which included the interpretive facilities and welcome stations, would be expanded. The facilities at the Woodlands Nature Center, Empire Farm, The Homeplace, the Golden Pond Visitor Center, North Welcome Station, and the South Welcome Station would be the first sites affected by the plan. At these facilities, items for sale would include promotional material, conveniences, and educational items. Promotional material would include logo items, regional crafts, and memorabilia. Conveniences would include items related to the enjoyment of the Land Between The Lakes. These items would include film, first aid supplies, and writing materials. Included in the educational items would be items related to the particular facility. For example bird seed and bird feeders could be sold at the Woodlands Nature Center. Rental equipment at the day-use sites would be related to the programming at the facility. Binoculars, cameras, tape recorders could be rented to individuals who visited the different sites. Snack food machines and snack counters would be placed within the existing facility.[78]

In making plans for any new attraction which could be added, it was decided that all new attractions would be zoned into very small areas. Intensive development including construction would occupy no more than a total of 500 of the 170,000 acres. Passive development which was defined as areas such as wildlife parks would include a total commitment of no more than 3,400 acres.[79] Except for group education facilities and alternative camping options which included rental tents and camping shelters, housing would be excluded. Hotels, motels, full service marinas, and resorts would be specifically excluded from the entire area. Food service operations would be added as a part of a main attraction already in existence in the area. The members of the group who wrote the Concept Plan asked for information from LBL employees and visitors about their reactions to the projections for the most popular facilities in the area. They were asked to submit plans for replacement and suggestions of how to supplement the existing facility. After all the ideas were discussed, the Concept Plan included four sites that would serve as models for future development. Cited as number one was the Homeplace because it was already the most popular facility. Its location adjacent to the remains of the Great Western Furnace and the Buffalo Range would allow ready development. It was suggested that a historic park was a logical extension of the facility and an enhanced historical theme was

---

[77]Ibid.

[78]Ibid.

[79]Ibid., Progress Report, 1989.

inherent in the site. The park might include a reconstruction of the Great Western Iron Furnace operation as it existed in 1850 and a Civil War interpretive facility could be added. Features of the moonshine era could be included in the presentation. A riverfront park, offering period rides in wagons and boats, craft shops, riverboat landing facilities, interpretive displays, and basic food service could be included in the facility.[80]

It was suggested that an assembly and activities complex be developed. The facility would be directed toward family and large-group recreation and would combine waterfront activities with new attractions. The foundation plan would include a large, quality beach which would be attractive to groups in the summer months. A day-use area would also include playing fields, playgrounds, concessions for refreshments, and recreation equipment rental. The locale would also serve as a meeting or picnic area for families, churches, and large group outings. The complex would include a large covered pavilion and an open-air amphitheater for major events such as arts and crafts festivals, water related competitions, and equipment shows.[81]

All the people who made suggestions for the development expressed strong interest in activities which included observation of wildlife. The live animal exhibits at the Woodlands Nature Center and the Buffalo Range had always been very popular sites and the people suggested that they should be maintained and enlarged. Because LBL had become a leader in restoration programs for waterfowl, mammals, and reptiles an Ecopark would conform to the guidelines. The Ecopark could build upon the Woodlands Nature Center programs, as well as the Wildlife Restoration Center. The Ecopark could include a botanical garden and a natural zoo in which visitors would have an excellent chance of seeing native animals in their natural habitat. Activity areas could be designed for photography, art, fishing, and other visitor interests.

The last significant proposal was a plan which would include an expansion of program capabilities and educational facilities. The general public could understand the regional resources and the historical development of the Tennessee River Valley area. Because the region has a rich and largely untapped local history, the region would provide opportunities for research and writing. The current resources management and education issues under study could be used by the general public as an information guide. The area could become a center for people at all age levels who could learn by becoming involved in participatory exhibits and demonstrations which would provide actual experience in conservation of natural resources, agricultural procedures, and energy management. One of the achievements would be that the participants could understand that all the subjects are interrelated. The project could include an adult education complex with primary emphasis placed on information and technology which might transfer to private industry and resource management agencies and institutions.[82]

A follow-up study was conducted by TVA when specialists from seven federal and seventeen state agencies were contacted for additional information. These people were interviewed by telephone and asked to comment on the effects of campground and facility

---

[80]Ibid.

[81]Ibid.

[82]Ibid.

amenities on the levels of use and the impacts on the local economics. TVA was trying to determine the effect of its programs on communities adjacent to the facility.[83] More than thirty-five people with extensive experience in the development of recreational activities commented on the proposed development, and none of these experts viewed any of the proposals in the new Concept Plan as negative. When they were requested to search the Concept Plan to determine if it could have a negative influence on the growth of business in the area, none saw any possible impediment to business. In each case studied, improvements in public conveniences were perceived as an enhancement of possible economic growth because of the increased number of tourists who would travel through the region.[84]

After deliberation, TVA officials concluded that since the natural resources, including the forest, wildlife, waters, and other resources, are the substructure upon which outdoor recreation, environmental education, and demonstration activities depend, visitors' needs would not be allowed to impair the natural resources of the area. TVA maintained its commitment to resource stewardship. The agency stated that it would only take measures which would both preserve and enhance full resource utilization for the present. Thus, the agency ensured the availability and quality of the natural resources for the future.[85]

The Concept Plan projected that the Land Between The Lakes could accommodate up to five million visits annually with minimal impact on the resources. In 1987, approximately 80 percent of all activity occurred on about 10 percent of the land base. Visitors came to the camp grounds, lake access areas, interpretive facilities, and roadways. That ratio was expected to remain about the same, with 80 percent of new use occurring at existing and planned facilities. It was thought that physical site improvements, such as paved parking lots and sidewalks, would eliminate many potential dangerous impacts because of increased use.[86]

The study concluded that the existing facilities could adequately accommodate the expected increased use of each site. TVA could monitor and change the visitation target if necessary. TVA also assured the public that under no circumstances would visitation be permitted to rise above the ability of the resource base or in any way produce environmental damage.[87]

In order for TVA to assess the economic impact of its Concept Plan, the USDA Forest Service and two universities were asked to do an independent analysis of the draft plan. The study was based on information gathered from visitors. The Corps of Engineers trained volunteers to distribute forms to visitors as they entered the facility. The people were requested to mail the completed forms directly to the University of Georgia for data assimilation by an optical scanning device. A computer program provided by Georgia Southern College was used to transform the spending information, including consumer prices as well as producer prices.

---

[83]Progress Reports, 1988-1989.

[84]Ibid.

[85]Ibid.

[86]ERAW, Concept Plan, 34.

[87]Progress Report, 1988.

The producer prices were then used to access the analysis capabilities by the USDA Forest Service at Fort Collins, Colorado. The study provided sector-by-sector and total estimates of changes in business activity that could result from the Concept Plan.[88]

The independent study revealed that the development proposals would produce a positive impact on the regional economy. The study predicted increases in direct spending on certain economic sectors in the region. The study determined that businesses most likely affected by the spending would be recreation and retail trade. Grocery and general merchandising stores, and more specialized businesses could expect to have more customers. Hotels, motels, and other lodging places would have increased use. Eating and drinking establishments would have more customers.[89]

The study also pointed out significant indirect and induced effects that could ripple through most of the 179 sectors which currently existed in the regional economy. The economic impact calculated in the study was $2.4 million which resulted from campground services, $40.9 million from services in facilities, and $214 million from the four major attractions. The study also estimated that 44 new jobs in the 12 county region would result from the camping services, 803 jobs from other facility services, 4,629 jobs from other attractions.[90]

The Concept Plan was scheduled to begin in 1987-1988 and the implementation would occur in phases until the 1990s. Beginning in the fiscal year 1988, TVA requested proposals from potential contractors and began to conduct feasibility studies of specific components of attractions. At the same time, TVA announced that it would aggressively seek federal funding and explore cooperative arrangements with public and private entities for additional funding. The agency intended to seek innovative cost-sharing arrangements involving multiple sources for future development. Nonprofit organizations and academic institutions with similar program components would be asked to sponsor some areas, and alliances with the private sector could be developed to provide the means to accomplish other areas of development. All new developments would be self-supporting and would require no additional federal funds for continued operation. Feasibility studies and detailed planning would be conducted with each potential cooperator to ensure that the development would be compatible with the Concept Plan goals. Studies would ensure that the development would not only be compatible with the plans but would also enhance appeals to potential patrons. The development program included a policy statement that the officials must guarantee that the facility remain financially solvent. Under no circumstances would land within the facility be sold.

The last statement concerning the policy of preserving the whole project intact was a very important step for TVA. For some time, it had been rumored that since the project was not living up to TVA's expectations some of the land would be sold to private developers. Once again, the rumor caused anger and consternation, especially in the area around the development. People had not forgotten the distress that had been caused when the land was taken in the 1960s. At that time, TVA was accused of buying land at low prices and later selling it for tremendous

---

[88]Ibid.

[89]Ibid.

[90]Ibid.

profits. Now, the people were waiting to see if the accusation was true. There were those who predicted that land along the Trace would be sold to developers. Those prophecies caused outcries in the press and angry words from the general public.

In this instance, TVA officials had anticipated the mood of the people and hastened to make their position clear. They would not sell land to developers. This statement of policy came at just the right time to help eradicate the negative views which existed in the region. On the whole, most people were not concerned with the proposals to allow more services. Most of the business community did not perceive expanded services as a threat to their private enterprises. When the news media contacted the business people and asked for a personal response, the individuals were quick to encourage development.[91]

After all the study and publicity, TVA was slow to implement programs. Plans were developed to support a more aggressive promotion and advertising effort by requiring cooperators to use some of the profits for regional marketing of the available facilities.[92] The planners were thinking in terms of developing a regional marketing plan to introduce the Land Between The Lakes to new market segments. Working in cooperation with the Land Between The Lakes Association and other tourism organizations, it was expected that there would be increased use of paid advertisements for facilities, attractions, and special events. Promotion and advertising would include television, radios, newspapers, and magazines. They encouraged the Tennessee and Kentucky departments of tourism to cooperate with publicizing the attractions of LBL. The planners tried to increase the visibility of the project.[93]

New visitor services were offered at the family campgrounds. Visitors were able to purchase ice, newspapers, tick repellent, and firewood. The Energy Lake Campground provided for the rental of rowboats and canoes. A gift shop, The Golden Pond Gift Shoppe, located in the Golden Pond Visitors Center, was opened to sell at retail prices handmade crafts and other items related to the region. The Land Between The Lakes Association purchased the initial inventory and contracted with the Bicentennial Volunteers, Inc., for the operation of the gift shop for one year. The shop was the first commercial establishment for retail sales established in the project.[94]

In 1988, TVA went through yet another reorganization program, and LBL was placed in the River Basin Operation in the Resource Development group within TVA. The director's title again became manager, and when Elizabeth Thach left the position at the end of the fiscal year, John L. Mechler was appointed acting manager for the remainder of the calendar year.[95]

After four years of work, a research project which was a cooperative endeavor between the U.S. Department of Agriculture and TVA was completed. The findings of the project were

---

[91]Newspaper accounts and television programs centered on the attitudes of the people. See The Tennessean, Nashville, Tennessee, June 12, 1989.

[92]Progress Report, 1988.

[93]Ibid.

[94]Ibid.

[95]Ibid.

published in scientific journals and the results were applied to tick control operations.[96]

Continued Problems with Tourism

Even though the planners had estimated an increase in the number of visitors to the attractions in 1988, the number declined to 2,046,998. The decrease was small, but it resulted in even more concern about the changes which had been suggested for the facility. Funding declined from $8,299,000 in 1987 to $8,167,000 in 1988. The Economic Research Associates expanded their report into a "Feasibility Land Between The Lakes Concept Plan" which was completed in September of 1988. It was expected that the Concept Plan would enable TVA and the LBL management team to make projection which would expand the facility. In the additional research, some interesting factors were uncovered. The peak season for the region was from June through August with an estimated 612,000 overnight guests. From March through May there were approximately 397,000 guests, and from September through November about 407,000 overnight guests. The key traffic points were along the I-24 corridor with an estimated annual vehicle count of 1.9 million at I-24 and State Road Kentucky 68 West. Approximately 5.3 million vehicles were counted at the I-24 junction with West Kentucky Parkway. In 1987 and 1988 little was being done to make the people aware of the attraction of the area. Because there were few signs and markers, people were not provided with a reason to leave the highway to visit the project.[97] Visitors stayed for about three hours. The goal of educating as well as entertaining the youth with the organized school programs in the spring and fall was not being accomplished. From all of the conclusions, it appears that the plans for the Historic Village Complex had the most potential, if in fact the plan was to integrate interest and involvement of the history of the area. No one doubted that the area was rich in historical lore that would attract both the young and the old. The Historic Village Complex which included plans for a variety of activities, shops, craft displays, music, entertainment, rides, food, and beverages would provide the resources for a well-planned program. The activities and entertainment had the potential of enticing visitors to the special events and attractions during the entire year. It cannot be refuted that the research established the fact that large numbers of people have a fascination with the past. The evidence to support this conclusion can be verified in the number of books, fiction and nonfiction, which deal with historic subjects. Also, numerous societies and associations are devoted to history in general, or to specific periods and events in history. Along with the history of the region, the Complex would have to choose people who could interact with the visitors and involve them in the activities. Displays of artifacts, pictures, and other objects are too passive in nature. The history must come alive through discussion and activities which include the visitors. The demonstrations and instruction should be handled in a group environment and should include all age groups.[98]

---

[96]Ibid.

[97]ERAW, Feasibility Plan, 19.

[98]TVA has not begun to implement the proposal which seems to have the most merit.

Another, and perhaps the most important consideration for the future development of the project was the economy of the country. All of the proposals were predicated on the assumption that if tourists wanted to come to the area because they could find appealing attractions, they would have the economic resources to make the journey. Even though the studies took into consideration the recession, inflation, and gasoline prices of the 1970s and early 1980s, the studies did not entertain the idea that the poor economic conditions would continue. Without doubt, the projections were that most of the adverse circumstances which negatively affected tourism would end as the country moved into the decade of the 1990s. That has not been the case, and the project is more vulnerable than ever to threats of less funding and fewer visitors. The one oversight in all the studies was the possibility of an extended recession.

Summary

From the settlement period to 1932-- not counting the atypical period of the Civil War-- the land between the rivers was not strongly affected by actions of the federal government. The people, isolated because of their geographic location, developed a unique culture rich in its European background with added cultural influences from Africans and Chinese. The people were generally satisfied with their standard of living and took great pride in their land and homes. The desire for radical change was not a part of their heritage. These people were often clannish and usually distrustful of strangers. Their self-esteem and status in the community depended upon their honesty and willingness to work. They were self-supporting and cringed at the thought of taking charity. They had a strong sense of social responsibility. They helped their neighbors, and with a certain reserve, they entertained strangers.

Accountability for their own actions, as well as those of close family members, was a part of the social fabric. World War II and the New Deal, and most of all TVA, were destined to change the lives of these people and transform the appearance of the countryside.

The land between the rivers lost its name and identity when the area was brought under the custody of TVA. The people moved and the settlements disappeared. When the people left to build and buy homes in other places, their unique way of life shifted and often disappeared. Many of their customs gradually began to vanish and have now been mostly forgotten. The "shiveree" or party for couples who had just married has disappeared. Certain patterns of speech and word usages began to vanish when the communities dispersed.

Some of those people who were forced out of their homes often looked upon TVA as the enemy. The enemy, they felt, had irrevocably changed their existence, and it had acted too swiftly and unjustly. TVA's most ardent detractors never changed their minds about what they considered the iniquitous behavior of the agency.

Other people resisted the agency's right to condemn and take their land, but they gradually recognized the inevitability of the situation and left the region with as much grace as they could muster. A very small number of people were glad to sell their land and move away from the area. Now, after more than two decades have passed since TVA became a predominant factor in the area, its actions can be viewed with more objectivity. Even those people who fought the formation of the Land Between The Lakes cannot deny that the project has resulted in many positive effects in the area. It has brought public attention to the area.

Tourists by the millions have visited the wilderness. It cannot be disputed that the facility has the potential to develop into one of the major attractions of the United States. Also, it has the capability for further development which can make the area one of the most important environmental, educational, and resource management attractions in the world.

Whenever the Land Between The Lakes is discussed the detractors often cite the loss of revenue to Stewart, Trigg, and Lyon Counties as one of the major factors which has hurt the region. Too often these people are not aware of the money which the states have received in lieu of taxes. Specifically, these people are not adequately informed as to how these funds are used by counties involved. Research indicates that the general public is unaware that TVA has historically made an effort to remunerate the state and local governments for the loss of taxable property. The reimbursement to the state is made by TVA, but the agency has no power to dictate how the state will handle those funds.[99] The estimated loss of taxes for 1988 in Lyon County was $25,183, and TVA's tax replacement was $311,323. The county received an excess over tax loss of $292,140. The estimated tax loss in Trigg County was $32,307, and TVA paid $363,856. The county received an excess of $331,549. In Stewart County where the estimate of taxes lost was $17,033, TVA paid $579,086. The county received an excess of $562,053. All three counties combined had an estimated former tax of $74,523. TVA paid the counties

---

[99]Data supplied to the author by TVA.

TAX REPLACEMENT PAYMENTS TO LAND BETWEEN THE LAKES COUNTIES
DUE TO TVA PROPERTY OWNERSHIP FOR FISCAL YEARS 1968-1988

Year	Lyon County	Trigg County	Stewart County	Total
1968	$ 41,999.00	$ 45,256.00	$ 7,752.00	$ 95,007.00
1969	57,462.00	57,684.00	13,711.00	128,857.00
1970	70,997.00	71,565.00	17,027.00	159,589.00
1971	86,450.00	84,138.00	50,704.00	221,292.00
1972	99,631.00	95,535.00	52,582.00	247,748.00
1973	83,628.00	92,650.00	52,749.00	229,027.00
1974	94,871.00	99,383.00	51,122.00	245,376.00
1975	115,030.00	114,648.00	51,122.00	280,800.00
1976	141,922.00	142,574.00	112,542.00	397,038.00
1977/a	231,361.00	231,961.00	163,404.00	626,726.00
1978	218,903.00	191,859.00	163,276.00	574,038.00
1979	245,246.00	251,357.00	/b	496,603.00
1980	227,467.00	280,008.00	249,323.00	756,798.00
1981	239,650.00	243,827.00	336,997.00	820,474.00
1982	249,055.00	248,657.00	402,599.00	900,311.00
1983	254,046.00	258,635.00	412,505.00	925,186.00
1984	197,512.00	206,012.00	412,307.00	815,831.00
1985	184,381.00	206,127.00	485,750.00	876,258.00
1986	319,365.00	354,605.00	503,892.00	1,177.862.00
1987	297,581.00	339,543.00	535,484.00	1,172,608.00
1988	317,323.00	363,856.00	579,086.00	1,260,265.00

/a Includes eighteen months.
/b The State of Tennessee was in the process of changing its method of allocating in lieu of tax monies received from TVA and did not redistribute funds to local governments during fiscal year 1979.

---

a total of $1,260,265 and an excess of tax replacement over tax loss of $1,185,742.[100]

These statistics indicate that the county governments of the three counties have not suffered a loss in tax revenue because of the development. Unquestionably, the counties have benefitted from the formation of LBL. A breakdown of the exact amount of money which is returned to the state for TVA holdings indicates that TVA does not wish to dispossess the state or local government. Its total payment in lieu of taxes for all its property including power property and reservoir land in the three counties was $1,838,558 in the fiscal year 1988.[101]

It is true that each of the counties involved lost citizens who had the potential to benefit the county through their presence and leadership capabilities. This specific loss cannot be studied or commented upon with any accuracy. Families moved out of the area and this movement had an impact on the social, cultural, and economic growth of the area. With the decrease in population, the counties had to consolidate schools, and lost state revenue when the number of school children decreased. All three counties have problems in competition with surrounding counties which have more money and larger schools.

It is also a fact that the unique culture of the land between the rivers was destroyed. Again, it is impossible to ascertain or adequately describe the effects of the loss. The cultural characteristics of the area are disappearing, and it is difficult to ferret out the traditions and attitudes which made this area reminiscent more of the eighteenth and nineteenth than the twentieth century. One cannot ignore the many individuals who suffered the frustration and anguish of losing their homes and community. In no way can we relate to their grief. One of the effects was hostility toward TVA. Time has affected the views of many of those people. Those who survive have become more reticent in their attitudes toward the agency, others cannot forgive. A study of the effects of the government's use of the right of eminent domain could be instituted around the cases in the land between the rivers. A study of those people and their reactions based upon the actions of TVA could present a matchless insight into ways which the government could circumvent extreme hostility when it is necessary to take an area out of the private domain.

The counties involved lost large areas of land. Roughly, each of the three counties contributed a third of the land that was needed for the development of the LBL project. In the case of Stewart County the loss posed a significant problem. Yet, the loss of land cannot distract us from the fact that the counties have benefitted from increased revenue from TVA. Even with escalation of land values in the region, it is possible that the coffers of the counties are richer from the TVA revenue than they would have been had the citizens remained in the area and paid taxes.

In the controversy over the loss of land, there are those who say that if TVA had taken less land, the private businesses catering to the tourists would have brought in more money than that which is presently supplied by TVA. This argument cannot be settled because it is not possible to determine what would have happened, but one must notice that one of the major problems is the lack of development of private businesses in the area. In 1991, it is generally agreed that businesses have not developed to serve those tourists who come to the area. It is

---

[100]Ibid.

[101]Ibid.

279

not plausible to assert that if other property had been excluded it would have developed into money-making enterprises catering to tourists. There are not enough facilities to lure tourists. Why have private developers virtually ignored the area? Why has recreation failed as a business? These are some of the questions which TVA needs to answer.

It is difficult to calculate the amount of revenue which is generated in the area by LBL. A summary of the direct and indirect economic impact from the development of the area was published by TVA in 1988. The report for the 1987 fiscal year showed the operating revenues at $1,543,900 and the total expenditure was $6,179,670 for the Land Between The Lakes. This total did not take into account certain expenditures and operating costs at the facility. Understandably, LBL is a government entity and is not in the business of making money. However, the report did not include the general overhead costs, general administrative costs, or the general maintenance and upkeep of the facilities. With a net operating loss of approximately $4,566,177, the management realized that expensive and detailed planning was needed at the facility. Because of TVA spending, the local and regional area is supported by the salaries of the people employed in the project. The number of people employed varies from season to season and year to year but approximately 137 full-time employees are contributing to the economy.

Frequently, the charge is made that TVA has not lived up to its promise to add more jobs for local residents at the facility and in the private sector. The accusation is made that many of the management personnel who make the most money are brought into the area by TVA when local talent is available to fill the positions. One of the most pressing problems for TVA, at this juncture, is to make an effort to recruit as many workers from the adjacent counties as possible. The area needs to see qualified residents in visible leadership roles.

Money spent on construction is said to have had a secondary or ripple effect throughout the local and regional areas. For every one million dollars in construction expenditures, 44.9 new jobs are created. By 1988, a total of 445 new jobs had been established. A total of $4.3 million had been spent in payrolls, and of that amount a $3.2 million sum was poured into the local and regional economy. Approximately $5.2 million had been spent on materials, supplies, and services and had the effect of creating two dollars and thirty-six cents for every dollar spent. Thus, an additional $12.3 million were spent in the local and regional economy.

The continuing operation of the facility with the implementation of the proposals from the Economic Research Associates is expected to provide direct benefits to the local economy in the form of new jobs, payrolls, purchases, and taxes.

The projections are that approximately 134 new jobs will be created by 1992. An additional payroll expenditure of $1,078,645 is stated as a minimum amount expected when the new programs are instituted. The goods and materials needed would amount to at least $1,481,535 and the estimated sales tax would be $34,075. The ripple effect of the expenditures would create 66 additional jobs in the local and regional economy. Direct payroll will be represented in the economy at a rate of .5719 per $1.00 of the payroll. This additional spending is expected to create an additional $616,877 in payrolls for other people. Direct purchases will be throughout the local and regional economy at approximately 1.96 times and will generate an additional 2.9 million dollars in spending.

Many positive results of establishing a facility which can conserve natural resources, promote research in the protection of wildlife, and generate interest in the history of the country are certainly still possible. At this moment, the members of the Biology Department at Austin Peay State University are involved in a joint effort with the people at LBL to carry on significant research. The Biology Department's Center for Field Biology, funded by the state of Tennessee, is able to furnish qualified trained personnel to meet the research demands of the project. This present historical study came about as a result of the leadership of Dr. Benjamin Stone, Director of the Center.

Some interesting and extremely important data are being gathered by the Center researchers who disseminate their findings to the country. Because of the on-going research, new information is being gathered and prepared for publication.

One of the most exciting proposals has been that TVA will make an effort to encourage more research, writing, and presentation of the history of the region. As this study indicates, the richness of the history of the region has not been exhausted. Extensive amounts of data are available, and the distinctive history of the region can be studied in greater detail if the agency will take a leadership role and initiate further study. The history should not be limited to just the people who inhabited the area. Extensive work is still to be done on the resources and culture of the region. One hopes that TVA will continue to encourage research into all these topics.

The Tennessee Valley Authority has launched a project which should be heralded by all citizens. With the sobering realization that our environment is in trouble, and that we continue to pollute some of the major unsullied areas of our world, TVA has, with difficulty, entered into a program of reclamation and preservation which is unequaled in any other part of the country. Because of the political and economic programs to reduce the national debt and decrease the commitment of the federal government in many social and economic programs at the local level, TVA has had a reduction in funding. That cutback has resulted in two problems. First, the proposed programs for development of the project have been put on hold. Second, adequate funding is still an absolute necessity and that need has forced the officials to try to discover sources of revenue which will enable the facility to maintain its present status and perhaps develop new programs in the future.

Two major concerns must be examined at this time. One is to convince the general public that the facility is a worthwhile endeavor and that federal money should be appropriated for the project. This task is made more difficult because of the sluggish national economy.

The Tennessee Valley Authority has been energetic in its attempts to inform the public that the Land Between The Lakes is of value to the entire nation. The final word is still out on how many people would like to use the facility. The agency is faced with the dilemma of preserving the area and at the same time appealing to the tourists. Researchers have developed excellent programs and now the citizens must assist TVA in delivering them.

Those Americans who are interested in protecting and preserving one of the most fascinating experiments in a three-fold plan of incorporating the preservation of an area, education and entertainment of the populace, and an economical plan for recreation must be alert to the needs of the program. The Land Between The Lakes needs the assistance and support of those who want to see it reach its goals. It can become one of the largest and most unique attractions in the United States, but its success rests upon the support of those who understand what it has to offer.

BOOKS

Ainsworth, Fred C., Leslie Perry and Joseph W. Kirkley. The War of the Rebellion: A Compilation of the Official Records of the Union and Confederate Armies. Washington D. C.: Government Printing Office, 1898.

Alexander, Augustus. Grant as a Soldier. St. Louis: The Author, 1915.

Ambrose Stephen. Halleck: Lincoln's Chief of Staff. Baton Rouge: Louisiana State University Press, 1962.

Aries, Phillipe. Centuries of Childhood: A Social History of Family Life. New York: Knopf, 1962.

Arnett, Hazel. I Hear America Sing: Great Folk Songs From the Revolution to Rock. New York: Praeger Publishers, 1975.

Arnow, Harriette Simpson. Flowering of the Cumberland. New York: Macmillan and Company, 1963.

Austin, Aleine. Matthew Lyon: "New Man" of the Democratic Revolution, 1749-1822. University Park: The Pennsylvania State University Press.

Axtell, James. The Invasion Within: The Contest of Cultures in Colonial North America. New York: Oxford University Press, 1985.

Bailey, Fred Arthur. Class and Tennessee's Confederate Generation. Chapel Hill: The University of North Carolina Press, 1987.

Banner, Lois. Women in Modern America: A Brief History. New York: Harcourt Brace Jovanovich, Inc., 1984.

Barney, William. Flawed Victory: A New Perspective on the Civil War. New York: Praeger, 1975.

Beringer, Richard, Herman Hallaway, Archer Jones, and William N. Still, Jr. Why the South Lost the Civil War. Athens: University of Georgia Press, 1986.

Berkhofer, Robert F., Jr. The White Man's Indian: Images of the American Indian from Columbus to the Present. Alfred A. Knopf, 1978.

Bestor, Arthur E. Backwoods Utopians: The Sectarian and Owenite Phases of Communitarian Socialism in America, 1663-1829. Philadelphia: University of Pennsylvania Press, 1950.

Black, Robert. Railroads of the Confederacy. Chapel Hill: University of North Carolina Press, 1952.

Burns, James McGregor. F. D. R.: The Lion and the Fox. New York: Harcourt, Brace, 1956.

Carson, Rachel. Silent Spring. Boston: Houghton Mifflin, 1962.

Catton, Bruce. Mr. Lincoln's Army. Garden City, New York: Doubleday, 1951. Grant Moves South. Boston: Little, Brown and Company, 1960.

Chester, Edward W. The Vascular Flora of Fort Donelson National Military Park, Stewart County, Tennessee. Knoxville, Tennessee: University of Tennessee Resource Management Report 80, 1986.

Clark, Bruce E. The Barkley Dam Site. Louisville: The Geological Society of Kentucky, 1962.

Coffin, Charles. <u>Four Years of Fighting</u>. New York: Arno Press, 1970.

Collins, Lewis. <u>History of Kentucky</u>. Cincinnati: Lewis Collins and J. A. & U. P. James, 1847.

Commoner, Barry. <u>The Closing Circle</u>. New York: Knopf, 1971.

Conkin, Paul K. <u>The New Deal</u>. New York: Crowell, 1967.

Connelly, Thomas L. <u>Army of the Heartland: The Army of Tennessee 1861-62</u>. Baton Rouge: Louisiana State University Press, 1967. <u>Autumn of Glory: The Army of Tennessee. 1862-65</u>. Baton Rouge: Louisiana State University Press, 1971. <u>The Politics of Command</u>. Baton Rouge: Louisiana State University Press, 1973.

Corlew, Robert E. <u>Tennessee</u>. Knoxville: The University of Tennessee Press, 1971.

Cramer, M. J. <u>Ulysses S. Grant: Conversations and Unpublished Letters</u>. New York: Eaton & Main, 1897.

Crummer, Wilbur. <u>With Grant at Fort Donelson, Shiloh, and Vicksburg</u>. Oak Park, Illinois: E. C. Crummer, 1915.

Cronon, William. <u>Changes in the Land: Indians, Colonists, and The Ecology of New England</u>. New York: Hill and Wang, 1983.

Cross, Whitney. <u>The Burned-Over District: The Social and Intellectual History of Enthusiastic Religion in Western New York, 1800-1850</u>. Ithaca, New York: Cornell University Press, 1950.

Cummings, Charles M. <u>Yankee Quaker, Confederate General: The Curious Career of Bushrod Rust Johnson</u>. Rutherford, New Jersey: Fairleigh Dickinson University Press, 1971.

Cutter, Irving. <u>A Short History of Midwifery</u>. Philadelphia: Saunders, 1964.

Dabney, Joseph Earl. <u>Spirits: A Chronicle of Corn Whiskey</u>. New York: Scribner's Sons, 1974.

Daniel, Larry J. <u>Cannoners in Gray: The Field Artillery of the Army of Tennessee</u>. University of Alabama: University of Alabama Press, 1984.

David, Donald. <u>Why the North Won the Civil War</u>. Baton Rouge: Louisiana State Univesity Press, 1960.

Davidson, Donald. <u>The Tennessee</u>. 2 vols, New York: Rhinehart, 1946.

Dodge, J. R. <u>Red Men of the Ohio Valley: An Aboriginal History</u>. Springfield, Ohio: Ruralist Publishing Company, 1859.

Donegan, Jane. <u>Women and Men Midwives</u>. Westport, Connecticut: Greenwood Press, 1978.

Douglas, Byrd. <u>Steamboating on the Cumberland</u>. Nashville: Tennessee Book Company, 1961.

Durham, Walter T. <u>Nashville: The Occupied City</u>. Nashville: Tennessee Historical Society, 1985.

Edmunds, R. David. <u>The Shawnee Prophet</u>. Lincoln: University of Nebraska Press, 1983.
Economics Research Associates. <u>A Feasibility Analysis of the Land Between The Lakes Concept Plan</u>. Land Between The Lakes: EDAW, Inc., 1988. General Service School. Fort Henry and Fort Donelson Campaigns 1962: Source Book Kansas: The General Services Schools Press, 1912.

Goodspeed. <u>Histories of Tennessee</u>. Nashville: The Goodspeed Publishing Company, 1886.

Goff, Richard. <u>Confederate Supply</u>. Durham, North Carolina: Duke University Press, 1984.

Grant, Ulysses S. <u>Personal Memoirs</u>. vol. II. New York: Webster, 1894.

283

Grantham, Dewey W. Southern Progressivism: The Reconciliation of Progress and Traditon. Knoxville: The University of Tennessee Press, 1983.

Hamer, Philip B., Tennessee: A History 1673-1932. vol. 1, New York: The American Historical Society, Inc., 1933.

Hamilton, James. The Battle of Fort Donelson. South Brunswick: T. Yoseloff, 1968.

Henry, J. Milton. The Land Between The Rivers. Knoxville: Tennessee Valley Authority, no date.

Hogan, William T. An Ecomonic History of the Iron and Steel Industry in the United States. vol. I. Washington D.C.: Heath and Company, 1971.

Holm, Jeanne, Maj. Gen. USAF(Ret.). Women in the Military: An Unfinished Revolution. Navota, California: Presidio Press, 1982.

Hook, John W. The Kentucky Flurspar District. Louisville: The Geological Society of Kentucky, 1962. "Indians in Colonial America," The Contest of Cultures in Colonial North America. D'Arcy McNickle Center for the History of the American Indian Occasional Papers in Curriculum Series 4, Chicago: The Newberry Library, 1986.

Horn, Stanley. Army of Tennessee. Norman: University of Oklahoma Press, 1953.

Jennings, Francis, The Invasion of America: Indians, Colonialism, and the Cant of Conquest. Chapel Hill: University of North Carolina Press, 1975. The Ambiguous Iroquois Empire: The Convenant Chain Confederation of Indian Tribes With English Colonies from Its Beginnings to the Lancaster Treaty of 1744. New York: W. W. Norton, 1984.

Johnson, Robert U., and Clarence C. Buel, Battles and Leaders of the Civil War. New York: Century Press, 1887.

Kanter, Rosabeth Moss. Commitment and Community: Communes and Utopias in Sociological Perspective. Cambridge, Mass.: Harvard University Press, 1972.

Kerber, Linda K. and Matthews, Jane. eds. Women's America: Refocusing the Past. New York: Oxford University Press, 1982.

Killebrew, J. B. An Introduction to the Resources of Tennessee. Nashville: Travel, Eastman and Howell, 1874.

Kiple, Kenneth, and Virginia King. Another Dimension in the Black Diaspora: Diet, Disease, and Racism. New York: Cambridge University Press, 1981.

Klein, Maury. History of the Louisville and Nashville Railroad. New York: McMillan, 1972.

Lafferty, Maude Ward. The Lure of Kentucky. Detroit: Singing Tree Press, 1971.

Laffin, John. Women in Battle. New York: Abelard-Shuman, 1967.

Leavitt, Judith Walzer. Brought to Bed: Childbearing in America, 1750-1950. New York: Oxford University Press, 1986.

Leavitt, Judith Walzer and Ronald Numbers, eds. Sickness and Health in America: Readings in the History of Medicine and Public Health. Madison: University of Wisconsin Press, 1978.

Leuchtenburg, William E. Franklin D. Roosevelt and the New Deal. New York: Harper and Row, 1963.

Lewis, N. N., and Madeline Kneberg. Tribes That Slumber. Knoxville: The University of Tennessee Press, 1958.

Martin, Calvin, ed. The American Indian and the Problem of History. New York: Oxford University Press, 1987.

McCloughlin, William G. Cherokee and Missionaries, 1789-1839. New Haven: Yale University Press, 1984.

McCrain, Geral R., and Audrey L. Grubb. An Analyis of Past and Present Vegetational Patterns and Historic Parameters at Fort Donelson National Battlefield with Recommendations for Restoration and Future Management. Raleigh, North Carolina: Resource Management Company, 1987.

McCraw, Thomas K. TVA and the Power Fight 1933-1939. New York: J. B. Lippincott Company, 1971.

McFeely, William. Grant: A Biography. New York: Norton, 1981.

McMillen, Sally G. Motherhood in the Old South: Pregnancy, Childbirth, and Infant Rearing. Baton Rouge: Louisiana State University Press, 1990.

McWhiney, Grady. Cracker Culture and Celtic Ways in the Old South. University of Alabama: University of Alabama Press, 1988.

Montell, William Lynwood. Ghosts along the Cumberland: Deathlore in the Kentucky Foothills. Knoxville: The University of Tennessee Press, 1975.

Moore, John R., ed. Economic Impact of TVA. Knoxville: The University of Tennessee Press, 1967.

Morse, Dan F. Reports of 1962 Excavations In Stewart County, Tennessee Portion of the Lake Barkley Reservoir. Knoxville: The University of Tennessee Press, 1985.

National Park Service. Survey of the Archeological Resources of Barkley Reservoir, Kentucky and Tennessee. Richmond: United States Department of the Interior, 1958.

National Park Service. The Vascular Flora of Fort Donelson National Military Park, Stewart County, Tennessee. Richmond: United States Department of the Interior, 1986.

Nevin, Allen. The War for the Union. (4) vols. New York: Scribners, 1959.

Parish, Peter. The American Civil War. New York: Holmes & Meier, 1975.

Parks, Joseph H. and Stanley J. Folmsbee. The Story of Tennessee. Norman, Oklahoma: Harlow Publishing Corporation, 1973.

Perrin, William H., ed. Counties of Christian and Trigg Kentucky. Chicago: F. A. Battery Publishing Company, 1884.

Plum, William. The Military Telegraph During the Civil War. Annapolis: Naval Institute Press, 1978.

Pratt, Fletcher. Civil War. Garden City, New York: Doubleday, 1955.

Ridley, Broomfield L. Battles and Sketches of the Army of the Tennessee. Mexico, Missouri: Missouri Press, 1906.

Rothstein, William. American Physicians in the Nineteenth Century: From Sect to Science. Baltimore: John Hopkins University Press, 1972.

Rowbotham, Sheila. Hidden From History: Rediscovering Women From the 17th Century to the Present. New York: Pantheon Books, 1974.

Segal, Charles M., and David C. Stinebeck, eds. Puritans, Indians and Manifest Destiny. New York: G. P. Putnam's Sons, 1977.

Schlesinger, Arthur. Age of Roosevelt. Boston: Houghton Mifflin, 1957.

Smith, Samuel D., Charles P. Stripling, and James M. Brannon. A Cultural Resource Survey of Tennessee's Western Highland Rim Iron Industry, 1790s-1930. Nashville, Tennessee: Department of Conservation, Division of Archeology, 1988.

Sochen, June. Herstory: A Woman's View of American History. vol. 1. New York: Alfred Publishing Co., Inc., 1974.

Tennessee Valley Authority. Technical Library Collection. vols. 1-34. Knoxville: Tennessee Valley Authority, 1968.

Tennessee Valley Authority. A History of the Tennessee Valley. Knoxville: Tennessee Valley Authority Information Office, 1983.

Tugwell, Rexford. The Democratic Roosevelt. Garden City, New York: Doubleday, 1957.

Tyler, Alice Felts. Freedom's Ferment: Phases of American Social History to 1860. Minneapolis: University of Minnesota Press, 1944.

Wertz, Richard. Lying-In: A History of Childbirth in America. New York: Free Press, 1977.

Wigginton, Eliot. The Foxfire Book. New York: Doubleday & Company, Inc., 1972.

Wigginton, Thomas A., and The Civl War Centennial Commission. Tennessee in the Civil War. Nashville: Civil War Centennial Commission, 1964.

Williams, Samuel Cole, ed. Adair's History of the American Indians. Johnson City, Tennessee: Watauga Press, 1930.

Wyeth, John Allen. That Devil Forrest: Life of General Nathan Bedford Forrest. New York: Harper and Brothers Publishers, 1959.

NEWSPAPERS

Banner, Nashville, Tennessee; January 1954 to August 1990

Caldwell County Times, Princeton, Kentucky; January 1954 to August 1990.

Cadiz Record, Cadiz, Kentucky; January 1954 to August 1990.

Commercial Appeal, Memphis, Tennessee; January 1954 to August 1990.

Courier Journal, Louisville, Kentucky; January 1954 to August 1990.

Democrat, Murray, Kentucky; January 1954 to August 1990.

Herald Ledger, Eddyville, Kentucky; January 1954 to July 1990.

Hustler, South Pittsburg, Tennessee; January 1954 to July 1990.

Journal, Knoxville, Tennessee; January 1955 to July 1990.

Kentucky New Era, Hopkinsville, Kentucky; January 1954 to July 1990.

Lakeside Ledger, Eddyville, Kentucky, July 1964 to August 1990.

Ledger-Times, Murray, Kentucky; January 1954 to July 1990.

Leaf Chronicle, Clarksville, Tennessee; January 1954 to July 1990.

Mayfield Messenger, Mayfield, Kentucky; January 1954 to July 1990.

Post and Times Herald, Washington D. C; January 1954 to July 1990.

Press-Chronicle, Johnson City, Tennessee; January 1954 to July 1990.

Marshall Courier, Benton, Kentucky; January 1954 to July 1990.

Messenger, Madisonville, Kentucky; January 1954 to August 1990.

Messenger & Inquirer, Owensboro, Kentucky; January 1960 to August 1990.

New Era, Hopkinsville, Kentucky; January 1954 to July 1990.

News, Birmingham, Alabama; January 1960 to August 1990.

News-Free Press, Chattanooga, Tennessee; January 1954 to July 1990.

News Sentinel, Knoxville, Tennessee; January 1954 to July 1990.

Oak Ridger, Oak Ridge, Tennessee; September 1954 to August 1990.
Paris Democrat, Paris, Tennessee; January 1954 to July 1990.
Park City News, Bowling Green, Kentucky; January 1956 to August 1990.
Press-Chronicle, Johnson City, Tennessee; January 1960 to August 1990.
Post, Paris, Tennessee; January 1954 to July 1990.
Post-Athenian, Athens, Tennessee; January 1954 to July 1990.
Press-Scimitar, Memphis, Tennessee; January 1954 to August 1990.
Press-Chronicle, Johnson City, Tennessee; January 1954 to July 1990.
Stewart-Houston Times, Dover, Tennessee; January 1954 to July 1990.
Star, Elizabethton, Tennessee; January 1960 to August 1990.
Sun, Jackson, Tennessee; January 1954 to July 1990.
Sun-Democrat, Paducah, Kentucky; January 1954 to July 1990.
The Tennessean, Nashville, Tennessee; January 1954 to July 1990.
Times, Chattanooga, Tennessee; January 1954 to July 1990.
Times, Kingsport, Tennessee; January 1954 to July 1990.
Times, Florence, Alabama; January 1954 to July 1990.
Times, New York, New York; January 1954 to July 1990.
The Commercial Appeal, Memphis, Tennessee; January 1954 to July 1990.
The Record, Cadiz, Kentucky; January 1954 to July 1990.
Tribune Democrat, Benton, Kentucky; January 1954 to July 1990.

UNPUBLISHED MATERIALS

Cook, J. C. Letters Confederate Collection. Nashville, Tennessee: Tennessee State Library and Archives.
Caldwell Court Records
Daniel, Buena Coleman. "The Iron Industry in Dickson County, Tennessee." M.A. Thesis, Austin Peay State University, 1971.
Davis, Jerilee, S. "The Charcoal Iron Industry of Montgomery and Stewart Counties." M.A. Thesis, Austin Peay State University, 1976.
Lyon County Court Records Lyon County Deed Books
Lumpkin, Martha Neville, ed. "Dear Darling Loulie": Letters of Cordelia Lewis Scales to Loulie W. Irby During and After the War Between the States. (held by author)
Trigg County Court Records Trigg County Deed Books
Stewart County Court Records
Stewart County Deed Books
Wallace, Betty Joe. "The Effects of the Civil War in Stewart County." M. A. Thesis, Austin Peay State University, 1976.

INDEX

A

Adair, James, 8
Adams, John Ouincy, 29, 58
Agriculture, 34-36, 87, 140
Agriculture Adjustment Act, 221
Alexander, Nathan, 22
Alexander, Robert, 12
almanacs, 88, 89
Anderson, Adna, 97, 98
Andrews, James, 22, 23
arbors, 35
Armstrong, Martin, 22
Armstrong, Thomas, 22
Ashland Furnace, 42
Atkins, H, Milton, 41
Atkins, Ira, 207, 208
Atkins, J. M. , 236
Austin Peay Memorial Highway, 236
Austin Peay State College, 236
Avedision, Michael, 215, 218

B

Baccus, Charles, 238
Bach, Jospeh, 22
Bagwell, Richard, 55
Baker, John, 22
Baker, Robert, 26, 28
Barkley, Alben W., 243
Barkley Dam, 197, 198, 199
Barkley Lake, 197, 198, 199
Barkley Reservoir, 200
Barksdale, Cook Company, 38, 39
Baxter, Robert, 37
Bass, Ross 207, 208, 210, 211
Bear Springs Furnace, 38, 39, 54
bees, 18, 19
beliefs, 167, 168
Bell, (Yeatman) Jane, 39
Bell, John, 38, 39, 60, 61
Bell, Montgomery, 37, 38
Bellwood Furnace, 38, 39, 54, 131
Benham, James, 25
Between The Lakes Development
      Association, 207-208
Bickerdyke, Mary, 126, 127

Bidwell, B. D., 98, 99
Big Rock, 54, 167
Bird, Amos, 22
Biushel, Littleberry, 62
Blair, John, 23
Bleidt, George, 200, 211, 234, 235, 241
Bobwhite Flour, 54
Bogard, Bill, 142
Bogard, Taylor, 142
Boundary disputes 10-14
Boyd's Landing, 29
Boyt, Sam, 22
Bradford, Simon, 37
Brandon, Christopher, 22
Brandon, George, 22
Brandon, Nathan 22, 93
Brandon, Irvin, 71
Bratt, E. C., 145
Breckenridge, John C., 60
Brian, Newell Company, 88
Broadbent, Simth Jr., 206, 207, 208, 209
Brooks, Henry, 260*
Brunsoni Furnace, 42
Bruton, Jesse, 22
Bryan, William J., 157
Buchanan, James, 60, 121
Buckner, Hiram, 93
Buckner, Simon B., 106, 112, 121-130
Buell, Don Carols, 108
Bumpus, Andrew Jackson, 54
Bumpus Mills, 54, 167
burial customs, 161
Burton, Jesse, 22
Byron Forge and Furnace, 42

C

cabins, 11
Cadiz, Kentucky, 27, 28, 53, 156
Camp Porter, 133
Camp Quarles, 93
Campbell, Thomas, 22
Campbell, Willaim, 200
Cannon, William, 27
Catlett, George, 30
"Carondelete", 115
Cass, Lewis, 61
Center Furnace, 42

Cerulean Springs, 21
charcoal production, 47-50
Chester, Edward Wayne, 10
childbirth, 76, 77
Chinese immigrants, 46, 47
Chittenden, Russ, 207
churches, 62, 63
    Dry Creek, 62
    Barron Creek, 62
    Crockett Creek, 62
"Cincinnati", 115
"City of Memphis", 115
Civil War
    effects 130-148
    events leading to, 90-115
    battles, 118-130
    Home Guard, 91-93
    military occupation, 145
Clark Furnace, 42
Clarksville, 19, 133, 134
class stucture, 69, 70
Clay, Henry, 58, 59, 220
Clement, Frank, 236
Clements, Erle, 197
Clinton, Thomas, 23
Cobb, Bradley Company, 38, 39
cockfighting, 64
Coglin, James, 22
Coker, Robert J., 219
Collins, John, 22
Combs, Burt, 203, 204
Commissary Ridge, 54, 55
Committee of Safety, 67
"Conestoga", 115
Cook, J. C., 93
Cooper, John Sherman, 213
Cooper, Robert, 24
Coppedge, Alexander, 61
corn, 14, 15
Cosey, Zeiner, 227, 228
cotton, 34
Craig, H. L., 62
crimes, 56
Crockarell, Douglas, 236
crops, 34, 35, 71, 72
    tobacco, 71, 72
Cross Creek Furnace, 40
Crutcher, Smith, 101
Cub Creek, 55
Cumberland Iron Works, 38, 39, 98, 166
customs 164, 165, 169, 170

D

"D. A. January", 115
Davis, David, 137, 138
Davis, Willliam, 66
Davidson County, 23
Dawson, Elisha, 22
Dawson, Richard P., 29
Denson, Jesse, 23
disease, 167, 168
Dill, Joe, 226
Dixon, Wallace, 37
doctors, 77, 78, 79, 80
Donelson, John, 10, 11
Donelson, Daniel S., 97, 98
Doris, John, 22
Doris, Joshua, 22
Douglas, Stephen A., 61, 62
Dover, 24, 53, 55, 88, 95, 96, 107, 167, 169
Dover Furnace, 38, 166
Downs, Elsa, 29

E

Eagle Hill Farm, 185
economic conditions, 159, 160
education, 61, 62
    schools, 61, 151, 152, 167, 168
    academies, 61
    curriculum, 62
Elam, Samuel, 68, 69
Elder, James, 21, 23
Ellender, Allen J., 232, 233-240
Ellington, Buford, 202, 203, 205, 208
Elliot, John, 22, 24
Ellis, William, 239
Emergency Relief Appropriations Act, 185
Empire Furnace, 40, 42
Erwin, Henry H., 91, 92
entertainment, 74
"Essex", 115
European Explorers, 5-8
    English, 7, 8
    French, 6
        Antoine Bonnefey, 7
        Martin Cartier, 7
        Andre Michaux, 9
    Spanish 7, 12
        Juan Padro, 7
Evans, Paul, 212

F

"Fanny Bullett", 115
farm goods, 61, 62, 63
Farmers Educational and Cooperative   Union,
175
Federal Music Project, 189
Federal Theater Project, 189
Fergeson, Robert, 25
Ferrell, John, 61
ferry rates, 67
Feutrell, Robert, 24
Fiftieth Tennessee Infantry
        Regiment, 93
fighting, 64
Fisher, Caleb, 22
floating book store, 31
Flood, Lilly, 247
Flood, Robert, 247
Floyd, John B., 120-130
folklore,
Foote, Adrew H., 115, 116, 119-130
Ford, Henry,
Forrest, Nathan Bedford, 121-130
Fort Campbell, 194, 195
Fort Donelson, 97-99, 101-107, 110, 113,
        114, 120-130, 205
Fort Heiman, 115, 117
Fort Henry, 97-99, 101-107, 110, 114, 118-
        120, 205
Forty-Ninth Tennessee Regiment, 139
Foster, Wilbur, 109
Fourteenth Tennessee Regiment, 93, 94
Fowler, Beman, 29
Free Soil Party, 59
French Broad River, 1
Fulton Furnace, 42

G

Gabrielson, Milton, 228-229
gambling, 65
General Field Order No. 5., 137
German settlers, 14
German prisoners, 185
Givins, Dickson, 26
Glasgow, Leslie, 237
Golden Pond, 26, 180, 181
Goodwin, Jesse, 25
Goodwin, Robert, 25
Goodwin, Samuel, 25

government, 33
Grace, Allan, 25
Grand Rivers 171, 172
Grant, Ulysses S., 114, 116, 119, 130-140
        133, 136
grapes, 35
Grasty, John, 25
Great Western Furnace, 40, 42, 68, 88
Griffin, Cleo, 248
Griggs, Charles, 22
Gristmills, 51-52
Griswold, Robert, 29
Grubb, Aubrey, 9
guerrilla bands, 140-144

H

Hall, Allen, 209
Halleck, Henry, 108, 114, 131-134
Harding, A. C., 132, 140
Harris, Isham G., 95, 96, 97
Harrison, William Henry, 59
Hart, Anthony, 22
Haynes, Milton A., 106
Hays, Robert, 22
Heflin, Lois, 73
Heiman, Adolphus, 99, 100
Hematite, 42
hemp, 35
Henderson, Richard, 5, 11
Henry, Milton J., preface
Henry, Gustavus H., 98
Hicks (Hichs), E. D., 37
Hinson, Joshua, 142, 143
hog killings, 86, 87
Holden, W. R., 217
Holland, Frank. 168
Holland, Otto S., 223
Holston River, 1
Home Guard, 92, 93, 94
homes, 15, 70
hominy, 16, 17
House Public Works
        Adminstration, 199
household goods, 5, 70, 71
Howers, Robert, 217, 255
Huling, James, 23
Humphries, Lurline, 178
hunting, 69, 164, 182, 183

I

"Iatan", 115
"Illinois", 115
Indian Mound, Tennessee, 1, 12, 55, 167
Irish immigrants, 46
Irby, Loulie W., 144, 145
Iron Industry, 36-47
iron masters, 42, 43
Iron Mountain Furnace, 42

J

Jackson, Andrew, 15, 30, 58, 220
Jackson, Rachel, 97
Jeffers, C. A.,
Jefferson, Thomas, 31
Johnson, Bushrod Rust, 97, 98
Johnson, Cave, 132, 133
Johnson, James L., 207
Johnson, Lyndon B., 215, 216, 222, 243
Johnson, Richard, 62
Johnston, Albert Sidney, 96, 105, 106, 108
Johnston, Henry, 22
Jones, A. R., 225
Jones, Joseph, 29
Jones, Ola, 227
Jordan, Irwin, and Company, 40
Jordan, G. H., 40
Jordan, W., 40

K

Kefauver, Estes, 212
Kelly, William, 37
Kennedy, John F., 201, 202, 209, 212, 213
Kentucky Dam, 195, 196, 197
"Keystone", 115
Kilgore, Eli, 25
killing hogs, 90, 91
Kingins, John, 22
Kirkman, Thomas, 41

L

Lack, James, 22
Lagow, Clark, 139
LaGrange Iron Works, 41, 166
"Lake Erie", 115

Lamb, Abner, 22
Land Between the Lakes, 203-280
    background, 203-205
    critics of TVA, 222, 223
    problems, 204, 205
    proposals, 263
    public confusion, 206, 207, 208
    public reaction,, 206, 207
    triumph of LBL, 250-282
    TVA assumes control, 220-226
    TVA support, 250-282
Land grants 11
Lash, Abraham, 25
Lathan, M. S., 137
Laura Furnace, 42
leadership, 80
Lee, Ann, 31
Lewis, D.H., 132
Lewis, E. H., 41
Lewis, G. T., 41
"Lexington", 115
Lick Skillet, 55
lifestyle, 56, 57
Lincoln, Abraham, 91
"Little Chicago", 216
Little Main River, 28
"Louisville", 115
Lowe, Wash, 93, 142, 143
Lower Cumberland Development Association, 201
lumber Industry, 47, 50, 157
Lumpkin, Martha Neville, 144, 145
lye, 14
Lyon, Chittenden, 32, 38, 49, 220
Lyon County, 29
Lyon, Harlan, 150-151
Lyon, Matthew, 29, 30-32, 220

M

Mammoth Furnace, 42
Manning, Martha, 22
Martin, James, 23
Martin, William, 23
Mason, Rodney, 143, 144
Massie, Jesse, 84
Mayberry, John, 25
merchant records, 84
    Babbitt, Good, and Company, 84
    William Cook, 82-86
    Wright Brothers, 84

291

Metacom (King Philip), 7, 8
McCarley, A. T., 217
McClelland, George B., 138, 139
McClernand, John, 115, 117, 121, 130
McCrain, Gerald, 9
McDougal, R., 65
McGavock, Randal W., 99, 100
McGee, M. C., 92
McGregory, Mark, 55
McNairy, John, 22
McNeese, John, 22
McWaters, Moses, 25
Messenger, John, 30
Milliken, Sherril W., 216, 217
Mills, James, 22
"Minnehan", 115
Mississippian Culture, 2
        Algonquin, 2
        Caddoan, 2
        Cherokee, 3, 4
        Chicksaw, 2
        Choctaw, 2
        Shawnee, 2
        Sioux, 3, 4
Mizell, Jane, 57
Mizell, Stephen, 57
Model, 88, 167, 169
money crops, 71, 72, 73
Montgomery County, 21
Morgan, Arthur, 186, 187
Morgan, Harcourt A., 186, 187
Morgan, Harold, 217, 233
Morgan, Joe, 239
mortality rates, 78, 79
Mosby, Henry S., 238
motherhood, 76, 77
Munsell, Luke, 10
Murphy, John W., 110
musseling, 173

N

Napier, G. W., 37
Napier, Richard C., 37
"Nashville Republican", 38
Native Americans, 1-8
        Archaic, 1
        Cherokee, 2, 3, 4, 7, 8
        Chickasaw, 2, 3
        Creek, 2, 3

        Shawnee, 1
        Woodland Cultures, 1
        Mississippian Cultures, 2
            Algonquin, 3
            Caddoan, 3
            Iroguoian, 3
            Muskhogean, 3
        Sioux, 2
Nelson, Robert, 23
Nelson, William, 21
Newberry, Johuah, 26, 27
New Deal, 183-188
Newell, D. S., 40
Newell and Prichett Company, 40
Nixon, Richard, 252-253
Nolin, John Nolin, 101
Norris, George, 185, 186
North Carolina, 1, 20

O

Ohio River, 1
O'Bryan, John, 207
Oglesby, R. J., 136, 137

P

Paris Landing, 116
Parker, Alton B., 157, 158
Parker, Nathan, 55
pauper houses, 151, 152
peddlers, 153
Perkins, Nicholas, 37
Petty, George, 23
Peytona Furnace, 41, 42
Phelps, S. L., 110
Phillips, Haskell, 239
Pierce, Franklin, 59, 60
pig iron, 43, 44
Pillow, Gideon, 106, 112, 120-130
Pipkin, Lewis, 22
Pitts, I. N., 216
"Pittsburg", 115
politics, 156, 157
Polk, James K., 59
Porter, W.D., 116
Pot Neck, 36, 37, 55
Prohibition, 156, 176-179
prosperity, 81, 82

Public Works Administration, 188, 189

R

racial tensions, 60, 61, 62,
Randolph Furnace and Forge, 40, 41
Rawlins, Johnathan A., 120
Ray, Homer, 238
Raylor, Eugene, 236
recreation, 64
religion, 62, 63, 165
remedies, 74
    bleeding, 75
    burns, 76
    colds, 76
    heart trouble, 76
    snake bite, 76, 77
Resettlement Administration, 194
    Rice, John, 22
Riggins, Emma D., 73
Riggins, Frazier, 236
Riggins, John, 139
roads, 145
Rorie, Hezekiah, 55
Roosevelt, Franklin, 185, 186, 187, 188
Rural Electrification Administration, 187
Rough and Ready Furnace, 39, 166

S

Saline Creek Furnace, 42
Scales, Cordelia Lewis, 144
schools, 151
Seventy-first Ohio Volunteers, 146
Sexton, Brittain, 22
sharecroppers, 149
Sharp, Lander, 26
Sharp, Thomas, 22
sheep, 154
Shepherd, Benjamin, 22
Sherman, William, 138, 139
Sills, David, 101
Silver Trail, 39
slaveholders, 65, 66, 81
slaves at Fort Henry and Fort
    Donelson, 104
slaves in the iron industry, 46
slave uprisings, 45, 65, 66
Small, Harry, 23
Smallpox, 10, 149, 150

Smith, Charles F., 108, 109
Smith, Daniel, 6, 11
Smith, George, 132
Smith, J. W., 128, 129
Smith, Samuel, 24
Snipe, Juanita, 241
Snyder, David, 240
social conditions, 169
soil conservation, 34
Stacker, John, 37
Stacker, Samuel, 37
Stacker, William, 37, 38, 98
Stacker, Wood, and Company, 61
"St. Louis", 124
Stewart Christopher C., 101
Stewart, Duncan, 21
Stewart, G. M., 150
Street, George, 29
Strum, Paul, 237
story telling, 160, 161
Stubblefield, Frank, 210, 211, 221
suffrage movement, 177, 178
sulpher mines, 172, 173
superstitions, 159, 160
supplies, 153

T

Tagert, James, 23
Tanning Industry, 51
tavern rates, 24, 28
Taylor, Zachery, 59
taxes, 33, 152
temple, 2
tenant farmers, 151, 152
Tennessee Valley Authority, 184-186, 195, 196, 214, 215
Terrell, Spot F., 129
Tharpe, 2
Thedford, R., 25
Thirteenth Amendment, 153
Thirtieth Tennessee Regiment, 98
Thomas, James M., 173
Thomson, William, 26
Tilghman, Lloyd, 105, 106, 116, 117
tobacco, 71, 72, 153
Tobacco Port, 22
Trail of These Hills, 254
tribal wars, 3
Travis, William, 239
Trigg County, Kentucky, 2, 24-29

Trigg Station, 25
Trigg, Stephen, 26
Turner, Henry, 22
"Tyler", 115
Tynor, Arthur, 22

U

Udall, Stewart, 206-209, 212
Union Furnace, 42
"Uncle Sam", 115
Utley, Francis, 226, 227, 228

V

Valley Forge Furnace, 40
Van Buren, Martin, 67, 68
Vance, Benjamin, 26
Vanleer, Samuel, 37, 38
Veasey, Jack E., 207
Veasey, M.E., 207
vegetables, 90
vegetation, 9, 10
Velasquez, Loreta (Henry T. Buford)
    111-112
Venable, Keith, 207
Vinson, J. R., 200
violence, 163, 164
Vogel, Herbert, 202, 203
Volstead Act, 179

W

"W.A.B", 115
Wagner, Aubrey J., 205, 211, 223, 224,   225
Walker Line, 11, 12, 13
Walker, Thomas, 5, 11
Wallace, Etheldred, 22
Wallace, Lew, 122, 125
Wallace, Rees, 181
Wallace, Roy, 181
Warner, James C. 162
waterways, 32
Webster, Daniel, 58
Wells, Hayen, 22
Wheeler, Joseph, 145, 146
Wheland and Company, 84
whiskey, 16, 17

White, Bob, 218
White, Pollard, 234
Whitfield, Bryan, 22
Whitehead, Corrinne, 246
Wilcox, F. M., 207
"Wildcat", 145
Williams, Caleb, 23
Williams, Gilbert, 54
Williams, John, 55
Williams, Isaac, 150
"Wilson", 115-122
Wilson, James, 53, 55
wine, 35
Wirt, Conrad, 205, 206
Wiseman, J. H., 219, 220
women work, 73, 74, 75, 164
Wood, Bob, 56
Woodland Cultures, 2
Woods, Joseph, 38
Woods, Robert, 38
Woods, Yeatman, and Co., 38
Work Progress Adm., 189
Work Project Adm., 189
World War I, 175, 176
World War II, 193, 194, 195
Wrangler Camp, 252
Wright Brothers, 84

Y

Yeatman, Jane, 37
Yeatman, Thomas, 37
Yuchi, 2

Iron Furnace Stack

Fig. 2

Charcoal Pit

Pig Iron

Tending a charcoal hearth.

Sow and Pigs

Fig. 3

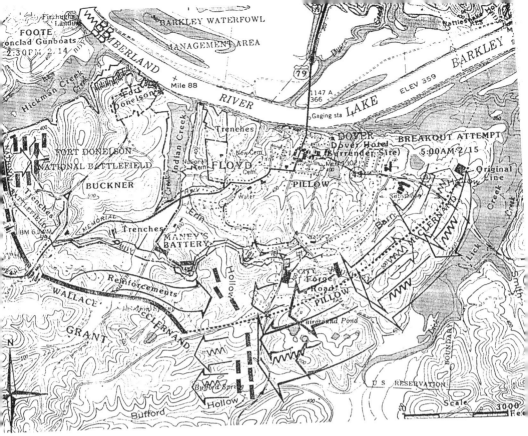

FORT DONELSON
14–15 February 1862

Fig. 4
General view of Fort Donelson

__NOTES__

__*NOTES*__

NOTES

__*NOTES*__

__*NOTES*__

__NOTES__

__NOTES___

__NOTES__

NOTES

The Miscellaneous Publications series of Austin Peay State University's Center for Field Biology is a medium for disseminating educational, scientific, or technical information which, because of length or content, is not appropriate for scientific journals or as part of the Center's symposium proceedings. Generally papers should relate to the natural history of the lower Cumberland and Tennessee River valleys of Kentucky and Tennessee; however, papers on similar topics from contiguous areas surrounding states also may be appropriate.

Publications may be obtained from: Publications Manager
The Center for Field Biology
Austin Peay State University
Clarksville, Tennessee 37044

Make checks payable to Austin Peay State University.

Persons interested in publishing in this series should contact the Center's Director at the above address.

Papers in the Miscellaneous Publications Series

1.   Chester, E. W., R. J. Schibig, and S. Simoni. 1987. The nut trees of Land Between The Lakes. An illustrated guide to the species of beech, chestnut, hickories, oaks, and walnuts of LBL. 49 pp. $3.00 + $1.00 shipping.

2.   Noel, S. M. 1987. A curriculum guide for understanding the woodland community. Student and teacher activities for a unit on woodland ecology. 66 pp. Free to teachers; $3.00 + $1.00 shipping to others.

3.   Noel, S. M., M. L. McReynolds, and E. W. Chester. 1990. The ferns and fern allies of Land Between The Lakes: a curriculum guide. An illustrated guide with activities for secondary teachers and students. 67 pp. Free to teachers; $3.00 + $1.00 shipping to others.

4.   Redmond, W. H., A. C. Echternacht, and A. F. Scott. 1990. Annotated checklist and update of the information on distributions, taxonomy, and habitats of Tennessee's herpetofauna, plus an extensive (1124 titles) annotated list of literature dealing with herpetology in the state. 173 pp. $4.00 + $1.00 shipping.

5.   Snyder, D. H. and F. J. Alsop, III. 1991. Birds of Land Between the Lakes. Accounts of 230 species of birds, with residency status and abundance information, basic descriptions, anecdotal commentaries, and suggestions on how and where to watch birds in the region. Illustrated with 125 color photographs. 234 pp. $7.00 + $1.00 shipping.

6.   Chester, E. W. 1992. An annotated catalogue of vascular plants known from Land Between The Lakes, Kentucky and Tennessee. $4.00 + $1.00 shipping.

7.   Harris, R. V. and S. M. Noel. 1992. The pond-dwelling vertebrates of Land Between The Lakes. $3.00 + $1.00 shipping.

8.   Wallace, B. J. 1992. Between the rivers: history of the Land Between The Lakes. 282 pp. $8.00 + $1.00 shipping.

AP - 403/4-92/Vaughn, Nashvlle/2M